CO-AXF-165

Programming
NETSCAPE
PLUG-INS

201 West 103rd Street
Indianapolis, Indiana 46290

Zan Oliphant

To Shirley Hubbard, Mitchell Harrison, and my family and friends in Juneau, Alaska.

Copyright © 1996 by Sams.net Publishing

FIRST EDITION

International Standard Book Number: 1-57521-098-3

Library of Congress Catalog Card Number: 96-67543

99 98 97 96   4 3 2 1

Interpretation of the printing code: the rightmost double-digit number is the year of the book's printing; the rightmost single-digit, the number of the book's printing. For example, a printing code of 96-1 shows that the first printing of the book occurred in 1996.

Composed in AGaramond and MCPdigital by Macmillan Computer Publishing

Printed in the United States of America

Publisher	*Richard K. Swadley*
Publishing Manager	*Mark Taber*
Managing Editor	*Cindy Morrow*
Marketing Manager	*John Pierce*
Assistant Marketing Manager	*Kristina Perry*

Acquisitions Editor
Sharon Cox

Development Editor
Jeff Koch

Software Development Specialist
Steve Straiger

Production Editor
Ryan Rader

Technical Reviewer
Alec Plumb

Editorial Coordinator
Bill Whitmer

Technical Edit Coordinator
Lynette Quinn

Editorial Assistants
Carol Ackerman
Andi Richter
Rhonda Tinch-Mize

Cover Designer
Tim Amrhein

Book Designer
Alyssa Yesh

Copy Writer
Peter Fuller

Production Team Supervisor
Brad Chinn

Production
Stephen Adams
Debra Bolhuis
Carol Bowers
Mona Brown
Bruce Clingaman
Tom Dinse
Jason Hand
Daniel Harris
Sonja Hart
Clint Lahnen
Ryan Oldfather
Casey Price
Laura Robbins
SA Springer
Mark Walchle
Jeff Yesh

Overview

I Getting Started

1	Introduction	3
2	Netscape Navigator Plug-Ins	7
3	Understanding MIME	17
4	Helper Applications and Network Communications	27

II The Netscape Plug-Ins Basics

5	Using a Plug-In	39
6	Plug-In Design and Architecture	51
7	Navigator Plug-In Design Considerations	59
8	The Plug-In Application Programming Interface (API)	69
9	Instance Initialization and Destruction	77
10	Stream Creation and Destruction	93
11	Reading From and Writing To Streams	121
12	Memory Management	135
13	Status Methods	145
14	LiveConnect	153
15	Miscellaneous Methods	163

III Real Examples

16	About the Sample Code	179
17	A Streaming Audio Sample	183
18	The Buffer Classes	203
19	The CPU Monitor Plug-In	217
20	A Plug-In with MCIWnd	235
21	Using MIDI with a Background Plug-In	249
22	Subclassing without Microsoft's Foundation Class Library	259
23	Netscape's LiveConnect Sample	271
24	Debugging with the Socket Spy	297

IV Plug-In Programming Resources for Windows

25	About Windows C++ Compilers	311
26	Writing a Plug-In with Borland C++ 5.*x*	315
27	Writing a Plug-In with Microsoft Visual C++ 4.*x*	329
28	Writing a Plug-In with Watcom C++ 10.*x*	341

V Appendixes

A	Netscape's Product Line	355
B	Today's Wide World of Plug-Ins	369
C	Glossary of Terms	383
	Index	389

Contents

I Getting Started

1 Introduction   **3**

What This Book Is About 4

    What Is a Netscape Navigator Plug-In? 4

    Can I Write a Plug-In in Java? 5

Who Should Use This Book? 5

How This Book Is Organized 5

The Book's CD-ROM 6

2 Netscape Navigator Plug-Ins   **7**

Introduction 8

Current Plug-In Categories 8

    Streaming versus File-Based Plug-In Architectures 9

Conclusion 14

What's Next? 15

3 Understanding MIME   **17**

Introduction 18

MIME Overview 18

    Content Types 19

Current MIME Types and Subtypes 20

Netscape Navigator and MIME Configuration 22

    New Types 23

    What About Plug-Ins? 23

A New MIME Type for Your Plug-In 24

    Initial Development 24

    Going Live 25

Registering a New Media Type 25

Conclusion 26

What's Next? 26

4 Helper Applications and Network Communications   **27**

Introduction 28

Netscape Helper Applications 28

Windows Sockets 29

Communication with Netscape 32

    Netscape's DDE Implementation 32

    OLE Automation in Netscape 33

What All of This Means to Plug-Ins 35

Conclusion 35

What's Next? 36

II   The Netscape Plug-Ins Basics

5   Using a Plug-In   39

Introduction 40

The EMBED Tag 40

RealAudio Extends the EMBED Tag Attributes 40

    CONTROLS 40

    AUTOSTART 48

    CONSOLE 48

    NOLABELS 50

The NOEMBED Tag 50

Conclusion 50

What's Next? 50

6   Plug-In Design and Architecture   51

Introduction 52

How It All Fits Together 52

LiveConnect 53

Runtime Loading 54

Plug-In Instances and Instance Data 54

Windows and Events 55

Seamless Web Page Embedding 55

Data Streams 55

    Sequential and Seekable Streams 56

Assisted Installation 57

Netscape's SDK 57

Conclusion 58

What's Next? 58

7   Navigator Plug-In Design Considerations   59

Introduction 60

Choosing a Development Language 60

Navigator Version Compatibility 61

Planning for Bandwidth Limitations 61

    Streaming Audio 61

Multiplatform Compatibility 62

Expanding to Java with LiveConnect 62

HTML EMBED Tag Attributes 63

    Current Attributes 63

    Adding Your Own Attributes 64

Multiple MIME Types 65

MIME Contention 65

File Base versus Streaming Plug-Ins 66

Streaming to the Navigator 66

Client/Server Design 66
Conclusion 67
What's Next? 67

8   The Plug-In Application Programming Interface (API)   69

Introduction 70
Who Is Calling Whom? 70
   Dynamically Loaded 70
   How Netscape Calls Your DLL 71
   NPWIN.CPP 71
   NP_Initialize 71
   Mapping Your API Calls to Netscape 72
   NP_GetEntryPoints 73
   Netscape Calls Your Code 74
   NP_Shutdown 74
A Quick Look at the Plug-In API Methods 74
Conclusion 76
What's Next? 76

9   Instance Initialization and Destruction   77

Introduction 78
Instance Data 78
Global Initialization and NPP_Initialize 79
Global Destruction and NPP_Shutdown 79
Instance Initialization and NPP_New 80
   MIME Type 80
   Instance Pointers 80
   Mode 81
   HTML Arguments 81
   Previously Saved Data 82
Instance Destruction with NPP_Destroy 82
   Saving Data with NPP_Destroy 82
Version Information with NPN_Version 84
API Quick Reference 84
   NPP_Initialize 84
   NPP_Shutdown 85
   NPP_New 86
   NPP_Destroy 88
   NPN_Version 90
Conclusion 91
What's Next? 91

10   Stream Creation and Destruction   93

Introduction 94
New Streams and Their Parameters 94

Stream Type 94
Stream Instance Structure 95
Seeking for Seek 96
Processing by Stream or by File 96
Life of a Stream Ends 96
Some Familiar Structures 97
Creating Your Own Streams 97
NPN_GetURL and NPN_PostURL 98
HTTP GET 99
HTTP POST 99
Emulate the Form with NPN_PostURL 102
Targeting Windows with NPN_GetURL and
    NPN_PostURL 104
API Quick Reference 105
NPP_NewStream 105
NPP_DestroyStream 107
NPN_NewStream 108
NPN_DestroyStream 109
NPN_GetURL 110
NPN_PostURL 112
New Navigator 3.0 Plug-In APIs 114
NPN_GetURLNotify 114
NPN_PostURLNotify 116
NPP_URLNotify 117
Conclusion 119
What's Next? 119

11   Reading From and Writing To Streams   121
Introduction 122
Getting Buffers From a Stream 122
NPP_WriteReady 122
NPP_Write 122
Killing a Stream 123
Getting Less Data 124
File-Based Processing 124
Local File Paths 124
Tricks with NP_ASFILE 125
Random Stream Access 126
Where the Offset Comes In 126
Writing to a Stream 127
API Quick Reference 127
NPP_WriteReady 127
NPP_Write 128
NPP_StreamAsFile 130

NPN_RequestRead 131

NPN_Write... 132

Conclusion 133

What's Next? 134

12 Memory Management   **135**

Introduction 136

Netscape's Memory APIs 136

Memory Allocation and Freeing 136

Flushing Navigator's Memory on the Macintosh 136

Windows 95 Memory Management 137

Address Space of a Process 137

Advanced Memory API 138

Your Plug-In as a Windows 95 DLL 140

API Quick Reference 140

NPN_MemAlloc 140

NPN_MemFree 141

NPN_MemFlush 142

Conclusion 143

What's Next? 143

13 Status Methods   **145**

Introduction 146

Giving Status 146

Your Own Progress Indicator 147

Netscape's User-Agent 148

What the Heck Is Mozilla? 149

API Quick Reference 150

NPN_Status 150

NPN_UserAgent 151

Conclusion 151

What's Next? 152

14 LiveConnect   **153**

Introduction 154

Calling Java Methods from Plug-Ins 155

Accessing Java Class Fields in C++ 155

Accessing Methods 155

Java Type Names 156

Calling Plug-In Methods from Java 156

Java Class: netscape.plugin.Plugin 157

Subclassing the Java Class: netscape.plugin.Plugin 158

Garbage Collection and Globals 158

API Quick Reference 158

NPP_GetJavaClass 158

NPN_GetJavaEnv 159
NPN_GetJavaPeer 160
Conclusion 161
What's Next? 161

15   Miscellaneous Methods   163

Introduction 164
Your Plug-In's Window 164
Subclassing a Window 164
Getting Instance Data 166
Subclassing with MFC 167
Printing and Your Plug-In 169
The Macintosh and Window Events 170
API Quick Reference 170
NPP_SetWindow 170
NPP_Print 172
NPP_HandleEvent 175
Conclusion 176
What's Next? 176

III   Real Examples

16   About the Sample Code   179

Introduction 180
Audio Streamer 180
Buffer Classes 180
Server CPU Monitor 181
Using MCIWnd in Windows 181
MIDI Background Music 181
Window Subclassing 181
Using LiveConnect 182
Socket Spy 182
Conclusion 182
What's Next? 182

17   A Streaming Audio Sample   183

Introduction 184
Where to Find the Files 184
The Design of NPWAVE 184
Plug-In Entry Points 185
CWave's Worker Thread 192
The Audio Driver 194
The CPluginWindow Class 195
Running the Audio Plug-In 199

Buffer Sizes 199

Multiple Instances 199

Automatic Starting of Audio 200

Conclusion 201

What's Next? 201

18   The Buffer Classes   203

Introduction 204

The Methods 204

Buffer Header 205

The Circular Buffer 205

`CBufferCircular` Methods 206

   `Constructor` 206

   `Destructor` 206

   `CBufferCircular::AllocateBuffers` 207

   `CBufferCircular::FreeBuffers` 208

   `CBufferCircular::AnyEmptyBuffers` 208

   `CBufferCircular::GetNextEmptyBuffer` 209

   `CBufferCircular::AnyFullBuffers` 209

   `CBufferCircular::GetNextFullBuffer` 210

   `CBufferCircular::GetLastFullBuffer` 210

   `CBufferCircular::ReturnUsedBuffer` 211

The FIFO Buffer 212

`CBufferFIFO` Methods 212

   `Constructor` 212

   `Destructor` 213

   `CBufferFIFO::AllocateBuffers` 213

   `CBufferFIFO::FreeBuffers` 213

   `CBufferFIFO::AnyEmptyBuffers` 214

   `CBufferFIFO::GetNextEmptyBuffer` 214

   `CBufferFIFO::AnyFullBuffers` 215

   `CBufferFIFO::GetNextFullBuffer` 215

   `CBufferFIFO::GetLastFullBuffer` 215

   `CBufferFIFO::ReturnUsedBuffer` 216

Conclusion 216

What's Next? 216

19   The CPU Monitor Plug-In   217

Introduction 218

Where to Find the Files 218

The Design of the CPU Monitor Plug-In 219

About `vmstat` 220

How `vmstat` Is Run with the CGI Program 220

The Plug-In Entry Points 221

NPP_New 221

NPP_Destroy 222

NPP_SetWindow 222

NPP_NewStream 223

NPP_WriteReady and NPP_Write 224

NPP_StreamAsFile 224

NPP_DestroyStream 225

The Main Object: CCpuMon 225

Construction and Destruction 225

Open 226

EndOfStream 226

Getting the Filename 226

Manually Updating the CPU Bar Chart 228

Close 228

The Window Object: CPluginWindow 228

Construction and Destruction 229

Window Initialization and Cleanup 229

Parsing vmstat Data 230

Drawing the Bar Chart 231

Handling the Update Button 232

Repainting the Window 232

Setting Up and Running the CPU Monitor Plug-In 232

Conclusion 233

What's Next? 234

20   A Plug-In with MCIWnd   235

Introduction 236

Where to Find the Files 236

The Design of the MCIWnd Plug-In 236

Multiple MIME Types 237

Plug-In Entry Points 238

NPP_New 238

NPP_Destroy 239

NPP_SetWindow 239

NPP_NewStream 240

NPP_WriteReady and NPP_Write 240

NPP_StreamAsFile 241

NPP_DestroyStream 241

The CMCIWnd Class 242

Construction and Destruction 242

Open 242

GotFileName 243

UpdateWindow 243

EndOfStream 244

A Bit about MCIWnd 244

Running the Plug-In 247

Conclusion 248

What's Next? 248

21   Using MIDI with a Background Plug-In   249

Introduction 250

Where to Find the Files 250

The Design of the Background MIDI Plug-In 251

Embedding as Hidden 251

Components 251

Plug-In Entry Points 252

NPP_New 252

NPP_Destroy 253

NPP_SetWindow 253

NPP_NewStream 254

NPP_WriteReady and NPP_Write 254

NPP_StreamAsFile 255

NPP_DestroyStream 255

The CMidi Class 255

Construction and Destruction 256

Open 256

GotFileName 256

EndOfStream 257

Running the Plug-In 257

Conclusion 258

What's Next? 258

22   Subclassing without Microsoft's Foundation Class Library   259

Introduction 260

Where to Find the Files 260

The Design of the Non-MFC Plug-In 261

Plug-In Entry Points 261

NPP_New 261

NPP_Destroy 262

NPP_SetWindow 263

NPP_NewStream 264

NPP_WriteReady and NPP_Write 264

NPP_StreamAsFile 265

NPP_DestroyStream 265

The CPluginWindow Class 266

Construction and Destruction 266

Open 266

Stub Methods 267

SubclassWindow 267

UnsubclassWindow 268

A Global Subclassing Procedure 268

Running the Plug-In 269

Conclusion 270

What's Next? 270

23   Netscape's LiveConnect Sample   **271**

Introduction 272

Where to Find the Files 272

Get a Java Compiler 273

The Design of the LiveConnect AVI Sample 273

Components 274

The Java Applet 274

AviTest 274

AviObserver 276

AviPlayer 277

Stub Code and Headers with javah 278

Native Plug-in Methods for Java 278

AviPlayer_setTimeOut 279

AviPlayer_play 279

AviPlayer_stop 279

AviPlayer_seek 280

AviPlayer_rewind 280

AviPlayer_forward 281

AviPlayer_frameForward 281

AviPlayer_frameBack 281

CPluginWindow 282

The Window Procedure 282

Constructor 284

Destructor 284

CPluginWindow::SetWindow 285

CPluginWindow::OnLButtonDown 285

CPluginWindow::OnRButtonDown 285

CPluginWindow::OnPaint 286

CPluginWindow::OnPaletteChange 287

CAvi 287

Constructor 287

Destructor 287

CAvi::Open 288

CAvi::Close 289

CAvi::Play 289

CAvi::Stop 290

CAvi::Seek 290

CAvi::Rewind 291
CAvi::Forward 291
CAvi::FrameForward 291
CAvi::FrameBack 292
Sizing, Positioning, and Updating 292
CAvi::SetFrequency 292
CAvi::OnStop 293
CAvi::OnPositionChange 294
Plug-In Entry Points 294
NPP_GetJavaClass 294
Running the Sample with JavaScript 294
Conclusion 296
What's Next? 296

24   Debugging with the Socket Spy   297

Introduction 298
The Socket Interface 298
Tricking Socket Applications 299
Using the Socket Spy with Netscape 299
Editing NETSCAPE.EXE 299
Getting the Files and Building 301
Under the Hood 302
The Data Files 305
Running the Socket Spy 306
Conclusion 307
What's Next? 307

IV Plug-In Programming Resources for Windows

25   About Windows C++ Compilers   311

Introduction 312
Resources 312
Calling Conventions 312
Plug-In Methods 312
Windows 95 DLL Entry Points 313
Class Libraries 313
Conclusion 313
What's Next? 314

26   Writing a Plug-In with Borland C++ 5.x   315

Introduction 316
Where to Find the Files 316
Preparing the Files for the Borland Compiler 316
The Example 317

Setting Up the Project 317
Compiling the Project 320
Testing Your Project 323
All Done 327
Using OWL 328
Conclusion 328
What's Next? 328

27   Writing a Plug-In with Microsoft Visual C++ 4.x   329

Introduction 330
Where to Find the Files 330
Modifying the Files 331
The Example 331
Setting up the Project 331
Compiling the Project 336
Testing Your Project 336
Conclusion 340
What's Next? 340

28   Writing a Plug-In with Watcom C++ 10.x   341

Introduction 342
Where to Find the Files 342
Modifying the Files 343
The Includes 343
The `sizeof` Operator 343
Change the Entry Point Definitions 343
The Example 343
Setting Up the Project 344
Compiling the Project 347
Testing Your Project 348
Conclusion 352
What's Next? 352

V Appendixes

A   Netscape's Product Line   355

Introduction 356
Navigator 356
Navigator 2.x 356
Navigator Gold 2.x 357
Navigator 3.0 Beta 357
Navigator Personal Edition 358

Navigator Dial-Up-Kit 358
Netscape Power Pack for Windows 359
Netscape SmartMarks 360
Netscape Chat 360
Collabra Share 360
Commercial Applications 361
Merchant System 361
Publishing System 361
Community System 362
IStore 362
Servers 362
SuiteSpot 363
FastTrack 363
Enterprise Server 364
Proxy Server 364
News Server 365
Mail Server 365
Catalog Server 365
Commerce Server 366
Communications Server 367
Conclusion 368
What's Next? 368

B **Today's Wide World of Plug-Ins** **369**

Introduction 370
Image Viewers 370
Document Viewers 373
Presentation 374
Animation 375
3-D and VRML 376
Audio 377
Video 379
Utilities 380

C **Glossary of Terms** **383**

Index **389**

Acknowledgments

On the professional side, I would like to thank the good people at Sams.net Publishing for giving me the opportunity and support to write this book. Special thanks to Alec Plumb at Netscape for helping with the technical nuts and bolts of the plug-in API. Also, any people involved with material covered in this book, such as plug-ins and Web sites, get my thanks. As for family and friends, thanks to my parents, Alexander and Sue; my brothers, Andrew and Brant; and my sister, Alexa; for their love and support in all of my ventures. Five thousand miles is a long way—I miss you guys. Thank you Chris Shablak and Stacy Feinerman for leaving the house when I asked, and thanks to all of my Florida friends who have been ignored for the last four months. Thanks Ross and Stephanie Holeman for understanding when I missed their wedding in Alaska. An unexpected thank you goes to South Miami Beach writer Larry Boytano, who during a 3 a.m. stroll through a seedy South Beach alley unknowingly inspired me to write this book. When I told Larry that I too wanted to write, he replied, "Well, why don't you?"

About the Author

Zan Oliphant is part of a rebel group of software consultants in South Florida, who specialize in Internet applications and multimedia device drivers. He has 10 years of experience in writing device drivers and applications for Windows, DOS, OS/2, Macintosh, and UNIX. Zan and his fellow PC programming cronies (left over from IBM's personal computer glory days in the Boca Raton area) are always looking for interesting opportunities. Contact Zan at zan@gate.net if you have a cool project for them.

Tell Us What You Think!

As a reader, you are the most important critic and commentator of our books. We value your opinion and want to know what we're doing right, what we could do better, what areas you'd like to see us publish in, and any other words of wisdom you're willing to pass our way. You can help us make strong books that meet your needs and give you the computer guidance you require.

Do you have access to CompuServe or the World Wide Web? Then check out our CompuServe forum by typing GO SAMS at any prompt. If you prefer the World Wide Web, check out our site at http://www.mcp.com.

> **NOTE**
>
> If you have a technical question about this book, call the technical support line at (800) 571-5840, ext. 3668.

As the team leader of the group that created this book, I welcome your comments. You can fax, e-mail, or write me directly to let me know what you did or didn't like about this book—as well as what we can do to make our books stronger. Here's the information:

FAX: (317) 581-4669

E-mail: programming_mgr@sams.mcp.com

Mail: Greg Wiegand
        Comments Department
        Sams.net Publishing
        201 W. 103rd Street
        Indianapolis, IN 46290

PART I

Getting Started

1   Introduction
2   Netscape Navigator Plug-Ins
3   Understanding MIME
4   Helper Applications and Network Communications

CHAPTER 1

Introduction

There's no doubt about it, the World Wide Web is here to stay. And from the way things look, Netscape Navigator will continue to be a major player in the ongoing Web Browser wars. Embracing and developing new Web standards keeps Netscape ahead of the pack. From Java to JavaScript, LiveConnect to the Plug-in API, and HTML to VRML, Netscape sets the pace. According to Netscape's management, this pace is not likely to slacken because they consider themselves a rabbit with a pickup truck bearing down on it. That truck would be Microsoft.

In the first quarter of 1996, Netscape introduced the Plug-in Application Programming Interface (API). This new interface, provided by Netscape Navigator 2.0 and above, allows software vendors to seamlessly embed their products in any given Web page. With the introduction of Navigator 2.0 Beta, a first wave of plug-ins quickly appeared, providing support for new image formats, interactive documents, presentations, animation, Virtual Reality Modeling Language (VRML), audio, video, and utilities. In the second quarter of 1996, Navigator 3.0 brought developers LiveConnect, which provides communication among Java, JavaScript, and plug-ins.

LiveConnect really defines the relationship between plug-ins, JavaScript, and Java. JavaScript, a fully interpreted language, is the slowest but most flexible and easy to learn. Java, using bytecodes, is faster, although it is still interpreted on a binary level. Both JavaScript and Java are totally platform independent. Now contrast that with a plug-in, which is extremely fast because it is object code but is also tied directly to the platform. LiveConnect provides communication for the three Navigator extensions so that each one can be used to its full potential.

What This Book Is About

Throughout the course of this book, you will learn how to write a plug-in code module for Netscape's Navigator. You will learn about a plug-in's architecture, design, and implementation using HTML, Java, and JavaScript. Plenty of examples are provided, complete with fully functional source code. Part IV of this book gives step by step directions for creating a plug-in from scratch with Microsoft, Borland, and Watcom compilers.

What Is a Netscape Navigator Plug-In?

Netscape Navigator plug-ins are dynamically loaded code modules that become part of the browser's code path. That is, after the plug-in is loaded, it becomes a direct part of the browser code. This technique provides the best possible speed, but it lacks in security and platform independence. Visually, a plug-in looks as if it is a seamless part of the Web page in which it is embedded. After users get the appropriate plug-in, they often are not aware that the plug-in is in operation.

Because plug-ins are object code, they must be written in a language that can be fully compiled. Also, in the case of Windows, the development environment must be capable of generating a Dynamic Link Library (DLL), complete with compiled resources. Keeping that in mind, this book is focused toward C++, which is the most popular Graphical User Interface (GUI) development language that fulfills these requirements. Additionally, because the original Netscape Plug-in SDK was written with Microsoft Visual C++ and its associated Microsoft Class Library (MFC), this book has a slant toward MFC.

Can I Write a Plug-In in Java?

It makes absolutely no sense to write a plug-in with Java. Navigator plug-ins and Java are totally different technologies. Plug-ins are native machine code and have absolutely no security restrictions, unlike Java. Think of a plug-in as a trusted code module—kind of like a shareware application. A user makes a conscious decision to download the plug-in, which is then automatically loaded by Netscape's Navigator the next time it is initialized. Java applets, on the other hand, are executed automatically, which creates bigger security problems.

Java applets are small binary modules that are downloaded whenever needed by the Web browser. In many cases, the user does not know or care that a Java applet is running. Plug-ins, on the other hand, are much larger code modules usually requiring an installation program. After a plug-in is installed, it need not be downloaded again.

Who Should Use This Book?

To get the most out of this book, you should be (or want to be) a C++ programmer. That doesn't mean that an avid JavaScript or Java programmer won't find good information in these pages concerning LiveConnect. It also doesn't mean that a programmer using another language won't be able to use the included plug-in API documentation. The C++ programmer will get the most benefit from the sample code and discussion, which is all in C++.

Also, this book is targeted toward Windows 95/NT programmers. All of the sample code is written for Windows 95/NT. Again, this does not exclude Windows 3.1, Macintosh, and UNIX programmers. All platform-specific APIs are well-documented.

How This Book Is Organized

You'll find that this book is organized into five parts, described in the following sections.

Getting Started

This section introduces different plug-in types with real-world examples. Multipurpose Internet Mail Extensions (MIME) are explained and Helper Applications are discussed with WinSock, DDE, and OLE interfaces documented. Using a plug-in with HTML is demonstrated using the RealAudio plug-in as an example.

The Netscape Plug-In Basics

The basics are the plug-in architecture, plug-in design, and a complete reference of all plug-in APIs up to Navigator 3.x. The API reference is complemented with a quick index on this book's inside front cover.

Real Examples

The sample code gives real-world examples of plug-ins, complete with source code. The samples include streaming audio, server CPU monitor, MIDI, video, Java, JavaScript, and a WinSock socket spy utility.

Plug-In Programming Resources for Windows

Resources for Windows discuss three Integrated Development Environments (IDEs) that are capable of generating a Navigator plug-in for Windows 95/NT. Full step-by-step instructions are provided for the Borland, Microsoft, and Watcom IDEs.

Appendixes

In the appendixes, you'll find data sheets for Netscape's current product line, a listing of today's available plug-ins, and a glossary of terms.

The Book's CD-ROM

A CD-ROM is included inside the back cover of this book. This CD-ROM contains all the source code required to compile the plug-in examples that are referenced in the book.

CHAPTER 2

Netscape Navigator Plug-Ins

Introduction

They're here and they're hot! For an architecture that is not yet one year old, the current number of available Netscape Navigator plug-ins is phenomenal. Vendors are rushing to support their file formats with Navigator plug-ins. While Adobe, Macromedia, Autodesk, Micrografx, Corel, Farallon, and Apple are expanding their software horizons with plug-ins, lesser-known vendors with cool names such as Totally Hip, Tumbleweed Software, and Starfish Software are gaining popularity.

For the most part, Navigator plug-ins are file format driven. That is, software vendors are developing plug-ins to support their own file formats (to make them more popular) or to support existing popular formats. Consider a plug-in called FIGleaf Inline from Carberry Technologies. This plug-in supports image file formats such as CGM, GIF, JPEG, PNG, TIFF, CCITT, GP4, BMP, WMF, EPSF, Sun Raster and more. All popular multimedia file types will eventually have Navigator plug-in support. In many cases, as you'll see throughout this book, supporting these new types is a simple matter of mapping the Navigator Plug-in API to the appropriate system level API.

This chapter takes a look at some existing (as of May 1996) plug-ins of each main category. For more plug-ins, take a look at Appendix B "Today's Wide Word of Plug-Ins." Additionally, you can get the most up-to-date plug-in lists on the Web. Netscape maintains a good list at its home page:

`http://www.netscape.com`

Just search for plug-ins, because the exact location of the list changes frequently. Another good source for existing Navigator plug-ins is BrowswerWatch, which is located at the following address:

`http://www.browserwatch.com`

If you are planning to develop a Navigator plug-in for profit, you should monitor as many plug-in related Web sites and news groups as possible. BrowserWatch provides an excellent source of Web browser and plug-in news. Sometimes, the origins of this site's news are from Netscape and other plug-in developers that want to remain anonymous. It's basically a forum for companies to leak information to developers without getting the marketing department involved in a formal press release.

Current Plug-In Categories

The majority of today's plug-ins fit nicely into the following eight categories:

> Image viewers
> Document viewers
> Presentation

Animation

3-D and VRML

Audio

Video

Utilities

Plug-ins that don't fit well into these categories can be thrown into the Utilities section, because any plug-in can essentially be considered a utility.

Streaming versus File-Based Plug-In Architectures

Today's plug-ins use two basic architectures. In this book, these architectures are called *streaming plug-ins* and *file-based plug-ins*. You will see many examples of both later in this book. A streaming plug-in processes data as it is downloaded from the Web server. A file-based plug-in must download a complete file before it can process the data. As a general rule, streaming plug-ins are most desirable because they make more efficient use of time.

For example, consider the audio player plug-in that ships with Navigator 3.*x*. This plug-in is file-based—that is, it operates on a number of audio file formats after the complete file has been downloaded. Now compare that to a real-time audio broadcast, which must be a streaming plug-in because there is never a file.

When you are designing your plug-in, use a streaming design as much as possible. Keep in mind that a client machine running a Web browser is much faster than today's fastest Internet access speeds. Try to utilize that CPU bandwidth while data is downloading.

Image Viewers

Image viewer plug-ins do exactly what the name implies: view images. This is a popular plug-in category and has many offerings.

Have you ever seen one of Berkeley System's slide show style screen savers? The company created a number of different products from Star Trek to Marvel Comics. The still images in these products are compressed using fractal technology from Iterated Systems. Iterated now has a plug-in for Navigator that offers great image compression. Figure 2.1 shows a picture of a skier displayed with Iterated Systems' Fractal Viewer plug-in. This graphic file is only 24KB in size! Notice the multitude of menu items available for special effects such as zoom, dither, flip, and rotate. The plug-in is available from `http://www.interated.com`.

Document Viewers

Document viewer plug-ins view documents created by other software applications. A company called Inso Corporation has created a plug-in for viewing Microsoft Word documents. This plug-in is very useful for sharing Word documents via a Web server. Corporations with Intranets can use plug-ins such as this for employee viewing of important internal documents. Figure 2.2 shows this chapter as it is being written using Inso's Word Viewer plug-in. Get this plug-in from `http://www.inso.com`.

Figure 2.1.
Iterated's Fractal Viewer plug-in in action.

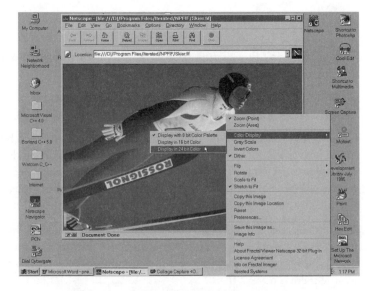

Figure 2.2.
Inso's Word Viewer is viewing this chapter as it is being written.

Presentation

Presentation plug-ins are usually implemented as a slide show viewer with screen transitions. These plug-ins are good for presentations, as you would expect. Using the Navigator Web Browser as a generic viewer for presentations allows users to see a corporate presentation with the familiar browser interface.

The ASAP WebShow plug-in (`http://www.spco.com`) from Software Publishing Corporation has the capability to expand the presentation to the full computer screen. This is a nice feature because the full computer screen is used for your presentation instead of sharing space with the Navigator. Figure 2.3 shows ASAP WebShow viewing a presentation in full screen mode.

Figure 2.3.
SPC's ASAP WebShow is viewing a presentation in full screen mode.

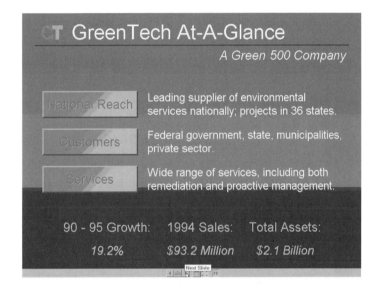

Animation

Shockwave from Macromedia is the big deal for animation plug-ins. Unfortunately, the Shockwave installation is very large, and it is difficult to download.

A company called Totally Hip has a smaller implementation of an animation plug-in. This is a true streaming based plug-in called Sizzler. The animation increases in resolution as more data downloads—similar to Netscape's GIF file support, but animated. In Figure 2.4, a fly is animated across a Web page. You can get this plug-in from `http://www.totallyhip.com`.

Figure 2.4.

A Web page using Totally Hip's Sizzler to animate a fly across the page.

3-D and VRML

The Virtual Reality Modeling Language (VRML) makes interactive three-dimensional Web pages a reality. This technology is so intense that it requires its own language—VRML, as opposed to the traditional HTML.

Netscape, a big believer in VRML, ships a plug-in called Live3D with its browser. This plug-in lets you "fly" through 3-D virtual worlds. Figure 2.5 shows the menu items used to control your navigation through some three-dimensional blocks faced with the Netscape logo. The Live3D plug-in is available from Netscape's home page: http://www.netscape.com.

Figure 2.5.

You can navigate through these Netscape blocks with Netscape's Live3D plug-in.

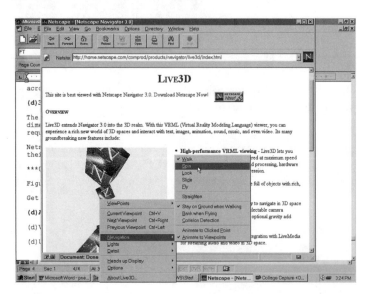

Audio

A number of streaming audio based plug-ins are available from vendors such as Voxware and RealAudio. These plug-ins provide excellent audio compression to make real-time audio over the Internet a reality.

For regular, run-of-the-mill file-based audio such as .WAV format, Netscape ships an audio player with the Navigator that supports a large array of audio formats. This player is displayed in Figure 2.6. You can see the VCR style controls for play, stop and pause in addition to volume control. The audio player plug-in ships with Navigator 3.x.

Figure 2.6.

Netscape's audio player that ships with Navigator 3.x.

Video

Streaming video plug-ins do exist from vendors such as VDOnet and Iterated Systems. You might not want to watch a movie through these plug-ins, but the frame rate that they achieve is impressive considering current Internet bandwidth.

Navigator 3.x for Windows ships with a player for .AVI video files. This is a file-based plug-in and it is not as impressive as the streaming video plug-ins, but everyone with Navigator 3.x will have it. Figure 2.7 shows Netscape's AVI player plug-in with a pop-up menu for controlling movie playback.

Utilities

Several interesting utility plug-ins exist for Netscape Navigator. Be sure to check out the remote control plug-ins from Carbon Copy/Net and Farallon. Also interesting are OLE-based plug-ins from ActiveX and OpenScape.

Starfish software makes a plug-in that tells you the time in locations around the world. This plug-in also gives you an animated map that indicates daylight and darkness. The map is shown in Figure 2.8. Get the Earthtime plug-in from Starfish at http://www.starfishsoftware.com.

Figure 2.7.
Netscape's video player that ships with Navigator 3.x.

Figure 2.8.
The EarthTime plug-in from Starfish Software.

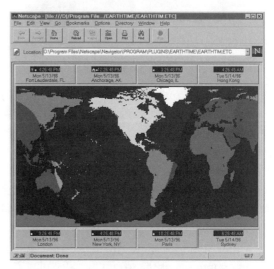

Conclusion

If you want to investigate more plug-ins, be sure to check out Appendix B, "Today's Wide World of Plug-Ins," and, of course, check the Web. Try to learn from other plug-in authors before you start writing your own plug-in. Notice whether plug-ins are stream or file based. See what file formats they support. Don't reinvent the wheel!

Throughout this book, you will learn how to write you own plug-ins using different streaming, buffering, and multimedia techniques. Some of this book's samples such as Chapter 20, "A Plug-In with MCIWnd," show how easy it is to write a very sophisticated plug-in with very little code.

Chapter 17, "A Streaming Audio Sample," is a fully streaming audio sample that demonstrates multithreaded 32-bit Windows programming and real-time data buffering. You can use these samples as a basis to write your own plug-ins for both private and commercial applications.

What's Next?

Most plug-ins get their start from a media file's MIME type. What is MIME? You'll find out in the next chapter.

CHAPTER 3

Understanding MIME

Introduction

As you will learn later in this book, Multipurpose Internet Mail Extensions (MIME) play an important part in the world of Netscape Navigator plug-ins. MIME was originally created for handling additional data types in electronic mail. With the advent of the World Wide Web, MIME was quickly adopted for use in Web servers and browsers.

A plug-in is registered by the Navigator using resource embedded MIME information. The file extension used for a given file is an important part of determining the file's MIME type. For example, a file in Microsoft wave audio format has no MIME information in the actual file. The MIME type—in this case, *audio/x-wav*—is determined by the file extension only.

Developers of plug-ins supporting new data types need to create a new MIME type for the data files. A new MIME type or subtype should be prefaced with an x-. The new type should be submitted to the Internet Assigned Numbers Authority (IANA) for formal review. In most cases, you only need a subtype. A new top-level type requires publication of an RFC and must go through the Internet standards process.

MIME Overview

When the standards for Internet mail were created in 1982, they provided for only ASCII characters and a 1000-character line limit, and they had a message length restriction. As time passed and technology such as multimedia came of age, a new electronic mail standard was needed to handle the large number of new data types. The MIME standard was adopted 10 years later in 1992.

Using the new MIME standard, a mail message can contain the following:

> Images
> Audio
> Video
> Binary data
> Multiple fonts
> Additional character sets
> Multiple objects in the same message
> Unlimited line and message length

To handle these new data types, MIME defines the following header fields:

- ■ `MIME-Version`: The MIME version to which the message conforms.
- ■ `Content-Type`: The MIME type and subtype for the data in the body of the message.
- ■ `Content-Transfer-Encoding`: Specifies how the data is encoded. For example, a common method of encoding binary files is BASE64. BASE64 uses four printable characters to represent three bytes of binary data.

- `Content-ID`: Content identification.
- `Content-Description`: Content description.

As a plug-in developer, you are really only concerned with the Content-Type and the file extension.

Content Types

The current MIME standard supports a number of top-level MIME types. Some of these types, such as `multipart` and `message`, apply only to electronic mail and might not have any Navigator plug-in applications. The current top level types are covered in the following sections.

text

The `text` type is a human-readable format used to represent text in a number of different character sets. Examples of text subtypes are `plain`, `richtext`, and `html`.

multipart

The `multipart` type allows a mail message to combine several different MIME types within a single message. This format has very little application for plug-ins.

application

The `application` type is a catch-all for binary data. If your plug-in uses binary data that is not an image, audio, or video, this one's for you. Some current application subtypes are `postscript`, `wordperfect5.1`, `mathmatica`, and `zip`.

message

The `message` type is used to encapsulate a mail message. Again, this is not of much use for plug-ins.

image

The `image` type handles still image or picture data in many different formats. This type plays an important role in displaying graphics on a Web browser. Some examples are `jpeg`, `gif`, and `tiff`.

audio

The `audio` type handles audio data, usually in PCM format. Most audio subtypes such as `x-wav` and `x-aiff` are still going through IANA approval. Approved audio subtypes are `basic` and `32kadpcm`.

video

The `video` type is used for transmitting video data. This video data can contain interleaved audio, depending on the video file format. `mpeg` and `quicktime` are examples of video subtypes.

Current MIME Types and Subtypes

The Content-Type header field is most important because it contains the MIME type and subtype. The syntax for this field is as follows:

```
type/subtype[;parameter]
```

The Internet Assigned Numbers Authority (IANA) is in charge of approving and tracking media types and subtypes for use in the MIME specification. IANA is operated by the Information Sciences Institute (ISI) of the University of Southern California (USC). You might want to visit their home page at http://www.isi.edu.

Figure 3.1.
The Information Sciences Institute home page.

For a current list of IANA approved media types, keep an eye on this file:

```
ftp://ftp.isi.edu/in-notes/iana/assignments/media-types/media-types
```

At the time of this writing, IANA's approved type and subtype list looks like this:

```
Type          Subtype             Description                    Reference
----          -------             -----------                    ---------
text          plain                                     [RFC1521,Borenstein]
              richtext                                  [RFC1521,Borenstein]
              enriched                                             [RFC1896]
              tab-separated-values                            [Paul Lindner]
              html                                                 [RFC1866]
              sgml                                                 [RFC1874]

multipart     mixed                                     [RFC1521,Borenstein]
              alternative                               [RFC1521,Borenstein]
              digest                                    [RFC1521,Borenstein]
              parallel                                  [RFC1521,Borenstein]
              appledouble                      [MacMime,Patrik Faltstrom]
              header-set                                     [Dave Crocker]
              form-data                                            [RFC1867]
              related                                              [RFC1872]
```

	report	[RFC1892]
	voice-message	[RFC1911]
message	rfc822	[RFC1521,Borenstein]
	partial	[RFC1521,Borenstein]
	external-body	[RFC1521,Borenstein]
	news	[RFC 1036, Henry Spencer]
application	octet-stream	[RFC1521,Borenstein]
	postscript	[RFC1521,Borenstein]
	oda	[RFC1521,Borenstein]
	atomicmail	[atomicmail,Borenstein]
	andrew-inset	[andrew-inset,Borenstein]
	slate	[slate,terry crowley]
	wita	[Wang Info Transfer,Larry Campbell]
	dec-dx	[Digital Doc Trans, Larry Campbell]
	dca-rft	[IBM Doc Content Arch, Larry Campbell]
	activemessage	[Ehud Shapiro]
	rtf	[Paul Lindner]
	applefile	[MacMime,Patrik Faltstrom]
	mac-binhex40	[MacMime,Patrik Faltstrom]
	news-message-id	[RFC1036, Henry Spencer]
	news-transmission	[RFC1036, Henry Spencer]
	wordperfect5.1	[Paul Lindner]
	pdf	[Paul Lindner]
	zip	[Paul Lindner]
	macwriteii	[Paul Lindner]
	msword	[Paul Lindner]
	remote-printing	[RFC1486,Rose]
	mathematica	[Van Nostern]
	cybercash	[Eastlake]
	commonground	[Glazer]
	iges	[Parks]
	riscos	[Smith]
	eshop	[Katz]
	x400-bp	[RFC1494]
	sgml	[RFC1874]
	cals-1840	[RFC1895]
	vnd.framemaker	[Wexler]
	vnd.mif	[Wexler]
	vnd.ms-excel	[Gill]
	vnd.ms-powerpoint	[Gill]
	vnd.ms-project	[Gill]
	vnd.ms-works	[Gill]
	vnd.ms-tnef	[Gill]
	vnd.svd	[Becker]
	vnd.music-niff	[Butler]
image	jpeg		[RFC1521,Borenstein]
	gif		[RFC1521,Borenstein]
	ief	Image Exchange Format	[RFC1314]
	g3fax		[RFC1494]
	tiff	Tag Image File Format	[Rose]
	cgm	Computer Graphics Metafile	[Francis]
	naplps		[Ferber]
	vnd.dwg		[Moline]
	vnd.svf		[Moline]
	vnd.dxf		[Moline]
audio	basic	[RFC1521,Borenstein]
	32kadpcm	[RFC1911]

```
video            mpeg                    [RFC1521,Borenstein]
                 quicktime                   [Paul Lindner]
                 vnd.vivo                          [Wolfe]
```

Notice that the reference field holds the Request for Comment (RFC) document numbers that contain further specification for the given media type. A number of places archive RFCs. Here is a convenient URL for reading RFCs:

```
http://www.uwaterloo.ca/uw_infoserv/rfc.html
```

For easy access to IANA information, check out their home page at this address:

```
http://www.isi.edu/div7/iana
```

Figure 3.2 shows IANA's home page at the time of this writing.

Figure 3.2.

The Internet Assigned Numbers Authority home page.

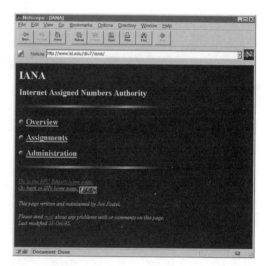

Netscape Navigator and MIME Configuration

Netscape Navigator provides a means for you to configure MIME types with helper applications. Figure 3.3 shows the Helpers configuration screen for Navigator 3.*x*. The first column indicates the file type or the MIME type. The second column determines the action that the browser should take when encountering this MIME type. These actions can be the name of a helper application or the keywords Ask User, Browser, and Save. The Action column can also contain the name of an external program to use as a helper application. The third column determines the file extension that is associated with the given MIME type.

You can toggle the associated action for a MIME type by selecting one of the four radio buttons: View in Browser, Save to Disk, Unknown: Prompt User, and Launch the Application. These buttons correspond to the column actions Browser, Save, Ask User, and the application name, respectively.

As you might have guessed, the `Browser` keyword indicates that the Web browser should handle the MIME type internally. Good examples of this are `image/gif` and `text/html`. `Save`, as the name says, simply saves the file to disk. The `Ask User` keyword prompts the user for action. The user can elect to save the file or configure an external helper application to handle the file.

A MIME type's action can be to launch an external helper application to handle the file. As you can see in Figure 3.3, when Launch the Application is selected, an entry field and Browse button are provided to enter the appropriate external application.

New Types

You can add a new type to the MIME configuration by clicking on the Create New Type button. This brings up a small dialog in which you can enter the new MIME type and MIME subtype. After the new type is entered, fill in the appropriate file extension and action.

Many Windows-based helper applications add new MIME types to Navigator's configuration through the use of DDE or OLE. This technique automates the process and avoids user intervention. See Chapter 4, "Helper Applications and Network Communications," for a listing of the appropriate DDE topics and OLE methods for automated MIME type configuration.

What About Plug-Ins?

Figure 3.3 shows the MIME configuration screen for the Windows version of Navigator 3.0. This version does not provide for plug-in to MIME type configuration. The Macintosh and UNIX versions 3.0 of Navigator have this capability, but this feature is slated for Windows in Navigator 4.*x*.

Figure 3.3.
Navigator's 3.x MIME type configuration screen.

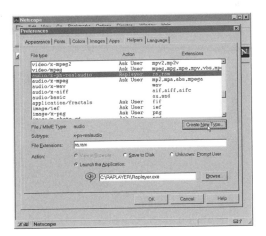

A New MIME Type for Your Plug-In

You will learn in the upcoming chapters that a plug-in requires three resources for the Navigator to recognize it. These resources are as follows:

    MIMEType

    FileExtents

    FileOpenName

Of the three, `MIMEType` and `FileExtents` help Navigator determine whether or not to load your plug-in code module. The `FileOpenName` resource is used for the Files of type: field in the File Open dialog.

Initial Development

Your initial plug-in development and testing usually does not involve a Web server. It is much easier to debug a plug-in using local data files instead of files on a server. To open a local data file in Netscape Navigator use the File|Open File main menu item to select your test data file. You can screen out files of the wrong extension by using the Files of type drop-down and selecting your type. Figure 3.4 shows an AVI file being opened.

Figure 3.4.
Navigator's File Open dialog.

When you are testing on a local machine you don't have to worry much about which MIME type you use. Just be sure that the browser doesn't already handle the type such as text/html. After a local file is opened, Navigator determines the MIME type by mapping the file extension to the MIME type, both of which are located in your plug-in's resource.

Going Live

When your plug-in is ready for the real world, things become a bit more complicated. File content type on a Web server is determined by the server, not by Netscape's Navigator. So your newly invented MIME type (called application/x-whatever) is not mapped to your newly created extension. This is a common plug-in developer's pitfall. The plug-in loads fine with a local file, but when the file is put on a Web server it doesn't load.

Many plug-in developers have server access and can simply add the new type to the server configuration. However, you should still go through the proper steps to register your new media type. That way, when your plug-in becomes wildly popular, Web servers will be aware of the new media type.

Registering a New Media Type

IANA has established a procedure for review and approval of new media types. To give you an idea of just what is required for this registration, here is an e-mail template:

```
To: IANA@isi.edu
Subject: Registration of new Media Type content-type/subtype

Media Type name:

Media subtype name:

Required parameters:

Optional parameters:

Encoding considerations:

Security considerations:

Publish specification:

Contact E-mail address:
```

In most cases, your plug-in uses an existing top-level media type. If it doesn't, you must explain why an existing type cannot be used. The published specification must be an Internet RFC or RFC-to-be for a new top-level media type.

A good source for further registration information is a document called *Media Type Registration Procedure*, which is located at the following address:

```
http://www.netscape.com/assist/helper_apps/rfc3
```

Conclusion

Now that you are a MIME expert, here are a few things to remember:

■ Try to use one of the existing top-level media types if it fits your needs. Most plug-ins can use `applicaton` for binary data.

■ Put an `x-` before your proposed new MIME subtype. Here is an example:

`application/x-whatever`

■ A new mime type must be configured on the Web server. You can temporarily use an existing type for server testing if you don't have server access.

■ Send your media type registration to `IANA@isi.edu`.

What's Next?

Another type of application that is MIME type-dependent is Netscape helper applications. Helper applications were the predecessor to Navigator plug-ins. Many of these helper applications use a direct socket interface. The next chapter focuses on Navigator helper applications and Windows socket programming.

CHAPTER 4

Helper Applications and Network Communications

Introduction

Netscape helper applications are the father to Netscape plug-ins. Helper applications are small stand-alone programs that enable you to use media types not handled by the Netscape browser. Helpers, like plug-ins, are started based on file extension and MIME type. You can configure which helper application is used for each MIME type within the Netscape Navigator.

Netscape network-based helpers use Berkeley sockets, Dynamic Data Exchange (DDE), Object Linking and Embedding (OLE), or a combination of the three to interact with the Internet. Some of these types of helpers are unaware of Netscape and use sockets directly, while others use DDE or OLE to communicate with the Navigator.

Development of a Navigator plug-in rarely requires the direct use of sockets, DDE, or OLE. This chapter is an overview of these techniques and is not meant as a reference.

Netscape Helper Applications

Netscape helper applications work in much the same way as Netscape plug-ins. When the Navigator encounters an unknown media type, it first consults an internal plug-in list. Finding no plug-ins, it turns to the Helpers configuration. If a helper application is associated with the given media type, it is started by the Navigator.

A helper application can be any software program that runs on your system. Many helpers have nothing to do with networking. Consider using Microsoft Paint as a bitmap viewer. Navigator encounters a bitmap file, downloads it, and opens Paint with the given filename. Paint operates on the local file normally.

Other helpers have little, if any, communication with the Netscape Browser and use the network sockets API. A good example of a sockets-based helper application is Progressive Networks' RealAudio Player, which is shown in Figure 4.1. The RealAudio Player plays real-time sound over the Internet.

Figure 4.1.

The RealAudio Player from Progressive Networks.

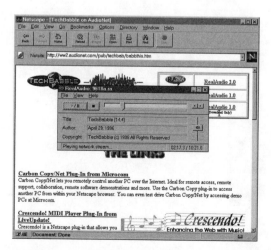

There are also helpers that rely heavily on the Navigator through the use of Netscape's Dynamic Data Exchange (DDE) or Object Linking and Embedding (OLE). These helpers can perform all network duties, such as loading URLs and writing to Web servers, strictly through the Navigator.

Windows Sockets

The Transmission Control Protocol (TCP) and Internet Protocol (IP) (known together as TCP/IP) were adopted in 1983 to network unlike computer architectures across the world. This network is, of course, the Internet. Although TCP/IP does provide an application layer, it proved to be complex and inconsistent across TCP/IP vendors. Enter Berkeley Software Distribution and its implementation of UNIX sockets, which simplified and standardized network programming. Berkeley socket implementations spread quickly to other platforms including Windows 3.x/95/NT.

The Windows socket interface is commonly known as WinSock. WinSock is implemented by dynamically linking to WINSOCK.DLL for 16-bit applications or WSOCK32.DLL for 32-bit applications. WinSock is a superset of the Berkeley socket API. The Windows extensions are prefaced with the letters *WSA*. Many of today's Windows Internet applications use WinSock for Internet communication. One good example is Netscape's Navigator.

Although this is not a WinSock programming book, it is interesting to take a look at the socket API names and brief descriptions. The WinSock APIs are divided into three sections. Table 4.1 shows the socket routines. The socket routines are used for basic socket communications including opening, closing, reading, and writing. Information such as host names and protocols can be determined with one of the database routines shown in Table 4.2. In Table 4.3, you can see that many of the Windows extensions (prefaced by WSA) were added to handle asynchronous calls and callbacks for Windows. These were needed to overcome the limitations of single-threaded Windows 3.1.

Table 4.1. Socket routines.

Socket	Description
accept	Accept a connection on a socket.
bind	Associate a local address with a socket.
closesocket	Close a socket.
connect	Establish a connection to a peer.
getpeername	Get the address of the peer to which a socket is connected.
getsockname	Get the local name for a socket.
getsockopt	Retrieve a socket option.
htonl	Convert a u_long from host to network byte order.
htons	Convert a u_short from host to network byte order.

continues

Table 4.1. continued

Socket	Description
inet_addr	Convert a string containing a dotted address into an in_addr.
inet_ntoa	Convert a network address into a string in dotted format.
ioctlsocket	Control the mode of a socket.
listen	Establish a socket to listen for incoming connection.
ntohl	Convert a u_long from network to host byte order.
ntohs	Convert a u_short from network to host byte order.
recv	Receive data from a socket.
recvfrom	Receive a datagram and store the source address.
select	Determine the status of one or more sockets, waiting if necessary.
send	Send data on a connected socket.
sendto	Send data to a specific destination.
setsockopt	Set a socket option.
shutdown	Disable sends and/or receives on a socket.
socket	Create a socket.

Table 4.2. Database routines.

Routine	Description
gethostbyaddr	Get host information corresponding to an address.
gethostbyname	Get host information corresponding to a hostname.
gethostname	Return the standard host name for the local machine.
getprotobyname	Get protocol information corresponding to a protocol name.
getprotobynumber	Get protocol information corresponding to a protocol number.
getservbyname	Get service information corresponding to a service name and protocol.
getservbyport	Get service information corresponding to a port and protocol.

Table 4.3. Windows extensions.

Extension	Description
WSAAsyncGetHostByAddr	Get host information corresponding to an address (asynchronous version).
WSAAsyncGetHostByName	Get host information corresponding to a hostname (asynchronous version).
WSAAsyncGetProtoByNumber	Get protocol information corresponding to a protocol number (asynchronous version).
WSAAsyncGetProtoByName	Get protocol information corresponding to a protocol name (asynchronous version).
WSAAsyncGetServByPort	Get service information corresponding to a port and protocol (asynchronous version).
WSAAsyncGetServByName	Get service information corresponding to a service name and port (asynchronous version).
WSAAsyncSelect	Request event notification for a socket.
WSACancelAsyncRequest	Cancel an incomplete asynchronous operation.
WSACancelBlockingCall	Cancel a blocking call that is currently in progress.
WSASetBlockingHook	Establish an application-specific blocking hook function.
WSAUnhookBlockingHook	Restore the default blocking hook function.
WSAGetLastError	Get the error status for the last operation that failed.
WSASetLastError	Set the error code, which can be retrieved by WSAGetLastError().
WSAIsBlocking	Determine whether a blocking call is in progress.
WSAStartup	Start a Windows sockets session.
WSACleanup	Terminate use of the Windows Sockets DLL.

These APIs are well documented in the Windows Sockets Specification found in the Microsoft Development Library. Although, as a plug-in developer, you might never need to make a single socket call, Netscape Navigator is using sockets on your plug-in's behalf.

TIP

The Socket Spy application (which is covered in Chapter 24, "Debugging with the Socket Spy") enables you to see data sent via sockets from any socket-based application. This can be helpful while debugging your plug-in.

Communication with Netscape

In many cases, socket-based helper applications have no communication with Netscape's Navigator. They are simply started by the Navigator and run as a totally separate program. Helpers that want tighter integration with Navigator use Dynamic Data Exchange (DDE) or Object Linking and Embedding (OLE). Applications using these interfaces might be able to avoid direct socket programming. Both interfaces are known as the Netscape Client API (NCAPI).

> **NOTE**
>
> This is not part of the Netscape plug-in API that you probably have bought this book to learn about. Just glance over this material, and you'll see the similarities to the plug-in API covered in Chapters 8 through 15.

Netscape's DDE Implementation

Navigator 1.*x* and above support DDE for communication with external programs. The external application must be both a DDE server and DDE client to take advantage of all DDE topics supported by Navigator. The DDE interface provides things such as getting URLs, progress notification, Navigator window information, and viewer registration. These DDE topics are shown in Table 4.4.

Table 4.4. Navigator DDE topics.

Topic	*Description*
WWW_Activate	Activate a Navigator window.
WWW_Alert	Display an alert box.
WWW_BeginProgress	Start sending progress topics.
WWW_CancelProgress	Notify Navigator to cancel download associated with the transaction.
WWW_EndProgress	Indicate that loading of the URL is complete.
WWW_Exit	Cause Navigator to attempt to exit.
WWW_GetWindowInfo	Get information about a Navigator window.
WWW_ListWindows	List all Navigator windows.
WWW_MakingProgress	Describe current progress with a range value.
WWW_OpenURL	Open a URL.

Topic	Description
WWW_ParseAnchor	Resolve a relative URL.
WWW_QueryURLFile	Return the URL from which a file was loaded.
WWW_QueryViewer	Query a viewer with a filename.
WWW_RegisterProtocol	Register a custom protocol.
WWW_RegisterURLEcho	Register a notification for URL loading.
WWW_RegisterViewer	Register a viewer with a MIME type.
WWW_RegisterWindowChange	Register a notification when a given Navigator window changes.
WWW_SetProgressRange	Set the progress range for progress messages.
WWW_ShowFile	Have Navigator load a file.
WWW_UnRegisterProtocol	Unregister the protocol registered with WWW_RegiesterProtocol.
WWW_UnRegisterURLEcho	Unregister echo registered with WWW_RegisterURLEcho.
WWW_UnRegisterViewer	Unregister viewer registered with WWW_RegisterViewer.
WWW_UnRegisterWindowChange	Unregister window changes registered with WWW_RegisterWindowChange.
WWW_URLEcho	Navigator loaded a URL.
WWW_Version	Check Navigator DDE version.
WWW_ViewDocFile	A file for a registered viewer.
WWW_WindowChange	A given Navigator window has changed.

Full documentation for Navigator DDE implementation can be found at the following address:

`http://home.netscape.com/newsref/std/ddeapi.html`

OLE Automation in Netscape

For Windows interprocess communication between Netscape's Navigator and an external application, OLE is the preferred mechanism. OLE is a bit more complicated to understand than DDE, but it provides tighter integration and a more object-oriented approach.

OLE automation is implemented in network, registry, viewer, and protocol objects. Of these, network and registry are implemented by the Navigator, while viewer and protocol are handled by the external application. Looking at the methods of these automation objects (shown in Tables 4.5 through 4.8), you see a superset of the DDE implementation.

Table 4.5. Network methods.

Method	Description
BytesReady	Inform the caller of the number of bytes prepared to be read.
Close	Disconnect any active connection and reset the Netscape.Network.1 object.
GetContentEncoding	Return the MIME encoding of the current load.
GetContentLength	Return the content length (total amount of bytes) of the current load.
GetContentType	Return the MIME type of the current load.
GetErrorMessage	Provide the caller with the Netscape internally generated error message.
GetExpires	Return when the data retrieved by this load is no longer considered valid.
GetFlagFancyFTP	Return whether or not FTP output will contain listing information such as file size, file type, and so on.
GetFlagFancyNews	Return whether or not Newsgroup listings will contain only newsgroups with an informative description.
GetFlagShowAllNews	Return whether or not all news articles will be listed.
GetLastModified	Return when the data retrieved by this load was last modified.
GetPassword	Determine the currently set password.
GetServerStatus	Determine the error status reported by the server.
GetStatus	Query the status of the current load.
GetUsername	Determine the currently set username.
IsFinished	Determine whether a load is complete.
Open	Initiate the retrieval of a URL from the network.
Read	Read data retrieved by Netscape.
Resolve	Generate an absolute (fully qualified) URL.
SetFlagFancyFTP	Inform Netscape whether or not FTP file listings will contain information such as file size, file type, and so on.
SetFlagFancyNews	Inform Netscape whether or not Newsgroup listings should also contain descriptions.
SetFlagShowAllNews	Inform Netscape whether or not all news articles will be listed when invoking Open with a news URL.
SetPassword	Set the current password in the Netscape.Network.1 object.
SetUsername	Set the current username in the Netscape.Network.1 object.

Table 4.6. Registry methods.

Method	Description
RegisterViewer	Register an OLE automation server to act as a streaming viewer for a particular MIME type.
RegisterProtocol	Register an OLE automation server to act as a protocol handler for a particular protocol type.

Table 4.7. Viewer methods.

Method	Description
Close	Inform the viewer that the download is now complete.
Initialize	Initialize the external streaming viewer.
Ready	Query the external streaming viewer about how much data it is ready to handle.
Write	Stream data to the external streaming viewer.

Table 4.8. Protocol methods.

Method	Description
Initialize	Initialize an external protocol handler to receive a URL.
Open	Inform the external protocol handler that it should open a URL.

What All of This Means to Plug-Ins

That is a lot of APIs, topics, and methods, but how do plug-ins fit into this picture? Plug-ins are code modules that become part of Netscape's Navigator. They are not separate applications such as helpers. Therefore, a large percentage of the subjects covered in this chapter are not used by a plug-in. That doesn't mean you can't use these techniques, but it will be a rare occasion when you do.

Conclusion

That was sure a quick tour of some serious information. Keep in mind that the techniques presented in this chapter are mainly for Netscape helper applications, not plug-ins. Plug-ins, a newer method of handling unknown media types within Netscape's Navigator, use a direct binary interface through the Navigator plug-in API.

What's Next?

The next chapter examines using a plug-in in a Web page with the appropriate HTML code. The RealAudio plug-in is used to show how the HTML EMBED tag works with a plug-in and how to extend EMBED tag attributes. This plug-in makes good use of a number of attributes to customize the look and feel of the Web page user interface.

PART II

The Netscape
Plug-Ins Basics

5   Using a Plug-In

6   Plug-In Design and Architecture

7   Navigator Plug-In Design Considerations

8   The Plug-In Application Programming Interface (API)

9   Instance Initialization and Destruction

10 Stream Creation and Destruction

11 Reading From and Writing To Streams

12 Memory Management

13 Status Methods

14 LiveConnect

15 Miscellaneous Methods

CHAPTER 5

Using a Plug-In

Introduction

In Chapter 4, you were introduced to the helper application RealAudio, created by a company called Progressive Networks. It just so happens that Progressive Networks also has a RealAudio plug-in that enables you to embed all the functionality of the helper application directly into your Web page.

The folks at Progressive Networks came up with a great tutorial for using a RealAudio plug-in for embedded audio. This tutorial serves as the basis for this chapter. You will see how the RealAudio plug-in makes extensive use of attributes with the HTML EMBED tag.

The EMBED Tag

To make it possible for plug-ins to coexist with other objects on a Web page, Netscape designers came up with the EMBED tag for HTML. This new tag allows your plug-in to become a seamless part of a Web page, with no difference to the user. It has the following syntax:

```
<EMBED src  height hidden palette pluginspace src type width units>
```

In this syntax, height, hidden, palette, pluginspace, src, type, width, and units are called *attributes* of the EMBED tag. These attributes, along with any others that your plug-in defines, are passed to the plug-in at load time. You can think of this as a command line similar to arguments passed into a text-based C program.

Attributes are passed in as *name=value* pairs. The attribute names are not case-sensitive. See Chapter 7, "Navigator Plug-In Design Considerations," for documentation on EMBED tag attributes.

RealAudio Extends the EMBED Tag Attributes

Plug-in developers are encouraged to extend the EMBED tag attributes to meet specific needs. The RealAudio plug-in makes full use of this feature by adding the CONTROLS, AUTOSTART, CONSOLE, and NOLABELS attributes. This is an excellent example of how to modify a plug-in's appearance based on the HTML code. Working examples of these RealAudio configurations can be found at the following address:

```
http://www.realaudio.com/products/ra2.0/plug_ins
```

Figure 5.1 shows the Web page located at this URL.

CONTROLS

The default user configuration of the RealAudio plug-in looks very much like that of its sibling, the RealAudio helper application. This configuration consists of multiple controls, title, author, copyright, and status information. Progressive Networks, realizing that many Web page authors do not need or want all of this control and information, made it possible to pick and choose sections of the RealAudio player for user interaction. To do this, they invented the CONTROLS attribute and assigned it 11 different values.

Figure 5.1.
*The "Using the RealAudio
Plug-in" Web page.*

CONTROLS=ALL

The first control type, CONTROLS=ALL, contains the whole ball of wax and, again, looks much like
the RealAudio. This is the default view if no CONTROLS attribute is specified. Audio can be played,
paused, and stopped via the appropriate buttons with VCR-style graphics. Information such as
title, author, copyright, modem speed, and stream position are displayed. Audio playback position can be changed with either a slider control or arrow buttons. Volume is changed with a vertical slider.

Figure 5.2 shows the results of using the following EMBED tag:

```
<EMBED SRC="all.rpm" WIDTH=300 HEIGHT=134>
```

Note that the CONTROLS attribute is not used, because ALL is the default.

Figure 5.2.
Using CONTROLS=ALL *with the
RealAudio plug-in.*

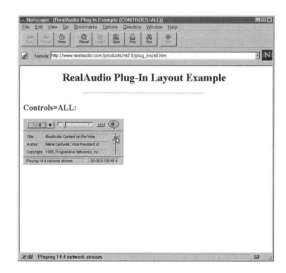

CONTROLS=ControlPanel

The next option, CONTROLS=ControlPanel, gives a user the basic Play/Pause button, Stop button, and Position slider. This is the same as the RealAudio helper application with none of the View main menu items checked.

Figure 5.3 shows the results of using the following EMBED tag:

```
<EMBED SRC="cpanel.rpm" WIDTH=350 HEIGHT=40 CONTROLS=ControlPanel>
```

Figure 5.3.

Using CONTROLS=
ControlPanel *with the
RealAudio plug-in.*

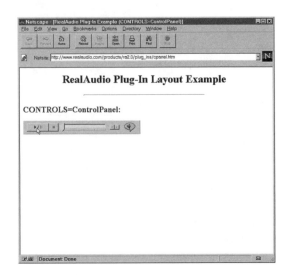

CONTROLS=InfoVolumePanel

CONTROLS=InfoVolumePanel shows the title, author, and copyright with a slider. This is the same as the RealAudio helper application with Info & Volume checked in the View main menu item.

Figure 5.4 shows the results of using the following EMBED tag:

```
<EMBED SRC = "infovol.rpm" WIDTH=350 HEIGHT=80
    CONTROLS=InfoVolumePanel console="Tester">
```

The EMBED line also includes the CONSOLE attribute. This attribute enables you to tie together multiple RealAudio controls. A full example of using the CONSOLE attribute is shown later in Figure 5.13.

CONTROLS=InfoPanel

CONTROLS=InfoPanel is the same as InfoVolumePanel minus the volume control. This panel displays the title, author, and copyright. Again, notice the floating Play/Pause and Stop buttons that are connected to the information panel with the CONSOLE attribute.

Figure 5.5 shows the results of using the following EMBED tag:

```
<EMBED SRC="infovol.rpm" WIDTH=320 HEIGHT=80
    CONTROLS=InfoPanel console="Tester">
```

Figure 5.4.

Using
CONTROLS=InfoVolumePanel
with the RealAudio plug-in.

Figure 5.5.

Using CONTROLS=InfoPanel
with the RealAudio plug-in.

CONTROLS=StatusBar

CONTROLS=StatusBar embeds a status bar. Status includes informational messages, position, and clip length. This is the same as the RealAudio helper application with the Status Bar of the View menu item checked.

Figure 5.6 shows the results of using the following EMBED tag:

```
<EMBED SRC="stat_bar.rpm" WIDTH=350 HEIGHT=22
    CONTROLS=StatusBar console="Tester">
```

Figure 5.6.

Using CONTROLS=StatusBar
with the RealAudio plug-in.

CONTROLS=PlayButton

CONTROLS=PlayButton is, as you would expect, an embedded play button. You can get some really cool effects by scattering audio controls throughout your Web page. Try embedding a control directly in a sentence.

Figure 5.7 shows the results of using the following EMBED tag:

```
<EMBED SRC="playbtn.rpm" WIDTH=40 HEIGHT=20
    CONTROLS=PlayButton>
```

Figure 5.7.

Using CONTROLS=PlayButton
with the RealAudio plug-in.

CONTROLS=StopButton

CONTROLS=StopButton provides an embedded Stop button. In most cases, you would also have an embedded Play button on the same page. Figure 5.8 includes both Stop and Play/Pause buttons. They are connected with the CONSOLE attribute.

Figure 5.8 shows the results of using the following EMBED tag:

```
<EMBED SRC="stopbtn.rpm" WIDTH=20 HEIGHT=20
    CONTROLS=StopButton console="Tester">
```

Figure 5.8.

Using CONTROLS=StopButton
with the RealAudio plug-in.

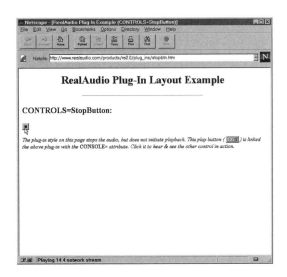

CONTROLS=VolumeSlider

CONTROLS=VolumeSlider provides a volume slider only. In some cases, you might not want to confuse the user with any other controls. Audio playback can be automatically started when the page is first viewed and stopped when the user leaves the page or when the audio stream is complete.

Figure 5.9 shows the results of using the following EMBED tag:

```
<EMBED SRC="volsldr.rpm" WIDTH=40 HEIGHT=80
    CONTROLS=VolumeSlider console="Tester">
```

CONTROLS=PositionSlider

CONTROLS=PositionSlider provides a position slider only. Again, as you can see in Figure 5.10, the CONSOLE attribute connects this slider to embedded PLAY/Pause and Stop buttons.

Figure 5.10 shows the results of using the following EMBED tag:

```
<EMBED SRC="positn.rpm" WIDTH=350 HEIGHT=40
    CONTROLS=PositionSlider console="Tester">
```

Figure 5.9.

Using CONTROLS= VolumeSlider *with the RealAudio plug-in.*

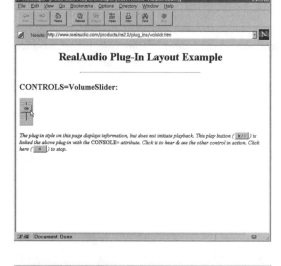

Figure 5.10.

Using CONTROLS= PositionSlider *with the RealAudio plug-in.*

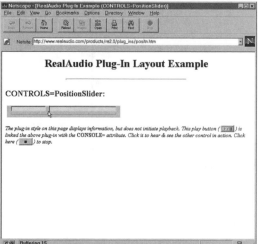

CONTROLS=PositionField

CONTROLS=PositionField embeds the field of the status bar that shows position and length. This is a handy status feature that you might want to hide in the corner of a Web page.

Figure 5.11 shows the results of using the following EMBED tag:

```
<EMBED SRC="pos_fld.rpm" WIDTH=100 HEIGHT=25
    CONTROLS=PositionField console="Tester">
```

Figure 5.11.

Using CONTROLS=
PositionField *with the*
RealAudio plug-in.

CONTROLS=StatusField

CONTROLS=StatusField embeds the field of the status bar that shows message text and progress indicators.

Figure 5.12 shows the results of using the following EMBED tag:

```
<EMBED SRC="stat_fld.rpm" WIDTH=350 HEIGHT=25
    CONTROLS=StatusField console="Tester">
```

Figure 5.12.

Using CONTROLS=StatusField
with the RealAudio plug-in.

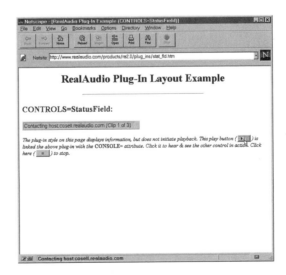

AUTOSTART

Many plug-ins support the AUTOSTART attribute. The RealAudio plug-in automatically begins playback when you add AUTOSTART=TRUE to the EMBED line. The AUTOSTART attribute looks like this in an EMBED tag:

```
<EMBED SRC="all.rpm" WIDTH=300 HEIGHT=134 AutoStart=True>
```

CONSOLE

Another really cool attribute that the RealAudio plug-in has is called CONSOLE. This attribute enables you to link two or more RealAudio plug-ins together. For example, you can have one stop button stop audio for any number of audio files. This attribute was used throughout the previous examples to link floating play and stop buttons to their respective audio files.

If you use a CONSOLE value of _master, it links that control to all audio files on the page. Figure 5.13 uses this technique.

Figure 5.13.

The CONSOLE *attribute hard at work.*

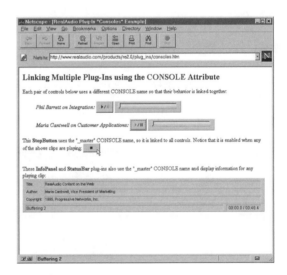

Here is the HTML code for the attribute shown in Figure 5.13:

```
<html>

<head>
<title>
RealAudio Plug-In "Consoles" Example
</title>
</head>

<body background="http://www.realaudio.com/pics/ihn_back.gif">

<H2>Linking Multiple Plug-Ins using the <FONT COLOR=C00000>CONSOLE</FONT>
Attribute</H2>
```

Each pair of controls below uses a different CONSOLE name so that their
behavior is linked together:

```
<BLOCKQUOTE>
<I>Phil Barrett on Integration: </I>

<EMBED SRC="console2.rpm" WIDTH=50 HEIGHT=33
    CONTROLS="PlayButton" CONSOLE=Clip2 ALIGN=absMiddle>

<EMBED SRC="empty2.rpm" WIDTH=200 HEIGHT=33
    CONTROLS="PositionSlider" CONSOLE=Clip2 ALIGN=absMiddle>

<P>
<I>Maria Cantwell on Customer Applications: </I>

<EMBED SRC="console3.rpm" WIDTH=50 HEIGHT=33
    CONTROLS="PlayButton" CONSOLE=Clip3 ALIGN=absMiddle>

<EMBED SRC="empty3.rpm" WIDTH=200 HEIGHT=33
    CONTROLS="PositionSlider" CONSOLE=Clip3 ALIGN=absMiddle>

</BLOCKQUOTE>
```

This <B>StopButton</B> uses the "_master" CONSOLE name, so it is linked
to all controls. Notice that it is enabled when any of the above clips
are playing: <EMBED SRC="empty4.rpm" WIDTH=50 HEIGHT=25 CONTROLS="StopButton"
CONSOLE="_master" ALIGN=absMiddle>

```
<BR clear=all>

<P>
```

These <B>InfoPanel</B> and <B>StatusBar</B> plug-ins also use the "_master"
CONSOLE name and display information for any playing clip:
<EMBED SRC="empty5.rpm" WIDTH=100% HEIGHT=75 CONTROLS="InfoPanel"
CONSOLE="_master" ALIGN=LEFT>

```
<BR CLEAR=ALL>

<EMBED SRC="empty6.rpm" WIDTH=100% HEIGHT=23 CONTROLS="StatusBar"

CONSOLE="_master"  ALIGN=LEFT>


</body>
</html>
```

NOTE

Chapter 9, "Instance Initialization and Destruction," mentions multi-instance plug-ins.
The RealAudio plug-in, using the CONSOLE attribute, is a great example of multi-instance
implementation and communications between plug-in instances.

NOLABELS

RealAudio also supports a NOLABELS attribute that, when set to TRUE, causes the InfoVolumePanel and InfoPanel controls not to display Title:, Author:, or Copyright labels. This is good for non-English implementations.

The NOEMBED Tag

Netscape Navigator 2.0 and above supports a NOEMBED tag that can be used for browsers that do not support plug-ins. For example, in the case of RealAudio, you might want the helper application to come up if plug-in support is not available.

Example:

```
<EMBED SRC="sample1.rpm" WIDTH=300 HEIGHT=134>
<NOEMBED><A SRC="sample1.ram"> Play the audio
using helper app! </A></NOEMBED>
```

Conclusion

There you have it—Progressive Networks RealAudio plug-in complete with EMBED attribute extensions. In Chapter 9, you'll learn how to parse Netscape's attributes, in addition to any of your own.

What's Next?

Now that you've seen how a plug-in is implemented with the HTML EMBED tag in a Web page, turn to the next chapter and read about Netscape's plug-in architecture. This chapter shows how HTML, Java, JavaScript, and the plug-in API all fit together.

CHAPTER 6

Plug-In Design and Architecture

Introduction

Netscape Navigator's plug-in architecture is based on dynamically loaded code modules. These modules reside in a subfolder or directory called PLUGINS that the Navigator reads during its initialization. Each module has a resource that determines which MIME type it can handle. When the Navigator finds this MIME type embedded in a Web page through HTML or as a single file, it loads the appropriate code module.

For embedded plug-ins, the HTML EMBED tag tells Navigator the size of the plug-in's window in a given Web page. This window is created by Navigator on behalf of the plug-in. The plug-in is given a handle to this newly created window for drawing and event processing.

When a plug-in is loaded, an instance of the plug-in is created with a call to the NPP_New API. The plug-in can be loaded multiple times, creating multiple instances. It is very common for a Web page to have more than one instance of a plug-in. Therefore, if your plug-in uses a restricted resource such as an audio card, you must allow for sharing of this resource across multiple plug-in instances.

Data streams are a big part of Netscape's plug-in architecture. Most plug-ins have data pushed from the server for processing, but others might choose to pull it down, perhaps in a random-access fashion. Just as a plug-in can have multiple instances, it can also have multiple streams per instance. The plug-in API also provides for stream instance data.

With the introduction of Netscape Navigator 3.0 comes LiveConnect. LiveConnect extends the plug-in architecture by adding communication between plug-ins, Java applets, and JavaScript. The Java Runtime Interface (JRI) plays an important part in this interface.

How It All Fits Together

As you can see in Figure 6.1, the Navigator 3.*x* plug-in architecture consists of a plug-in code module, Navigator, Java Applet and Java Runtime Interface (JRI), JavaScript, and HTML. A bare minimum plug-in could go without Java, JavaScript, and HTML. For example, many of this book's examples don't use Java or JavaScript and, if opened directly by the plug-in supported media file, would not use HTML either.

The core of the plug-in interface is the plug-in Application Programming Interface (API). These APIs are prefixed by NPN_ for methods located within the Navigator and NPP_ for methods in the plug-in. All APIs up to Navigator 3.*x* are well-documented in upcoming chapters of this book. Using the APIs, the plug-in becomes part of Navigator's code. With the introduction of Netscape Navigator 3.0 came new APIs and LiveConnect. LiveConnect joins plug-ins with Java and JavaScript.

Figure 6.1.

Netscape's Navigator 3.x plug-in architecture.

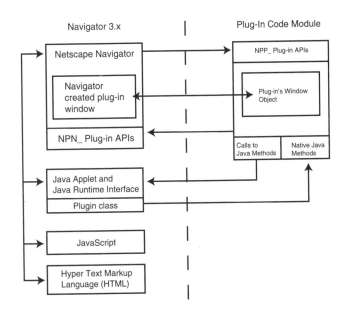

LiveConnect

Netscape's LiveConnect enables you to integrate Java, JavaScript, and plug-ins. New plug-in methods for LiveConnect are `NPP_GetJavaClass`, `NPN_GetJavaEnv`, and `NPN_GetJavaPeer`. Chapter 14, "LiveConnect," documents these Java-specific APIs for plug-ins and gives more details on the LiveConnect interface. Also, a LiveConnect example written by Netscape is presented in Chapter 23, "Netscape's LiveConnect Sample."

For the purposes of this chapter, you should understand what LiveConnect does. With LiveConnect you can perform the following tasks:

■ Call a Java method from a plug-in.

■ Call a *native* method located in a plug-in from Java.

■ Call Java methods from JavaScript.

■ Call JavaScript methods from Java.

As you can see, LiveConnect is for extending JavaScript and Java as much as it is for extending plug-ins. If you refer back to Figure 6.1, you can see that there is no direct connection between plug-ins and JavaScript. Any plug-in to JavaScript communication must go through Java.

To learn more about LiveConnect, refer to this book's LiveConnect Plug-in API reference and sample chapters. Also, make sure to get the latest Software Development Kit (SDK) from Netscape and read the documentation. The Netscape SDK has the most up-to-date LiveConnect information.

Runtime Loading

When the Navigator initializes itself, it checks for installed plug-ins in the PLUGINS subdirectory or folder. Navigator does not load any plug-ins at this time; it just parses out the resource information containing the plug-in's supported MIME types, file extensions, and the name for the file open dialog. At the time of this writing, Macintosh plug-ins allow a user to configure plug-in/MIME type association, while Windows does not. Navigator release 4.0 for Windows is slated to have this feature, according to Netscape sources.

The release of Navigator Beta 4 for Windows contains an updated version of the Help|About Plug-ins menu item. The About Plug-ins feature tells you what plug-in you have installed. Also provided is the full path of each plug-in and its MIME type, its description, its suffixes, and whether it is enabled. Only after Navigator finds a MIME type to which a plug-in is registered is the plug-in loaded into memory and executed. Figure 6.2 shows the Windows Navigator Beta 4 About Plug-ins screen.

Figure 6.2.

Windows Navigator Beta 4 About Plug-ins screen.

Plug-In Instances and Instance Data

It is important to realize that your plug-in can be loaded multiple times, depending on a given Web page. For example, a Web page might contain three audio files of the same type. Navigator then creates three instances of the audio plug-in using the NPP_New API. Each of these instances has its own instance data that is allocated by the plug-in and attached to a Navigator-maintained instance data pointer. Each time Navigator calls one of your plug-in methods, you must dereference the Navigator-provided instance pointer and get access to your instance data. All of the examples in this book show how to do this.

In many cases, your plug-in code can be oblivious to other instances. However, in some cases, a plug-in needs to communicate among its instances. The RealAudio plug-in does this by allowing a Web author to load a console instance to control other instances associated with audio files. You can read more about the RealAudio plug-in in Chapter 5, "Using a Plug-In."

Windows and Events

It is important to understand that Navigator creates a window for your plug-in's use. You are provided a handle to this window during a call to the NPP_SetWindow method. The size of this window is determined by the HTML EMBED tag attributes WIDTH and HEIGHT. Relative window position is also determined by the HTML code. Window and event processing differ between UNIX, Windows, and Macintosh.

In Windows and UNIX, a child window is created in the window hierarchy. This child window automatically sees all window events. In the Windows programming environment, you can sub-class the Navigator-created window to process any given window event.

The Macintosh environment is a little different. A Macintosh window is shared between the plug-in and the Navigator, which means that your plug-in must only draw in the specified area of this shared window. You must save, set up, and restore the shared drawing environment around any drawing operations. Events are provided to the Macintosh plug-in with the NPP_HandleEvent API.

Seamless Web Page Embedding

The big advantage of a Navigator plug-in over a Navigator helper application is its capability to embed itself directly in the Navigator displayed Web page. This feature is similar to how a Java applet provides seamless Web page integration. A plug-in differs from Java in that the plug-in's code is native to the local machine and is installed. A Java applet is downloaded before each use and is platform independent.

A plug-in can run in either embedded, full page, or hidden modes. Of these modes, embedded is used most often because it provides seamless Web page integration. Full page mode allows a plug-in to run by itself, taking the whole Navigator display area. Hidden mode, as the name implies, is for plug-ins that have no visible attributes. An example of a hidden plug-in is the Background MIDI Player found in this book's sample code.

Data Streams

Netscape Navigator plug-ins are built around the concept of client/server data streaming. A stream is a constant flow of data. One of the first implementations of streams was for the UNIX I/O subsystem, which provided a full-duplex, modular connection to a given device driver. As multimedia becomes more prevalent on the home computer, streaming becomes very important to handle data flow for audio and video.

A simple stream can be implemented with a pool of fixed-length buffers. The producer of data continuously fills empty buffers, buffer order is maintained, and data is delivered to the consumer. Such problems as overruns (no more empty buffers) or underruns (no more full buffers) make the life of the stream more complicated.

The Navigator plug-in API provides many methods for managing data streams both to and from a plug-in. For a stream that sends data from the Navigator to a plug-in (the most common type of stream), you can create it with NPP_NewStream, get data from it with NPP_Write, and destroy it with NPP_DestroyStream. A stream that sends data from a plug-in to the Navigator (new with the Navigator 3.0 plug-in API) uses NPN_NewStream for creation, NPN_Write to write data to the stream, and NPN_DestroyStream to destroy it. Additionally, your plug-in can have multiple incoming and outgoing streams running concurrently. Read about the streaming methods in Chapter 10, "Stream Creation and Destruction," and Chapter 11, "Reading From and Writing To Streams." Be sure to check out the code samples in Chapter 17, "A Streaming Audio Sample," and Chapter 18, "The Buffer Classes," to see how your plug-in can handle a real-time data stream from the Navigator.

> **NOTE**
>
> All of the streaming samples in this book operate on single streams. If you are writing a plug-in that handles multiple streams, be sure to add code for multiple stream management. This book's samples relate a single stream to the whole plug-in instance object. A multiple stream plug-in should use a separate stream object to manage each stream. Some of the API code examples in Chapter 10 show this technique, but sample code in Chapters 17 through 23 does not.

Sequential and Seekable Streams

After a plug-in is loaded, for all intents and purposes it is part of the Navigator client. A plug-in is compiled machine code and requires no interpretation, as is required by platform-independent languages such as Java. Being this tightly coupled allows a very high-speed bond to the Navigator client and, in turn, the Web server. Data flows between the plug-in and Navigator in either sequential or seekable streams.

As you'll see in Chapter 10, a plug-in can change the stream type to seekable by setting *stype to NP_SEEK. Setting this mode allows a plug-in to pull data from a server with calls to the NPN_RequestRead method. This technique puts the onus on a plug-in to continuously call Navigator for data buffers and is not considered a true continuously flowing stream. A seekable stream is generally slower than a sequential stream, which is driven by Navigator with calls to the plug-in implemented method NPP_Write. Your plug-in should only use seekable streams when the random access benefits outweigh the performance penalty. Seekable streams also have many other usage problems that you'll find out about in Chapter 10.

When Navigator creates a stream for your plug-in, it is in sequential mode. In most cases, a sequential type stream is created for each plug-in instance. Your plug-in is automatically notified by the NPP_Write API as chunks of data come across the network. This data flow can come from the Internet via TCP/IP, a Local Area Network (LAN), a local client file, or Navigator's file cache. A sequential stream, as the name implies, is a continuous sequential stream of data true to the streaming definition. In most cases, this is the preferred stream type for a plug-in to use.

> **NOTE**
>
> Navigator's cache plays an important role in your plug-in's performance. Netscape Navigator 2.0 has both a memory-based and a disk-based caching system. The caching scheme is based on whole files. If you abort a file download, it is not saved to cache. Both cache sizes are user configurable.
>
> Navigator 3.0 introduced LiveCache. LiveCache provides progressive caching, which enables you to continue where you left off if a file download is aborted. LiveCache also enables you to preload content from slow devices such as CD-ROM for fast access and viewing.

Assisted Installation

A common problem with plug-ins is that users don't know where to find them. To view a Web page that needs a specific plug-in, the user must have that plug-in installed on his or her local machine. To make it easy for users to install new plug-ins, Navigator provides an assisted installation feature. This is automatically activated when a user displays an HTML page that requires a plug-in that is not currently installed.

When a user hits a Web page that requires a plug-in not found in that user's current plug-in installation, a dialog is automatically opened, allowing the user to select either Plug-in Info or Cancel. If the Plug-in Info button is clicked, Navigator loads a new URL to get the given plug-in. This URL can be specified in the PLUGINSPACE attribute of the EMBED tag (see the next chapter for further documentation). If no PLUGINSPACE attribute is used, Navigator goes to a current plug-in list.

Netscape's SDK

You should download Netscape's Plug-in SDK to use in conjunction with this book. The SDK contains the authoritative and most up-to-date plug-in documentation. This SDK is currently located at the following FTP site:

```
ftp://ftpXX.netscape.com/pub/navigator/sdk
```

In this address, ftpXX is any one of Netscape's 20 or so FTP servers.

The Plug-in SDK provides the following benefits:

- Documentation in HTML format
- Header and source files
- Source code examples
- Special tools for LiveConnect

Conclusion

This chapter discussed Netscape Navigator's plug-in architecture. The block diagram in Figure 6.1 showed Navigator's current plug-in architecture up to Navigator 3.*x*.

Navigator 3.*x* introduced a major plug-in enhancement called LiveConnect. LiveConnect allows direct communication between Java, JavaScript, and plug-ins. You should get the current Netscape Navigator Plug-in SDK for the best information on LiveConnect.

Remember that plug-ins are dynamically loaded code modules. A plug-in that is loaded more than once is considered to have multiple instances. Navigator creates a child window in UNIX and MS Windows, but it shares the main window with a Macintosh plug-in.

Try to process your data in a streaming fashion by allowing the Web server to push data to your plug-in with a sequential mode stream.

What's Next?

The next chapter focuses on design issues for your plug-in. Network bandwidth, MIME considerations, HTML attributes, and plug-in types are discussed.

CHAPTER 7

Navigator Plug-In Design Considerations

Introduction

You should think about a few things before you jump into the wonderful world of Netscape Navigator plug-in development. The tools you use, the compatibility, and the performance will affect your plug-in's success in the quickly growing plug-in market. As you design your Netscape Navigator plug-in, consider the following factors:

■ What development language should you use? Most Navigator plug-ins today are written in C++. In fact, all of this book's examples are in C++. You can use C or even assembler. Any language that is capable of generating machine language for your given platform will work.

■ Another thing to think about is Navigator capability. Will your plug-in work with Navigator 2.*x*? How about 3.*x*? Make sure you have a good reason for not supporting these older Navigator versions.

■ Bandwidth requirements for your plug-in should be well-planned. Can your plug-in handle a 28.8K baud Internet connection? How about 14.4K?

■ Do you want a Java or JavaScript interface to your plug-in?

■ What about MIME types? How many should you support? Is MIME contention an issue?

■ Can you write your plug-in so that it processes data in a real-time streaming fashion? Or, must a user wait for a complete file to download?

■ Does your plug-in require a CGI program?

This chapter will help you think about these questions.

Choosing a Development Language

Unlike a Java applet, a plug-in is native machine code and is not interpreted, which means that you can write a plug-in in any language that compiles to native machine code. However, there are some issues that make certain languages easier to use than others.

For example, in Windows a plug-in must be a Dynamic Link Library (DLL). The development language you use must be capable of generating a DLL code module to build a stand-alone plug-in. Many languages such as Microsoft's Visual Basic and Borland's Delphi are quite capable of generating Windows DLLs, but these languages might not be able to properly generate the special resources required for plug-ins. You might be better off using one of these high-level languages to generate an OLE library for use with a third party plug-in such as ActiveX from NCompass or OpenScape from BusinessWeb. (See Appendix B for more on these plug-ins.)

The best-documented language for Navigator plug-in development is C++. This book, along with Netscape's Plug-in SDK, uses C++ exclusively. Assembler can be used inline or in separate routines. In some cases, such as software decompression, an assembler routine might provide the performance you need. Other possibilities should be considered. Perhaps a hybrid solution using C++ to call routines implemented in other languages could work as well.

It is possible to modify this book's example code so that you can use the C language for your plug-in development. However, for the most part, modifying for C is probably harder than learning a few simple things about C++ to use it in plug-in development.

Navigator Version Compatibility

What version of Netscape's Navigator should your plug-in support? Plug-in support was introduced with Navigator 2.*x*. Navigator 3.*x* brought many new and cool features such as LiveConnect and streaming data from a plug-in to the Navigator. Can you design your plug-in so that it works with both Navigator 2.*x* and Navigator 3.*x*? What about Navigator 4.*x*! Your plug-in can also "turn on" more features, depending on the Navigator version under which it is running.

Be sure to check out the NPN_Version API for determining the current Navigator version. Also keep in mind that the version number returned by NPN_Version does not correspond to the Navigator version (such as 2.0, 3.0, and so on) but to the plug-in API it supports. You see more on this in Chapter 9, "Instance Initialization and Destruction."

Planning for Bandwidth Limitations

What about network bandwidth? Is your plug-in geared toward Internet usage for cases in which a typical Internet Service Provider (ISP) is connecting users at 14.4K baud or 28.8K baud? Or perhaps you are developing a plug-in for your company's local Intranet. Intranet plug-ins, used mostly on local area networks, need not worry about slow modem connections. Multimedia audio and video formats have huge bandwidth requirements. Most of today's multimedia data throughput minimums were defined by CD-ROM speeds, not by comparatively slow Internet connections. Data compression for audio and video media types has never been more important.

Streaming Audio

Let's look at audio and how you can stream it in real-time. A common modem speed today is 14,400 bits per second. Low quality audio is generally sampled at 11,025 samples per second, using one byte per sample. A speed of 11,025 samples per second is 11,025 bytes per second, and that is 88,200 bits per second:

```
11,025 bytes/second * 8 bits/byte = 88,200 bits/second
```

How are you going to fit 88,200 bps through a 14,400 bps Internet connection? The answer, of course, is data compression.

Using the preceding numbers, a 7 to 1 compression ratio would squeak you by:

```
88,200 bps / 14,400 bps ~ 7
```

Some of today's plug-in vendors are claiming compression ratios as high as 50 to 1! This more than ample compression is obtained through the use of *lossy compression*, or removing some data such as dead space between words. In fact, much of what you see on the Web today uses lossy compression, such as JPEG, AVI video, and audio compression.

Remember that the preceding numbers were taken from a perfect world. You won't get 14,400 bps from a 14.4K modem. Other factors such as TCP/IP error correction, the speed of your computer, and server load also play an important part in actual throughput.

Multiplatform Compatibility

Multiplatform compatibility is a big design consideration that determines your plug-in's marketability. Although this book is geared toward Windows plug-ins, Netscape's Plug-in API was designed for platform independence. You will see how they do this in Chapter 8, "The Plug-In Application Programming Interface (API)." Great efforts were made by the Netscape development staff to keep the API set consistent across the Macintosh, UNIX, and Windows platforms. Rumors of more platforms (such as OS/2) being supported for Navigator are now coming across the Internet.

If you are a Windows developer, don't be too quick to rule out a version of your plug-in for the Macintosh and UNIX platforms. Try to develop your plug-in with an eye toward other platforms. Consider using Java in conjunction with your plug-in for a user interface. Tight integration between Java and the plug-in comes with LiveConnect as shown in Chapter 14, "LiveConnect." You should only use native operating system level APIs when there is no other recourse.

Expanding to Java with LiveConnect

Netscape introduced LiveConnect with the release of the 3.0 Navigator. LiveConnect allows Navigator plug-ins, Java, and JavaScript to communicate with each other. How can this technology benefit your development efforts? Does it make sense to add a Java extension to your plug-in, or are you doing it strictly for the hype value?

Using Java in conjunction with a plug-in can certainly reduce your development efforts. The most dramatic reduction would occur with a Java/Plug-in applet that uses a plug-in for platform-specific duties and Java for an interactive user interface. In that case, you only have to port the hardware-dependent plug-in, while the user-interface written in Java is untouched.

Netscape's LiveConnect AVI video player is a simple example of using Java and JavaScript for the user interface and leaving the video implementation to a plug-in. The LiveConnect video player is documented in Chapter 23.

HTML EMBED Tag Attributes

An embedded plug-in is started by the EMBED tag in the Web page's HTML code. When the plug-in is loaded, it is displayed as part of the HTML document rather than within another window. This technique is very similar to how graphics are embedded in a Web page. As you design your plug-in, you should think about which EMBED tag attributes your plug-in will support. Additionally, define new attributes that are specific to your plug-in.

Current Attributes

The next few sections document Netscape's current EMBED tag attributes. The EMBED tag has the following syntax:

```
<EMBED attributes> … </EMBED>
```

HEIGHT="value"

> *Example*   HEIGHT=50

The HEIGHT attribute defines the vertical size of the plug-in window in units defined by the UNITS attribute. Default UNITS are pixels.

HIDDEN=true or HIDDEN=false

> *Example*   HIDDEN

The HIDDEN attribute determines whether the plug-in is visible. A value of true indicates that the plug-in is hidden and not visible. This overrides any HEIGHT or WIDTH parameters and makes the plug-in zero in size. An example of a hidden plug-in is a Web page background MIDI player (a sample in this book). Be sure to use the HIDDEN attribute to define an invisible plug-in rather than defining HEIGHT and WIDTH to zero. If you use the HIDDEN attribute with no parameters, it defaults to true.

PALETTE=foreground or PALETTE=background

> *Example*   PALETTE=background

The PALETTE attribute is for the Windows platform. This attribute instructs the plug-in to realize its palette as either a foreground or background palette. It is useful for embedding multiple palette-aware plug-ins in a single page. The default value is background.

PLUGINSPAGE="URL"

> *Example*   PLUGINSPAGE=http://www.yourcompany.com

The PLUGINSPAGE attribute is used by the assisted installation feature if the plug-in registered for the MIME type of a given EMBED tag is not found. Its argument is a standard Universal Resource Locator (URL) that usually contains the location of the needed plug-in.

> **NOTE**
>
> This attribute is not implemented in Navigator 2.*x*.

SRC="URL"

Example   SRC=sound.wav

The SRC attribute indicates, with its Universal Resource Locator (URL), the location of a plug-in's data file. The MIME type of this data file determines which plug-in is loaded to handle the file. Usually, the MIME type is determined by the file's extension. The EMBED tag must use either the SRC or TYPE attribute.

TYPE="type"

Example   TYPE=audio/x-wav

The TYPE attribute is used instead of SRC to load a plug-in. The TYPE attribute is used for plug-ins that do not require a data file for startup. The argument for this attribute is a MIME type that maps to a plug-in. The EMBED tag must use either the SRC or TYPE attribute.

WIDTH="value"

Example   WIDTH=200

The WIDTH attribute defines the horizontal size of the plug-in window in units defined by the UNITS attribute. Default UNITS are pixels.

UNITS="value"

Example   UNITS=en

The UNITS attribute defines which measurement units are used by the HEIGHT and WIDTH attributes. The value can be either pixels or en. pixels are the default. An en is half the point size.

Adding Your Own Attributes

It is a simple matter to add attributes for your plug-in's private use. Just put them in the EMBED command line. Navigator ignores all nonstandard attributes while parsing the HTML EMBED tag. You get any additional name=value pairs during your plug-in's NPP_New API.

For example, many plug-ins use the AUTOSTART and LOOP attributes. These attributes can be added to the EMBED tag like this:

```
<EMBED SRC="video.avi" WIDTH=320 HEIGHT=200 LOOP=true AUTOSTART=true>
```

Notice how additional private attributes can be put in the EMBED tag command line just like standard attributes. For an example of extensive use of private attributes, check out Chapter 5, "Using a Plug-In," which shows how the RealAudio plug-in uses this technique.

Multiple MIME Types

Your plug-in can support more than one MIME type. This feature can be really handy for plug-ins that support more than one file format. Consider Netscape's LiveAudio plug-in, which is included with Navigator 3.*x*. This plug-in currently supports seven different MIME types! The most popular audio formats for UNIX, Macintosh, and Windows are covered. Table 7.1 shows the MIME types, descriptions, and suffixes supported by the LiveAudio plug-in.

Table 7.1. LiveAudio MIME types.

Mime Type	Description	Suffixes
audio/basicl	AU	au
audio/x-aiff	AIFF	aiff, aif
audio/aiff	AIFF	aiff, aif
audio/x-wav	WAV	wav
audio/wav	WAV	wav
audio/x-midi	MIDI	midi, mid
audio/midi	MIDI	midi, mid

MIME Contention

MIME contention occurs when more than one installed plug-in supports the same MIME type. The Macintosh Navigator has solved this problem by letting the user configure appropriate plug-ins for each MIME type. At the time of this writing, Windows and UNIX do not yet have this plug-in user configuration.

When designing your plug-in, you should be aware of these MIME contention issues. The best defense is a good installation program and user documentation until Netscape resolves this problem.

File Base versus Streaming Plug-Ins

Try to design for a streaming plug-in rather than a file-based plug-in whenever possible. A streaming plug-in processes data on a buffer by buffer basis as it is downloaded from the network. The advantages of using this design are twofold. First, your plug-in can operate in real-time such as the RealAudio plug-in. And second, your plug-in can take advantage of processing time while the data file is being downloaded.

Although it is preferred, in many cases it does not make sense to use a streaming plug-in design. Consider a plug-in that plays AVI video files. Because the AVI format was designed for CD-ROM streaming at 150KB per second (not your common Internet connection speed), it is not possible to play this file format in real-time over the Internet. As you will see with Netscape's AVI player plug-in example, this type of plug-in is file-based.

Streaming to the Navigator

Navigator 3.*x* enables you to stream data from your plug-in to the Navigator. Do this by creating a new stream with `NPN_NewStream`, writing to it with `NPN_Write`, and destroying it with `NPN_DestroyStream`. These APIs are fully documented later in this book.

Why would you ever want to do this? Maybe you could create a plug-in that reads raw data from a Web server, converts it to HTML, and streams that HTML data to the Navigator for display. For example, you could write a plug-in that displays UNIX manual pages in a nice HTML format.

Your plug-in can make Web pages on-the-fly using this technique.

Client/Server Design

With the addition of a Common Gateway Interface (CGI) program residing on the Web server, your plug-in implementation can have a true client/server design. Your CGI server back-end can do things such as database searches while the browser client handles the display.

You can send data to your CGI program with `NPN_GetURL` or `NPN_PostURL`. Navigator 3.*x* adds `NPN_GetURLNotify`, `NPN_PostURLNotify`, and `NPP_URLNotify` to the mix for better error checking.

Be sure to check out the Server CPU Monitor sample for an example of using these APIs with a CGI program.

Conclusion

This chapter gave you some ideas to contemplate while designing your plug-in. Navigator compatibility, development languages, bandwidth requirements, LiveConnect, EMBED attributes, and MIME types should all be considered for your plug-in's development and design. Streaming plug-ins are generally considered much cooler than file-based plug-ins. You can use a CGI program for any needed server software.

The best way to get ideas for your plug-in is from existing plug-ins that are already written. Check out Appendix B and try to get one example of each type. Always be on the lookout for new and interesting plug-ins listed by Netscape, BrowserWatch, and other sites.

What's Next?

Chapter 8, "The Plug-In Application Programming Interface (API)," and Chapters 9 through 15 document all Netscape Navigator plug-in APIs up to Navigator version 3.*x*. Be sure to use the API index on the inside of this book's front cover to quickly locate these APIs.

The Plug-In Application Programming Interface (API)

Introduction

In order to maintain similarity across multiple platforms, the Windows plug-in Application Programming Interface (API) is not built in the usual Windows fashion. A Netscape Navigator plug-in is implemented in a dynamically linked code module. In Windows, this module is the standard dynamic link library, or DLL. Microsoft designed the dynamic link library with an eye toward implementations such as a Netscape plug-in, but Netscape has taken a slightly different approach.

This chapter explains the difference between a Netscape API and a plug-in API. Implementations are included for both types of APIs and how code is called. Additionally, all APIs (including platform-specific) are briefly explained. More detailed documentation is continued throughout the next chapters.

Who Is Calling Whom?

If you scan through the plug-in documentation, you might notice that there are two types of APIs. The first type begins with the convention NPP_. These routines are implemented by your plug-in and are called from the Navigator. The letters NPP stand for *Netscape Plug-in: Plug-in Defined.* The second type begins with the convention NPN_. These routines are implemented by the Navigator and are called from your plug-in. The letters NPN stand for *Netscape Plug-in: Navigator Defined.* Figure 8.1 shows the calling direction for NPN_ and NPP_ plug-in APIs.

Figure 8.1.
API calling techniques.

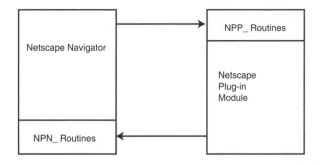

Dynamically Loaded

All plug-in types—whether they are UNIX, Macintosh, or Windows 3.1/95/NT—are dynamically loaded code modules. As explained previously in this book, this architecture has been proven over the years as an effective technique to save system resources by calling code only on demand. As a Windows developer, you are probably familiar with a Windows dynamically linked library (DLL), and you might have used them in your projects.

Routines are called within a DLL through entry points defined during compile time. An application might implicitly load a DLL by linking to a stub library during compile time, or explicitly load a DLL by using a Windows API such as LoadLibrary followed with calls to GetProcAddress to retrieve function addresses.

How Netscape Calls Your DLL

Unfortunately, these linking methods are very specific to Windows and did not fit Netscape's criteria for cross-platform equivalence. If you look at a typical plug-in DLL's header, you'll notice only three entry points:

```
NP_GETENTRYPOINTS
NP_SHUTDOWN
NP_INITIALIZE
```

That certainly doesn't give Netscape much to work with—or does it?

NPWIN.CPP

A file is provided by Netscape for Windows developers. It's called NPWIN.CPP and can be found on this book's CD-ROM or via Netscape's plug-in developer's kit. This file contains code for Windows DLL entry points. You might want to review this file before proceeding.

Because NPWIN.CPP is intended as a layer to hide Windows platform-specific entry points from your plug-in, Netscape asks developers not to touch this file. To ensure that this code is not changed, Netscape has mentioned that it might convert NPWIN.CPP to a binary library in the future.

NP_Initialize

Immediately after the plug-in is loaded, the DLL routine NP_Initialize is called. This routine has one parameter, a pointer to an NPNetscapeFuncs structure:

```
NPError WINAPI NP_EXPORT NP_Initialize (NPNetscapeFuncs* pFuncs)
```

The NPNetscapeFuncs structure, which is located in the Netscape provided header file npupp.h, is defined in the Navigator 3.0 Plug-in SDK as follows:

```
typedef struct _NPNetscapeFuncs {
    uint16 size;
    uint16 version;
    NPN_GetURLUPP geturl;
    NPN_PostURLUPP posturl;
    NPN_RequestReadUPP requestread;
    NPN_NewStreamUPP newstream;
    NPN_WriteUPP write;
    NPN_DestroyStreamUPP destroystream;
    NPN_StatusUPP status;
    NPN_UserAgentUPP uagent;
    NPN_MemAllocUPP memalloc;
    NPN_MemFreeUPP memfree;
    NPN_MemFlushUPP memflush;
    NPN_ReloadPluginsUPP reloadplugins;
    NPN_GetJavaEnvUPP getJavaEnv;
    NPN_GetJavaPeerUPP getJavaPeer;
    NPN_GetURLNotifyUPP geturlnotify;
    NPN_PostURLNotifyUPP posturlnotify;
#ifdef XP_UNIX
    NPN_GetValueUPP getvalue;
#endif /* XP_UNIX */
} NPNetscapeFuncs;
```

The first things to notice are the structure members size and version. The size is simply a sizeof NPNetscapeFuncs. During NP_Initialize, the size is checked against your plug-in's internal NPNetscapeFuncs structure to assure compatibility:

```
if(pFuncs->size < sizeof NPNetscapeFuncs)
    return NPERR_INVALID_FUNCTABLE_ERROR;
```

The version is checked in a similar fashion:

```
if(HIBYTE(pFuncs->version) > NP_VERSION_MAJOR)
    return NPERR_INCOMPATIBLE_VERSION_ERROR;
```

NOTE

The version numbers indicated by NP_VERSION_MAJOR and NP_VERSION_MINOR can't be directly correlated to the version of the Navigator. These values refer to the version of the API. When the major version number of the API increases, it is a breaking change. Plug-ins written for version 0 of the API (the current major version number) won't work if the API in the Navigator progresses to major version 1. Minor version changes indicate nonbreaking changes in the API. Thus, the major version number returned by Atlas (Navigator 3.*x*) continues to be 0, while the minor version is incremented with each change to the API. NP_VERSION_MAJOR and NP_VERSION_MINOR are predefined in the header file, so those numbers indicate the version of the API against which the plug-in was compiled.

Further down in the structure, notice the 12 function pointer prototypes beginning with NPN_. You remember that NPN stands for a routine within the Navigator. This structure holds function pointers to all Navigator entry points that are called by your plug-in. A global pointer to this structure is maintained by your plug-in for future calls to the Navigator:

```
g_pNavigatorFuncs = pFuncs; // save it for future reference
```

The NP_Initialize routine ends with a call to your internal NPP_Initialize method, which is documented in Chapter 9, "Instance Initialization and Destruction."

Mapping Your API Calls to Netscape

As your plug-in is running, it makes calls to the Navigator. For instance, a call to allocate memory from the Navigator is NPN_MemAlloc (see Chapter 12, "Memory Management"). NPN_MemAlloc is really a routine within your plug-in. Look again in the file NPWIN.CPP and find the following routine:

```
void* NPN_MemAlloc(uint32 size)
{
    return g_pNavigatorFuncs->memalloc(size);
}
```

Notice that this routine simply maps your call to NPN_MemAlloc to the previously mentioned structure of function pointers NPNetscapeFuncs and calls the routine memalloc through the use of the saved pointer, g_pNavigatorFuncs.

NP_GetEntryPoints

After NP_Initialize is called and returns successfully, the DLL entry point routine NP_GetEntryPoints is called. Just as NP_Initialize gives you the means to call Navigator routines, NP_GetEntryPoints allows Netscape to call your plug-in's routines without using standard DLL calling conventions. Look at the prototype for this routine:

NPError WINAPI NP_EXPORT NP_GetEntryPoints (NPPluginFuncs* pFuncs)

As with NP_Initialize, a pointer to a structure is passed. In this case, it's a pointer to the structure NPPluginFuncs, which is currently defined as follows:

```
typedef struct _NPPluginFuncs {
    uint16 size;
    uint16 version;
    NPP_NewUPP newp;
    NPP_DestroyUPP destroy;
    NPP_SetWindowUPP setwindow;
    NPP_NewStreamUPP newstream;
    NPP_DestroyStreamUPP destroystream;
    NPP_StreamAsFileUPP asfile;
    NPP_WriteReadyUPP writeready;
    NPP_WriteUPP write;
    NPP_PrintUPP print;
    NPP_HandleEventUPP event;
    NPP_URLNotifyUPP urlnotify;
    JRIGlobalRef javaClass;
} NPPluginFuncs;
```

Again, the first two members are size and version provided for compatibility checking. In this case, your plug-in only checks the structure size because the version refers to the plug-in:

```
if (pFuncs->size < sizeof NPPluginFuncs)
    return NPERR_INVALID_FUNCTABLE_ERROR;
```

Later in the structure, notice the function pointers and prototypes to such routines as NPP_NewUPP newp. The prototype for these routines begins with NPP_, identifying them as calls from the Navigator to your plug-in's methods.

The function pointers in this structure are filled by the plug-in with the appropriate internal routines during NP_GetEntryPoints:

```
pFuncs->version       = (NP_VERSION_MAJOR << 8) | NP_VERSION_MINOR;
pFuncs->newp          = NPP_New;
pFuncs->destroy       = NPP_Destroy;
pFuncs->setwindow     = NPP_SetWindow;
pFuncs->newstream     = NPP_NewStream;
pFuncs->destroystream = NPP_DestroyStream;
pFuncs->asfile        = NPP_StreamAsFile;
```

```
pFuncs->writeready    = NPP_WriteReady;
pFuncs->write         = NPP_Write;
pFuncs->print         = NPP_Print;
pFuncs->event         = NULL;        /* reserved */
```

Versions `NP_VERSION_MAJOR` and `NP_VERSION_MINOR` are defined in `NPAPI.H` and indicate the plug-in API release and point version, respectively.

Netscape Calls Your Code

After `NP_GetEntryPoints` returns, the Navigator's structure `NPPluginFuncs` has been filled with valid function pointers that will be directly called as needed. If you are using a compiler other than Microsoft's, you should make sure that your plug-in APIs are prototyped correctly for your compiler. See Part IV of this book, "Plug-In Programming Resources for Windows," for more information.

Because the plug-in is running, you no longer a need to use the standard Windows DLL interface. No other DLL entry points are used until your plug-in is unloaded from memory. At this point, `NP_Shutdown` is called.

NP_Shutdown

The last of the Windows DLL entry points, `NP_Shutdown`, is called immediately before the plug-in is unloaded and simply calls your internal `NPP_Shutdown` routine (see Chapter 9, "Instance Initialization and Destruction"), in addition to zeroing out the global functions pointer:

```
NPError WINAPI NP_EXPORT NP_Shutdown()
{
    NPP_Shutdown();

    g_pNavigatorFuncs = NULL;

    return NPERR_NO_ERROR;
}
```

A Quick Look at the Plug-In API Methods

Throughout the next chapters, all plug-in APIs up to the Navigator 3.0 plug-in API are fully documented. Table 8.1 shows plug-in implemented APIs and Table 8.2 shows Netscape implemented APIs.

Table 8.1. The plug-in APIs, which are called from Netscape.

API Name	Description
NPP_Destroy	Deletes an instance of a plug-in.
NPP_DestroyStream	Called when a data stream is complete.

API Name	Description
NPP_GetJavaClass	Returns the plug-in associated Java class.
NPP_HandleEvent	Macintosh-only event handler.
NPP_Initialize	Global initialization.
NPP_New	Creates a new instance of a plug-in.
NPP_NewStream	Called when a new stream has been created.
NPP_Print	Print handler.
NPP_SetWindow	Called during plug-ins window activity.
NPP_Shutdown	Global termination.
NPP_StreamAsFile	Gives the filename for the stream.
NPP_URLNotify	Notifies the completion of a URL request.
NPP_Write	Called to write data to a plug-in.
NPP_WriteReady	Determines whether a plug-in is ready for data.

Table 8.2. The Netscape APIs, which are called from the plug-in.

API Name	Description
NPN_DestroyStream	Terminates a data stream.
NPN_GetJavaEnv	Returns the Java execution environment.
NPN_GetJavaPeer	Returns the plug-in associated Java object.
NPN_GetURL	Requests that a new stream be created.
NPN_GetURLNotify	Requests that a new stream be created with notification.
NPN_MemAlloc	Allocated memory.
NPN_MemFlush	Macintosh-only flush memory.
NPN_MemFree	Frees memory.
NPN_NewStream	Creates a new stream of data.
NPN_PostURL	Posts data to a URL.
NPN_PostURLNotify	Posts data to a URL and notifies of result.
NPN_RequestRead	Requests bytes from a stream.
NPN_Status	Displays a status message.
NPN_UserAgent	Gets Navigator's user agent field.
NPN_Version	Gets the Navigators plug-in version.
NPN_Write	Writes to a stream.

Conclusion

In this chapter, you've learned how a plug-in code module fits into the Netscape Navigator in the Windows environment through the use of a dynamic link library. The Application Programming Interface (API) has been reviewed for calls both to and from the plug-in module.

Additionally, you should realize that your Windows DLL is not called in the traditional DLL entry point fashion, but rather through direct function pointers retrieved by the Navigator. Structures to accomplish this are found in the Netscape SDK file NPUPP.H.

Calls from your plug-in to the Navigator, although more straightforward, use the same technique with function pointers.

What's Next?

In Tables 8.1 and 8.2, APIs both to and from your plug-in are defined in alphabetical order and grouped by the types NPP and NPN. The next six chapters fully document all APIs, with each chapter covering a group of APIs based on their purpose. The next chapters cover instance initialization and destroying, stream creation and destruction, reading from and writing to the server, Netscape's memory management, status APIs, LiveConnect, and miscellaneous APIs.

CHAPTER 9

Instance Initialization and Destruction

Introduction

When Netscape encounters an unknown MIME type, it checks the plug-in registry and determines which plug-in, if any, to load. After loading the plug-in, the Navigator must call initialization routines within the newly loaded code module. Conversely, after finishing with the plug-in, API routines are called to free system resources previously allocated, and the module is unloaded from system memory.

Typically, a plug-in allocates a block of instance data for itself for reference throughout its operation. Many other system resources can also be allocated during initialization, including memory, files, and multimedia devices. These resources are freed during the plug-in destruction process.

This chapter covers the following initialization and destruction routines:

```
NPP_Initialize

NPP_Shutdown

NPP_New

NPP_Destroy

NPN_Version
```

At the end of the chapter, you find a quick reference to these functions, including sample code.

Instance Data

The plug-in architecture relies heavily on instance data. An "instance" of your plug-in is created every time a new URL of your MIME type is encountered by the Web browser. A new data block is allocated by your code for every instance. In many cases, multiple instances of your plug-in might be active at the same time! Consider the following HTML code:

```html
<html>
<head>
   <title>My Plug-in Test Page</title>
</head>
<body>

<h2 align=center>First Plug-in Instance</h2>

<center><p><embed SRC=audio1.wav WIDTH=400 HEIGHT=60></p></center>

<h2 align=center>Second Plug-in Instance</h2>

<h2 align=center><embed SRC=audio2.wav WIDTH=400 HEIGHT=60></h2>

</body>
</html>
```

NOTE

This HTML code embeds a plug-in that plays Microsoft's .WAV audio files. A plug-in like this can be found, with its source code, on the CD-ROM included with this book.

This code causes the Navigator to load two instances of the plug-in registered for the MIME type audio/x-wav. Each instance of the plug-in will have a private copy of data. In the case of an audio player plug-in, assuming a single audio card, one instance might be active and control the audio card while another might be waiting. If desired, control of the card can be changed to another instance by user input on the plug-in's embedded window.

WARNING

A bug in Navigator 2.x allows only one plug-in instance to be created from a Web page that embeds two identical URLs in a single page. The workaround is to copy the second object and rename it, thus creating unique URLs.

Global Initialization and `NPP_Initialize`

API mapping, which is covered in Chapter 8, "The Plug-In Application Programming Interface (API)," is performed first before any standard initialization routines are called. After this is done, your routine `NPP_Initialize` is called. `NPP_Initialize` is called only one time, when the plug-in code is loaded into memory. Therefore, you should use this function for global initializations only. In many cases, you won't even need or want to do anything during this time.

Some plug-ins might need communication between multiple instances. The `NPP_Initialize` routine can be used to allocate a global data structure to be shared across instances. Windows 95 and NT developers should be careful to serialize access to this data:

```
// Use critical sections to serialize access to global plug-in data. Watch out
// for deadlocks! Many plug-in APIs are re-entrant.
EnterCriticalSection (&CritSect);

pGlobalData->fFlag = TRUE;
pGlobalData->nState = RUNNING;

LeaveCriticalSection (&CritSect);
```

Global Destruction and `NPP_Shutdown`

Immediately before your plug-in is unloaded from memory, `NPP_Shutdown` is called. This routine enables you to free any resources created with `NPP_Initialize`.

NOTE

In a Windows DLL, NPP_Initialize and NPP_Shutdown originate from the DLL entry
points NP_Initialize and NP_Shutdown, respectively.

Instance Initialization and NPP_New

After NPP_Initialize is complete, NPP_New is called. NPP_New enables you to allocate per instance
resources. Additionally, this routine provides your plug-in with valuable information relating your
instance.

MIME Type

The first thing that NPP_New tells you is which MIME type caused the creation of this plug-in
instance. This is important because a single plug-in can support multiple MIME types. It helps to
know which one you are dealing with.

An example MIME type is audio/x-wav.

Instance Pointers

The second parameter of NPP_New is a pointer to a structure called NPP. This structure contains
pointers to both your plug-in's instance data and Netscape's. This structure is currently defined
as follows:

```
typedef struct _NPP
{
    void*   pdata;      // Plug-in's instance data
    void*   ndata;      // Netscape's instance data
} NPP_t;

typedef NPP_t*  NPP;
```

NOTE

It's interesting to note that Netscape gives a pointer to its instance data also, but at this
time it is undocumented. Happy hacking!

This structure comes into NPP_New with the plug-in's instance data pointer set to NULL. Your job
is to create a block of instance data for the plug-in and attach it to the supplied pointer. It might
look something like this:

```
myInstance* myinstance = (myInstance *)NPN_MemAlloc (sizeof(myInstance));
instance->pdata = myinstance;
```

Notice the usage of Netscape's memory allocation routine NPN_MemAlloc. This API is covered in Chapter 12, "Memory Management." In some cases, you might not need to use NPN_MemAlloc, and you could perhaps use malloc(), but why take the risk?

Mode

The third parameter of NPP_New contains the mode in which your plug-in is running. These modes are as follows:

- NP_EMBED: The plug-in window is embedded into a larger HTML document window.
- NP_FULL: The plug-in window is full page and not part of an HTML document.
- NP_BACKGROUND: The plug-in is hidden and runs in the background.

> **NOTE**
>
> Netscape Navigator 2.x has not implemented NP_BACKGROUND. Look for this feature in 3.x and above.

HTML Arguments

The fourth, fifth, and sixth NPP_New parameters are relevant only to the plug-in mode of NP_EMBED. These parameters contain a pre-parsed version of the HTML code following the embed tag.

Of these parameters, the first, argc, contains the argument count. This count starts after the embed tag.

The second, argn, is an array of pointers that reference the first value of a name/value pair.

The third, argv, is an array of pointers that reference the second value of a name/value pair.

> **WARNING**
>
> Netscape makes no guarantee that the HTML arguments are valid in any mode but NP_EMBED. Always check for NP_EMBED before you attempt to access any of these arguments.

Consider the following HTML line:

```
<embed SRC=audio1.wav WIDTH=400 HEIGHT=60>
```

HTML arguments from this line look like this:

```
argc = 3

argn[0] = "SRC"            argv[0] = "audio1.wav"
argn[1] = "WIDTH"          argv[1] = "400"
argn[2] = "HEIGHT"         argv[2] = "60"
```

To ease HTML coding for users of your plug-in, you might want to parse these strings without reference to case.

Previously Saved Data

The seventh and last parameter of NPP_New is a pointer to a structure called NPSavedData. This structure, if allocated, points to a block of data saved from a previous instance. You can access your saved data like this:

```
… NPSavedData* pSavedData, …

if (pSavedData)
{
    if (pSavedData->len == sizeof(MyData))
    {
        MyData* mydata = (MyData *)pSavedData->buf;
    }
}
```

> **WARNING**
>
> Netscape Navigator 2.*x* gives a GPF if you return an error from NPP_New. This bug is in Windows Navigators only and has been fixed in 3.*x*.

Instance Destruction with NPP_Destroy

Whatever is created must be destroyed. Netscape provides for your plug-in's instance data destruction by calling NPP_Destroy. During this call, you can free instance data, unsubclass Netscape's client window, delete objects, and perform any other cleanup duties.

> **WARNING**
>
> Resizing a Web page can cause your plug-in to be destroyed and re-created in Netscape Navigator 2.*x*.

Saving Data with NPP_Destroy

In many cases, you might want to save data between your plug-in instances. This can be accomplished through the use of the NPSavedData structure pointer passed to you in NPP_Destroy. The structure is currently defined as follows:

```
typedef struct _NPSavedData
{
    int32   len;
```

```
    void*   buf;
} NPSavedData;
```

NPP_Destroy is actually passed only the address of a pointer to the NPSavedData structure. It's up to your code to allocate the structure and point it to your saved data. Perhaps, you could use something like this:

```
(*save) = (NPSavedData *) NPN_MemAlloc (sizeof(NPSavedData));
(*save)->buf = myinstance;
(*save)->len = sizeof(MyInstance);
```

In this example, you save your whole instance. Often, you might want to define a special structure just for saved data. Make sure that you use NPN_MemAlloc to allocate this memory. NPN_MemAlloc registers the memory block with Netscape, which can free it later.

If you use the new operator to allocate a saved memory object, you need to overload it within that class. The following class, called CNetscapeMemObject, does this:

```
#ifndef NETSCAPEMEMOBJECT_H
#define NETSCAPEMEMOBJECT_H

#include <defines.h>

#ifndef _NPAPI_H_
#include "npapi.h"
#endif

class CNetscapeMemObject
{
    public:
        void* operator new(size_t size)
            { return NPN_MemAlloc( size ); };
        void operator delete( void* theThing, size_t size )
            { NPN_MemFree( theThing ); };
};

#endif
```

Any class derived from this class will inherit its behavior. You can use this as a base class for your saved memory object.

In some rare cases, you might never see the saved memory block again. Netscape makes no guarantee that this data will ever return. In light of that, make sure you use this technique for noncritical data such as a volume setting or a video frame number.

NOTE

The data in the saved data buffer must be flat. That is, it must not contain pointers to any data that it owns. Navigator would not be able to resolve those references if it had to free some memory, which would lead to a memory leak.

> **WARNING**
>
> Saved data does not work for the mode of NP_FULL; it only works for NP_EMBED in Netscape Navigator 2.*x*.

Version Information with NPN_Version

NPN_Version is a simple method designed to tell you the plug-in API's major and minor version numbers, in addition to your plug-in's major and minor numbers. A major version is a major product release and a minor version is usually a point release. The major and minor plug-in API version numbers do not correspond to the release versions of the Navigator.

It's interesting to note that the code for NPN_Version resides fully within your plug-in. If you remember from the previous chapter, NPN stands for an API within the Navigator, but this is an exception to the rule. The Navigator version information, however, was brought to you from Netscape via your plug-in's initialization routine.

Windows developers can find the code for NPN_Version in NPWIN.CPP:

```
void NPN_Version (int* plugin_major,
    int* plugin_minor,
    int* netscape_major,
    int* netscape_minor)
{
    *plugin_major   = NP_VERSION_MAJOR;
    *plugin_minor   = NP_VERSION_MINOR;
    *netscape_major = HIBYTE(g_pNavigatorFuncs->version);
    *netscape_minor = LOBYTE(g_pNavigatorFuncs->version);
}
```

The same block of code is also in NPMac.cpp for Macintosh developers in the Macintosh SDK.

You can see that your plug-in's version information is simply defined from NPAPI.H, while the Netscape plug-in API version numbers are within the Navigator function pointer structure, having been retrieved earlier.

API Quick Reference

The following sections give in-depth information on the APIs used in this chapter.

NPP_Initialize

Compatibility	Windows 3.1/95/NT, Macintosh, UNIX.
API Type	Plug-in implemented method.
Purpose	Use this routine to perform any load time initialization for your code module.

Syntax	`NPError NPP_Initialize (void)`
Includes	`#include <npapi.h>`
Description	Called from the Navigator only once after the code module is loaded. In the case of a Windows DLL, this routine is called from the `NP_Initialize` DLL entry point located in the Netscape Windows SDK file NPWIN.CPP.

This is the first API called in your plug-in code.

Any error codes returned (aside from `NPERR_NO_ERROR`) cause the plug-in to be unloaded by the Navigator.

Returns	`NPERR_NO_ERROR`: No error.
	`NPERR_GENERIC_ERROR`: An unknown error occurred.
	`NPERR_OUT_OF_MEMORY_ERROR`: Out of memory.
See Also	`NPP_Shutdown`
Example	`#include <npapi.h>`

```
MyGlobalData* pGlobalData;

//
// One time initialization of plug-in
//
NPError NPP_Initialize(void)
{
    if (pGlobalData = NPN_MemAlloc
(sizeof(MyGlobalData))
        return NPERR_NO_ERROR;

    return NPERR_OUT_OF_MEMORY_ERROR
}
```

NPP_Shutdown

Compatibility	Windows 3.1/95/NT, Macintosh, UNIX.
API Type	Plug-in implemented method.
Purpose	Perform any final global resource freeing before plug-in is unloaded.
Syntax	`void NPP_Shutdown (void)`
Includes	`#include <npapi.h>`
Description	This function is called immediately before the plug-in is un-loaded. It is called only once. Use it to free any global resources. In the case of a Windows DLL, this routine is called from the

`NP_Shutdown` DLL entry point located in the Netscape Windows SDK file NPWIN.CPP.

Returns	None.
See also	`NPP_Initialize`
Example	

```
#include <npapi.h>


MyGlobalData* pGlobalData;


//
// Cleanup plug-in library
//
void NPP_Shutdown(void)
{
    if (pGlobalData)
        NPN_MemFree (pGlobalData)

}
```

NPP_New

Compatibility	Windows 3.1/95/NT, Macintosh, UNIX.
API Type	Plug-in implemented method.
Purpose	Creates new instance data to associate with a plug-in instance.
Syntax	

```
NPError NPP_New (NPMIMEType pluginType,
    NPP instance,
    uint16 mode,
    int16 argc,
    char* argn[],
    char* argv[],
    NPSavedData* saved)
```

NPMIMEType pluginType: A character pointer to the plug-in's MIME type.

NPP instance: A pointer to structure NPP, which contains pointers to both the plug-in's and Netscape's private instance data.

uint16 mode: An unsigned short determining the plug-in's mode. Current modes are NP_FULL, NP_EMBED, and NP_BACKGROUND.

int16 argc: A short determining the number of HTML arguments for an embedded plug-in.

char* argn[]: A character pointer to an array of strings representing the first of a name pair from HTML code for an embedded plug-in.

char* argv[]: A character pointer to an array of strings representing the second of a name/value pair from HTML code for an embedded plug-in.

NPSavedData* saved: A pointer to an NPSavedData structure containing the length and a pointer to plug-in data saved previously with NPP_Destroy.

Includes

```
#include <npapi.h>
```

Description

NPP_New is called immediately after NPP_Initialize. The routine resides in your plug-in module and is designed to provide your plug-in instance with relevant startup information such as MIME type, mode, and HTML arguments.

NPP_New also gives a plug-in developer the capability for allocation of both instance data and data objects. A pointer to this data is returned to the Navigator and is later passed to your APIs for future reference.

Saved data from a previous call to NPP_Destroy can be returned via the NPP_New call.

Returns

NPERR_NO_ERROR: No error.

NPERR_GENERIC_ERROR: An unknown error occurred.

NPERR_INVALID_INSTANCE_ERROR: The instance value is invalid.

NPERR_OUT_OF_MEMORY_ERROR: Out of memory.

See Also

NPP_Destroy

Example

```
#include <npapi.h>
//
// Create a new instance for our plug-in
//
NPError NP_LOADDS NPP_New (NPMIMEType pluginType,
    NPP instance,
    uint16 mode,
    int16 argc,
    char* argn[],
    char* argv[],
    NPSavedData* saved)
{
    // Check for spurious calls from Netscape

    if (instance == NULL)
        return NPERR_INVALID_INSTANCE_ERROR;

    // Allocate instance data for this plug-in instance
```

```
MyInstance* myinstance = (MyInstance *)NPN_MemAlloc
(sizeof(MyInstance));

myinstance->pWindow = NULL;     // the window pointer
myinstance->pObject = new CPluginObject ();   //
➥Allocate main plug-in object
myinstance->mode = mode;  // Save the mode: NP_FULL,
➥NP_EMBED, NP_HIDDEN


if (mode == NP_EMBED)
{
    // Embedded plug-ins have HTML arguments

    // Extract them here…(argc, argn, argv)
}

// Save our instance pointer which will be passed back
➥in all calls

instance->pdata = myinstance;

return NPERR_NO_ERROR;
}
```

NPP_Destroy

Compatibility	Windows 3.1/95/NT, Macintosh, UNIX.
API Type	Plug-in implemented method.
Purpose	Frees any instance data allocated via NPP_New. Frees any per instance resources.
Syntax	NPError NPP_Destroy (NPP instance, NPSavedData** save)

NPP instance: A pointer to structure NPP, which contains pointers to both the plug-in's and Netscape's private instance data.

NPSavedData save:** A pointer to a pointer that references an NPSavedData structure containing the length and a pointer to plug-in instance data.

Includes	#include <npapi.h>
Description	NPP_Destroy is called to free all per instance data and resources. This call usually, but not always, indicates that Navigator is done with your plug-in. Typically, this routine is used to delete

objects attached to a plug-in instance, free instance memory, and in the case of Windows, unsubclass Netscape's plug-in window.

NPP_Destroy provides a mechanism to save data for a later instance of the plug-in via the NPSavedData structure. A pointer to this structure should be returned during the next NPP_New call. Be sure to use NPN_MemAlloc to allocate the saved structure because you might not have the opportunity to free it. Netscape frees the memory in this case.

The saved data is given to the next call to NPP_New whose SRC is the same as that associated with this instance of the plug-in. For example, if this is a movie plug-in, the saved data only shows up the next time that the same movie is viewed.

Returns

NPERR_NO_ERROR: No error.

NPERR_GENERIC_ERROR: An unknown error occurred.

NPERR_OUT_OF_MEMORY_ERROR: Out of memory.

See Also

NPP_New

Example

```
#include <npapi.h>


//
// Destroy a plug-in instance
//
NPError NP_LOADDS NPP_Destroy(NPP instance, NPSavedData**
➥save)
{
    MyInstance* myinstance = (MyInstance *)instance-
➥>pdata;

    // In windows, unsubclass the window

    myinstance->pWindow->UnSubclassNetscapesWindow ();
    myinstance->pWindow->CleanupWindow();

    // Delete objects

    delete myinstance->pWindow;
    delete myinstance->pObject

    // Allocate a save structure and attach our instance
➥to it for next time.

    (*save) = (NPSavedData *)NPN_MemAlloc
➥(sizeof(NPSavedData));
```

```
(*save)->buf = myinstance;
(*save)->len = sizeof(MyInstance);

return NPERR_NO_ERROR;
}
```

NPN_Version

Compatibility   Windows 3.1/95/NT, Macintosh, UNIX.

API Type   Navigator implemented method.

Purpose   Retrieves the major and minor version numbers for both the Navigator plug-in API and your plug-in.

Syntax
```
void NPN_Version (int* plugin_major,
    int* plugin_minor,
    int* netscape_major,
    int* netscape_minor);
```

int* plugin_major: An integer pointer to your plug-in's major version number.

int* plugin_minor: An integer pointer to your plug-in's minor version number.

int* netscape_major: An integer pointer to the Navigator plug-in API's major version number.

int* netscape_minor: An integer pointer to the Navigator plug-in API's minor version number.

Includes   `#include <npapi.h>`

Description   This routine does not actually call the Navigator. It calls local code in your plug-in that stored version information during plug-in initialization. A major version is a major code release number, and a minor version is a point release.

For example, Navigator plug-in API version 0.6 would be major 0, minor 6.

Returns   None.

See Also   None.

Example
```
#include <npapi.h>
    .

    .

    .
int plugin_major, plugin_minor, netscape_major,
netscape_minor;
```

//

```
// Get our version info.
//
NPN_Version (&plugin_major, &plugin_minor,
&netscape_major, &netscape_minor);
.
.
.
```

Conclusion

In this chapter, you've learned how your plug-in is loaded, initialized, destroyed, and unloaded. Remember that NPP_Initialize and NPP_Shutdown are called only once for the time that your plug-in is loaded and unloaded from memory. NPP_New and NPP_Destroy are called for each new instance of your plug-in. Multiple instances of a plug-in are quite common.

Also, keep in mind that NPN_Version returns the Navigator's plug-in API version, not the Navigator browser version.

What's Next?

Now that you've mastered instance initialization and destruction, it's time to move on to stream creation and destruction. In the next chapter, you learn about the following topics:

■ New stream notification through the use of NPP_NewStream.

■ Stream destruction notification with NPP_DestroyStream.

■ Initiating new streams and stream destruction with NPN_NewStream and NPN_DestroyStream.

■ Starting a stream with NPN_GetURL and sending data to a URL with NPN_PostURL.

CHAPTER 10

Stream Creation and Destruction

Introduction

This chapter introduces the plug-in APIs that are responsible for creating and destroying streams both directly and indirectly. You will learn how to get valuable information from a new stream, such as the MIME type, last modification date, and whether it supports seeking with byte range requests. Stream instance structures are reviewed along with stream type return values.

Additionally, the APIs NPN_GetURL and NPN_PostURL, in addition to the new Navigator 3.0 APIs NPN_GetURLNotify, NPN_PostURLNotify, and NPP_URLNotify, are introduced with many code examples. You will learn how these APIs are also responsible for the creation of new data streams.

This chapter also introduces you to the following APIs:

NPP_NewStream

NPP_DestroyStream

NPN_NewStream

NPN_DestroyStream

NPN_GetURL

NPN_PostURL

NPN_GetURLNotify

NPN_PostURLNotify

NPP_URLNotify

The end of the chapter contains a quick reference with code examples for each of these APIs.

New Streams and Their Parameters

When the Navigator encounters a URL with a MIME type of your plug-in's registration, a stream is created to send the URL's data to your streaming routines. You are notified of a new stream with a call to your plug-in's API NPP_NewStream.

NPP_NewStream provides your code module with the parameters type, stream, seekable, and stype. These values contain important information concerning your stream.

Stream Type

The type value is a pointer to a buffer containing the MIME type that caused the creation of the stream. These can be one of the types that your plug-in registered with Netscape or a totally unrelated MIME type, perhaps originating from a call to NPN_GetURL. This type might not match the MIME type sent to a new plug-in instance via the NPP_New call.

> **WARNING**
>
> In Navigator 2.*x*, if the stream results from a call to GetURL, the type field might be
> invalid. (It will return the type of the stream that launched the plug-in.) This has been
> fixed in Atlas (Navigator 3.*x*).

Stream Instance Structure

A stream instance structure is passed to you with the stream parameter. This is a pointer to an
NPStream structure currently defined as follows:

```
typedef struct _NPStream
{
    void*       pdata;
    void*       ndata;
    const char* url;
    uint32      end;
    uint32      lastmodified;
} NPStream;
```

Within this structure, you notice some familiar friends: pdata and ndata. ndata points to the
Navigator's instance data, and pdata is an extra pointer for your plug-in's use in streaming. For
example, you might want to allocate an object and attach it to pdata so that your plug-in can
easily manage a given stream. This technique is especially useful in tracking multiple streams within
a plug-in.

```
stream->pdata = new MyStreamTrackingObject;
```

Also note url, end, and lastmodified. The url member tells you which URL is responsible for the
creation of this stream. This can be handy for requesting more URLs via NPN_GetURL. The end
member gives you the size of the requested stream. The lastmodified member indicates when the
file associated with the URL was last modified.

> **WARNING**
>
> Navigator gives as much information about the stream as it knows during a call to
> NPP_NewStream. When the stream is just beginning, it might not have received the size
> information yet. When the stream is generated on-the-fly by a CGI program, Navigator
> might not know how big the stream is going to be until it's actually finished. Therefore,
> you should be careful when using the end member of the NPStream structure.

Seeking for Seek

The `seekable` parameter of `NPP_NewStream` indicates whether the stream supports seeks or byte range requests. Byte range requests are performed through the use of `NPN_RequestRead`, which is documented in later chapters. Unfortunately, requesting a random block of a file is very new to the world of Web servers. At the time of this writing, most servers do not support it. You can, however, seek within a file that is already on the local system. Additionally, a stream is `seekable` if it has previously been cached on the local system.

Processing by Stream or by File

Speaking of local files, you might be interested in the `stype` parameter. This is a pointer to a value that is filled with the requested mode of streaming. The values are as follows:

- `NP_NORMAL`: This value is the default and does not need to be set. `NP_NORMAL` implies that your plug-in will process the data in a streaming manner or as it comes to you.
- `NP_SEEK`: This value asks for seeking capabilities as discussed previously.
- `NP_ASFILE`: This value tells the Navigator that you want to wait for the whole file to be completely downloaded before beginning processing. This type corresponds with the `NPP_StreamAsFile` API, which is called when the file is ready. The file is temporarily stored within Netscape's file caching mechanism for processing.

  `NP_ASFILE` streams display all of the behavior of `NP_NORMAL` streams such as calls to `NPP_WriteReady` and `NPP_Write`. The difference is that they also call `NPP_StreamAsFile` just before `NPP_DestroyStream`.

- `NP_ASFILEONLY`: This is a new type for the Navigator 3.0 plug-in API. This type is much more efficient than `NP_ASFILE` because it prevents a file from streaming if it is already on the system's local drive, which allows your plug-in to access the file with normal system-level file I/O instead of using Navigator's built-in streaming mechanism.

NOTE

Netscape recommends that plug-ins use a full streaming technique whenever possible. This is especially true for files located on Internet servers. Users might not want to wait for the full file download, as in `NP_ASFILE`.

Life of a Stream Ends

When a stream is complete or interrupted, Netscape makes a call to your `NPP_DestroyStream` API. Although it is called in streams of type `NP_ASFILE`, this API is really only relevant to plug-ins that process data in a streaming fashion. Plug-ins that are file based are notified to begin processing with a call to `NPP_StreamAsFile`.

If you are writing a streaming-based plug-in, you should pay close attention to NPP_DestroyStream. For example, if your plug-in is processing data buffers as they come across the net and a user stops the transfer, the plug-in needs to know that no more data is coming. File-based plug-ins don't care because they don't begin processing until the file is fully downloaded.

Some Familiar Structures

NPP_DestroyStream contains three parameters: instance, stream, and reason. The instance structure is the same as with most APIs. The stream structure is identical to when it left NPP_NewStream. The reason parameter tells you why the stream is being destroyed.

The following are possible reasons for stream destruction:

> NPRES_NETWORK_ERR
>
> NPRES_USER_BREAK
>
> NPRES_DONE

NPRES_NETWORK_ERR, as the name says, is a network error. This could be caused by someone picking up a phone during a modem connection. NPRES_USER_BREAK is caused by the user aborting the streaming process by pressing the Stop button, going to another link, or even ending the application. NPRES_DONE indicates that the file has been fully transferred.

> ### WARNING
>
> Netscape 2.*x* SDK release notes state that the reason is wrong in some cases. This bug might have been fixed in later releases of 2.*x*, but you should be wary of reason.

Creating Your Own Streams

With the release of Netscape's Navigator 3.0 plug-in API comes the methods NPN_NewStream, NPN_DestroyStream, and NPN_Write. These methods were present in the 2.0 API release, but they did not work at that time. You can use these APIs to create and manage a data stream from your plug-in to the Navigator. One good application would be using a plug-in as a filter.

Chapter 19, "The CPU Monitor Plug-In," gives an example of a plug-in running a CGI program through the use of NPN_GetURL. This program runs a UNIX command called vmstat and gets the results of the command from a Navigator-created data stream. The plug-in then displays this data with a bar graph within the plug-in's window. You can use part of this technique to make your plug-in act as a filter for the Navigator.

For the sake of this discussion, assume that your boss wants to view UNIX-style man pages within Netscape's Web Broswer. Your plug-in can run a CGI program as in the CPU Monitor plug-in that runs man with a given command. After Navigator streams back the results of the CGI program, your plug-in can buffer this data and create a stream to Netscape's Navigator. The plug-in acts as a filter because it can take raw man text and convert it to formatted HTML for display by the Navigator. The following code shows some highlights for using this technique:

```
//
// Send HTML formatted data to the Navigator
//

  .
  .
  .

// Allocate and clear an NPStream structure

NPStream stream;
memset (&stream, 0, sizeof(NPStream));

// Create a new stream of MIME type "text/html"
// and target a blank web page

NPError rc = NPN_NewStream (instance, "text/html", "_blank", &stream);

// Write the previously formatted HTML data to the Navigator

bytesWritten = NPN_Write (instance, &stream, htmlLen, htmlBuffer);

  .
  .
  .

// Destroy the stream when finished

rc = NPN_DestroyStream (instance, &stream, NP_RESDONE);
```

At the time of this writing, Navigator 3.0 is still in beta and the APIs as shown in the preceding code block are not yet fully functional. Because of this, you won't find any working code examples of a plug-in acting as a filter in this book.

NPN_GetURL **and** NPN_PostURL

Both NPN_GetURL and NPN_PostURL are resolved to HTTP server methods by the Navigator. Server methods indicate what to do with the object referenced by the given URL. As the names imply, NPN_GetURL resolves to a GET and NPN_PostURL resolves to a POST. (If you want to read up on other HTTP methods, a good place to start is *The World Wide Web Consortium* at http://www.w3.org.)

The main difference between GET and POST is that GET is used mostly for requesting URL objects, while POST is the preferred method of sending data to a server. That doesn't mean GET is never used to send data. In fact, many HTML programs embed data within the URL in the form of *name=value* pairs. For example, a Yahoo search for the string "Netscape" yields the following:

```
http://search.yahoo.com/bin/search?p=Netscape
```

Although GET is restricted to inserting data directly in the URL string, POST is more advanced and appends data after the POST header.

HTTP GET

The GET server method is used for most requests for URLs. For example, if you type `http://www.yahoo.com` in your Web browser, the browser sends the following GET request to the HTTP server:

```
GET / HTTP/1.0
If-Modified-Since: Monday, 25-Mar-96 23:48:32 GMT; length=5683
Connection: Keep-Alive
User-Agent: Mozilla/2.01 (Win95; I)
Host: www.yahoo.com
Accept: image/gif, image/x-xbitmap, image/jpeg, image/pjpeg, */*
```

Although the specifics of this GET header are relevant to HTTP syntax and beyond the scope of this book, you can get a good idea of what the browser is looking for by reading the text.

After the GET request is sent, the browser waits patiently for word from the server. In the case of Yahoo, you end up with the following:

```
HTTP/1.0 200 OK
Last-Modified: Wed, 27 Mar 1996 09:33:06 GMT
Content-Type: text/html
Content-Length: 5688

<HTML>
.
.
.
</HTML>
```

Reading through the text, you can see the last modification date, content type, and content length. The actual HTML code has been removed for the sake of brevity. Within the HTML code are mode URL objects such as graphics, which cause your browser to issue more GET commands.

> **TIP**
>
> If want to see what is sent back and forth through a Windows 95 socket connection, check out WSOCK00.DLL and its associated source code on this book's CD-ROM. This socket spy utility dumps data files corresponding to socket transfers to your local hard drive. Chapter 24, "Debugging with the Socket Spy," details how to use this utility.

HTTP POST

The POST HTTP method is the preferred method for sending data to HTTP servers. Sending data to a server in this manner requires a server script or program using the Common Gateway

Interface (CGI). A CGI program lives in a special directory that is set up by the server administrator. If you don't have access to a server, check out the National Center for Supercomputing Applications (NCSA) Fill-Out Form Support Page, which is currently located at the following address:

```
http://www.ncsa.uiuc.edu/SDG/Software/Mosaic/Docs/fill-out-forms/overview.html
```

You can test your programming skills using Netscape's `NPN_PostURL` by emulating one of the NCSA sample forms. For example, take a look at the form shown in Figure 10.1.

Figure 10.1.

An example form that posts data to a CGI program from NCSA.

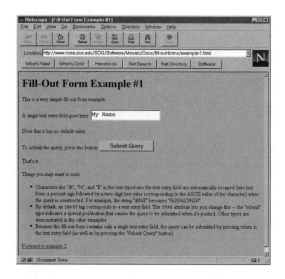

If you view the HTML source for this example, you see the following simple `FORM` defined:

```
<FORM METHOD="POST" ACTION="http://hoohoo.ncsa.uiuc.edu/cgi-bin/post-query">

A single text entry field goes here: <INPUT NAME="entry"> <P>

Note that it has no default value. <P>

To submit the query, press this button: <INPUT TYPE="submit"
VALUE="Submit Query">. <P>

</FORM>
```

Notice `FORM METHOD="POST"`, which corresponds to an `HTTP POST`. Also notice `ACTION="http://hoohoo.ncsa.uiuc.edu/cgi-bin/post-query"`. The `ACTION` points to a URL containing the CGI program to process the `FORM`.

When a user clicks on the Submit Query button, the following `POST` is sent to the CGI program `post-query`:

```
POST /cgi-bin/post-query HTTP/1.0
Referer: http://www.ncsa.uiuc.edu/SDG/Software/Mosaic/Docs/
➥fill-out-forms/example-1.html
Connection: Keep-Alive
User-Agent: Mozilla/2.01 (Win95; I)
```

```
Host: hoohoo.ncsa.uiuc.edu
Accept: image/gif, image/x-xbitmap, image/jpeg, image/pjpeg, */*
Content-type: application/x-www-form-urlencoded
Content-length: 13
```

```
entry=My+Name
```

The post-query program is written in C and can be found at the following ftp site:

```
ftp://ftp.ncsa.uiuc.edu/Web/httpd/Unix/ncsa_httpd/cgi/cgi-src/post-query.c
```

Take a look at the post-query.c source code from NCSA:

```c
#include <stdio.h>

#define MAX_ENTRIES 10000

typedef struct {
    char *name;
    char *val;
} entry;

char *makeword(char *line, char stop);
char *fmakeword(FILE *f, char stop, int *len);
char x2c(char *what);
void unescape_url(char *url);
void plustospace(char *str);

main(int argc, char *argv[]) {
    entry entries[MAX_ENTRIES];
    register int x,m=0;
    int cl;

    printf("Content-type: text/html%c%c",10,10);

    if(strcmp(getenv("REQUEST_METHOD"),"POST")) {
        printf("This script should be referenced with a METHOD of POST.\n");
        printf("If you don't understand this, see this ");
        printf("<A HREF=\"http://www.ncsa.uiuc.edu/SDG/Software/Mosaic/Docs/
        ↪fill-out-forms/overview.html\">forms overview</A>.%c",10);
        exit(1);
    }
    if(strcmp(getenv("CONTENT_TYPE"),"application/x-www-form-urlencoded")) {
        printf("This script can only be used to decode form results. \n");
        exit(1);
    }
    cl = atoi(getenv("CONTENT_LENGTH"));

    for(x=0;cl && (!feof(stdin));x++) {
        m=x;
        entries[x].val = fmakeword(stdin,'&',&cl);
        plustospace(entries[x].val);
        unescape_url(entries[x].val);
        entries[x].name = makeword(entries[x].val,'=');
    }

    printf("<H1>Query Results</H1>");
    printf("You submitted the following name/value pairs:<p>%c",10);
    printf("<ul>%c",10);
```

```
for(x=0; x <= m; x++)
    printf("<li> <code>%s = %s</code>%c",entries[x].name,
            entries[x].val,10);
printf("</ul>%c",10);
}
```

This CGI program is the back-end of the form shown in Figure 10.1. Here are some things to note:

■ A POST method CGI program communicates with the HTTP server through the use of environment variables, standard input, and standard output. Look at the repeated calls to getenv to retrieve REQUEST_METHOD, CONTENT_TYPE, and CONTENT_LENGTH. In the form example shown in Figure 10.1, the REQUEST_METHOD is POST, CONTENT_TYPE is application/x-www-form-urlencoded, and CONTENT_LENGTH is 13.

■ After CONTENT_LENGTH is determined, a for loop is entered to parse the given *name=value* pairs. Note the calls to fmakeword, plustospace, unescape_url, and makeword. The source code for these routines can be found in the file util.c, which is available from the same FTP site as post-query.c.

Emulate the Form with NPN_PostURL

You can produce the same output as the form in Figure 10.1 through the use of NPN_PostURL. Try the following in a test plug-in:

1. Make a buffer with the appropriate content type, content length, and data. You can use a CString to make string building easier. Make sure to include a new line after content type and two new lines after content length:

```
CString csPost = "Content-type: application/x-www-form-urlencoded\n";
csPost += "Content-length: 13\n\n";
csPost += "Entry=My+Name\n";
```

2. Use NPN_PostURL to send the data to the URL

```
// Send data to the server

NPError rc = NPN_PostURL (instance,
    "http://hoohoo.ncsa.uiuc.edu/cgi-bin/post-query",
    "_blank",
    csPost.GetLength(),
    csPost.GetBuffer(csPost.GetLength()),
    TRUE);
```

3. If everything went well, Netscape should connect to the server and display the results shown in Figure 10.2.

If, by the time you are reading this book, NCSA's example has gone away, simply find yourself another FORM example that uses the POST method. Or, if you are lucky enough to have access to an HTTP server, just write your own CGI program.

Figure 10.2.

NCSA's CGI program responds to a call from NPN_PostURL.

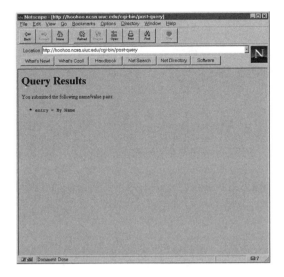

WARNING

You cannot use a buffer with NPN_PostURL for Netscape Navigator version 2.*x*, as the previous example suggests. If you do, because of a bug in this version, an extra blank line is appended to the end of the Accept: line. The previous example's POST request would look like this:

```
POST /cgi-bin/post-query HTTP/1.0
Referer: http://www.ncsa.uiuc.edu/SDG/Software/Mosaic/Docs/
➥fill-out-forms/example-1.html
Connection: Keep-Alive
User-Agent: Mozilla/2.01 (Win95; I)
Host: hoohoo.ncsa.uiuc.edu
Accept: image/gif, image/x-xbitmap, image/jpeg, image/pjpeg, */*

Content-type: application/x-www-form-urlencoded
Content-length: 13

entry=My+Name
```

It would no longer look like this:

```
POST /cgi-bin/post-query HTTP/1.0
Referer: http://www.ncsa.uiuc.edu/SDG/Software/Mosaic/Docs/
➥fill-out-forms/example-1.html
Connection: Keep-Alive
User-Agent: Mozilla/2.01 (Win95; I)
Host: hoohoo.ncsa.uiuc.edu
Accept: image/gif, image/x-xbitmap, image/jpeg, image/pjpeg, */*
Content-type: application/x-www-form-urlencoded
Content-length: 13

entry=My+Name
```

HTTP servers are very sensitive to new line placement and will not work in this case. The solution is to use a temporary file instead of a buffer. The code example for the NPN_PostURL API at the end of this chapter shows how to do this.

Targeting Windows with NPN_GetURL and NPN_PostURL

Both NPN_GetURL and NPN_PostURL provide a means for targeting windows. Target windows are windows within the Navigator that receive the data stream associated with a given URL. In most cases, you use the value of NULL for your window target. Using NULL ensures that the data stream is written to your plug-in via NPP_Write. Otherwise, you might specify a number of target windows relating to the TARGET tag within your HTML code or use one of the "magic" target window names.

The following are the current magic target windows:

    _blank

    _new

    _self

    _current

    _parent

    _top

Of these, _blank and _new are synonymous and cause the Navigator to create a new unnamed window instance of itself. The targets _self and _current are also synonyms. They cause the link to load in the same window in which the anchor was clicked.

The target _parent loads the link in the immediate FRAMESET parent of the document, and _top makes the link load in the full body of the window.

For more information on frames and magic window names from Netscape, please consult the following addresses:

http://home.netscape.com/assist/net sites/frames.html

http://home.netscape.com/eng/mozilla/2.0/relnotes/demo/targets/html

WARNING

Although target windows work well with NPN_GetURL in Netscape Navigator 2.*x*, they are totally unreliable with NPN_PostURL. Use them at your own risk!

API Quick Reference

The following sections give in-depth information on the APIs used in this chapter.

NPP_NewStream

Compatibility	UNIX, Macintosh, Windows 3.1/95/NT
API Type	Plug-in routine called from the Navigator.
Purpose	Notifies your plug-in instance of a new stream.
Syntax	

```
NPError NPP_NewStream (NPP instance,
        NPMIMEType type,
        NPStream *stream,
        NPBool seekable,
        uint16 *stype)
```

NPP instance: A pointer to structure NPP that references both the plug-in's and Netscape's private instance data.

NPMIMEType type: A character pointer to the MIME type that caused the creation of the stream.

NPStream* stream: A pointer to structure NPStream that references both the plug-in's and Netscape's stream instance data. This structure also contains the name of the URL that created this stream, its last modification date, and the content length in bytes.

NPBool seekable: Indicates whether the stream is seekable. A value of TRUE is considered seekable.

uint16* stype: The stream instance can request a new stream mode by setting this type. The current types are as follows:

> NP_NORMAL: Normal stream. This is the default.

> NP_SEEK: Request a seekable stream. Actual seeking depends on your server.

> NP_ASFILE: Request that the data is sent as a whole file rather than a stream. This mode is preserved for compatibility with the 2.0 API. For Navigator 3.0, use NP_ASFILEONLY.

> NP_ASFILEONLY: New for Navigator API 3.0. This mode is more efficient than the older NP_ASFILE. If the file is local, it is not streamed and no calls to NPP_WriteReady and NPP_Write are made.

Includes	#include <npapi.h>

Description   NPP_NewStream is a routine within your plug-in that is called by the Navigator to inform you of a new stream. This stream might have been created by a user action or a plug-in call such as NPN_GetURL.

As with most plug-in APIs, a pointer to your instance data is included with a call to NPP_NewStream. Similar to this, a pointer to a stream instance is also included in the call. You can attach your plug-in's per stream private data to the Navigator-supplied stream->pdata pointer.

Other information such as MIME type, URL, last modification date, content length in bytes, and seekability are provided for your plug-in during this call.

You can indicate how the stream should be handled with the stype parameter. Current types are normal streaming (NP_NORMAL), full file download (NP_ASFILE), or seeking (NP_SEEK).

Returns   NPERR_NO_ERROR: No error.

NPERR_GENERIC_ERROR: An unknown error occurred.

NPERR_INVALID_INSTANCE_ERROR: The instance value is invalid.

NPERR_OUT_OF_MEMORY_ERROR: Out of memory.

See Also   NPP_DestroyStream, NPN_NewStream, NPN_GetURL

Example
```
#include <npapi.h>

//
// A new stream has been created - check it out.
//

NPError NP_LOADDS NPP_NewStream (NPP instance,
    NPMIMEType type,
    NPStream *stream,
    NPBool seekable,
    uint16 *stype)
{
    // Check for spurious calls from Netscape

    if (instance == NULL)
        return NPERR_INVALID_INSTANCE_ERROR;

    // Retrieve instance data

    MyInstance* myinstance = (MyInstance *)instance->pdata;

    // Take any action during this time

    if (myinstance->pObject)
        myinstance->pObject->NewStream (stream->url);

    return NPERR_NO_ERROR;
}
```

NPP_DestroyStream

Compatibility	UNIX, Macintosh, Windows 3.1/95/NT
API Type	Plug-in routine called from the Navigator.
Purpose	Notifies your plug-in instance that a stream is being destroyed. Usually called when a stream is complete.
Syntax	NPError NPP_DestroyStream (NPP instance, NPStream *stream, NPError reason)

NPP instance: A pointer to structure NPP that references both the plug-in's and Netscape's private instance data.

NPStream* stream: A pointer to structure NPStream that references both the plug-in's and Netscape's stream instance data. This structure also contains the name of the URL that created this stream, its last modification date, and the content length in bytes.

NPError reason: A parameter indicating the reason why the stream was destroyed, which can be one of the following:

> NPRES_NETWORK_ERR: A network error occurred.

> NPRES_USER_BREAK: The user aborted the stream.

> NPRES_DONE: The stream finished normally.

Includes	#include <npapi.h>
Description	Navigator calls NPP_DestroyStream when a stream has been closed and deleted by either a network error, a user action, or normal completion.

A streaming-based plug-in would be notified that the stream is complete and take any appropriate action. The parameter end in the NPStream structure contains the content length that is returned from the server. Usually, content length corresponds to the file size on the server.

NP_ASFILE streams still get a call to NPP_DestroyStream after the call to NPP_StreamAsFile.

Returns	NPERR_NO_ERROR: No error.

NPERR_GENERIC_ERROR: An unknown error occurred.

NPERR_INVALID_INSTANCE_ERROR: The instance value is invalid.

NPERR_OUT_OF_MEMORY_ERROR: Out of memory.

See Also   NPP_NewStream, NPN_DestroyStream

Example   #include <npapi.h>

```
//
// A stream was destroyed.
//

NPError NP_LOADDS NPP_DestroyStream (NPP instance,
    NPStream *stream,
    NPError reason)
{
    // Check for spurious calls from Netscape

    if (instance == NULL)
        return NPERR_INVALID_INSTANCE_ERROR;

    // Retrieve instance data

    MyInstance* myinstance = (MyInstance *)instance->pdata;

    // Take any action during this time

    if (myinstance->pObject)
        myinstance->pObject->EndofStream (stream->url, reason);

    return NPERR_NO_ERROR;
}
```

NPN_NewStream

Compatibility   UNIX, Macintosh, Windows 3.1/95/NT. Navigator 3.0 and above only.

API Type   Navigator routine called from the plug-in.

Purpose   Creates a new stream for streaming data from the plug-in to the Navigator.

Syntax
```
NPError NPN_NewStream (NPP instance,
    NPMIMEType type
    const char* target,
    NPStream* stream)
```

NPP instance: A pointer to structure NPP that references both the plug-in's and Netscape's private instance data.

NPMIMEType type: A character pointer to the MIME type associated with this new stream.

const char* target: The target window or frame. See the description for NPN_GetURL later in this chapter for target names and definitions.

NPStream* stream: A pointer to structure NPStream that references both the plug-in's and Netscape's stream instance data. This structure also contains the URL, last modification date, and content length in bytes.

Includes   `#include <npapi.h>`

Description   The `NPN_NewStream` API allows your plug-in to create a stream for streaming data from your plug-in to the Navigator.

Returns   `NPERR_NO_ERROR`: No error.

           `NPERR_GENERIC_ERROR`: An unknown error occurred.

           `NPERR_INVALID_INSTANCE_ERROR`: The instance value is invalid.

           `NPERR_OUT_OF_MEMORY_ERROR`: Out of memory.

See Also   `NPP_NewStream, NPN_DestroyStream`

Example
```
#include <npapi.h>
   .
   .
   .
//
// Create a new stream
//

NPStream stream;
memset (&stream, 0, sizeof(NPStream));

// Create a new stream of MIME type "text/html"
// and target a blank web page

NPError rc = NPN_NewStream (instance, "text/html", "_blank",
➡&stream);

   .
   .
   .
```

NPN_DestroyStream

Compatibility   UNIX, Macintosh, Windows 3.1/95/NT. Navigator 3.0 and above only.

API Type   Navigator routine called from the plug-in.

Purpose   Closes and deletes a stream previously created with `NPN_NewStream`.

Syntax   `NPError NPN_DestroyStream (NPP instance, NPStream* stream,`
           `➡NPError reason)`

           `NPP instance`: A pointer to structure `NPP` that references both the plug-in's and Netscape's private instance data.

           `NPStream* stream`: A pointer to structure `NPStream` that references both the plug-in's and Netscape's stream instance data. This structure also contains the URL, last modification date, and content length in bytes.

NPError reason: A parameter indicating the reason why the stream was destroyed, which can be one of the following:

NPRES_NETWORK_ERR: A network error occurred.

NPRES_USER_BREAK: The user aborted the stream.

NPRES_DONE: The stream finished normally.

Includes	`#include <npapi.h>`
Description	The NPN_DestroyStream method is new starting with Naviagator 3.0. This API allows your plug-in to destroy a stream.
Returns	NPERR_NO_ERROR: No error.
	NPERR_GENERIC_ERROR: An unknown error occurred.
	NPERR_INVALID_INSTANCE_ERROR: The instance value is invalid.
	NPERR_OUT_OF_MEMORY_ERROR: Out of memory.
See Also	NPP_DestroyStream, NPN_NewStream

Example

```
#include <npapi.h>
    .
    .
    .
//
// Destroy a stream
//

// Set the reason

reason = NPRES_USER_BREAK;

// Call the Navigator to destroy the stream

NPError rc = NPN_DestroyStream (instance, stream, reason)
    .
    .
    .
```

NPN_GetURL

Compatibility	UNIX, Macintosh, Windows 3.1/95/NT
API Type	Navigator routine called from the plug-in.
Purpose	Requests the creation of a new stream for the specified URL. This operation is asynchronous.
	Sends a GET request to the Web server.
Syntax	`NPError NPN_GetURL (NPP instance, const char* url, const char* `➥`window)`

NPP instance: A pointer to structure NPP that references both the plug-in's and Netscape's private instance data. This is the same instance value that is passed to every NPP_ call.

const char* url: A pointer to a constant string containing the URL for the GET request.

const char* window: A pointer to a user-supplied constant string indicating the display location of the stream. This parameter will be renamed target in future SDKs. See the following description for more information on this parameter.

Includes

#include <npapi.h>

Description

Use NPN_GetURL to start a new stream of data to a specified window.

The window target should be NULL if you want the new stream to be passed to the current instance of your plug-in regardless of the new URL's MIME type. This allows your plug-in to read files of different MIME types such as text/html.

You can specify the name of a target window for the new stream. This new stream may or may not be handled by your plug-in, depending on the MIME type and any magic target names.

Window target names can be passed in as parameters to the plug-in with the EMBED tag. Magic target names can be used in the NPN_GetURL call, as in the following examples:

_blank creates a new blank Netscape window for the URL data. This window is not named. A synonym for this target is _new.

_self causes the link to load in the same window. A synonym for this target is _current.

_parent loads the link in the immediate FRAMESET parent of this document. It defaults to acting like _self if the document has no parent.

_top makes the link load in the full body of the window.

Returns

NPERR_NO_ERROR: No error.

NPERR_GENERIC_ERROR: An unknown error occurred.

NPERR_INVALID_INSTANCE_ERROR: The instance value is invalid.

NPERR_OUT_OF_MEMORY_ERROR: Out of memory.

See Also

NPN_PostURL, NPN_GetURLNotify, NPN_PostURLNotify, NPP_URLNotify

| *Example* | ```
#include <npapi.h>
 .
 .
 .
//
// Get a URL
//

// Get the new URL and have the data streamed into the top most
➥frame window

NPError rc = NPN_GetURL (instance, "http://www.gate.net/
➥~zan/outofb.wav", "_top");

 .
 .
 .
``` |

NPN_PostURL

Compatibility UNIX, Macintosh, Windows 3.1/95/NT

API Type Navigator routine called from the plug-in.

Purpose Use NPN_PostURL to send data to a URL. This API resolves to a POST request to a Web server. The routine is useful for sending data to a CGI script.

Syntax
```
NPError NPN_PostURL (NPP instance,
      const char* url,
      const char* window,
      uint32 len,
      const char* buf,
      NPBool file)
```

NPP instance: A pointer to structure NPP that references both the plug-in's and Netscape's private instance data.

const char* url: A pointer to a constant string containing the URL for the POST request.

const char* window: A pointer to a user-supplied constant string indicating the display location of the stream. This parameter will be renamed target in future SDKs.

uint32 len: Corresponds to the length of the following data buffer.

const char* buf: A constant pointer to a buffer with the data for posting.

NPBool file: If this Boolean is set to TRUE, the previous buffer contains a local filename for the Navigator to read instead of a data buffer. If it is FALSE, the buffer contains raw data.
```

Includes `#include <npapi.h>`

Description NPN_PostURL sends a number of bytes to a URL with the server command POST.

If file is set to TRUE, a local temporary file is used to hold the post data. This file is deleted by Netscape after the post. If file is set to FALSE, a raw data buffer is used.

Whether you use a local file or a raw data buffer, the format is specific to a POST command, as in the following example:

```
char buf[] = "Content-type: application/x-www-form-
↪urlencoded\nContent-length:
27\n\nName=John+Doe&Data=whatever\n";
```

Be sure to check the beginning of this chapter for problems with this API in Navigator 2.*x*.

The window target should be NULL if you want the new stream to be passed to the current instance of your plug-in regardless of the new URL's MIME type. This allows your plug-in to read files of different MIME types such as HTML.

You can specify the name of a target window for the new stream. This new stream may or may not be handled by your plug-in, depending on the MIME type and any magic target names.

Window target names can be passed in as parameters to the plug-in with the EMBED tag. Magic target names can be used in the NPN_PostURL call, as in the following examples:

_blank creates a new blank Netscape window for the URL data. This window is not named. A synonym for this target is _new.

_self causes the link to load in the same window. A synonym for this target is _current.

_parent loads the link in the immediate FRAMESET parent of this document. It defaults to acting like _self if the document has no parent.

_top makes the link load in the full body of the window.

Returns NPERR_NO_ERROR: No error.

NPERR_GENERIC_ERROR: An unknown error occurred.

NPERR_INVALID_INSTANCE_ERROR: The instance value is invalid.

NPERR_OUT_OF_MEMORY_ERROR: Out of memory.

See Also NPN_GetURL, NPN_GetURLNotify, NPN_PostURLNotify, NPP_URLNotify

Example

```
#include <npapi.h>
   .
   .
   .
//
// Post data to a URL using the file technique
//

// Setup some strings

CString csFile = "posturl.txt";
CString csPost = "Content-type: application/x-www-form-
➥urlencoded\n";

csPost += "Content-length: 18\n\n";
csPost += "Entry=Zan+Oliphant\n";

// Create a temp. file and write to it

Cfile TmpFile (csFile.GetBuffer(csFile.GetLength()),
    CFile::modeCreate ¦ CFile::modeReadWrite ¦
➥CFile::shareDenyNone);
TmpFile.Write (csPost.GetBuffer(csPost.GetLength()),
csPost.GetLength());
TmpFile.Close();

// Send data to the server

NPError rc = NPN_PostURL (instance,
    "http://hoohoo.ncsa.uiuc.edu/cgi-bin/post-query",
    NULL,
    csFile.GetLength(),
    csFile.GetBuffer(csFile.GetLength()),
    TRUE);
   .
   .
   .
```

New Navigator 3.0 Plug-In APIs

NPN_GetURLNotify

Compatibility   UNIX, Macintosh, Windows 3.1/95/NT, Navigator 3.0 and above.

API Type   Navigator routine called from the plug-in.

Purpose   Requests the creation of a new stream for the specified URL and gets a result notification through a future call to NPP_URLNotify. This operation is asynchronous.

Sends a GET request to the Web server.

| *Syntax* | ```
NPError NPN_GetURLNotify (NPP instance,
    const char* url,
    const char* target,
    void* notifyData);
``` |

NPP instance: A pointer to structure NPP that references both the plug-in's and Netscape's private instance data.

const char* url: A pointer to a constant string containing the URL for the GET request.

const char* target: A pointer to a user-supplied constant string indicating the display location of the stream.

void* notifyData: A plug-in private value that can be used to uniquely identify the request. This will be returned to the plug-in as a parameter to the corresponding NPP_URLNotify call.

Includes `#include <npapi.h>`

Description The NPN_GetURLNotify API has the identical function as NPN_GetURL, but it provides for a result notification with a future call to NPP_URLNotify.

In order for your plug-in to correctly associate a NPN_GetURLNotify with the proper NPP_URLNotify, a new parameter called notifyData has been added to this API. You can attach a data block to this void pointer such as a pointer to an object or stream.

See the previous reference on NPN_GetURL for the base functionality of NPN_GetURLNotify.

Returns NPERR_NO_ERROR: No error.

NPERR_GENERIC_ERROR: An unknown error occurred.

NPERR_INVALID_INSTANCE_ERROR: The instance value is invalid.

NPERR_OUT_OF_MEMORY_ERROR: Out of memory.

See Also NPN_GetURL, NPN_PostURL, NPN_PostURLNotify, NPP_URLNotify

Example
```
#include <npapi.h>
    .
    .
    .
//
// Get a URL with a result notification
//

// Get the new URL and have the data streamed into
// the existing plug-in instance by using NULL for
// the target.
```
```

```
NPError rc = NPN_GetURLNotify (instance,
    "http://www.gate.net/~zan/outofb.wav",
    NULL,
    pMyPrivateData);
```

.
.
.

NPN_PostURLNotify

Compatibility   UNIX, Macintosh, Windows 3.1/95/NT, Navigator 3.0 and above.

API Type   Navigator routine called from the plug-in.

Purpose   Use NPN_PostURL to send data to a URL with a result notification sent
back to your plug-in with NPP_URLNotify. This API resolves to a POST
request to a Web server. The method is useful for sending data to a
CGI script.

Syntax
```
NPError NPN_PostURL (NPP instance,
    const char* url,
    const char* target,
    uint32 len,
    const char* buf,
    NPBool file,
    void* notifyData);
```

NPP instance: A pointer to structure NPP that references both the plug-
in's and Netscape's private instance data.

const char* url: A pointer to a constant string containing the URL for
the POST request.

const char* window: A pointer to a user-supplied constant string
indicating the display location of the stream. This parameter will be
renamed target in future SDKs.

uint32 len: Corresponds to the length of the following data buffer.

const char* buf: A constant pointer to a buffer with the data for
posting.

NPBool file: If this Boolean is set to TRUE, the previous buffer contains
a local filename for the Navigator to read instead of a data buffer. If it is
FALSE, the buffer contains raw data.

void* notifyData: This is a plug-in private value that can be used to
uniquely identify the request. It is returned to the plug-in as a parameter to the corresponding NPP_URLNotify call.

Includes   #include <npapi.h>

Description   The NPN_PostURLNotify API has the same function as NPN_PostURL, but provides for a result notification with a future call to NPP_URLNotify.

See the previous reference on NPN_PostURL for the base functionality of NPN_PostURLNotify.

Returns   NPERR_NO_ERROR: No error.

NPERR_GENERIC_ERROR: An unknown error occurred.

NPERR_INVALID_INSTANCE_ERROR: The instance value is invalid.

NPERR_OUT_OF_MEMORY_ERROR: Out of memory.

See Also   NPN_GetURL, NPN_PostURL, NPN_GetURLNotify, NPP_URLNotify

Example
```
#include <npapi.h>
  .
  .
  .
//
// Post data to a URL
//

// Setup some strings

CString csPost = "Content-type: application/x-www-form-
➥urlencoded\n";

csPost += "Content-length: 18\n\n";
csPost += "Entry=Zan+Oliphant\n";

// Send data to the server

NPError rc = NPN_PostURL (instance,
    "http://hoohoo.ncsa.uiuc.edu/cgi-bin/post-query",
    NULL,
    csPost.GetLength(),
    csPost.GetBuffer(csPost.GetLength()),
    FALSE,
    pMyPrivateData);
  .
  .
  .
```

NPP_URLNotify

Compatibility   UNIX, Macintosh, Windows 3.1/95/NT, Navigator 3.0 and above.

API Type   Plug-in method called from the Navigator.

Purpose   Notifies your plug-in of the completion of a URL request through either NPN_GetURLNotify or NPN_PostURLNotify.

| *Syntax* | ```
void NPP_URLNotify (NPP instance,
    const char* url,
    NPReason reason,
    void* notifyData);
``` |

NPP instance: A pointer to structure NPP that references both the plug-in's and Netscape's private instance data.

const char* url: A pointer to a constant string containing the URL that was requested.

void* notifyData: A plug-in private value that can be used to uniquely identify the request. This was previously set by the plug-in during either NPN_GetURLNotify or NPN_PostURLNotify.

Includes   `#include <npapi.h>`

Description   The NPP_URLNotify method is called when the Navigator completes a NPN_GetURLNotify or NPN_PostURLNotify request to inform the plug-in that the request has completed for the reason specified by reason.

The following values are currently defined for reason:

■   NPRES_NETWORK_ERR: The request could not be completed because a network error occurred. For example, the URL could not be found.

■   NPRES_USER_BR: The request was halted due to a user action such as clicking on the Stop button.

■   NPRES_D: The request completed normally.

Returns   None.

See Also   NPN_GetURLNotify, NPN_PostURLNotify

Example
```
#include <npapi.h>

//
// Process the URL notification
//

void NPP_URLNotify (NPP instance,
    const char* url,
    NPReason reason,
    void* notifyData);
{
    // Check for spurious calls from Netscape

    if (instance == NULL)
        return NPERR_INVALID_INSTANCE_ERROR;

    // Retrieve instance data

    MyInstance* myinstance = (MyInstance *)instance->pdata;
```
```

```
        // If the reason indicates no error, process

    if (reason == NPRES_DONE)
    {
        myinstance->URLRequestComplete (url, notifyData);
    }

    return NPERR_NO_ERROR;
}
```

Conclusion

This chapter showed you how to create and destroy streams both implicitly and explicitly. Data structures were defined and parameters both to and from the Navigator were covered. Special attention was given to sending data to HTTP servers with NPN_PostURL.

Make sure to take note of the warnings about use of these APIs. Netscape Navigator 2.*x* has a few bugs and does not support some of the streaming APIs.

What's Next?

Now that you're an expert at creating streams, it's time to move on to reading and writing to them. In the next chapter, you will see how both NPP and NPN type APIs enable you to move data to and from the server. The next chapter covers the APIs NPP_StreamAsFile, NPP_WriteReady, NPP_Write, NPN_RequestRead, and NPN_Write.

Reading From and Writing To Streams

Introduction

After a stream has been created, it can be written to freely by either your plug-in or Netscape's Navigator. In most cases, the data flow direction of a stream is from the Navigator and to the plug-in.

This chapter covers the methods used for stream reading and writing. In this chapter, you will learn the difference between processing a file in a streaming manner or waiting for the complete file download. APIs for pulling data from the server and allowing the server to push data to your plug-in are introduced.

The following APIs are covered in this chapter:

> NPP_WriteReady
>
> NPP_Write
>
> NPP_StreamAsFile
>
> NPN_RequestRead
>
> NPN_Write

Getting Buffers From a Stream

The plug-in API provides the methods NPP_WriteReady and NPP_Write to write streamed data to your plug-in. Both of these methods are *plug-in implemented*, which means that they are methods in your plug-in that are called from the Navigator.

NPP_WriteReady

After a stream has been created, your plug-in sits patiently waiting for data. This wait can be long or short, depending on your connection's speed. When the data arrives, the first call made to the plug-in is NPP_WriteReady. This API lets the plug-in know that data is on the way and asks how much data the plug-in can handle in one chunk. The size of this chunk can be anywhere from 1 to over 2 billion bytes (the maximum size of a 32-bit signed digit). Generally, your plug-in should request buffer sizes that make sense for a given data type. For example, if you are streaming compressed audio data and sending 4096-byte buffers to the CODEC, it makes sense to ask Netscape for the same size buffer. In most cases, Navigator passes your plug-in data in chunks no larger than 8KB buffers. You also might return 0 to Navigator to temporarily stop the data flow. Navigator tries again at regular intervals with calls to NPP_WriteReady to see whether your plug-in is again ready for data.

NPP_Write

Following the call to NPP_WriteReady is a call to another plug-in method, NPP_Write. The parameters passed to NPP_Write contain a pointer to the actual stream data for processing and the length of that data. You can immediately process the data or copy it for later use. The stream data provided by the Navigator is only valid for the duration of the NPP_Write call. If you plan to access any of this data at a later time, your plug-in must copy it to a separate buffer.

It is important to realize that the return value from NPP_WriteReady is the amount that your plug-in must consume on each call to NPP_Write, not the upper limit of data written by Navigator during NPP_Write. For example, if a plug-in returns 8KB from NPP_WriteReady, Navigator might respond with a 10KB write with NPP_Write. Normally, this is not a problem; just copy the data you want (8KB, in this case), and return the amount of data consumed (again 8KB). Just make sure you don't key your code from the Netscape buffer size and expect it to be less than or equal to the size you specified in NPP_WriteReady.

> **NOTE**
>
> In some plug-ins, a secondary buffer management scheme is needed to handle real-time data streaming. Data from NPP_Write is saved to establish a low water mark to begin processing. A scheme such as this is used in Chapter 17, "A Streaming Audio Sample." The source code for this example is available on this book's CD-ROM.

Another interesting parameter passed to NPP_Write is offset. Use this value to see how far you are into the stream. In most cases, this offset is incremented by the size of each buffer. One exception to this rule is the case of a seekable stream as indicated by the NP_SEEK definition. A seekable stream is random access in nature and is not really a true data stream. Therefore, the offset still relates to file position, but it is not necessarily incremented during each call to NPP_Write.

Killing a Stream

At some time in the life of a plug-in, it might be necessary to kill a stream before it is complete. This is accomplished by returning a negative value from NPP_Write. Consider a case in which your plug-in cannot handle a specific data type within its MIME type. The file's header can be read and the stream can be aborted, followed by an error message to the user. This technique avoids a long wait for an unsupported file format.

Killing a stream in this manner from within your plug-in is the same as having a user click the Stop button on the browser.

> **NOTE**
>
> Returning a negative value from NPP_Write with the Macintosh Navigator 2.x creates problems and should be avoided on this platform and the Navigator version.

Getting Less Data

In some cases, your plug-in might get less data in the NPP_Write call than was requested in NPP_WriteReady. The most common case is during the end of the stream when it might not end on an even buffer boundary. If you are getting 4KB buffers and the file that is being streamed is not divisible by 4KB, of course you will get a remainder. This scenario is usually not a problem, considering that your buffer will be larger.

File-Based Processing

A mechanism exists to let your plug-in process a file as a whole file rather than a stream of data. If possible, this practice should be avoided because it makes the user wait for the complete file to download before any processing can begin. In some data types, this is unavoidable, but many can be processed in a streaming manner.

When your plug-in requires a complete file, a plug-in indicates this to the Navigator by setting *stype to NP_ASFILE in your NPP_NewStream method. If you do this, a call is made to your NPP_StreamAsFile method when the file has completed downloading. NPP_StreamAsFile is not called for NP_SEEK or NP_NORMAL. The Navigator 3.0 Plug-in API introduces a new type called NP_ASFILEONLY. This new type is similar to NP_ASFILE, but it is more efficient because it intelligently avoids streaming local files. Consult Chapter 10, "Stream Creation and Destruction," for more information on *stype values.

Local File Paths

NPP_StreamAsFile is passed a pointer to a fully qualified path of the file on the local system. This file might have originated on the local machine, and perhaps it was opened through the File|Open File in Browser menu item. In this case, the file lives on the local machine and the path to it is the actual fully qualified filename. Otherwise, the file might have been downloaded from an HTTP server and resides in Netscape's cache directory with an obscure filename. The real filename can always be found by parsing the URL in the NPStream structure.

> **TIP**
>
> Even when you use a stream of type NP_ASFILE and the NPP_StreamAsFile method, data is still streamed through the Navigator. Although, in many cases, this is not a problem, consider a CD-ROM or file server with very large video files. You certainly don't want to read the file twice; once through Netscape and once with your plug-in is too much. You can avoid this problem by using NP_ASFILEONLY if your plug-in is running under Navigator 3.0 and above.

To avoid this scenario in Navigator 2.*x*, follow these steps:

1. Check the URL in `NPP_NewStream` and see whether it starts with `file:`. For example, here is a local file:

   ```
   file:///D¦/Program Files/Netscape/Navigator/Program/bach.wav
   ```

2. If it is a local file, don't set the type to `NP_ASFILE`. Just leave it as `NP_NORMAL`. If it's not a local file, forget this plan.

3. Parse out a real local filename from the URL and save it within your plug-in's instance data. For example, you need to convert the previous URL to the following:

   ```
   D:\Program Files\Netscape\Navigator\Program\bach.wav
   ```

4. As the streaming begins, request one byte in `NPP_WriteReady`.

5. Return a negative value from `NPP_Write`, thereby destroying the stream.

6. Process the file normally.

Feel free to use this technique for all local file processing. Remember that you can avoid this process by using `NP_ASFILEONLY` with the Navigator Plug-in API 3.0 and above (Plug-in API Major Version of 0, Plug-in API Minor Version greater than or equal to 8).

Tricks with `NP_ASFILE`

Another interesting thing that a stream of type `NP_ASFILE` can do is create a local file within Netscape's cache while still letting the plug-in process the file as a stream. Stream types of `NP_ASFILE` let your plug-in process stream buffers normally through the use of `NPP_WriteReady` and `NPP_Write`.

The advantage of this technique is that it allows you to continue processing the file in Netscape's cache after the stream is complete. The name of this cached file is passed to your plug-in during the `NPP_StreamAsFile` method. Of course, you can always cache downloaded files yourself either in memory or on disk.

NOTE

Netscape caches files in a subdirectory called Cache. The directory and cache size can be changed via the Options|Network Preferences menu item. As a plug-in developer, you should be aware that using Netscape's file caching for large files tends to blow away a lot of little files such as HTML code. Because the caching scheme is First In First Out (FIFO), your big files squeeze other files out. In addition, a file is not cached unless it has been completely streamed and, in the case of plug-ins, is type `NP_ASFILE`.

Random Stream Access

One of the more interesting APIs of Netscape's plug-in design is NPN_RequestRead. This method allows a plug-in to read specific portions of a file without downloading it. This isn't a big deal for local files, but what if you could pick through large files on an HTTP server? Imagine being able to scan through a large audio file. Perhaps, you might listen to half of a speech tonight and the other half tomorrow night. The second time around, instead of downloading the entire first half again, a plug-in simply starts in the middle of the file. In the world of streams, this random access is called *seeking*.

> **WARNING**
>
> Before you get too excited, at the time of this writing there are no HTTP servers that can handle file seeking through what are known as *byte range requests*. Because the implementation for this on the server side is very straightforward, you should see this feature very soon—if not by the time you are reading this book.

NPN_RequestRead can be called on seekable streams only. To determine whether a stream supports seeks, simply check to see whether the seekable parameter of NPP_NewStream is set to TRUE. If it is, be sure to set stype of the same API to the stream type NP_SEEK.

To seek within a stream, you must first build a linked list of byte range structures. If you are only requesting one contiguous range of bytes, your list only consists of one member. The structure to build the list is called NPByteRange and is defined as follows:

```
typedef struct _NPByteRange
{
    int32                   offset;
    uint32                  length;
    struct _NPByteRange*    next;

} NPByteRange;
```

Fill the structure with the byte offset of the beginning of the byte range. Positive values are from the first byte in the file, and negative values are from the last byte. The next pointer references the following NPByteRange structure, if any. To add another request, simply allocate another structure and attach it to the next pointer. As with most linked lists, be sure to set next to NULL for the last structure.

Where the Offset Comes In

As with a normal stream, a successful return of data from an NPN_RequestRead comes through the NPP_WriteReady and NPP_Write methods. You might remember from NPP_Write that there was an odd little parameter called offset. In a nonseeking stream, this parameter is not very exciting because it simply increments along with each buffer. With seeking streams, its task is more important. If you've made a multiple-byte request call with `NPN_RequestRead`, you can match each request by the offset values in both `NPP_Write` and the `NPByteRange` structure.

Writing to a Stream

Navigator 3.0 introduces `NPN_Write` to be used in conjunction with `NPN_NewStream` and `NPN_DestroyStream`. `NPN_Write` allows your plug-in to write data to a stream for consumption by Netscape. Although, at the time of this writing, this method is not working properly, it should work when Navigator 3.0 is out of beta. See Chapter 10 for an example of how you might use these new methods.

API Quick Reference

The following sections give in-depth information on the APIs used in this chapter.

NPP_WriteReady

Compatibility	Windows 3.1/95/NT, Macintosh, UNIX, Navigator 2.0 and above.
API Type	Plug-in implemented method.
Purpose	Determines whether your plug-in is ready to receive data, and how much data it is willing to receive.
Syntax	`int32 NPP_WriteReady (NPP instance, NPStream* stream)`

NPP instance: A pointer to structure `NPP` that references both the plug-in's and Netscape's private instance data.

NPStream* stream: A pointer to structure `NPStream` that references both the plug-in's and Netscape's stream instance data. This structure also contains the URL, last modification date, and content length in bytes.

Includes	`#include <npapi.h>`
Description	`NPP_WriteReady` is called by the Navigator to ask your plug-in how much data it is willing to receive. This amount is indicated by the return value. `NPP_WriteReady` is usually, but not always, followed closely by a call to `NPP_Write` with the actual data. Your plug-in can get a larger data buffer than requested during `NPP_Write`, but it is only required to consume the amount returned by the previous call to `NPP_WriteReady`.

Even if you are processing a stream as `NP_ASFILE`, a call is made to `NPP_WriteReady`. In this case, you should simply return with a very large value to indicate to the Navigator that your plug-in will not process data in a streaming manner and doesn't care how much is written at one time.

Don't be afraid to return a value of zero to prevent Navigator from sending more data. This is a stream overrun and a valid case. Navigator will try again later.

Returns   int32 bytes: Data length in bytes that the plug-in is ready to receive.

See Also   NPP_Write

Example
```
//
// NPP_WriteReady
//

int32 NP_LOADDS NPP_WriteReady (NPP instance,
    NPStream *stream)
{
    if (instance == NULL)
        return 0;

    // Retrieve instance data

    MyInstance* myinstance = (MyInstance *)instance->pdata;

    // Retrieve per stream data

    MyStream* mystream = (MyStream *)stream->pdata;

    // Take any action during this time

    if (mystream)
        return mystream->PrepareForWrite ();
    else
        return 0;
}
```

NPP_Write

Compatibility   Windows 3.1/95/NT, Macintosh, UNIX, Navigator 2.0 and above.

API Type   Plug-in implemented method.

Purpose   Called from the Navigator to give your plug-in its requested buffer from NPP_WriteReady.

Syntax
```
int32 NPP_Write (NPP instance,
    NPStream* stream,
    int32 offset,
    int32 len,
    void* buffer)
```

NPP instance: A pointer to structure NPP that references both the plug-in's and Netscape's private instance data.

NPStream* stream: A pointer to structure NPStream that references both the plug-in's and Netscape's stream instance data. This structure also contains the URL, last modification date, and content length in bytes.

int32 offset: A byte offset within the data stream. Useful for verifying range requests from NPN_RequestRead or verifying stream progress.

int32 len: The length in bytes of the following buffer.

void* buffer: A pointer to the buffer containing stream data.

Includes	#include <npapi.h>
Description	NPP_Write is called to give your plug-in the data that it requested from NPP_WriteReady. Although the length of this data can be more or less than the requested amount, your plug-in must consume at least the amount requested from NPP_WriteReady or the entire buffer.

The offset parameter verifies how many bytes have been streamed. In a nonseeking stream, this value grows according to the size of each buffer written. In a seeking stream that uses byte range requests, offset can be used to verify read requests from NPN_RequestRead.

The plug-in returns the number of bytes written, which is the amount of data that the plug-in consumed during the NPP_Write method. A negative value can be returned to request the destruction of the stream.

Returns	int32 bytes: The number of bytes written or a negative value to destroy the stream.
See Also	NPP_WriteReady
Example	

```
//
// NPP_Write
//

int32 NP_LOADDS NPP_Write (NPP instance,
    NPStream* stream,
    int32 offset,
    int32 len,
    void* buffer)

    if (instance == NULL)
        return -1;

    // Retrieve instance data

    MyInstance* myinstance = (MyInstance *)instance->pdata;

    // Retrieve per stream data

    MyStream* mystream = (MyStream *)stream->pdata;

    // Take any action during this time
```

```
                    if (mystream)
                        return mystream->WriteData (offset, len, buffer);
                    else
                        return -1;
                }
```

NPP_StreamAsFile

Compatibility   Windows 3.1/95/NT, Macintosh, UNIX, Navigator 2.0 and above.

API Type   Plug-in implemented method.

Purpose   Provides a filename for a file-based plug-in of type NP_ASFILE, or for Navigator 3.0 and above it provides NP_ASFILEONLY.

Syntax
```
void NP_LOADDS NPP_StreamAsFile (NPP instance,
    NPStream* stream,
    const char* fname)
```

NPP instance: A pointer to structure NPP that references both the plug-in's and Netscape's private instance data.

NPStream* stream: A pointer to structure NPStream that references both the plug-in's and Netscape's stream instance data. This structure also contains the URL, last modification date, and content length in bytes.

const char* fname: A pointer to a buffer containing a fully qualified path of the filename on the client.

Includes   `#include <npapi.h>`

Description   If you set *stype in NPP_NewStream to NP_ASFILE or NP_ASFILEONLY for Navigator 3.0, NPP_StreamAsFile is called upon completion of the stream and gives you a fully qualified path to the local filename.

NPP_StreamAsFile and NPP_DestroyStream are very similar methods. Both are called on completion of the stream. For local files, NPP_DestroyStream could be used, instead of NPP_StreamAsFile, by retrieving the local filename from the given URL. In the case of a remote file that was downloaded by the Navigator, you must use NPP_StreamAsFile to get the filename within Netscape's file cache.

It is interesting to note that although you might have indicated that your plug-in will wait for the end of stream with NP_ASFILE, NPP_WriteReady and NPP_Write are still called in the normal fashion, allowing you to see the data as it is streamed.

This method is not called for streams of type NP_NORMAL.

Returns	None.
See Also	NPP_DestroyStream, NPP_Write, NPP_WriteReady
Example	

```
//
// NPP_StreamAsFile
//
//

void NP_LOADDS NPP_StreamAsFile(NPP instance,
    NPStream *stream,
    const char* fname)
{
    // Check for bogus filename

    if (fname == NULL)
        return;

    if (fname[0] == NULL)
        return;

    if (instance == NULL)
        return;

    // Retrieve instance data

    MyInstance* myinstance = (MyInstance *)instance->pdata;

    // Retrieve per stream data

    MyStream* mystream = (MyStream *)stream->pdata;

    // Take any action during this time

    if (mystream)
        mystream ->ProcessFile (fname);

    return;

}
```

NPN_RequestRead

Compatibility	Windows 3.1/95/NT, Macintosh, UNIX, Navigator 2.0 and above.
API Type	Navigator implemented method.
Purpose	Requests a range of bytes from a seekable stream that will be written to the plug-in in subsequent NPP_Write calls.
Syntax	NPError NPN_RequestRead (NPStream* stream, NPByteRange* rangeList)

NPStream* stream: A pointer to structure NPStream that references both the plug-in's and Netscape's stream instance data. This structure also contains the URL, last modification date, and content length in bytes.

NPByteRange* rangeList: A pointer to the head of a linked list of
NPByteRange structures. Each structure corresponds to a separate byte
range request.

Includes #include <npapi.h>

Description NPN_RequestRead requests one or more byte range reads that result in
calls to NPP_WriteReady and NPP_Write. For multiple requests, a linked
list of NPByteRange structures is created, with each structure representing a separate request.

The stream used in the call must be valid and must be of type NP_SEEK,
which is set in the method NPP_NewStream.

Returns NPERR_NO_ERROR: The call was successful.

NPERR_GENERIC_ERROR: An error occurred.

See Also NPP_WriteReady

Example
```
//
// NPN_RequestRead
//
    .
    .
    .

    // Build a linked list of ranges for three reads.

    NPByteRange range1, range2, range3;

    range.offset = 55000;
    range.length = 1045;
    range.next = &range2;

    range2.offset = 245000;
    range2.length = 4000;
    range2.next = &range3;

    range3.offset = 500000;
    range3.length = 100000;
    range3.next = NULL;

    NPError rc = NPN_RequestRead (stream, &range1);
    .
    .
    .
```

NPN_Write

Compatibility Windows 3.1/95/NT, Macintosh, UNIX, Navigator 3.0 and above.

API Type Navigator implemented method.

Purpose Called by your plug-in to write to a stream for consumption by the
Navigator. This stream was created by a previous call to
NPN_NewStream.

Syntax

```
int32 NPN_Write (NPP instance, NPStream* stream, int32 len,
void* buffer)
```

NPP instance: A pointer to structure NPP that references both the plug-in's and Netscape's private instance data.

NPStream* stream: A pointer to structure NPStream that references both the plug-in's and Netscape's stream instance data. This structure also contains the URL, last modification date, and content length in bytes.

int32 len: The length in bytes of the buffer to be written.

void* buffer: A pointer to the buffer to be written.

Includes

```
#include <npapi.h>
```

Description

Use NPN_Write to write data to a stream for consumption by the Navigator. This new Navigator 3.0 API should be used in conjunction with NPN_NewStream and NPN_DestroyStream. See Chapter 10 for an example including these three methods.

If NPN_Write returns a negative value indicating an error, you should terminate the stream immediately with a call to NPN_DestroyStream.

Returns

int32 bytes: The number of bytes actually written.

int32 (negative value): An error occurred.

See Also

NPP_WriteReady, NPP_Write

Example

```
//
// NPN_Write
//
    .
    .
    .
    // Write some HTML code to the Navigator

    char Buffer[] = "<html>\n<body>\n\n<h2 align=center>Stuff</
h2>\n\n</bod
➥y>\n</html>"
    int32 bytes = NPN_Write (instance, stream, strlen(Buffer),
Buffer);

    .
    .
```

Conclusion

This chapter has shown you how to read and write streams. In most cases, a plug-in uses a server push model in which the HTTP server pumps data to the Navigator, which in turn calls your plug-in's API NPP_Write. A client pull technique was also discussed using the API NPN_RequestRead. This API is used strictly for seekable streams.

What's Next?

The next chapter discusses Netscape's memory management methods for your plug-in. You'll learn why you need to use them to avoid memory leaks from your plug-in code module. The `NPN_MemAlloc`, `NPN_MemFlush`, and `NPN_MemFree` APIs are covered.

Memory Management

Introduction

Netscape provides a plug-in developer with a set of three memory management APIs. For Macintosh developers, these APIs allow plug-ins to force Netscape to release system memory. Windows and Macintosh developers both need the Navigator's memory APIs to implement the save feature used by both `NPP_Destroy` and `NPP_New`.

Windows 95 plug-in developers have many system memory management functions to choose from. Of these, some of the most interesting are direct access to virtual memory and memory mapped files.

The following APIs are covered in this chapter:

```
NPN_MemAlloc

NPN_MemFree

NPN_MemFlush
```

Netscape's Memory APIs

Netscape provides plug-in developers with some basic memory management APIs to facilitate a saved memory feature. In many cases, you won't have to use these provided APIs. If you want to take advantage of saved memory between instances and don't want to worry about freeing memory that was allocated by a nonpresent instance, these plug-in APIs are the way to go.

In some cases, aside from the save feature, Netscape's provided memory management APIs are essential. Consider a Macintosh with the virtual memory feature turned off. This configuration is quite common for Mac users. If your plug-in attempts a memory allocation via a standard system call, it might find no memory available to back up this request. Instead, use the `NPN_MemAlloc` method. On a resource-restricted system, this API frees memory from Netscape's cache to try to fulfill the memory request.

In the world of Windows, the preceding scenario can also be the case with virtual memory turned off or with a full hard drive.

Memory Allocation and Freeing

To allocate a block of memory from Netscape, simply call the method `NPN_MemAlloc` with the single parameter being the size of the requested memory block. To free this memory block, call the `NPN_MemFree` method with a pointer to the previously allocated block.

Flushing Navigator's Memory on the Macintosh

The Macintosh has a special API called `NPN_MemFlush`. This method is provided for cases when calling `NPN_MemAlloc` is not possible. System APIs on the Mac can cause indirect allocation of memory. If these fail because of lack of memory, your recourse is to flush out Netscape's cache using `NPN_MemFlush` to retrieve the necessary amount of memory. Call `NPN_MemFlush` repeatedly until it returns zero to free as much memory as possible from the Navigator.

Windows 95 Memory Management

In Windows 95, you might never need to use Netscape's memory management APIs. A failed memory request from Windows 95 usually indicates much bigger problems than can be solved with Navigator giving up whatever memory it has allocated for cache. Additionally, the `new` operator certainly doesn't know about using `NPN_MemAlloc`. Although a tricky C++ programmer could simply override the new operator, Microsoft's Foundation Class Library beat you to it. Saving data between plug-in instances is probably the only case in Windows 95 to use Netscape's memory management APIs.

Address Space of a Process

In Windows 95, your plug-in is part of the Navigator's process address space. Each process has its own address space totally independent of other processes. Your plug-in's process, which is shared with Netscape, has a 2GB range of addresses for memory allocation. In addition to runtime memory allocation, your plug-in's DLL and the Netscape .EXE file are loaded in this range of addresses.

Although a 32-bit pointer can address 4GB of memory, a Windows 95 process can only access 2GB. The rest of the address range is used by page tables, VxDs, system DLLs, memory mapped files, 16-bit Windows support, and MS-DOS. Figure 12.1 shows the process address space for Windows 95.

Figure 12.1.

Windows 95 process address space.

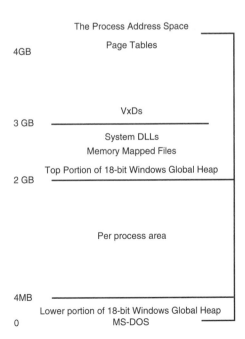

Advanced Memory API

Windows 95 provides many layers of memory management. These layers support such things as Windows 3.*x*, C Runtime Memory Functions, Heap Manager API, Virtual Memory API, and Memory Mapped File API. At the end of all this is either your hard disk or physical memory. Figure 12.2 shows layered memory management for Win32.

Figure 12.2.

Windows 95 memory management layers.

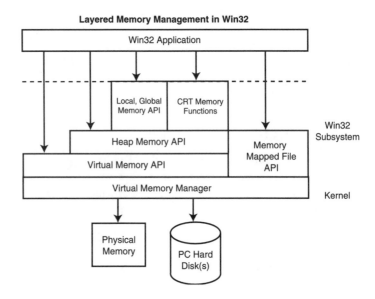

Layered Memory Management in Win32

Which Memory Management Functions to Use

With all those layers, it can be somewhat overwhelming to figure out what to use for plug-in development. In most cases, the `new` and `delete` operators combined with `malloc` and `free` are all you need. However, there are some really interesting memory management APIs that a Windows 95 developer might want to take advantage of—in particular, the Virtual Memory API and the Memory Mapped File API.

Using Virtual Memory Directly

Windows 95 manages virtual memory in what are called *pages*, or 4096-byte sections. Each of these pages can be in memory or swapped to disk at any given time. An address within your Windows 95 application really references a set of page tables. A 32-bit address within your process is broken down into a page directory index, page table index, and page index. The first 10 bits are the directory index, the next 10 bits are the table index, and the last 12 bits are the page index.

The following example shows how a virtual address of 0x009c8788 is resolved into directory, table, and page indices:

```
Address = 0x009C8788 (in hex)
Address = 0000 0000 1001 1100 1000 0111 1000 1000 (in binary)

Directory Index  = 0000 0000 10
Table Index      = 01 1100 1000
Page Index       = 0111 1000 1000
```

The problem with using virtual memory without any heap management functions is that any allocation—even 1 byte—will allocate a page of 4096 bytes. Fortunately, the C runtime does a nice job of suballocating these pages for you with the help of the Heap Memory API.

Although malloc is great for small chunks of memory, what if you require a very large memory allocation? For example, if you know that you need at least 1MB of memory but definitely no more than 100MB, it would be nice to keep this memory as a contiguous range of addresses. If you allocate 100MB with malloc, memory is immediately committed and your swap file probably grows accordingly. Using a virtual memory API such as VirtualAlloc enables you to reserve the 100MB range but only commit it as necessary. The 100MB limit might seem like a lot, but remember that your process can address 2GB; 100MB is only about five percent of that, and the memory address range is just reserved and uses no system resources.

Using a Memory Mapped File

With all that address space within your process, another Windows 95 feature called memory mapped files is possible. Memory mapped files allow you to map a file to your process's address space and access the file through pointers as if it is memory. Because a very large memory mapped file is read into memory by Windows in only 4096 byte pages, resource use is minimized and the application benefits by seeing the whole file in memory. A memory mapped file is also allocated in shared memory, which allows interprocess communication.

> **NOTE**
>
> The Microsoft Developer Network CD-ROMs are an excellent source of information on advanced Windows 95 memory management features.

Old Friends: LocalAlloc and GlobalAlloc

If you are coming from a Windows 3.*x* programming background, as most Windows 95 programmers are, you might be tempted to use LocalAlloc and GlobalAlloc instead of the C Runtime routine malloc. In the past, many problems occurred with malloc for Windows 16-bit programming. With Windows 95, you can safely use malloc and free. In fact, LocalAlloc and GlobalAlloc are somewhat obsolete and both resolve to the same routine within the Windows kernel. Keep in mind that Windows 95 has a 32-bit flat memory module with no concept of near or far pointers. Also, because in MFC C++ the new operator resolves to a `malloc`, you really can't avoid using `malloc` even if you want to.

Your Plug-In as a Windows 95 DLL

A Windows 95 plug-in is implemented as a Dynamic Link Library (DLL). Unlike Windows 3.*x*, a Windows 95 DLL data segment is not shared by default. In most cases, you won't care whether your plug-in is loaded by another process. Although it is very rare for a user to bring up another copy of Netscape and load your plug-in through another process, you still need to handle this case.

If your plug-in will have catastrophic failure when loaded by another process, you should keep track of how many times the plug-in is loaded. A simple way to do this is by creating an additional data segment within your DLL and setting it to SHARED. Use the SECTIONS keyword in your .DEF file and name your new segment as follows:

```
SECTIONS  .newseg  READ WRITE SHARED
```

In your C code, use pragmas to define any variables in this new segment:

```
#pragma data_seg (".newseg")
int ProcessCount = 0;
#pragma data_seg ()
```

Make sure to initialize any variables in this new segment, or they will be put in the uninitialized data section. Use the NPP_Initialize and NPP_Shutdown methods accordingly to increment and decrement a process count.

API Quick Reference

The following sections give in-depth information on the APIs used in this chapter.

NPN_MemAlloc

Compatibility	Windows 3.1/95/NT, Macintosh, UNIX.
API Type	Navigator implemented method.
Purpose	Called from the plug-in to allocate memory within the Navigator's memory space.
Syntax	`void* NPN_MemAlloc (uint32 size)`
	`uint32 size`: An unsigned long indicating the size of memory for allocation.

Includes   `#include <npapi.h>`

Description   `NPN_MemAlloc` is called from the plug-in to request a block of memory from the Navigator. This method is only needed for cases in which the plug-in might not have the opportunity to free the memory block. One such case is the `NPP_Destroy` method's save option. When your plug-in allocates memory for this feature, it must allocate the memory with `NPN_MemAlloc` to guarantee eventual freeing of the memory block. If your plug-in is never called again, the Navigator ensures that memory is freed.

Returns   `void*`: A pointer to the allocated memory block.

See Also   `NPN_MemFlush` (Macintosh only), `NPN_MemFree`

Example

```
//
// Use NPN_MemAlloc for a saved memory block
//
    .
    .
    .

    // First allocate the structure for saved data

    MySavedData* mysaveddata = (MySavedData*)NPN_MemAlloc
➥(sizeof(MySavedData));

    // Then allocate a NPSavedData structure

    (*save) = (NPSavedData *)NPN_MemAlloc (sizeof(NPSavedData));
    (*save)->buf = mysaveddata;
    (*save)->len = sizeof(MySavedData);

    .
    .
    .
```

NPN_MemFree

Compatibility   Windows 3.1/95/NT, Macintosh, UNIX.

API Type   Navigator implemented method.

Purpose   Called from the plug-in to free memory previously allocated with the NPN_MemAlloc method.

Syntax   `void NPN_MemFree (void* ptr)`

`void* ptr`: A pointer to a memory block allocated with `NPN_MemAlloc`.

Includes   `#include <npapi.h>`

Description　Use NPN_MemFree to free a memory block that was allocated with NPN_MemAlloc. Make sure NPN_MemAlloc and NPN_MemFree are used as pairs. Do not attempt to use NPN_MemFree on a block of memory allocated with malloc or the new operator.

Returns　None.

See Also　NPN_MemFlush (Macintosh only), NPN_MemAlloc

Example
```
//
// Free a saved block of memory allocated with NPN_MemAlloc
//

    .
    .
    .

if (saved)
{
    if (saved->len == sizeof (MySavedData)
    {
        MySavedData* mysaveddata = saved->buf;

        .
        . Get whatever you need…
        .

        // Free both memory blocks with NPN_MemFree

        NPN_MemFree (saved->buf);
        NPN_MemFree (saved);
    }
}
    .
    .
    .
```

NPN_MemFlush

Compatibility　Macintosh only.

API Type　Navigator implemented method.

Purpose　Used to free memory in the Navigator and allow more memory for the plug-in.

Syntax　uint32 NPN_MemFlush (uint32 size)

uint32 size:　An unsigned long indicating the amount of memory required by the plug-in.

Includes　#include <npapi.h>

Description   In the Macintosh environment, it is quite common to turn off virtual memory. This practice can lead to a memory-starved system. Netscape allocates some unessential memory for such things as cache that can be freed for use by the plug-in. In a regular call to NPN_MemAlloc, Navigator memory is freed to accommodate a plug-in's request. A Macintosh System API might also attempt to allocate memory. If these system allocations fail, the plug-in developer might call NPN_MemFlush to free more memory from the Navigator.

Call NPN_MemFlush repeatedly until it returns zero to request that the Navigator free as much memory as possible.

Returns   None.

See Also   NPN_MemAlloc, NPN_MemFree

Example
```
//
// Get the maximum amount of memory from the Navigator with
NPN_MemFlush
//

    .
    .
    .

    while (NPN_MemFlush (0xFFFF));

    .
    .
    .
```

Conclusion

Of the plug-in memory management APIs, NPN_MemAlloc and NPN_MemFree are used by the Windows, UNIX, and Macintosh environments, and the NPN_MemFlush API is used in the Macintosh environment only.

In most cases, these methods are used for the purposes of allocating and freeing memory to use in saves between plug-in instances.

The NPN_MemFlush method allows the Macintosh plug-in to request that Navigator free any non-critical memory.

What's Next?

Netscape provides a method to give the browser user plug-in status and another method to query the user agent field. The NPN_Status and NPN_UserAgent methods are covered in the next chapter.

Status Methods

Introduction

With the sometimes lengthy delays you can encounter when using today's World Wide Web, it's important to continuously update the user with the status of the current operation. Netscape Navigator accomplishes this with a line of text at the bottom of the browser. Everything from URLs to transfer status is displayed in this line. Your plug-in also has the opportunity to give status in this area with the NPN_Status method.

A Web browser's User-Agent field is sent to an HTTP server during client server communications. This field is very important for generating universal statistics on browser usage. A plug-in can access this information with the NPN_UserAgent method.

This chapter covers the following APIs:

    NPN_Status

    NPN_UserAgent

Giving Status

As an avid Netscape Navigator user, it would be hard for you not to notice the status line on the bottom of the user interface. This single line of text gives the user all kinds of information, from URLs to progress reports (see Figure 13.1).

Figure 13.1.

Netscape's status line showing a URL during a Yahoo search request.

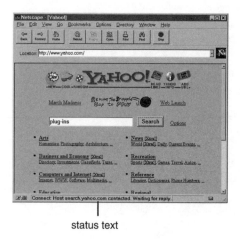

status text

Your plug-in is given the capability to print status in the same area as the Navigator with the NPN_Status API. This API is very simple to use. Just provide a character buffer with whatever information you would like to display and Navigator will show it to the user.

WARNING

Because you might end up fighting the browser for use of the status line, any critical error messages should be displayed in another fashion.

Your Own Progress Indicator

One of the coolest things that you can put in the status line is a file progress indicator. The parameters stream->end, offset, and len are provided during NPP_Write and can be used to create your own progress indicator based on data streaming to your plug-in. Here is a Windows sample method to accomplish this:

```
//
// ShowProgress
//
void CWorker::ShowProgress (NPP instance,
    uint32 FileSize,
    int32 Offset,
    int32 len)
{
    DWORD dwCurTick = GetTickCount ();

    if (dwLastTickCount)
    {
        float BytesPerSecond =  (float)len / ((float)(dwCurTick - this->dwLastTi
➥ckCount) / (float)1000.0);

        int SecsRemain = (int)((FileSize - Offset) / BytesPerSecond);

        int MinutesRemain = SecsRemain / 60;

        SecsRemain -= MinutesRemain * 60;

        int PercentComplete = (int)((float)Offset / (float)FileSize * 100);

        CString OutPut;

        OutPut.Format ("%d%% of %dK (at%8.0f bps, %02d:%02d remaining)",
            PercentComplete,
            FileSize / 1024,
            BytesPerSecond * 8,
            MinutesRemain,
            SecsRemain);

        NPN_Status (instance, OutPut.GetBuffer(OutPut.GetLength()));
    }

    // Dont forget to zero out dwLastTickCount after each destroy stream

    this->dwLastTickCount = dwCurTick;

}
```

This code produces a status line very similar to the one Navigator shows during its file progress. The only difference is that this sample displays file progress in bits per second (bps) rather than Navigator's traditional kilobytes per second (kbps). Using bps provides a nice ratio because it relates directly to the speed of the user's modem.

If you are not developing for Windows, simply replace `GetTickCount()` with your operating system's equivalent API. Don't forget to zero out `dwLastTickCount` during initialization and when the stream is destroyed!

Calling the progress method is a simple matter of adding the following line (or your equivalent) to `NPP_Write`:

```
data->pWorker->ShowProgress (instance, stream->end, offset, len);
```

Netscape's User-Agent

When Web browsers communicate with an HTTP server, a User-Agent field is included with most requests. The User-Agent field tells the HTTP server the name of the agent software, its version, and its operating system. This information is very useful for generating statistics on browser usage.

> **NOTE**
>
> A good place to view such statistics is called BrowserWatch (see Figure 13.2) and can be found at the following address:
>
> ```
> http://www.browserwatch.com
> ```
>
> BrowserWatch is a great resource for plug-in developers on all platforms. It's also a good way to find out what Netscape is working on with stats from the User-Agent field. Other fun things from BrowserWatch are Browser News, Plug-in Plaza!, Net Fame, Browser Listing, and Browser Stats. You can bet Bill Gates and Marc Andreessen are checking out pages such as BrowserWatch!
>
> Note your User-Agent at the top of the page:
>
> ```
> HTTP_USER_AGENT: Mozilla/3.0B2 (Win95; I)
> ```
>
> Also interesting is your IP address:
>
> ```
> Client outside the MSKCC network: 198.206.134.109 (dfbf12-46.gate.net)
> ```
>
> When you have completed your plug-in, be sure to contact these guys and get it in Plug-in Plaza!

Figure 13.2.

The BrowserWatch home page.

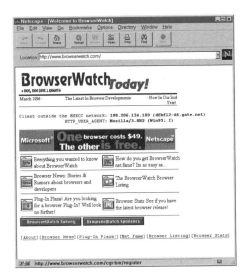

One of the most frequently used HTTP requests is GET. As you learned from previous chapters, NPN_GetURL can be used by a plug-in to generate a GET request. The request that the Navigator sends to the server might look something like this:

```
GET / HTTP/1.0
Connection: Keep-Alive
User-Agent: Mozilla/3.0B2 (Win95; I)
Host: www.browserwatch.com
Accept: image/gif, image/x-xbitmap, image/jpeg, image/pjpeg, */*
```

In this case, the User-Agent is Mozilla/3.0B2 (Win95; I).

What the Heck Is Mozilla?

Mozilla is Netscape's mascot. He is a fire-breathing Godzilla-like creature who appears now and then on Netscape's home page. It's rumored that this mascot was chosen to stomp out the competition. That would be NSCA Mosaic at the time.

> **NOTE**
>
> Netscape's co-founder, Marc Andreessen, previously worked at the National Center for Supercomputing Applications (NCSA) for a mere pittance of $6.85 an hour. As you might already know, NCSA produced the Web's first popular browser, called NCSA Mosaic. After Marc graduated from the University of Illinois, he was recruited by Jim Clark, founder of Silicon Graphics. The pair formed Netscape Communications and proceeded to recruit young developers from the NCSA project. Netscape's biggest competitor at the time was NCSA Mosaic—written by Netscape developers themselves! As they sort of competed with themselves, they came up with Mozilla.

API Quick Reference

The following sections give in-depth information on the APIs used in this chapter.

NPN_Status

Compatibility	Windows 3.1/95/NT, Macintosh, UNIX.
API Type	Navigator method called from a plug-in.
Purpose	Prints a user status message, which appears in the lower section of the Navigator's user interface.
Syntax	`void NPN_Status (NPP instance, const char* message)`

NPP instance: A pointer to structure NPP that references both the plug-in's and Netscape's private instance data.

const char* message: A pointer to a buffer containing the status message.

Includes	`#include <npapi.h>`
Description	During the normal use of Netscape's Navigator, status messages are constantly displayed to the user in the bottom portion of the user interface. Your plug-in can also display a message in this area using NPN_Status with a message string.

Unfortunately, you might have to compete with Netscape's messages in the same area.

Returns	None.
See Also	`NPN_UserAgent`
Example	

```
//
// Give the user some status
//

    .
    .
    .

    CString OutPut;

    // Format the output

    OutPut.Format ("%d%% of %dK (at%8.0f bps,
➥%02d:%02d remaining)",
        PercentComplete,
        FileSize / 1024,
        BytesPerSecond * 8,
```

```
                          MinutesRemain,
                          SecsRemain);

              NPN_Status (instance, OutPut.GetBuffer(OutPut.GetLength()));


          .
          .
          .
```

NPN_UserAgent

Compatibility	Windows 3.1/95/NT, Macintosh, UNIX.
API Type	Navigator method called from a plug-in.
Purpose	Retrieves the User-Agent field from the Navigator.
Syntax	`const char* NPN_UserAgent (NPP instance)`

NPP instance: A pointer to structure NPP that references both the plug-in's and Netscape's private instance data.

Includes	`#include <npapi.h>`
Description	Use this method to get the Navigator's User-Agent field, which is sent out in HTTP server requests. This field is used mostly for browser statistics.
Returns	`const char*`: A pointer to a buffer containing the Navigator's User-Agent field.
See Also	`NPN_Status`
Example	```

```
//
// Get the User-Agent
//
          .
          .
          .

const char* p = NPN_UserAgent (instance);


          .
          .
          .
```

Conclusion

A plug-in can give the browser user status through the traditional status line provided by the Navigator. The user should be made aware of any lengthy operations and, when possible, the percentage complete of the current operation should be given.

The User-Agent field provides a plug-in with the best source of information regarding the correct version of the browser hosting your plug-in.

What's Next?

The next chapter is a collection of APIs that didn't really fit into any of the previous chapters. The `NPP_SetWindow`, `NPP_Print`, and `NPP_HandleEvent` APIs are covered in Chapter 14.

LiveConnect

Introduction

Netscape's introduction of LiveConnect with the 3.0 version of Navigator brings plug-ins, Java applets, and JavaScript programs closer together. LiveConnect provides communication between the three software modules by allowing direct access to methods. As you can see in Figure 14.1, LiveConnect has two interfaces. The first interface, located between a plug-in and a Java applet, allows a plug-in to call Java methods and Java to call the plug-in's methods. The second interface, between Java and JavaScript, allows Java to call JavaScript methods and JavaScript to call Java methods.

Figure 14.1.

LiveConnect interfacing plug-ins, Java, and JavaScript.

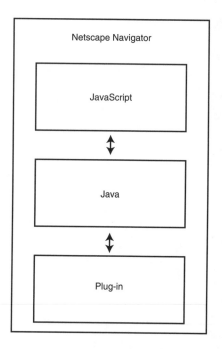

Notice that there is no direct interface between plug-ins and JavaScript. These two must communicate through an intermediate Java applet. This book doesn't attempt to document the Java/JavaScript interface, but instead it concentrates on the plug-in to Java interface.

> **NOTE**
>
> Be sure to download Netscape's latest plug-in SDK to supplement any information in this book.

Calling Java Methods from Plug-Ins

To call a Java method from a plug-in, you must use the javah tool that comes in Netscape's plug-in SDK. Running this tool on Java methods generates the appropriate header files for your C++ code to call the Java methods.

For example, if you want to call methods from the java.lang.String class, run javah like this:

```
javah -jri java.lang.String
```

This generates the file java_lang_String.h, with accessor macros defined for all methods and fields that are accessible in the Java class. The javah tools also generate java_lang_String.c, which contains all of the stub implementations associated with java_lang_String.h

Accessing Java Class Fields in C++

The type denoting the Java class becomes the C++ class with the same name. Fields can be accessed with inline accessor methods with the following form:

```
class ClassName : …
{
    ResultType    // getter method
    fieldName (JRIEnv* env) {…}

    void  // setter method
    fieldName (JRIEnv* env, ResultType value) {…}
}
```

You can get the count field of the String class (created previously with the javah tool) like this:

```
jint cnt = myString->count (env);
```

And you can set the same field like this:

```
myString->count (env, cnt);
```

Refer to Netscape documentation for C language information.

Accessing Methods

Java methods can be accessed much like fields. Calling the substring method of the Java String class looks like this in C++:

```
java_lang_String* sub = str->substring (env, 5, 9);
```

Overloaded Methods

The `javah` tool handles overloaded methods in Java by generating symbols that have an index appended to all but the first method. Using an index avoids complex symbol *name mangling* as is typical in the C++ language. C++ creates new function names based on the original name to differentiate between permutations of overloaded functions. Refer to Netscape documentation for further information on `javah` symbol names for overloaded methods.

Java Type Names

When you are dealing with Java methods from C or C++, you should use the Java names for primitive types. By using these Java-specific types, you can keep your C/C++ platform independent. Noteworthy new type sizes to C/C++ programmers are double-byte characters and eight-byte longs. These types are defined in `jri_md.h`, which is included by `jri.h`. The Java primitive types and their C/C++ equivalents are shown in Table 14.1.

Table 14.1. The Java primitive types.

Java Type	C/C++ Type	Size
boolean	jbool	1 byte
byte	jbyte	1 byte
char	jchar	2 bytes
short	jshort	2 bytes
int	jint	4 bytes
long	jlong	8 bytes
float	jfloat	4 bytes
double	jdouble	8 bytes

Calling Plug-In Methods from Java

Methods that Java calls within your plug-in are called Plug-in Native Methods. To Java programs, plug-ins appear as instances of the class `netscape.plugin.Plugin`. This class is a Java reflection of a plug-in. Plug-ins can subclass this class and add new native plug-in methods to it. JavaScript can manipulate a plug-in through this class.

Java Class: `netscape.plugin.Plugin`

The following sections document the Java class `netscape.plugin.Plugin`, which allows Java to call methods implemented in a plug-in.

Constructor: `Plugin`

```
public Plugin()
```

The constructor initializes this Java class.

Method: `getPeer`

```
public int getPeer()
```

This method returns the native NPP object—the plug-in instance that is the native part of a Java `Plugin` object. This field is set by the system, but it can be read from plug-in native methods by the following call:

```
NPP instance = (NPP)self->getPeer (env);
```

Method: `init`

```
public void init()
```

This method is called when the plug-in is initialized. You never need to call this method directly; it is called when the plug-in is created.

destroy

```
public void destroy()
```

This method is called when the plug-in is destroyed. You never need to call this method directly; it is called when the plug-in is destroyed. At the point where this method is called, the plug-in is still active.

isActive

```
public boolean isActive()
```

This method determines whether the Java reflection of a plug-in still refers to an active plug-in. Plug-in instances are destroyed whenever the page containing the plug-in is left, thereby causing the plug-in to no longer be active.

getWindow

```
public JSObject getWindow()
```

This method returns the JavaScript window in which the plug-in is embedded.

Subclassing the Java Class: `netscape.plugin.Plugin`

A plug-in that interfaces with Java might choose to provide the previous `Plugin` Java class or a subclass of it. This class allows Java to call into the plug-in. You can choose not to provide Java with this class but still call into Java.

For an example of subclassing the `netscape.plugin.Plugin` Java class, see Chapter 23, "Netscape's LiveConnect Sample," which also shows implementation of native plug-in methods.

The `NPP_GetJavaClass` plug-in API (documented later in this chapter) associates the Java class with your plug-in.

Garbage Collection and Globals

Garbage collection is a feature of the Java programming language that automatically frees any memory allocations made during the life of the program. Because the C and C++ languages do not have this feature, some memory management issues are involved with C/C++ and Netscape's Java Runtime Interface. You must be especially careful while using global memory in C/C++ to reference Java objects. Check out the latest documentation from Netscape on garbage collection and globals. This information is changing as Netscape continues to enhance LiveConnect.

API Quick Reference

The following sections give in-depth information on the APIs used in this chapter.

NPP_GetJavaClass

Compatibility	Windows 3.1/95/NT, Macintosh, UNIX, Navigator 3.0 and above.
API Type	Plug-in implemented method.
Purpose	Returns the Java class associated with the plug-in.
Syntax	`jref NPP_GetJavaClass (void)`
Includes	`#include <npapi.h>`
Description	In order for Java to call a native method in your plug-in, you must associate a Java class with your plug-in by using `NPP_GetJavaClass`. This API gets the Java environment and then calls the initializer routine for the plug-in implemented Java class. The initializer returns a reference to the Java class, which is also returned by `NPP_GetJavaClass`. This initializer routine is located in stub code generated by the `javah` tool.

Returns	`jref`: This is a reference to the Java class representing this plug-in. It is a `typedef` for a `void` pointer.
	`NULL`: You return `NULL` to indicate that a Java class is not associated with your plug-in.
See Also	`NPN_GetJavaEnv`
	`NPN_GetJavaPeer`
Example	

```
//
// Get the Java class for this plug-in.
//
jref NPP_GetJavaClass(void)
{
    // First, get the Java environment

    JRIEnv* env = NPN_GetJavaEnv();

    // Call the native class initializer which returns a
    // Java class reference. This routine is stub code generated
    // by the javah tool.

    return init_AviPlayer(env);
}
```

NPN_GetJavaEnv

Compatibility	Windows 3.1/95/NT, Macintosh, UNIX, Navigator 3.0 and above.
API Type	Navigator implemented method.
Purpose	This API returns the Java execution environment needed to make any calls to Java methods from your plug-in using the Java Runtime Interface (JRI).
Syntax	`JRIEnv* NPN_GetJavaEnv (void);`
Includes	`#include <npapi.h>`
Description	The `NPN_GetJavaEnv` API returns a handle to the current Java execution environment, which is supervised by the Java interpreter. The first time you call this, the interpreter might need to initialize itself if the browser has not yet run a Java applet.
	The Java execution environment encapsulates the current Java thread of execution. Only use the environment handle within the thread that it was requested on.
Returns	`JRIEnv*`: This is the handle to your current Java execution environment.

See Also	NPP_GetJavaClass
	NPN_GetJavaPeer
| *Example* | ```
//
// Get the Java execution environment
//
    .
    .
    .

    JRIEnv* env = NPN_GetJavaEnv ();

    .
    .
    .
``` |

NPN_GetJavaPeer

Compatibility	Windows 3.1/95/NT, Macintosh, UNIX, Navigator 3.0 and above.
API Type	Navigator implemented method.
Purpose	This API returns the Java object associated with the plug-in instance.
Syntax	jref NPN_GetJavaPeer (NPP instance);
Includes	#include <npapi.h>
Description	NPN_GetJavaPeer allows your plug-in to access the Java object associated with it by the NPP_GetJavaClass API.
	The Java instance is not created until this call is made for the first time. This avoids starting the Java interpreter if you never need the instance.
	JavaScript implicitly calls this routine if it needs to communicate with a plug-in on the page.
Returns	jref: This is a reference to the Java class representing this plug-in. This is a typedef for a void pointer.
See Also	NPP_GetJavaClass
	NPN_GetJavaEnv
| *Example* | ```
//
// Get this plug-in's Java object
//
    .
    .
    .

    AviPlayer* javaAviInst;

    javaAviInst = (AviPlayer*)NPN_GetJavaPeer (_pluginInstance);

    .
    .
    .
``` |

Conclusion

LiveConnect ties together plug-ins, Java applets, and JavaScript programs. A LiveConnect plug-in interfaces with Java with C/C++ glue generated by Netscape's `javah` tool. A plug-in can call Java methods, and Java can call plug-in methods. Be sure to use the Java primitive types when dealing with Java methods in your plug-in.

It is important that you supplement this book with current information from Netscape to properly implement a LiveConnect plug-in.

What's Next?

The next chapter is a collection of APIs that didn't really fit into any of the previous chapters. The `NPP_SetWindow`, `NPP_Print`, and `NPP_HandleEvent` APIs are covered.

CHAPTER 15

Miscellaneous Methods

Introduction

Your plug-in's window is created by the Netscape browser. To receive window events in the Microsoft Windows environment, you must subclass the plug-in window using the Windows API SetWindowLong method or the Microsoft Foundation Class Library SubclassWindow method. The Macintosh does not provide for window subclassing and must use the plug-in method NPP_HandleEvent to get window events.

Printing is handled jointly by your plug-in and the browser in the case of an embedded plug-in. For full-page plug-in types, printing is solely up to the plug-in.

The following APIs are covered in this chapter:

```
NPP_SetWindow

NPP_Print

NPP_HandleEvent
```

Your Plug-In's Window

If your plug-in is of type NP_EMBED or NP_FULL, the Navigator creates a window on its behalf. The size of the window depends on the type. An embedded window's size is specified in the HTML code, as in the following example:

```
<embed SRC=sound.wav WIDTH=400 HEIGHT=60>
```

This code causes the browser to create a window of width 400 and height 60. A NP_FULL type plug-in refers to a full Navigator page. Full page plug-ins fill the whole page display area of the browser. Regardless of the size, it is the browser that creates the window, not your plug-in. This creates some special challenges to the plug-in developer.

Because the plug-in does not create the window, it needs a way to receive events from any user actions relating to the window. In the world of Microsoft Windows, this is accomplished through subclassing the window. Macintosh plug-ins receive events through a Macintosh-specific API called NPP_HandleEvent.

Subclassing a Window

In Microsoft Windows, every window has a class associated with it. This class is defined by a WNDCLASS structure and a call to RegisterClass. Within this structure is an address of the window procedure that is called for windows of this class. This window procedure is called whenever a message for the window needs to be processed.

A plug-in is contained in a Windows DLL. This DLL is loaded and called by the Netscape Navigator and becomes part of the Navigator's process. Being part of this process allows the plug-in and browser to easily share system resources such as memory and files. In addition, being in the same process space allows a plug-in to subclass a window procedure that is in the Navigator's code. Through a series of APIs, the plug-in can instruct Windows to call a window procedure within the plug-in's code before it calls the window procedure in the browser's code. The new window procedure is hooked in as shown in Figure 15.1.

Figure 15.1.

A plug-in's window procedure subclassing the Navigator-created plug-in window.

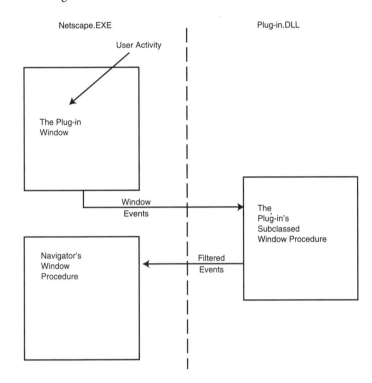

Immediately after Netscape Navigator creates a window for your plug-in, it calls the NPP_SetWindow API. This API passes a window handle for the newly created window. If you are not using Microsoft's Foundation Class Library (MFC), you must subclass Netscape's window with the SetWindowLong API. This function replaces the window procedure with one inside your plug-in DLL. You can call it like this:

```
instance->lpfnOldWndProc = (FARPROC)SetWindowLong (hWnd,
    GWL_WNDPROC,
    (DWORD)SubclassFunc);
```

In this example, SetWindowLong replaces the window procedure for the window specified by hWnd with the new procedure SubclassFunc. Note the saving of the old window procedure within lpfnOldWndProc, which is returned by SetWindowLong. The new procedure located within your DLL's code would be structured something like this:

```
LONG NP_LOADDS WINAPI SubClassFunc (HWND hWnd,
    WORD Message,
    WORD wParam,
    LONG lParam)
{
    PluginInstance* instance = GetInstance(hWnd);

    switch (Message)
    {
    case:
        //
        // Any message specific code would go in this switch statement.
        //
        break;
    default:
        break;
    }
    return CallWindowProc (instance->lpfnOldWndProc,
        hWnd,
        Message,
        wParam,
        lParam);
}
```

At the end of SubClassFunc is a call to the Windows API CallWindowProc. As you might have guessed, this API calls the old window procedure, located in the Navigator, with the saved procedure pointer instance->lpfnOldWndProc.

When your plug-in's instance is being destroyed, you should remove the subclass from the window. This is done with the same API, SetWindowLong, and is called as follows:

```
SetWindowLong (instance->hWnd, GWL_WNDPROC, instance->lpfnOldWndProc);
```

Here the saved old window procedure is replacing the new one installed previously.

Getting Instance Data

One obstacle with using a subclassed window procedure without MFC is getting your plug-in's instance data. Most Netscape methods provide your plug-in with instance data with a passed parameter of instance. This is a pointer to a structure containing references to both the plug-in's and Netscape's instance data. However, the subclassed window procedure is not called directly from the Navigator. It is called by Windows itself. Windows does not pass a pointer to your instance data.

The most obvious solution is to provide a global reference to your instance data in the DLL's global data. Unfortunately, this won't do the trick, because plug-ins support multiple window instances. A single pointer to an instance is overwritten when the next window is created.

Another potential way is to use extra window bytes allocated with the RegisterClass API. You could have stored a pointer to your instance data within these extra bytes if Netscape had allocated any extra window bytes for a plug-in's use—which it didn't.

The Netscape Way

Netscape provides a technique for retrieving your instance data using a linked list to store pointers to your instance for each plug-in window. The non-MFC example of NPSHELL.CPP (provided on this book's CD-ROM) gives an example of this technique with two routines: `AssociateInstance` and `GetInstance`. `AssociateInstance` is called during the `NPP_SetWindow` method for any new windows. It associates an instance pointer to a window handle. `GetInstance`, called during the new window procedure, scans through the linked list until the same window handle is found, and then it returns an instance pointer. You can see a call to `GetInstance` in the previous example of `SubClassFunc`.

Another Way

If Netscape's linked list approach causes your head to spin, another way to store window-specific data is by storing it in the window's property list. The `SetProp` API attaches properties to a window by calling it with a window handle, property string, and pointer to your data. When you need to get your instance data again, simply call `GetProp` with the window handle and property string. Your instance pointer is returned. Don't forget to call `RemoveProp` to remove your data when the window is destroyed.

> **NOTE**
>
> `SetProp`, `GetProp`, and `RemoveProp` are well-documented in the Windows API documentation. Another source of information is called *Safe Subclassing in Win32* by Kyle Marsh. This article can be found on Microsoft's Development Library CD-ROM.

Subclassing with MFC

Microsoft's Foundation Class Library makes subclassing a window much easier. Problems with instance data are gone, because MFC enables you to create a window object with an associated message map. This window object is defined in your code as a child of `CWnd`. You can store any data you need, including a pointer to the plug-in's instance data within this object. MFC shields you from the complexities of associating data with a particular window.

To use this technique, first create a new window class derived from `CWnd` in your header file. Here is a very simple example:

```
class CPluginWindow : public CWnd
{
protected:
    MyInstance*  instance;

public:
    CPluginWindow ();
    ~CPluginWindow ();
```

```
    void StoreData (MyData *);

    //{{AFX_MSG( CMainWindow )
    afx_msg void OnPlay();
    afx_msg void OnStop();
    //}}AFX_MSG

    DECLARE_MESSAGE_MAP()
};
```

Notice the pointer to your instance data: `MyInstance* instance`. This pointer is set with a call to the method `StoreData`. A message map is declared with methods `OnPlay` and `OnStop`.

When the plug-in method `NPP_SetWindow` is called for the first time, construct your object `CPluginWindow` and attach a pointer to your instance data. Remember, constructing a `CWnd` derived class does not actually create a window. This is important because `CPluginWindow` will be subclassed to an already existing window:

```
instance->pWindow = new CPluginWindow ();
```

Then call the inherited `CWnd` method `SubclassWindow`, and give it a handle to the plug-in window create by the Navigator:

```
instance->pWindow->SubclassWindow ((HWND)window->window);
```

Finally, save a pointer to your instance data in your new `CPluginWindow` with a call to `StoreData` or your equivalent method:

```
instance->pWindow->StoreData (instance);
```

MFC handles the rest by calling your appropriate method defined in the message map and, upon completion, returning control to the original Navigator window procedure.

Remember to unsubclass the window during destruction of the window's instance in `NPP_Destroy` with a call to `CWnd`'s `UnsubclassWindow`:

```
instance->pWindow->UnsubclassWindow ();
```

WARNING

Netscape's current documentation instructs you to unsubclass your window during a call to `NPP_SetWindow` when the Navigator window handle (`window->window`) is set to `NULL`. Unfortunately, for Navigator 2.*x* and early betas of 3.*x*, a call is made to `NPP_SetWindow` during printing with a `NULL` window handle without another call to `NPP_SetWindow` to allow plug-ins to re-subclass. The workaround is to unsubclass only during an `NPP_Destory`.

Printing and Your Plug-In

When a user requests a print action and your plug-in is a visible type and is loaded, a call is made to your plug-in's NPP_Print method. To receive this call, your plug-in must be of type NP_FULL or NP_EMBED.

For plug-ins of type NP_FULL, printing is handled totally by the plug-in code. A NULL pointer is passed to the NPP_Print method for the printInfo parameter. The plug-in is in charge of all printing-related tasks such as displaying the printer dialog, getting the printer, creating the printer device context, scaling data, and so on.

Plug-ins of type NP_EMBED print jointly with the Navigator. An embedded plug-in is, by definition, embedded in another document. The Navigator must print its portion of this document and, in turn, the plug-in prints the embedded portion. A plug-in might opt to print nothing, which simply leaves a space in the printout.

When NPP_Print is called for an embedded plug-in, the API parameter printInfo points to the structure NPPrint. This structure contains the plug-in mode and a union of structures NPFullPrint and NPEmbedPrint:

```
typedef struct _NPPrint
{
    uint16          mode;       /* NP_FULL or NP_EMBED */
    union
    {
        NPFullPrint    fullPrint;  /* if mode is NP_FULL */
        NPEmbedPrint   embedPrint; /* if mode is NP_EMBED */
    } print;

} NPPrint;
```

> **WARNING**
>
> At the time of this writing, NPPrint is broken. NPPrint only references a plug-in type of NP_EMBED, because a type NP_FULL is passed a NULL pointer for the structure NPPrint. This means that the mode is invalid and the union only references the structure NPEmbedPrint.

The structure NPEmbedPrint is currently defined as follows:

```
typedef struct _NPEmbedPrint
{
    NPWindow    window;
    void*       platformPrint;      /* Platform-specific printing info */
} NPEmbedPrint;
```

In this case, the window structure member is a structure of type NPWindow and the platformPrint structure member is the printer's device context (DC). NPWindow is currently defined as follows:

```
typedef struct _NPWindow
{
    void*   window;             /* platform specific window handle */
    uint32  x;                  /* position of top left corner relative
                                   to a netscape page */
    uint32  y;
    uint32  width;              /* maximum window size */
    uint32  height;
    NPRect  clipRect;           /* clipping rectangle in port coordinates */

} NPWindow;
```

NPWindow provides a window handle, x/y coordinates for the top left corner of the plug-in window relative to a browser page, window width and height, and a clipping rectangle.

In Microsoft Windows, all window coordinates are in TWIPs. A TWIP is one twentieth of a printer's point. A point is 1/72 of an inch, so a TWIP is 1/1440 of an inch. You must use the appropriate conversions to get back to logical coordinates.

The Macintosh and Window Events

Because of the Macintosh windowing architecture, it is not possible to receive events using subclassing. To provide window events to a Macintosh plug-in, Netscape has included the Mac-specific plug-in method NPP_HandleEvent.

NPP_HandleEvent is passed a pointer to a Macintosh EventRecord structure. The EventRecord.what field can be any of the normal Macintosh event types or a Netscape-specific event. Currently, the following types are used:

> getFocusEvent
>
> loseFocusEvent
>
> adjustCursorEvent

getFocusEvent informs your plug-in that it will get key events. If you don't want to get key events, just return a FALSE when passed a getFocusEvent.

The event loseFocusEvent lets a plug-in know that it is no longer in focus.

The adjustCursorEvent event is passed to your plug-in as the mouse moves over your window. You can hide the cursor by returning FALSE.

API Quick Reference

The following sections give in-depth information on the APIs used in this chapter.

NPP_SetWindow

> ***Compatibility***   Windows 3.1/95/NT, Macintosh, UNIX.
>
> ***API Type***   Plug-in method called from the Navigator.

Purpose	Informs a plug-in that a new window was created, the window was moved or sized, or the window was destroyed.
Syntax	NPError NPP_SetWindow (NPP instance, NPWindow* window)

NPP instance: A pointer to structure NPP that references both the plug-in's and Netscape's private instance data.

NPWindow* window: A pointer to structure NPWindow that contains a platform-specific window handle, top left corner, window width, height, and a clipping rectangle.

Includes	#include <npapi.h>
Description	This method is called to inform you that a window was created for your plug-in. A handle is provided to allow you to subclass this window. Normally, this window is a subwindow of the Navigator window hierarchy.

NPP_SetWindow is only called for plug-in types of NP_FULL (indicating a Navigator full page) or NP_EMBED (indicating an embedded window). NP_BACKGROUND type plug-ins do not have an associated window.

If the window is moved or resized, NPP_SetWindow is called with the new window position and size.

Your window can be destroyed. This is indicated by a call to NPP_SetWindow with the platform-specific window handle set to NULL.

At times, NPP_SetWindow might be called without any new information. Your plug-in should maintain window state information to handle such cases.

Returns	NPERR_NO_ERROR: No error.

NPERR_GENERIC_ERROR: An unknown error occurred.

NPERR_OUT_OF_MEMORY_ERROR: Out of memory.

NPERR_INVALID_INSTANCE_DATA: Invalid instance data.

See Also	NPP_HandleEvent (for Macintosh developers)
Example	

```
//
// NPP_SetWindow
//

NPError NP_LOADDS NPP_SetWindow (NPP instance, NPWindow* window)
{
    if (!window)
        return NPERR_GENERIC_ERROR;
```

```
        if (!instance)
            return  NPERR_INVALID_INSTANCE_ERROR;

        // Retrieve instance data

        MyInstance* myinstance = (MyInstance *)instance->pdata;

        if (!myinstance)
            return NPERR_GENERIC_ERROR;

        if (!window->window && !myinstance->pWindow)  // spurious
➥entry
            return NPERR_NO_ERROR;

        if (!window->window && myinstance->pWindow)
        {
            // The window was destroyed. Don't do anything.

            return NPERR_NO_ERROR;
        }

        if (!myinstance->pWindow && window->window)
        {
            // The first call to NPP_SetWindow. We need to create
➥our window
            // and subclass it to Navigator's window.

            myinstance->pWindow = new CPluginWindow ();

            myinstance->pWindow->SubclassWindow ((HWND)window-
➥>window);
            myinstance->pWindow->InitWindow ();

            // Save a pointer to our instance in our new window
➥class's data

            myinstance->pWindow->StoreData (myinstance);
        }

        // Resize or move the window. In some cases the window may
        // not have changed.

        data->pWindow->InvalidateRect (NULL);
        data->pWindow->UpdateWindow ();

        return NPERR_NO_ERROR;
    }
```

NPP_Print

Compatibility   Windows 3.1/95/NT, Macintosh, UNIX.

API Type   Plug-in method called from the Navigator.

Purpose   Called when the user requests a print action while your plug-in is
loaded. The plug-in can be of type NP_EMBED, in which the Navigator
prints jointly with the plug-in, or type NP_FULL, in which the plug-in
must handle all printing related functions.

Syntax

```
void NP_LOADDS NPP_Print (NPP instance, NPPrint* platformPrint)
```

NPP instance: A pointer to structure NPP that references both the plug-in's and Netscape's private instance data.

NPPrint* platformPrint: A pointer to structure NPPrint that contains the plug-in's current mode and references to either structures NPFullPrint or NPEmbedPrint, depending on this mode.

This parameter can be NULL for plug-in type NP_FULL.

Includes

```
#include <npapi.h>
```

Description

A call to NPP_Print results from the user requesting a print action on a Web page where your plug-in is loaded. The plug-in must be either type NP_FULL or NP_EMBED.

NP_FULL plug-ins are expected to handle all printing-related tasks. These include displaying the printer dialog, getting the correct printer, creating a printer device context (DC), scaling data, and so on. In most cases, a print request for NP_FULL is passed a NULL pointer for the parameter printInfo.

NP_EMBED type plug-ins print in conjunction with the Navigator. In addition to printing its part of the page, Netscape handles other print functions including displaying the print dialog, getting the printer, creating the DC, and so on. Your plug-in is passed a reference to structure NPEmbedPrint that contains a printer DC in the platformPrint member and your plug-in's window to be printed in the window member.

In Microsoft Windows, all window coordinates are in TWIPs. A TWIP is one twentieth of a printer's point. Because a point is 1/72 of an inch, a TWIP is 1/1440 of an inch. You must use the appropriate conversions to get back to logical coordinates.

Returns

None.

See Also

Platform-specific printing documentation.

Example

```
//
// NPP_Print
//

void NP_LOADDS NPP_Print (NPP instance, NPPrint* printInfo)
{
    // Make sure we have an instance

    if(!instance)
        return;

    // Retrieve instance data
```

```
     MyInstance* myinstance = (MyInstance *)instance->pdata;

 if (!printInfo)
 {
     // A NULL value for printInfo indicates an NP_FULL type
➥print.
     // Verify we are in the NP_FULL mode.

     if (myinstance->mode != NP_FULL)
         return;

     //
     //
     // Here would go your printing code for NP_FULL.
➥Navigator
     // provides no assistance in this case.
     //
     //
 }
 else
 {
     // Must be NP_EMBED. printInfo contains the printer DC
➥and
     // print window.

     NPWindow* printWindow = &(printInfo-
>print.embedPrint.window);
     void* platformPrint = printInfo-
>print.embedPrint.platformPrint;

     // Create a pen

     LOGBRUSH lb;
     lb.lbStyle = BS_SOLID;
     lb.lbHatch = 0;

     HPEN hPen = ExtCreatePen (PS_COSMETIC ¦ PS_SOLID, 1,
➥&lb, 0, NULL);

     // Get the printer DC from platformPrint.

     HDC hDC = (HDC)(DWORD)platformPrint;

     HPEN hPenOld = (HPEN)SelectObject (hDC, hPen);

     // Draw a rectangle

     BOOL result = Rectangle (hDC,
         (int)(printWindow->x),
         (int)(printWindow->y),
         (int)(printWindow->x + printWindow->width),
         (int)(printWindow->y + printWindow->height));

     // Print some simple text

     char buf[] = "Hello From My Plug-in";

     TextOut (hDC,
         printWindow->x + 180,
```

```
                                printWindow->y + 180,
                                buf,
                                strlen(buf));

                // Cleanup

                SelectObject(hDC, hPenOld);
                DeleteObject(hPen);
            }
        }
```

NPP_HandleEvent

Compatibility	Macintosh only.
API Type	Plug-in method called from the Navigator.
Purpose	Provides a Macintosh plug-in with window events.
Syntax	`int16 NPP_HandleEvent (NPP instance, void* event)`

NPP instance: A pointer to structure NPP that references both the plug-in's and Netscape's private instance data.

void* event: A pointer to a Macintosh EventRecord structure.

Includes	`#include <npapi.h>`
Description	In Windows, the window handle alone is sufficient for event processing through the technique of window subclassing. On the Macintosh, the native window is shared between the plug-in and the Netscape client. Subclassing is not possible, so the Navigator provides events to the plug-in with calls to the NPP_HandleEvent API.

The parameter event is a pointer to a Macintosh EventRecord structure. The EventRecord.what field can be any of the normal Macintosh event types or a Navigator-specific type such as getFocusEvent, lostFocusEvent, and adjustCursorEvent.

The getFocusEvent event informs your plug-in that it will get key events. Conversely, lostFocusEvent means that you are no longer in focus and will not get key events. If you don't want to receive key events, return FALSE when passed a getFocusEvent.

The adjustCursorEvent is passed to your plug-in as the mouse moves over your plug-in's window. To hide the cursor, return FALSE; otherwise, return TRUE.

The return value for all standard Macintosh events is ignored except for key events. With key events, return TRUE only if your plug-in has handled that event.

Returns	TRUE: The event was handled.
	FALSE: The event was not handled.
See Also	Macintosh-specific documentation.
Example	

```
//
// Handle a Macintosh Event
//

int16 NPP_HandleEvent (NPP instance, void* event)
{
    NPBool eventHandled = FALSE;

    // Make sure we have an instance

    if(!instance)
        return  eventHandled;

    // Retreive instance data

    MyInstance* myinstance = (MyInstance *)instance->pdata;

    //
    //
    // Process the Macintosh event…
    //
    //

    return eventHandled;

}
```

Conclusion

The Macintosh receives window events through calls to the Macintosh-specific plug-in API NPP_HandleEvent. Windows plug-ins get their events by subclassing the plug-in window given a window handle in the plug-in method NPP_SetWindow.

During window event processing, plug-in instance data is easy to retrieve using Microsoft's Foundation Class Library. Without MFC, instance data is more difficult to access and must be done through a linked list or a window's property list.

Printing can be performed solely by the plug-in (which is the case with types of NP_FULL) or in conjunction with the browser (which is the case with an embedded plug-in).

What's Next?

That about wraps up the plug-in API documentation. The next few chapters introduce you to sample plug-in code that uses the plug-in API. All of the samples are included on the book's CD-ROM.

The next chapter explains how the sample code is structured and what samples are provided.

PART III

Real Examples

16 About the Sample Code

17 A Streaming Audio Sample

18 The Buffer Classes

19 The CPU Monitor Plug-In

20 A Plug-In with MCIWnd

21 Using MIDI with a Background Plug-In

22 Subclassing without Microsoft's Foundation Class Library

23 Netscape's LiveConnect Sample

24 Debugging with the Socket Spy

CHAPTER 16

About the Sample Code

Introduction

This book and its CD-ROM contain many examples of working Navigator plug-ins. These plug-in samples can serve as a basis for your plug-in development because each one demonstrates a different technique.

All of the samples were written for Windows 95/NT using Microsoft Visual C++ 4.0. If you are using compilers from Borland or Watcom, you can still use the samples, but you should refer to the chapters covering those compilers in this book to properly port your code.

The plug-in samples demonstrate two basic design types. As you probably remember from earlier chapters, these are streaming plug-ins and file-based plug-ins. The streaming plug-in example in Chapter 17, "A Streaming Audio Sample," plays audio in real-time over the Internet (depending on the speed of your connection). This plug-in uses a buffer class that is examined in Chapter 18, "The Buffer Classes." The next few plug-in samples are file-based. They are a server CPU monitor, an MCIWnd sample, a MIDI sample, and a LiveConnect sample from Netscape using Java and JavaScript. Chapter 24 documents how to build your own Socket Spy for debugging.

Each sample contains the source file locations on the CD-ROM, plug-in design discussion with a block diagram, and documentation for each code section. There are many notes about the caveats of Windows plug-in development that can save you time in your development efforts.

Audio Streamer

If you are new to Windows 95/NT multithreaded programming, Chapter 17, "A Streaming Audio Sample," is for you. This plug-in creates a separate worker thread that feeds the audio driver buffers. The thread is fully synchronized using semaphores and critical sections. Discussion covers potential deadlock situations and how to avoid them.

The Audio Streamer is a good basis for any plug-in that streams data from Navigator to a device. For example, you can use the same model for streaming real-time video data. Additionally, you might want to add audio decompression using Window's Audio Compression Manager (ACM). After adding ACM, your audio plug-in should come close to commercial performance. Or, perhaps you want to add real-time audio/video capability to your corporate Intranet without paying for a commercially available plug-in.

Buffer Classes

Chapter 18, "The Buffer Classes," explains two different buffer classes for use with a real-time streaming plug-in. These classes allow your plug-in to easily preread a configurable number and size of data buffers from Netscape's Navigator. The audio streaming sample can use either of the classes, depending on your preference. The buffer classes demonstrate circular and FIFO buffering schemes.

Server CPU Monitor

Chapter 19, "The CPU Monitor Plug-In," demonstrates client/server communications with a plug-in using a Common Gateway Interface (CGI) program on the server. This plug-in uses the NPN_GetURL API to request server load status. The CGI program, written in C, calls out to the UNIX command vmstat for system statistics. These statistics are sent back to the plug-in for graphical display.

It would be cool to extend this idea with a better user interface, using more of the available vmstat data. Although the sample uses only CPU percentages, your plug-in can display information about kernel threads, virtual memory, interrupts, system calls, and context switches. Don't limit yourself to vmstat. The results of any command line server command can be displayed with a Navigator plug-in.

Using MCIWnd in Windows

MCIWnd is a Windows class for Microsoft Windows that makes it very easy to code multimedia controller plug-ins. The example in Chapter 20, "Writing a Plug-In with MCIWnd," shows how to make a plug-in that can handle AVI video, WAV audio, and MIDI playback with very little code. The sample is also a good example of a plug-in that handles multiple MIME types.

Using MCIWnd for a plug-in might be more suitable to an Intranet with relatively high bandwidth. For example, you can make a really great video plug-in for your company that plays AVI videos over the LAN. With MCIWnd, you can modify video controls easily, using the provided messages, macros, and functions. Impress your boss!

MIDI Background Music

Using the Musical Instrument Device Interface (MIDI) can add real spice to your Web page with extremely low bandwidth requirements. Many of today's hottest computer games use a combination of MIDI and PCM audio to add cool effects. Most audio cards such as Sound Blaster support real-time MIDI and PCM audio mixing, which means that you can play MIDI background music with bursts of PCM audio intermixed.

The MIDI background sample in Chapter 21, "Using MIDI with a Background Plug-In," is a good example of using the HIDDEN attribute of the EMBED tag.

Window Subclassing

Chapter 22, "Subclassing without Microsoft's Foundation Class Library," gives an example of subclassing your plug-in's window using standard Windows APIs. This technique avoids using a class library for window subclassing and takes advantage of Windows APIs such as SetWindowLong, SetProp, GetProp, CallWindowProc, and RemoveProp. Use this example for the basis of creating a very small plug-in of less than 25KB in size.

Using LiveConnect

Netscape's 3.0 Plug-in SDK includes support for LiveConnect. LiveConnect facilitates the communication between Java, JavaScript, and plug-ins. Using Netscape's javah tool along with a Java compiler and C or C++ compilers allows Java to call plug-in implemented classes and allows plug-ins to call Java implemented classes.

Chapter 23, "Netscape's LiveConnect Sample," examines Netscape's Windows AVI video player that is included with the 3.0 plug-in SDK. Because LiveConnect is still in beta at the time of this writing, you should supplement any information on LiveConnect found in this book with current documentation from Netscape's Web site.

Socket Spy

Debugging a plug-in can be a very frustrating experience. When you request an action from the Navigator (for example, NPN_PostURL), Navigator translates your request to the proper HTTP format and sends it via sockets and TCP/IP to the Web server. In return, data is sent back to Navigator and, if your lucky, to your plug-in.

The problem with this multilayered approach is that sometimes you don't know what is actually sent to the Web server (or any IP address). You can use expensive hardware, such as a protocol analyzer, to overcome this problem or do it in software with the Socket Spy (as shown in Chapter 24, "Debugging with the Socket Spy").

The Socket Spy is truly a software hack that will horrify many traditionalists, but it works well. Socket Spy is just a fancy name for a DLL that is inserted between a Windows socket application and WinSock. The ugliness or beauty of it is that you must use a binary editor to make your WinSock application load the Socket Spy DLL instead of WinSock (wsock32.dll for 32-bit WinSock). This enables you to source-level debug any socket calls made from a WinSock application. With Navigator and your plug-in, this technique allows you to "spy" on the Navigator to WinSock data while you are debugging your plug-in.

Conclusion

That was an overview of the sample plug-in chapters. Feel free to use any code or ideas presented in this section for your plug-in development. You certainly should consider running Navigator with Socket Spy to aid in debugging.

What's Next?

The next chapters in this section give detailed examples of the topics mentioned here. All source code for the examples is included on the CD-ROM.

CHAPTER 17

A Streaming Audio Sample

Introduction

NPWAVE is a Windows 95 plug-in for Netscape Navigator 2.*x* and above. This plug-in allows audio to play as it is streamed, rather than waiting for the complete file to download. Audio buffers are passed on to the Windows audio driver as they are received. Audio can be started and paused with buttons on the plug-in window.

The plug-in is made up of three classes: CWave, CPluginWindow, and CBuffer. CWave manages the plug-in and its use of Windows audio resources. CPluginWindow is a small class derived from CWnd that is used to subclass the plug-in window. CBuffer is a generic circular buffer management class. It is explained further in the next chapter.

Audio buffers are passed to the plug-in with the help of a worker thread. This thread interacts with CWave and CBuffer to provide the audio driver with data. The audio driver is opened with a callback routine specified. The callback informs the plug-in when a buffer is exhausted so that the buffer can be recycled.

The plug-in was built with Microsoft Visual C++ 4.0. Other compilers should work as well, such as Borland or Visual C++ 2.*x*.

Where to Find the Files

All the necessary files for building NPWAVE.DLL are located on the CD-ROM. These files are in the \CODE\WAVE, \CODE\INC, and \CODE\COMMON directories. You need the following files:

```
\code\wave:
     npshell.cpp - Plug-in entry point methods.
     npwave.cpp, npwave.h - The audio class CWave
     npbuffer.cpp, npbuffer.h - The buffer class CBuffer
     npwindow.cpp, npwindow.h - The window class CPluginWindow
     npwave.def - DLL module definition file
     npwave.rc - Resources
     npwave.mak - Makefile for Microsoft Visual C++
\code\inc
     npapi.h - Plug-in API prototypes and associated structures
     npupp.h - Plug-in API prototypes
     stdafx.h - Standard include files
\code\common
     npwin.cpp - DLL entry point to plug-in API mapping
     stdafx.cpp - Includes standard include files
```

The Design of NPWAVE

The main objective of NPWAVE is to play audio while streaming data from the HTTP server. Audio buffers are sent to the audio driver as they come in from the server. The user does not have to wait for the file to download before hearing audio.

This example is intended as a learning tool and, as such, does not provide for audio compression, which is needed for many applications. Audio compression can easily be added using Microsoft's Audio Compression Manager (ACM).

The current version of NPWAVE supports standard .WAV file formats. Without compression, using 11,025 samples per second audio data, a bandwidth of 88,200 bps is required to use NPWAVE in real time. Of course, you can use the plug-in on your local hard drive or a LAN to easily make this bandwidth requirement.

As you can see in Figure 17.1, the audio plug-in consists of several main components that fit together to create a working audio streamer:

- Netscape's plug-in entry points
- `CWave` class
- Thread and associated routine
- Audio driver procedure
- `CBuffer` class and associated buffers
- `CPluginWindow` class

Figure 17.1.
The components of the audio plug-in.

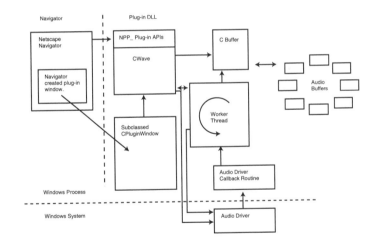

Plug-In Entry Points

As you might remember from Chapter 8, "The Plug-In Application Programming Interface (API)," Navigator uses a file called npwin.cpp to provide access to APIs both within your plug-in and within the Navigator. Methods that reside in the plug-in are prefaced with `NPP_`, and methods in the Navigator are prefaced with `NPN_`. The audio plug-in uses only `NPP_` type methods. No calls are made to the Navigator from the plug-in.

A file called npshell.cpp contains these methods. Some methods, such as `NPP_Print` and `NPP_StreamAsFile`, are not used but stubs are still provided for the Navigator to call. If you don't provide these stubs, Navigator traps.

Creating a New Instance

The first two methods called in the audio plug-in are NPP_Initialize and NPP_New. NPP_Initialize does nothing and is provided as a stub method. NPP_New enables you to create a plug-in instance and save it for later reference.

Rather than having a separate instance structure, NPWAVE uses the CWave class to hold its instance data. It's simple to allocate a CWave object with the new operator and attach it to Netscape's instance structure:

```
// Create a new CWave object
CWave* pWave = new CWave (pInstance);

// Attach it to the instance structure
pInstance->pdata = pWave;
```

After this, if the plug-in was started in embedded mode, the HTML line is checked for an autostart parameter. If autostart is set to true, the audio begins playing as soon as the plug-in is loaded. Otherwise, the user must click on Play to start the audio. You can add as many HTML arguments as you like. For example, a loop=true named pair could make the plug-in loop the audio clip.

The New Stream

After a new instance is created, NPP_NewStream is called to inform the plug-in of a new audio stream. During this method, after retrieving the plug-in's instance data, the Open method of CWave is called to inform the CWave class of a new stream.

Subclassing Navigator's Window

NPP_SetWindow is called after the new stream is created. During this API, the plug-in creates a CWnd child called CPluginWindow and attaches a pointer referencing this object to the instance object, CWave:

```
// Get instance data

CWave* pWave = (CWave *)pInstance->pdata;
.
.
.
// Create our plug-in's window class

pWave->pWindow = new CPluginWindow (pWave);
```

Notice that a pointer to CWave is passed to CPluginWindow during creation. This pointer allows easy access to CWave from the window class.

When you create a child of CWnd, it is important to remember that just a window object—not actually a window—is created. Because of this, the plug-in can attach this newly created class to the Navigator's window using window subclassing. Navigator has already created the plug-in window before the call to NPP_SetWindow. You can override Navigator's window procedure by subclassing it with CPluginWindow:

```
// Subclass the plug-in window

pWave->pWindow->SubclassWindow ((HWND)window->window);
```

Data from the Navigator

When the stream starts, data is written to the plug-in with calls to both NPP_WriteReady and NPP_Write. As you might remember, NPP_WriteReady asks the plug-in how much data it is willing to receive, and NPP_Write sends the actual data. The audio plug-in hands off these APIs to CWave's methods, IsBufferAvailable and FillBuffer, respectively.

Stream completion, usually indicating total consumption of a file by the plug-in, is indicated by a call to NPP_DestroyStream. This method calls the CWave method EndOfStream.

This Is the End My Friend

Calls to NPP_Destroy and NPP_Shutdown tell the plug-in to clean up all system resources. The user has caused the plug-in to unload, perhaps moving on to more exciting things. Such is the life of a Web surfer.

This plug-in uses NPP_Destroy to unsubclass the window and delete it. The Close method of CWave is also called, after which CWave is deleted:

```
if (pWave->pWindow)
{
    // Unsubclass the window, clean it up and delete it.

    pWave->pWindow->UnsubclassWindow ();
    pWave->pWindow->CleanupWindow();

    delete pWave->pWindow;
}
// Close the audio driver and delete the audio object.

pWave->Close ();
delete pWave;
```

CWave

The real guts of NPWAVE are in the CWave class. CWave is located in the file npwave.cpp. This class handles audio buffer management, the audio driver, and a thread. Most CWave methods are called from npshell.cpp. Methods called from npshell.cpp are as follows:

```
CWave::CWave
CWave::~CWave
CWave::Open
CWave::IsBufferAvailable
CWave::FillBuffer
CWave::EndOfStream
CWave::Close
```

Opening CWave

CWave is created with the new operator in the file npshell.cpp. CWave's constructor initializes variables and gets a pointer to the plug-in's instance, NPP. Don't look for where this instance is used because it is not used in this case. Because many Navigator methods require the NPP instance structure, it's handy to have around just in case.

Next, after construction, a call is made to CWave::Open. This method is called from the NPP_NewStream API. It initializes a critical section, enters it, and creates a circular buffer with the CBuffer class:

```
// Protect data with critical sections

InitializeCriticalSection (&CritSect);

// Create a new CBuffer and have it make a circular buffer.

EnterCriticalSection (&CritSect);

pCBuffer = new CBuffer;
pCBuffer->AllocateCircularBuffer (MAX_BUFFER_SIZE, MAX_BUFFERS);

LeaveCriticalSection (&CritSect);
```

A call to CWave::Open requires a stream pointer of NPStream*. Like the instance pointer, this is never used but is nice to have within the class.

CRITICAL SECTIONS IN WINDOWS 95

Windows 95 introduces multithreading to the Windows programming world. The NPWAVE plug-in uses an additional thread to feed the audio driver buffers of audio data. This worker thread and the main thread from Netscape both need to access the CWave object. MFC objects are not thread safe at object level, but only at class level.

CWave is a class that can be used to create a CWave object. When multiple threads access a single CWave object, you must provide synchronization to this object and protect its data members. Throughout the NPWAVE plug-in, this is provided with the use of critical sections. Critical sections are an efficient mechanism of mutual-exclusion between threads.

To use critical sections, you must first create a critical section object with the Windows API InitializeCriticalSection. After it is created, a thread uses EnterCriticalSection to request ownership and LeaveCriticalSection to release ownership. If the thread is not granted ownership, it waits indefinitely until it is granted ownership. Call DeleteCriticalSection when you are done with it to release system resources.

You can also use the MFC CCriticalSection object, which works in a very similar manner. Consult the MFC Class Library Reference for further details.

Getting and Filling Buffers

`NPP_WriteReady` and `NPP_Write` call the `CWave` methods, `IsBufferAvailable` and `FillBuffer`, respectively. `IsBufferAvailble`, as the name implies, checks for an available empty buffer by calling the `CBuffer` object. `CBuffer` is explained in detail in the next chapter. Critical sections are used to protect `CBuffer`:

```
int32 CWave::IsBufferAvailable (void)
{
    ulBufSize = 0;

    EnterCriticalSection (&CritSect);

    if (pCBuffer->AnyEmptyBuffers ())
        ulBufSize = MAX_BUFFER_SIZE - STRUCT_SIZE;
    else
        ulBufSize = 0;

    LeaveCriticalSection (&CritSect);

    return ulBufSize;
}
```

The available buffer size is returned. Each buffer has a header whose size is subtracted from the total buffer size.

Next called is `FillBuffer` with the actual audio data. This method's job is to get the data from the Navigator and start the play for autostart-type plug-ins. First, it gets a buffer and sets the length. If this is the first buffer, the .WAV information is extracted:

```
// Get an empty buffer

BUFFER* pBuff = (BUFFER*)pCBuffer->GetNextEmptyBuffer();

if (pBuff)
{
    // Got a buffer, now copy the audio data.

    pBuff->pvData = &pBuff->ulData;
    memcpy (pBuff->pvData, pvNetscapeData, len);

    // Always set the length, it could be any value under
    // your buffer size.

    pBuff->ulDataSize = len;

    if (++ulBufferFullCount == 1)    // First buffer, parse wav header
    {
        pBuff->ulFlags |= BUFFER_FIRST;

        if (!ParseWaveHeader (pBuff))
        {
            // Bad format, bail out...
```

```
            bRc = FALSE;
            goto ExitFillBuffer;
        }
    }}
```

Next, an autostart condition is handled. If there are enough buffers to start, the thread is started with a call to PlayTheAudio:

```
if (bAutoStart)
{
    // Start it if we have enough buffers.

    if (ulBufferFullCount >= ulLowWaterMark &&
        usState != AUDIO_PLAYING && usState != AUDIO_PAUSED)
    {
        BOOL rc = PlayTheAudio ();
    }
}
```

Finally, a data underrun is handled:

```
if (bDataUnderrun)
{
    // The audio data can't keep up with the device. Get enough
    // buffers to clear our low water mark and restart the thread.

    if (ulBufferFullCount > ulLowWaterMark)
    {
        ulBufferFullCount = 1;   // Start over
        pBuff->ulFlags |= BUFFER_FIRST;
    }

    if (ulBufferFullCount == ulLowWaterMark)
    {
        bDataUnderrun = FALSE;
        BOOL fSuccess = SetEvent (hEvent);
    }
}
```

An underrun occurs when the NPWAVE plug-in is starved for data. The bDataUnderrun flag is set by the driver callback routine when it can't get any more buffers. If an underrun occurs and the buffer count is over the minimum amount of buffers for starting (ulLowWaterMark), the thread is restarted with a call to SetEvent.

The End of the Stream

EndOfStream is called from NPP_DestroyStream. This method is in charge of marking the last audio buffer and starting any autostart streams.

Mark the last buffer:

```
EnterCriticalSection (&CritSect);

// Mark the last full buffer. Once the audio driver proc sees the
// last buffer it will signal the thread to close the audio driver
// and exit gracefully.

BUFFER* pBuff = (BUFFER*)pCBuffer->GetLastFullBuffer();
```

```
if (pBuff)
    pBuff->ulFlags |= BUFFER_LAST;

LeaveCriticalSection (&CritSect);
```

Remember that a call to NPP_DestroyStream does not mean to stop playing; it just means that the data is done. In light of this, the last audio buffer is flagged. When the thread sees this flag, it closes the audio driver and exits.

Again, autostart is handled:

```
// In some cases we will not clear our low water marker for an auto start
// by the end of stream. Play what we have (if anything).

if (bAutoStart)
{
    if (usState == AUDIO_WAITING_FOR_START && ulBufferFullCount > 0)
    {
        BOOL rc = PlayTheAudio ();
    }
}
```

Closing Down the Plug-In

Shutting down a multithreaded plug-in is an exercise in caution. Exit processing bugs have caused many a project to run late. Always make sure you think of all possibilities for deadlocks on exit. A thread context will switch on order of milliseconds. Beware of thoughts such as "That would never happen," or "That window of opportunity is too small to deadlock." It might not happen to you, but someone could be in for a real treat.

The Close method is called from NPP_Destroy, which instructs the plug-in to free its instance and all associated resources:

```
BOOL CWave::Close (void)
{
    // Don't try to grab our critical section in this routine.
    // waveOutReset may cause buffers to be returned with WOM_DONE
    // messages which get a critical section in the driver proc.

    hEventCloseSync = CreateEvent (NULL, FALSE, FALSE, NULL);

    if (pThread)
    {
        bKillThread = TRUE;
        BOOL fSuccess = SetEvent (hEvent);
        DWORD dwRc = WaitForSingleObject (hEventCloseSync, INFINITE);
    }

    if (hWave)
    {
        // We are going to wait for the WOM_CLOSE message in the driver callback
        // proc. Otherwise we may try to access an invalid CWave object while
        // processing WOM_CLOSE. Although this may not be necessary, it is a good
        // safety measure.

        waveOutReset (hWave);    // Stop any current play (returns all buffers)
        waveOutClose (hWave);    // Close the audio device.
```

```
        DWORD dwRc = WaitForSingleObject (hEventCloseSync, INFINITE);
    }

    CloseHandle (hEventCloseSync);

    // It's safe now to free the audio buffers. The audio driver
    // has returned all buffers.

    pCBuffer->FreeCircularBuffer();
    delete pCBuffer;

    return TRUE;
}
```

During this method, a synchronization event is created for two purposes. First, it allows the worker thread to exit gracefully while the main thread waits. If the main thread did not wait, the whole object could be deleted before the worker thread was switched back in, causing a trap. Second, the event allows all audio buffers to be returned while the main thread waits. Windows 95 does the audio driver synchronization for you, but you might as well be safe.

Finally, at the end of the method, the plug-in can safely free all audio buffers without fear of trapping.

CWave's Worker Thread

The worker thread routine, although not part of the CWave class, is located in the same file and has direct access to the object. The thread calls the following methods:

```
CBuffer::GetNextFullBuffer
CWave::SendDataToDriver
```

An infinite while loop keeps the thread alive throughout its mission. The worker thread first waits for another thread to wake it:

```
// Wait for someone to start us...

DWORD dwRc = WaitForSingleObject (pWav->hEvent, INFINITE);
```

The thread starting the worker is either the main Navigator calling thread or the audio driver callback thread. After waking, the kill flag is checked, and if it is set, the thread exits:

```
if (pWav->bKillThread)
{
    // Main thread wants us dead

    BOOL fSuccess = SetEvent (pWav->hEventCloseSync);
    AfxEndThread (0);
}
```

Notice the call to SetEvent to signal the main thread that the kill is acknowledged.

The next order of business is to check whether the audio driver has played and returned the last audio buffer. If so, this thread is done and exits:

```
EnterCriticalSection (&pWav->CritSect);

if (pWav->bPlayedLastBuffer)
{
    // The last buffer was played. We are done.
    // Close the audio device and exit this thread.

    waveOutClose (pWav->hWave);
    pWav->hWave = 0;
    pWav->pThread = 0;

    LeaveCriticalSection (&pWav->CritSect);

    AfxEndThread (0);
}
```

The audio driver is closed with waveOutClose, and the thread exits with AfxEndThread.

If the thread still lives after all of these potential deaths, it's time to send the audio driver some data. First, call CBuffer::GetNextFullBuffer to get a buffer, and if that is successful, the buffer is sent to the driver with CWave::SendDataToDriver. The first buffer in the audio stream is denoted by the BUFFER_FIRST flag. When the thread sees that it is the first buffer, it sends a few more buffers to keep the audio driver happy for awhile. Those extra buffers might not be available. In that case, CWave::SendDataToDriver sees the NULL buffer pointer and simply returns the following:

```
else
{
    // Get another buffer and send it to the audio driver.

    BUFFER* pBuf = (BUFFER*)pWav->pCBuffer->GetNextFullBuffer ();

    if (pBuf)
    {
        pWav->SendDataToDriver (pBuf);

        if (pBuf->ulFlags & BUFFER_FIRST)
        {
            pBuf->ulFlags &= ~BUFFER_FIRST;

            // Send the audio driver a bunch of
            // buffers to chew on for awhile.

            for (int i=0; i<STARTING_BUFFERS; i++)
            {
                pBuf = (BUFFER*)pWav->pCBuffer->GetNextFullBuffer ();
                pWav->SendDataToDriver (pBuf);
            }
        }
        pWav->bDataUnderrun = FALSE;
    }
}
```

On completion of these tasks, the worker thread loops back and waits again.

The Audio Driver

You've already learned about CWave::PlayTheAudio. This method is called when the plug-in is starting the audio playback. It opens the default audio device and creates the worker thread:

```
BOOL CWave::PlayTheAudio (void)
{
    // Open the audio device

        MMRESULT mmRc = waveOutOpen (&hWave,
            WAVE_MAPPER,
            &WaveFormat,
            (DWORD)DriverCallback,
            (DWORD)this,
            CALLBACK_FUNCTION);

        if (mmRc)
            return FALSE;

    // Create the thread

    usState = AUDIO_PLAYING;

    CreateWriteThread ();

    return TRUE;
}
```

Look at the call to waveOutOpen. This Windows API opens a waveform device. In this case, it is the default audio device, WAVE_MAPPER. A pointer to a WAVEFORMATEX structure previously filled is supplied along with the address of a callback routine (DriverCallback) and a reference to the CWave object (this).

Audio Driver Callback Messages

The audio driver callback routine is an important piece of the NPWAVE plug-in equation. This routine processes three basic driver messages:

> WOM_CLOSE
>
> WOM_OPEN
>
> WOM_DONE

WOM_CLOSE is sent after a call to waveOutClose. This message indicates that all audio buffers have been returned and the driver is closing. During this message, the plug-in driver callback signals the main thread that it is safe to continue with exiting:

```
case WOM_CLOSE:    // Driver was closed with waveOutClose
{
    BOOL fSuccess = SetEvent (pWav->hEventCloseSync);
    break;
}
```

WOM_OPEN is sent after a call to waveOutOpen. The plug-in callback does nothing for this message.

WOM_DONE is sent when the driver has finished with a data block. During this message, the callback signals the worker thread to continue processing buffers. If the last buffer is detected, the flag bPlayedLastBuffer is set to TRUE. When the thread sees this flag set, it exits:

```
case WOM_DONE:     // Driver is finished with last data block
{
    EnterCriticalSection (&pWav->CritSect);

    WAVEHDR* pWaveHdr = (WAVEHDR*)dw1;
    BUFFER* pBuff = (BUFFER*)pWaveHdr->dwUser;

    // Clean up preparation performed by the waveOutPrepareHeader function

    waveOutUnprepareHeader (pWav->hWave, pWaveHdr, sizeof(WAVEHDR));

    if (pBuff->ulFlags & BUFFER_LAST)
    {
        pWav->bPlayedLastBuffer = TRUE;

        BOOL fSuccess = SetEvent (pWav->hEvent);    // Release the thread
    }
    else
    {
        pWav->pCBuffer->ReturnUsedBuffer (pBuff);

        if (pWav->pCBuffer->AnyFullBuffers ())
            BOOL fSuccess = SetEvent (pWav->hEvent);    // Release the thread
        else
            pWav->bDataUnderrun = TRUE;
    }

    LeaveCriticalSection (&pWav->CritSect);

    break;
}
```

During WOM_DONE processing, the CBuffer::ReturnUsedBuffer and CBuffer::AnyFullBuffers methods are called. ReturnUsedBuffer gives the used buffer back to the buffer pool. AnyFullBuffers checks to ensure that more buffers are available. If not, an underrun condition is flagged.

The audio driver callback allows the audio plug-in to efficiently manage its memory by returning consumed buffers. This technique also lets the plug-in send multiple buffers on startup to prevent potential audio breakup during high system load.

The CPluginWindow Class

As shown in Figure 17.2, the NPWAVE plug-in has an extremely simple user interface. This interface consists of a Play button and a Pause button. These buttons are children of the plug-in's window. The window was created by the Navigator, and it is sized depending on the plug-in's type. To access this window, the plug-in creates a CPluginWindow object and subclasses it to the Navigator's window.

Figure 17.2.

The audio plug-in's user interface.

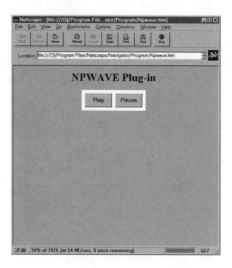

Clicking the Play button starts the audio playing. Pause, as the name implies, pauses the audio playback. A pause is resumed with another click to the Play button.

CPluginWindow is a small class with a message map for window message processing. The class lives in a file called npwindow.cpp. CPluginWindow's message map looks for the plug-in defined messages ID_AUDIO_PLAY and ID_AUDIO_PAUSE. These messages are generated when the Play or Pause buttons are clicked. ID_AUDIO_PLAY resolves to the OnPlay method, and ID_AUDIO_PAUSE resolves to the OnPause method. Here is the message map:

```
BEGIN_MESSAGE_MAP( CPluginWindow, CWnd )
    //{{AFX_MSG_MAP( CMainWindow )
    ON_COMMAND(ID_AUDIO_PLAY,OnPlay)
    ON_COMMAND(ID_AUDIO_PAUSE,OnPause)
    //}}AFX_MSG_MAP
END_MESSAGE_MAP()
```

OnPlay

When the Play button is clicked, the OnPlay method simply calls the CWave::Play method:

```
//
// OnPlay - The "Play" button was clicked
//
void CPluginWindow::OnPlay()
{
    if (pWave)
        if (!pWave->Play ())
            AfxMessageBox ("Can't play now !");
}
```

Notice that a pointer to CWave is used to call the Play method. This pointer was acquired during creation. CWave's Play method looks like this:

```
BOOL CWave::Play (void)
{
    if (usState == AUDIO_PAUSED)
    {
        MMRESULT mmRc = waveOutRestart (hWave);

        usState = AUDIO_PLAYING;
    }
    else if (!bAutoStart)
    {
        if (usState == AUDIO_WAITING_FOR_START && ulBufferFullCount > 0)
        {
            BOOL rc = PlayTheAudio ();

            if (!rc)
                return FALSE;
        }
        else
            return FALSE;
    }
    return TRUE;
}
```

OnPause

In a paused condition, the audio is restarted using waveOutRestart. Otherwise, PlayTheAudio is called. PlayTheAudio opens the audio device with a call to waveOutOpen and creates the worker thread. The thread, in turn, passes buffers to the audio driver.

The OnPause method is called when the Pause button is clicked. It looks like this:

```
//
// OnPause - The "Pause" button was clicked
//
void CPluginWindow::OnPause()
{
    if (pWave)
        if (!pWave->Pause ())
            AfxMessageBox ("Can't pause now !");
}
```

OnPause in turn calls CWave::Pause, which looks like this:

```
BOOL CWave::Pause (void)
{
    if (usState == AUDIO_PLAYING)
    {
        MMRESULT mmRc = waveOutPause (hWave);

        usState = AUDIO_PAUSED;
    }
    else
        return FALSE;

    return TRUE;
}
```

The Pause method calls the waveOutPause API, which temporarily suspends audio playback.

The Buttons

The buttons are created in the `CPluginWindow::InitWindow` method by creating `Cbutton` objects with the appropriate parameters:

```
void CPluginWindow::InitWindow()
{
    CRect rect (10,10,90,50);

    cbPlay = new CButton();

    cbPlay->Create("Play",
        BS_PUSHBUTTON | WS_VISIBLE,
        rect,
        this,
        ID_AUDIO_PLAY);

    rect.SetRect (100,10,180,50);

    cbPause = new CButton();

    cbPause->Create("Pause",
        BS_PUSHBUTTON | WS_VISIBLE,
        rect,
        this,
        ID_AUDIO_PAUSE);
}
```

Writers of commercial-grade plug-ins probably want to have some really cool bitmap buttons using `CBitmapButton`, instead of these plain examples. The buttons are simply deleted during a call to the `CPluginWindow::CleanupWindow` method:

```
void CPluginWindow::CleanupWindow ()
{
    delete cbPlay;
    delete cbPause;
}
```

NOTE

You might have noticed in the file npshell.cpp an object called `theApp`. It was allocated globally at the beginning of npshell.cpp like this:

```
CWinApp theApp;
```

Interestingly enough, the object is never accessed. Why?

Well, for one thing, those buttons created in `CPluginWindow` would not work properly. To use MFC routines in a DLL, the class library must be initialized. When you use Visual C's MFC AppWizard to create a DLL, a `CWinApp` is provided for you with a source file for overriding members of `CWinApp`, such as the constructor.

Because the NPWAVE DLL was not created using AppWizard, it simply declares a `CWinApp` object, fulfilling the required MFC initialization.

Running the Audio Plug-In

Any Netscape plug-in should support multiple instances. In some cases, as with the audio plug-in, a single resource is shared among these instances. Because the audio plug-in shares a single audio device, only one plug-in instance can use this device at any given time. To play another audio instance, you must either allow the stream to complete, or click the Stop button on the Navigator.

Buffer Sizes

When you click the Stop button on the Navigator, the audio does not immediately stop because a number of audio buffers are queued in the plug-in. The size and amount of these buffers can be configured in the npwave.h file. Feel free to change these values and see how it affects playback performance:

```
#define    MAX_BUFFER_SIZE    (1024 * 16) + STRUCT_SIZE
#define    MAX_BUFFERS        20
#define    LOW_WATER          10
#define    STARTING_BUFFERS   4
```

With the preceding values, there are 20 buffers with a size of 16KB each. Total memory required for a stream is 320KB. If you are playing 8-bit PCM at 11025 samples per second, each 16KB buffer holds about 1.5 seconds of audio. Notice the STARTING_BUFFERS define is set to 4. This value instructs the plug-in to send four full buffers to the audio driver on start. Four buffers is about six seconds of audio data. The LOW_WATER define tells the plug-in to wait for this many full buffers before starting or restarting audio playback.

Multiple Instances

Your plug-in can have a number of instance configurations depending on the way it is run. Here are some possibilities:

- Single instance full page
- Multiple instance full page
- Single instance embedded
- Multiple instance embedded

A multiple instance full page scenario is usually created by the user creating a new Navigator instance with File|New Web Browser. With the audio plug-in, it looks like the one in Figure 17.3.

A multiple-instance embedded plug-in can have more than one instance within the same Web page. You might even run into multiple pages of multiple embedded plug-ins! Figure 17.4 shows a single page with multiple embedded audio plug-ins.

Figure 17.3.
Multiple instances of full page audio plug-ins.

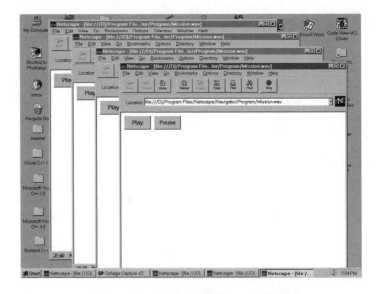

Figure 17.4.
Multiple embedded instances of the audio plug-in.

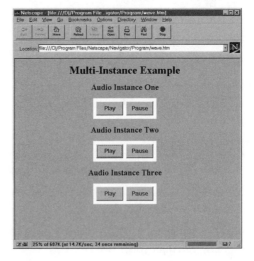

The importance of separate instance data and very careful protection of shared resources is shown in these examples.

Automatic Starting of Audio

Another little function that the audio plug-in supports in embedded mode is an autostart flag. This flag, if set to true, makes the audio playback start as soon as the page is loaded. You can pass any HTML parameters in your HTML embed statement. Each named pair is passed into your plug-in. For example, the autostart=true statement is passed to the audio plug-in like this:

```
<embed SRC=mission.wav WIDTH=190 HEIGHT=60 autostart=true>
```

Conclusion

The sample audio plug-in, NPWAVE.DLL, is a Window's 95 multithreaded DLL. Multithreaded applications require careful protection for shared resources through the use of synchronization objects. This chapter gave an example of safe interaction between threads and MFC objects.

Real-time data streaming and data processing really shows off the power of a Netscape Navigator plug-in module. Although this audio example might not perform in a real-time fashion using a typical 28.8 baud modem, a savvy programmer can add compression to stream data at whatever bandwidth is available.

What's Next?

The fundamental design of the NPWAVE plug-in allows for generic streaming and buffering of any data type. Buffering is implemented with a circular buffer via the CBuffer class. This generic class is the topic of the next chapter.

CHAPTER 18

The Buffer Classes

Introduction

Depending on the device, many data-streaming applications require your plug-in to internally buffer data. Consider the audio plug-in sample in Chapter 17. The audio driver requires multiple buffers on startup and a continuous feed of data. Audio buffers are cached up to a maximum buffer number. Buffers are then sent to the driver with a thread that is totally independent of the main Navigator thread. This scheme allows the plug-in to pre-read any amount of data.

Pre-reading data in a real-time streaming application is a must. Even with the fastest Internet connections, data flow can be halted for several seconds. How much should be pre-read is highly dependent on the device requiring the data. For example, setting up the audio sample to have 20 buffers at 16KB each allows the plug-in to cache 320KB of data, which translates to 30 seconds of playing time with 11khz 8-bit mono audio.

This chapter covers the `CBufferCircular` and `CBufferFIFO` classes. These classes are fully inter-changeable into the sample audio plug-in and can also be used in other applications. Both classes have exactly the same methods, but they differ in the buffer management implementation. `CBufferCircular` uses a recycling circular buffer scheme and `CBufferFIFO` uses a First In First Out (FIFO) scheme.

It should be noted that these classes are intended as learning tools and are not commercial-grade source code. The methods are short and to the point, without much in the way of error checking. If you plan to use these classes in your code, pay special attention to the technical notes throughout this chapter, which warn of potential pitfalls.

The Methods

Although the audio sample is currently set up to use the `CBufferCircular` class, it is a very simple task to switch to the `CBufferFIFO` class. In npwave.cpp, you can find where `CBufferCircular` is allocated in the `CWave::Open` method:

```
pCBuffer = new CBufferCircular;
```

Then, you can change the line to look like this:

```
pCBuffer = new CBufferFIFO;
```

That's all there is to it. Notice that this is possible because the methods are interchangeable between classes. These methods are as follows:

- ■ `(Constructor)` class constructor.
- ■ `(Destructor)` class destructor.
- ■ `AllocateBuffers` sets up the buffer sizes and amounts.
- ■ `FreeBuffers` frees the buffers.
- ■ `AnyEmptyBuffers` returns `TRUE` if there any empty buffers.

- AnyFullBuffers returns TRUE is there are any full buffers.
- GetNextEmptyBuffer returns a pointer to the next empty buffer.
- GetNextFullBuffer returns a pointer to the next full buffer.
- GetLastFullBuffer returns a pointer to the last full buffer.
- ReturnUsedBuffer returns a consumed buffer.

Buffer Header

To effectively manage these buffers, a small header structure is attached to the first part of each buffer:

```
typedef struct _cbuff
{
    struct _cbuff* pNextBuffer;
    ULONG ulFlags;

} CBUFF;
```

This header can be expanded for additional needs. In the sample audio plug-in, the expanded version is as follows:

```
typedef struct _buffer
{
    struct _buffer* pNextBuffer;
    ULONG ulFlags;
    ULONG ulBufferSize;
    ULONG ulDataSize;
    WAVEHDR WaveHdr;
    void* pvData;
    ULONG ulData;

} BUFFER;
```

Make sure that the first part of the expanded structure contains a next pointer and flags in that order. The buffer classes only care about these two members.

The Circular Buffer

The audio sample's default configuration uses the circular buffer class, CBufferCircular. This class is contained in the files npbfcirc.cpp and npbfcirc.h.

The circular buffer allocates a linked list of buffers in which the last buffer allocated points to the first. All buffers are allocated at initialization and continuously recycled throughout the life of the stream. Because memory is allocated only once, performance of this technique is slightly faster than the FIFO class CBufferFIFO.

An allocated CBufferCircular might look something like the one in Figure 18.1 in memory.

Figure 18.1.
Memory blocks allocated with
`CBufferCircular.`

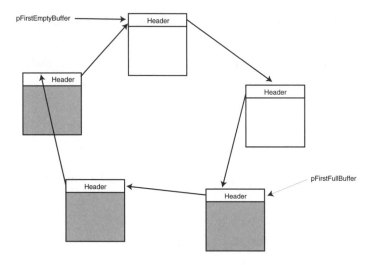

As you can see in Figure 18.1, `pFirstFullBuffer` points to the first buffer with valid data and `pFirstEmptyBuffer` points to the first buffer available for use. As the data is streaming, full buffers are consumed by a device and empty buffers are filled by the Navigator.

CBufferCircular **Methods**

The circular buffer class uses the standard C runtime memory management routines: `malloc` and `free`. All memory is allocated at the same time and freed at the same time.

Constructor

The constructor initializes the buffer pointers:

```
//
// Constructor
//
CBufferCircular::CBufferCircular ()
{
    pFirstEmptyBuffer = pFirstFullBuffer = NULL;
}
```

Destructor

The destructor checks to make sure that memory is freed, and if it is not, frees the memory implicitly:

```
//
// Destructor
//
CBufferCircular::~CBufferCircular ()
{
```

```
    if (pFirstEmptyBuffer)
        this->FreeBuffers ();     // Forgot to free us.
}
```

CBufferCircular::AllocateBuffers

The first method allocates buffers and chains them together to form a circular linked list:

```
//
// AllocateBuffers
//
BOOL CBufferCircular::AllocateBuffers (ULONG ulBuffSize,
    USHORT usNumberOfBuffers)
{
    CBUFF*    pBuff;

    for (int i=1; i<usNumberOfBuffers; i++, pBuff=pBuff->pNextBuffer)
    {
        if (i == 1)
        {
            pFirstEmptyBuffer = pBuff = (CBUFF*) malloc (ulBuffSize);
            memset (pFirstEmptyBuffer, 0, ulBuffSize);
        }

        pBuff->pNextBuffer = (CBUFF*) malloc (ulBuffSize);
        memset (pBuff->pNextBuffer, 0, ulBuffSize);
    }

    // Last buffer points to first, a circular buffer scheme.

    pBuff->pNextBuffer = pFirstEmptyBuffer;

    return TRUE;
}
```

> **NOTE**
>
> `CBufferCircular::AllocateBuffers` only works if `usNumberOfBuffers` is greater than one. Also, there is no protection against a memory leak if the method is called twice. If you use this code, you might want to add these checks.

The first empty buffer pointer (`pFirstEmptyBuffer`) is set, and the last buffer allocated points to the first, completing the circle.

Notice that the buffer size and amount of buffers is passed to the method, allowing any number of configurations. You can also allocate a circular buffer with respect to the data type. For example, if you are streaming 11khz 8-bit mono audio data, 10 16KB buffers might be sufficient, but 44khz 16-bit stereo might require 20 64KB buffers. It depends entirely on your application and performance requirements.

CBufferCircular::FreeBuffers

When you are done with the circular buffer, call FreeBuffers. This method scans through the chain and frees all memory:

```
//
// FreeBuffers
//
BOOL CBufferCircular::FreeBuffers (void)
{
    CBUFF*      pBuff=pFirstEmptyBuffer, *pBuffNext;

    do
    {
        pBuffNext = pBuff->pNextBuffer;
        free (pBuff);
        pBuff = pBuffNext;

    } while (pBuff != pFirstEmptyBuffer);

    pFirstEmptyBuffer = pFirstFullBuffer = NULL;

    return TRUE;
}
```

NOTE

CBufferCircular::FreeBuffers has no protection against being called when there are no buffers. You might want to add this check to this method in order to avoid a potential memory protection fault.

CBufferCircular::AnyEmptyBuffers

While data is streaming, the plug-in continuously calls AnyEmptyBuffers, which returns TRUE if there are any empty buffers. This is analogous to an NPP_WriteReady called from the Navigator:

```
//
// AnyEmptyBuffers
//
BOOL CBufferCircular::AnyEmptyBuffers (void)
{
    if (pFirstEmptyBuffer->ulFlags & BUFFER_FULL)
        return FALSE;
    else
        return TRUE;
}
```

To determine whether any empty buffers are available, the flags are checked for the first empty buffer, pFirstEmptyBuffer. This buffer can be full in the case of data overrun. Streaming for a local disk drive almost always produces a situation in which all buffers are full.

CBufferCircular::GetNextEmptyBuffer

When AnyEmptyBuffers returns TRUE, a call to GetNextEmptyBuffer is made, which returns a pointer to the next empty buffer:

```
//
// GetNextEmptyBuffer
//
void* CBufferCircular::GetNextEmptyBuffer (void)
{
    CBUFF*      pBuff=pFirstEmptyBuffer;

    if (!(pBuff->ulFlags & BUFFER_FULL))
    {
        if (!pFirstFullBuffer)
            pFirstFullBuffer = pFirstEmptyBuffer;

            pBuff->ulFlags |= BUFFER_FULL;

        // Next buffer please...

        pFirstEmptyBuffer = pFirstEmptyBuffer->pNextBuffer;

        return pBuff;
    }
    else
        return NULL;
}
```

The method double-checks the flags on the first empty buffer, making sure it is not full. If pFirstFullBuffer is NULL, it is set to this buffer, making it the first buffer in the stream. The buffer is flagged as full, and pFirstEmptyBuffer is pointed to the next buffer.

CBufferCircular::AnyFullBuffers

The consumer of stream data, which could be another thread, calls AnyFullBuffers and returns TRUE if data is available:

```
//
// AnyFullBuffers
//
BOOL CBufferCircular::AnyFullBuffers (void)
{
    if (pFirstFullBuffer->ulFlags & BUFFER_FULL)
        return TRUE;
    else
        return FALSE;
}
```

NOTE

`CBufferCircular::AnyFullBuffers` should really make sure that `pFirstFullbuffer` is not NULL and does exist. You might want to add this check to your implementation of this code.

The first full buffer pointer is checked for data with the `BUFFER_FULL` flag.

CBufferCircular::GetNextFullBuffer

After determining that there is some data, `GetNextFullBuffer` is called and returns a pointer to a full data buffer:

```
//
// GetNextFullBuffer
//
void* CBufferCircular::GetNextFullBuffer (void)
{
    CBUFF*      pBuff=pFirstFullBuffer;

    if (pBuff->ulFlags & BUFFER_FULL)
    {
        // Next buffer please...

        pFirstFullBuffer = pFirstFullBuffer->pNextBuffer;

        return pBuff;
    }
    else
        return NULL;
}
```

NOTE

Your calling code should assure that `CBufferCircular::AnyFullBuffers` is called before `CBufferCircular::GetNextFullBuffer`.

`GetNextFullBuffer` verifies that `pFirstFullBuffer` contains data by checking the `BUFFER_FULL` flag. It then points `pFirstFullBuffer` to the next buffer and returns a valid buffer pointer.

CBufferCircular::GetLastFullBuffer

When a stream is finished, it calls `NPP_DestroyStream` to signal stream completion. The fact that the stream is complete does not mean your plug-in is done consuming buffers. The plug-in needs to flag the last full buffer so that the device knows to stop. `GetLastFullBuffer` is provided to retrieve the last full buffer for this purpose:

```
//
// GetLastFullBuffer
//
void* CBufferCircular::GetLastFullBuffer (void)
{
    CBUFF*      pBuff=pFirstFullBuffer;

    if (!(pBuff->ulFlags & BUFFER_FULL))
        return NULL;

    for (; pBuff->pNextBuffer->ulFlags & BUFFER_FULL; pBuff=pBuff->pNextBuffer)
    {
        if (pBuff->pNextBuffer->ulFlags & BUFFER_ACTIVE)
            return pBuff;    // Buffer is in the driver
                             // (already consumed, but still full)

        if (pBuff->pNextBuffer == pFirstFullBuffer)
            return pBuff;    // All buffers are full
    }

    return pBuff;
}
```

GetLastFullBuffer scans through the buffer circle starting with pFirstFullBuffer. It stops when an empty buffer is found or a complete circle has been made. The flag BUFFER_ACTIVE is used to denote a buffer that is technically full but is already sent to the device. For the purpose of GetLastFullBuffer, these are considered empty.

CBufferCircular::ReturnUsedBuffer

When a device is totally finished with a buffer, the buffer is returned for recycling with a call to ReturnUsedBuffer:

```
//
// ReturnUsedBuffer
//
BOOL CBufferCircular::ReturnUsedBuffer (void* pvBuffer)
{
    CBUFF*      pBuff=pFirstEmptyBuffer;

    do
    {
        if (pvBuffer == (void*)pBuff)
        {
            // Found it, flag as empty and return.

            pBuff->ulFlags &= ~(BUFFER_FULL | BUFFER_ACTIVE);
            return TRUE;
        }

        pBuff=pBuff->pNextBuffer;

    } while (pBuff != pFirstEmptyBuffer);

    return FALSE;
}
```

This method scans the list, finds the given buffer, and turns off the BUFFER_FULL and BUFFER_ACTIVE flags.

The FIFO Buffer

The other buffer class, CBufferFIFO, is located in the files npbffifo.cpp and npbffifo.h. These files are part of the sample audio plug-in. This class is not used, but it can easily be swapped in as discussed earlier in this chapter.

The FIFO buffer also uses a linked list of buffers. Unlike the circular buffer, the FIFO buffer is a chain of buffers with a NULL terminated end buffer. Buffers are not recycled but are allocated and freed as needed. This provides for a somewhat simpler implementation at a slight performance penalty.

An allocated CBufferFIFO might look something the one in Figure 18.2 in memory.

Figure 18.2.
Memory blocks allocated with
CBufferFIFO.

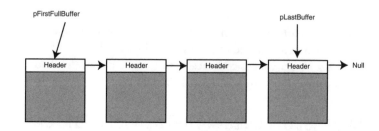

In Figure 18.2, pFirstFullBuffer points to the first buffer with valid data and pLastBuffer points to the last buffer with valid data. No empty or active buffers are maintained.

CBufferFIFO Methods

The FIFO buffer class uses the standard C runtime memory management routines: malloc and free. Unlike with CBufferCircular, memory is allocated as needed and freed immediately after use.

Constructor

The constructor initializes pointers and counters:

```
//
// Constructor
//
CBufferFIFO::CBufferFIFO ()
{
    pFirstFullBuffer = pLastBuffer = NULL;
    usBufferCount = 0;
}
```

Destructor

As it did with `CBufferCircular`, the destructor ensures that memory has been freed:

```
//
// Destructor
//
CBufferFIFO::~CBufferFIFO ()
{
    if (pFirstFullBuffer)
        this->FreeBuffers ();     // Forgot to free us.
}
```

CBufferFIFO::AllocateBuffers

No buffers are really allocated in this method. The buffer size and count is stored for later reference during buffer allocation:

```
//
// AllocateBuffers
//
BOOL CBufferFIFO::AllocateBuffers (ULONG ulBuffSize, USHORT usNumberOfBuffers)
{
    this->ulBuffSize = ulBuffSize;
    this->usNumberOfBuffers = usNumberOfBuffers;

    return TRUE;
}
```

CBufferFIFO::FreeBuffers

`FreeBuffers` is almost identical to `CBufferCircular::FreeBuffers`. The real difference is that the starting pointer is `pFirstFullBuffer` instead of `pFirstEmptyBuffer`:

```
//
// FreeBuffers
//
BOOL CBufferFIFO::FreeBuffers (void)
{
    CBUFF*      pBuff=pFirstFullBuffer, *pBuffNext;

    if (!pBuff)
        return TRUE;

    do
    {
        pBuffNext = pBuff->pNextBuffer;
        free (pBuff);
        pBuff = pBuffNext;

    } while (pBuff);

    pFirstFullBuffer = NULL;

    return TRUE;
}
```

CBufferFIFO::AnyEmptyBuffers

This method is much simpler than `CBufferCircular::AnyEmptyBuffers`. The FIFO buffer class allocates memory on the fly. Therefore, as long as the maximum buffers limit is not exceeded, the method returns TRUE.

```
//
// AnyEmptyBuffers
//
BOOL CBufferFIFO::AnyEmptyBuffers (void)
{
    if (usBufferCount <= usNumberOfBuffers)
        return TRUE;
    else
        return FALSE;
}
```

CBufferFIFO::GetNextEmptyBuffer

A new buffer is allocated and attached to the end of the chain. If there are no buffers to chain to, pLastBuffer is NULL and a new chain is created by resetting pFirstFullBuffer.

The buffer is zeroed, it is flagged as full, and buffer count is incremented:

```
//
// GetNextEmptyBuffer
//
void* CBufferFIFO::GetNextEmptyBuffer (void)
{
    CBUFF*      pBuff=pLastBuffer;

    if (pBuff)
    {
        pBuff->pNextBuffer = (CBUFF*)malloc (ulBuffSize);
        pBuff = pBuff->pNextBuffer;
        pLastBuffer = pBuff;
    }
    else
    {
        pFirstFullBuffer = pLastBuffer = (CBUFF*)malloc (ulBuffSize);
        pBuff = pFirstFullBuffer;
    }

    if (!pBuff)
        return NULL;

    memset (pBuff, 0, ulBuffSize);

    pBuff->ulFlags = BUFFER_FULL;

    usBufferCount++;

    return pBuff;
}
```

CBufferFIFO::AnyFullBuffers

Check to make sure that the first full buffer is indeed full, and return TRUE if it is. pFirstFullBuffer is NULL if no buffers are available:

```
//
// AnyFullBuffers
//
BOOL CBufferFIFO::AnyFullBuffers (void)
{
    if (pFirstFullBuffer)
    {
        if (pFirstFullBuffer->ulFlags & BUFFER_FULL)
            return TRUE;
        else
            return FALSE;
    }
    else
        return FALSE;
}
```

CBufferFIFO::GetNextFullBuffer

Make sure that pFirstFullBuffer points to a full buffer. If it does, detach the buffer from the chain by moving pFirstFullBuffer onto the next buffer (if any):

```
//
// GetNextFullBuffer
//
void* CBufferFIFO::GetNextFullBuffer (void)
{
    CBUFF*      pBuff=pFirstFullBuffer;

    if (!pBuff)
        return NULL;

    if (pBuff->ulFlags & BUFFER_FULL)
    {
        // Detach this full buffer from the list and send it out

        if (!(pFirstFullBuffer = pFirstFullBuffer->pNextBuffer))
            pLastBuffer = NULL;

        return pBuff;
    }
    else
        return NULL;
}
```

CBufferFIFO::GetLastFullBuffer

The last full buffer is always maintained by the FIFO class. It just returns pLastBuffer:

```
//
// GetLastFullBuffer
//
```

```
void* CBufferFIFO::GetLastFullBuffer (void)
{
    return pLastBuffer;
}
```

CBufferFIFO::ReturnUsedBuffer

Finally, a returned buffer is freed by the C runtime. Also, the buffer counter is decremented to allow for more buffer allocations:

```
//
// ReturnUsedBuffer
//
BOOL CBufferFIFO::ReturnUsedBuffer (void* pvBuffer)
{
    // Just free the memory and decrement the counter

    if (pvBuffer)
    {
        free (pvBuffer);
        usBufferCount—;
        return TRUE;
    }

    return FALSE;
}
```

Conclusion

Use the CBufferFIFO class or its partner CBufferCircular for your plug-in streaming needs. Be sure to call the methods in the correct order. This order is best illustrated in the audio plug-in sample file, npwave.cpp.

Tune your buffer sizes to effectively manage the data stream. For example, a MIDI buffer size would be very small compared to a much larger video buffer size.

Add your plug-in specific data to the buffer header while still maintaining compatibility with the CBUFF structure found in npbfcirc.h or npbffifo.h.

Don't forget to protect these buffer objects with critical sections for multithreaded plug-ins.

What's Next?

The next chapter outlines the Server CPU Monitor plug-in. This plug-in is not a streaming plug-in. It uses NPN_GetURL to retrieve server CPU statistics that are determined via the UNIX command vmstat, running with a server CGI program.

CHAPTER 19

The CPU Monitor Plug-In

Introduction

Most UNIX and NT Web servers have an interesting system-level command called vmstat. This operating system utility provides a plethora of system-level information such as thread status, virtual memory statistics, interrupts, system calls, context switches, and CPU usage—all the important performance data for a preemptive multitasking operating system. This chapter is about the CPU Monitor plug-in sample, which uses vmstat to retrieve Web Server CPU statistics.

The CPU Monitor works in conjunction with a CGI program to display a bar chart in a Navigator Web page showing relative user, system, and idle CPU time within a time slice specified by the vmstat command. The plug-in runs a CGI program by calling it with NPN_GetURL. The CGI program in turn runs vmstat and output is sent back to the Navigator.

This plug-in is file-based; that is, it gets data from a Navigator cached file. The plug-in API NPP_StreamAsFile is used, rather than NPP_WriteReady and NPP_Write as in the audio plug-in sample.

Where to Find the Files

All the necessary files for building NPCPUMON.DLL are located on the CD-ROM. These files are in the \CODE\CPUMON, \CODE\INC, and \CODE\COMMON directories. You will need the files shown in the following lists.

For the directory \CODE\CPUMON, you need these files:

- npshell.cpp: Plug-in entry point methods
- npcpumon.cpp, npcpumon.h: The CPU monitor class CCpuMon
- npwindow.cpp, npwindow.h: The window class CPluginWindow
- npcpumon.def: The DLL module definition file
- npcpumon.rc: Resources
- npcpumon.mak: Makefile for Microsoft Visual C++
- unixprog.c: The CGI program

For the directory \CODE\INC, you need these files:

- npapi.h: Plug-in API prototypes and associated structures
- npupp.h: Plug-in API prototypes
- stdafx.h: Standard include files

For the directory \CODE\COMMON, you need these files:

- npwin.cpp: DLL entry point to plug-in API mapping
- stdafx.cpp: Includes standard include files

The Design of the CPU Monitor Plug-In

The CPU Monitor plug-in is a much simpler Windows 95 plug-in implementation than the audio sample plug-in. Because no threads or callbacks are used, synchronization is not necessary. The CPU monitor does not process data on the fly with NPP_WriteReady and NPP_Write, but instead uses NPP_StreamAsFile. A filename is passed via this API that is opened and read using the standard I/O functions fopen and fgets.

This plug-in actually runs a piece of software on the HTTP server using the Common Gateway Interface (CGI), which is a small program written in C, via the NPN_GetURL plug-in API. The program kicks off vmstat with a one second interval. Standard output is routed back to the Navigator, as it is with any CGI program.

When vmstat's data comes back, the plug-in displays the CPU usage in a bar chart on the plug-in window. A button called Update is also on this window. When you click this button, it repeats the process, runs the CGI program with NPN_GetURL, and displays the results on the window.

As you can see in Figure 19.1, two classes are used for this plug-in: CCpuMon and CPluginWindow. You might remember CPluginWindow from the audio sample. This class has the same name but a slightly different implementation. The name is kept because, as in the audio sample, the resulting object is used to subclass the Navigator-created plug-in window. The CCpuMon class is the central class that handles calls from both CPluginWindow and NPP_ type APIs from the file npshell.cpp.

Figure 19.1.

The components of the CPU monitor plug-in.

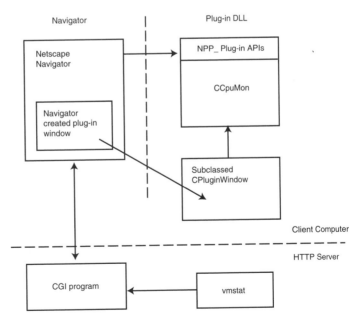

About `vmstat`

The heart of the CPU monitor plug-in is the UNIX-based `vmstat` command. This command reports statistics about kernel threads, virtual memory statistics, interrupts, system calls, context switches, and CPU usage. The sample plug-in uses only CPU usage statistics. You might be interested in adding page faults or system call statistics as a programming exercise.

The CPU monitor CGI program runs `vmstat` for a one second interval with two reports. The first report contains the statistics since system startup, and the second report contains statistics for the requested time interval. It is run like this:

`vmstat 1 2`

In this statement, 1 is one second and 2 is two reports.

It takes at least one second for the `vmstat` program to finish, because it must calculate the statistics over a one second interval. When it is completed, the output might look something like this:

```
procs     memory              page                 disk        faults      cpu
 r b w   avm   fre  re at  pi  po  fr  de  sr d0 s1 s2 s3  in  sy  cs us sy id
 0 0 0     0  1280   0  5   3   3   1   0  16  4  8 10  0 223 607 134 20 25 55
 0 0 0     0  1280   0  0  32   0   0   0   0  0  1  0  0 112 319  79  3 10 87
```

Kind of cryptic isn't it? The CPU monitor plug-in only uses the last three numbers of the second report. These numbers are in the `cpu` section under `us`, `sy`, and `id`. In this case, `us` indicates user, `sy` is system, and `id` is idle. Because these three number always total 100, each is a percentage of total CPU time.

How `vmstat` Is Run with the CGI Program

A very basic C program runs `vmstat` using the `system` call. It looks like this:

```c
#include <stdio.h>

#define    INTERVAL    1

main ()
{
    char buff[100];

    printf ("Content-type: text/plain%c%c", 10,10);
    fflush (stdout);

    printf ("VMSTAT %d second intervals.\n", INTERVAL);
    fflush (stdout);

    sprintf (buff, "vmstat %d 2",INTERVAL);

    system (buff);
}
```

It is necessary to flush standard output with `fflush` because the order of output might be wrong if you don't. For example, the `Content-type:` section of the header might come *after* the vmstat output. Notice that the content type (or MIME type) is text/plain. Why? It could be anything. The plug-in makes a call to NPN_GetURL with a NULL window parameter, which guarantees that the plug-in will get the resulting URL data regardless of the MIME type.

Take note of the header printf:

```
printf ("Content-type: text/plain%c%c", 10,10);
```

Those two decimal 10s produce two line feeds, which are needed for a proper HTTP header. After this header, any output that the program generates goes to the Web Browser. In this case, it is the vmstat output.

The Plug-In Entry Points

You'll notice a familiar file in the CPU monitor plug-in called npshell.cpp. This file contains the entry points for the plug-in. It is very much similar to the audio plug-in's npshell.cpp.

Of the standard plug-in API entry points, NPP_Initialize, NPP_Shutdown, NPP_WriteReady, and NPP_Print are not used by the plug-in.

NPP_New

During the NPP_New API, the plug-in allocates a CCpuMon object with the new operator, saves it to Netscape's NPP structure, and saves the mode. Nothing is done with the HTML attributes for embedded plug-ins.

```
//
// NPP_New - Create a new plug-in instance.
//
NPError NP_LOADDS NPP_New (NPMIMEType pluginType,
    NPP pInstance,
    uint16 mode,
    int16 argc,
    char* argn[],
    char* argv[],
    NPSavedData* saved)
{
    if (pInstance == NULL)
        return NPERR_INVALID_INSTANCE_ERROR;

    // Create a new CCpuMon object

    CCpuMon* pCpuMon = new CCpuMon (pInstance);

    // Attach it to the instance structure

    pInstance->pdata = pCpuMon;

    // No window yet

    pCpuMon->pWindow = NULL;
```

```
    // Save our plug-in's mode

    pCpuMon->mode = mode;

    return NPERR_NO_ERROR;
}
```

NPP_Destroy

The NPP_Destroy method is typical of the audio plug-in in which the window is unsubclassed, and then its cleanup method is called and deleted. After that, the CCpuMon object is closed and deleted:

```
//
// NPP_Destroy - Destroy our plug-in instance.
//
NPError NP_LOADDS NPP_Destroy (NPP pInstance, NPSavedData** save)
{
    CCpuMon* pCpuMon = (CCpuMon *)pInstance->pdata;

    if (pCpuMon)
    {
        if (pCpuMon->pWindow)
        {
            // Unsubclass the window, clean it up and delete it.

            pCpuMon->pWindow->UnsubclassWindow ();
            pCpuMon->pWindow->CleanupWindow();

            delete pCpuMon->pWindow;
        }

        pCpuMon->Close ();

        delete pCpuMon;
        pInstance->pdata = NULL;
    }
    return NPERR_NO_ERROR;
}
```

NPP_SetWindow

The NPP_SetWindow method is identical to the audio plug-in sample. Instance data is retrieved, and during the first call, a CPluginWindow object is created and subclassed to the Navigator-created plug-in window. After this, the window is initialized with a call to CPluginWindow::InitWindow.

```
//
// NPP_SetWindow - A window was created, resized, or destroyed.
//
NPError NP_LOADDS NPP_SetWindow (NPP pInstance, NPWindow* window)
{
    if (!window)
        return NPERR_GENERIC_ERROR;
```

```
    if (!pInstance)
        return NPERR_INVALID_INSTANCE_ERROR;

    // Get instance data

    CCpuMon* pCpuMon = (CCpuMon *)pInstance->pdata;

    if (!pCpuMon)
        return NPERR_GENERIC_ERROR;

    // Spurious entry - just return

    if (!window->window && !pCpuMon->pWindow)
        return NPERR_NO_ERROR;

    // Window should have been destroyed, but because of a bug in
    // Navigator, we consider this a spurious entry.

    if (!window->window && pCpuMon->pWindow)
        return NPERR_NO_ERROR;

    if (!pCpuMon->pWindow && window->window)
    {
        // Create our plug-in's window class and
        // subclass it to Navigators.

        pCpuMon->pWindow = new CPluginWindow (pCpuMon);

        BOOL rc = pCpuMon->pWindow->SubclassWindow ((HWND)window->window);

        // Init window and give the object a pointer to
        // the cpu monitor object.

        pCpuMon->pWindow->InitWindow ();
    }

    // Redraw the window.

    pCpuMon->pWindow->InvalidateRect (NULL);
    pCpuMon->pWindow->UpdateWindow();

    return NPERR_NO_ERROR;
}
```

NPP_NewStream

In NPP_NewStream, the stype is set to NP_ASFILE. This allows the use of NPP_StreamAsFile. The CCpuMon object is opened with CCpuMon::Open.

```
//
// NPP_NewStream - A new stream was created.
//
NPError NP_LOADDS NPP_NewStream(NPP pInstance,
    NPMIMEType type,
    NPStream* pStream,
```

```
        NPBool seekable,
        uint16* stype)
{
    if(!pInstance)
        return NPERR_INVALID_INSTANCE_ERROR;

    CCpuMon* pCpuMon = (CCpuMon *)pInstance->pdata;

    *stype = NP_ASFILE;

    if (pCpuMon)
        pCpuMon->Open (pStream);

    return NPERR_NO_ERROR;
}
```

NPP_WriteReady **and** NPP_Write

Although NPP_WriteReady and NPP_Write are not really used, this plug-in returns a large value to NPP_WriteReady so that the Navigator will write data. NPP_Write just returns the length written and does nothing with the data. You can still use these methods even with a file-based plug-in.

```
//
// NPP_WriteReady - Returns amount of data we can handle for the next NPP_Write
//
int32 NP_LOADDS    NPP_WriteReady (NPP pInstance, NPStream *stream)
{
    return 0x0FFFFFFF;
}

//
// NPP_Write
//
int32 NP_LOADDS NPP_Write (NPP pInstance,
    NPStream *stream,
    int32 offset,
    int32 len,
    void *buffer)
{
    return len;
}
```

NPP_StreamAsFile

The plug-in has been waiting for the name of the file containing data in Navigator's file cache. Here CCpuMon::GotFileName is called to process this file.

```
//
// NPP_StreamAsFile
//
void NP_LOADDS NPP_StreamAsFile (NPP pInstance,
    NPStream* stream,
    const char* fname)
```

```
{
    CCpuMon* pCpuMon = (CCpuMon *)pInstance->pdata;

    if (pCpuMon)
        pCpuMon->GotFileName (fname);
}
```

NPP_DestroyStream

`CCpuMon::EndOfStream` is called during `NPP_DestroyStream`. This plug-in doesn't really care when the stream ends. The call was made for any future implementation.

```
//
// NPP_DestroyStream
//
NPError NP_LOADDS NPP_DestroyStream (NPP pInstance,
    NPStream *stream,
    NPError reason)
{
    CCpuMon* pCpuMon = (CCpuMon *)pInstance->pdata;

    if (pCpuMon)
        pCpuMon->EndOfStream ();

    return NPERR_NO_ERROR;
}
```

The Main Object: CCpuMon

The `CCpuMon` class is the central controller for the plug-in. Its methods are called from both npshell.cpp and `CPluginWindow`. Some of these methods are just stubs for future code. The methods are as follows:

> CCpuMon::CCpuMon
>
> CCpuMon::~CCpuMon
>
> CCpuMon::Open
>
> CCpuMon::EndOfStream
>
> CCpuMon::GotFileName
>
> CCpuMon::RequestUpdate
>
> CCpuMon::Close

Construction and Destruction

The constructor for `CCpuMon` gets a pointer to the Navigator instance structure, NPP. This reference is needed for a future call to NPN_GetURL. The destructor does nothing.

```
//
// Constructor - Initialize variables. Get the instance pointer for any
//               NPN type calls.
//
CCpuMon::CCpuMon (NPP pInstance)
{
    this->pInstance = pInstance;

    bRunningCGIProgram = FALSE;
}

//
// Destructor
//
CCpuMon::~CCpuMon ()
{
}
```

Open

The Open method is called from npshell.cpp during the NPP_NewStream API. This method saves a pointer to the stream instance structure, NPStream. The stream reference is never used.

```
//
// Open - Get ready for data, called from Netscape's NPP_NewStream
//
BOOL CCpuMon::Open (NPStream* pStream)
{
    this->pStream = pStream;

    return TRUE;
}
```

EndOfStream

The CCpuMon::EndOfStream method is called during the NPP_DestroyStream API. It is not currently used.

```
//
// EndOfStream - Called from NPP_DestroyStream. The stream is done. Our plug-in
//               has all the data.
//
BOOL CCpuMon::EndOfStream (void)
{
    // CPU Monitor is file based, just return.

    return TRUE;
}
```

Getting the Filename

A call to the method CCpuMon::GotFileName is made during the NPP_StreamAsFile API. The filename and path are provided during the call. This file can live in either Netscape's file cache or another directory, depending on where the file was opened. If the file was opened locally, there is no need to cache and the real file path is given.

During the life of the CPU Monitor plug-in, GotFileName is called at least two times. In both cases, the file is first opened using fopen. The first file is the one that started the plug-in. This file must have the appropriate MIME type extension for this plug-in. Within this file must be the URL of the CGI program. This URL is retrieved using fgets, after which the newline character is stripped. The URL is stored in ProgramURL, and NPN_GetURL is called.

The plug-in knows that it is the second call or greater when the bRunningCGIProgram flag is set to TRUE. If it is set to TRUE, CPluginWindow::UpdateChart is called to draw the CPU bar chart.

```
//
// GotFileName - Called from NPP_StreamAsFile with a local filename
//
BOOL CCpuMon::GotFileName (const char* fname)
{
    // Open the file in ASCII read only

    FILE* fp = fopen (fname, "r");

    if (fp)
    {
        if (bRunningCGIProgram)
        {
            // CGI program is running, update the chart

            pWindow->UpdateChart (fp);
            fclose (fp);

            return TRUE;
        }

        if (fgets (ProgramURL, sizeof(ProgramURL), fp))
        {
            // The first file starts us. It must contain the URL
            // for the CGI program.

            fclose (fp);

            char* p = strchr(ProgramURL, '\n');  // Remove newline

            if (p)
                *p = NULL;

            // Flag the CGI program as running and get the URL

            bRunningCGIProgram = TRUE;
```

```
            NPError rc = NPN_GetURL (pInstance, ProgramURL, NULL);
        }
    }

    return TRUE;
}
```

Manually Updating the CPU Bar Chart

The user of the CPU monitor plug-in can continuously update the bar chart by clicking on the Update button. Each button click resolves to a CPluginWindow::OnUpdate, which then calls CCpuMon::RequestUpdate. This method calls NPN_GetURL with the CGI program's URL. Remember that NPN_GetURL is an asynchronous call, so multiple update requests can be queued. Try clicking the Update button really fast. It can be quite entertaining!

```
//
// RequestUpdate - Called from CPluginWindow::OnUpdate when the update button
//                 is clicked.
//
BOOL CCpuMon::RequestUpdate (void)
{
    if (!bRunningCGIProgram)
        return FALSE;

    NPError rc = NPN_GetURL (pInstance, ProgramURL, NULL);

    if (rc)
        return FALSE;

    return TRUE;
}
```

Close

CCpuMon::Close is not used, but it is provided for future implementation.

```
//
// Close - Called from NPP_Destroy. This plug-in instance is history. Free
//         all resources.
//
BOOL CCpuMon::Close (void)
{
    return TRUE;
}
```

The Window Object: CPluginWindow

The CPluginWindow object is used to subclass to the Navigator-created plug-in window. This object creates and deletes the Update button for user interaction. It parses the vmstat data and displays it on a bar chart in the window. The methods in this class are as follows:

```
CPluginWindow::CPluginWindow

CPluginWindow::~CPluginWindow
```

```
CPluginWindow::InitWindow

CPluginWindow::CleanupWindow

CPluginWindow::UpdateChart

CPluginWindow::DrawRects

CPluginWindow::OnPaint
```

Construction and Destruction

The constructor saves a pointer to CCpuMon for calls resulting from clicking the Update button. The vmstat structure is zeroed during construction. Nothing is done during destruction.

```
//
// Constructor
//
CPluginWindow::CPluginWindow (CCpuMon *pCpuMon)
{
    this->pCpuMon = pCpuMon;

    memset (&vmstat, 0, sizeof(VMSTAT));
}

//
// Destructor
//
CPluginWindow::~CPluginWindow()
{
}
```

Window Initialization and Cleanup

InitWindow and CleanupWindow are called from npshell.cpp. The InitWindow method creates a CButton for the Update button, and CleanupWindow deletes it.

```
//
// InitWindow - Create the button
//
void CPluginWindow::InitWindow()
{
    CRect rect(30,70,110,110);
    cbUpdate = new CButton();
    cbUpdate->Create("Update",
        BS_PUSHBUTTON | WS_VISIBLE,
        rect,
        this,
        ID_UPDATE_CHART);
}

//
// CleanupWindow - Delete the button
//
void CPluginWindow::CleanupWindow ()
{
    delete cbUpdate;
}
```

Parsing vmstat Data

UpdateChart is called from CCpuMon::GotFileName with a pointer to the file containing the raw vmstat output. A beep is produced so that the user knows when the update is complete. The vmstat data is generated from the CGI program discussed previously. The data looks something like this:

```
VMSTAT 1 second interval
 procs     memory              page                disk         faults       cpu
 r b w   avm   fre  re at  pi  po  fr  de  sr d0 s1 s2 s3  in  sy  cs us sy id
 2 0 0     0   292   0  5   2   0   0   0  16  4  8 10  0 222 607 133 20 25 55
 2 0 0     0   292   1  6  40  20  84   0  40  0  7  0  0 357 662 174 46 25 28
```

The first line in the data block is checked for the VMSTAT signature, after which the fifth line is retrieved by five calls to fgets:

```
//
// UpdateChart - Parse out the vmstat data
//
BOOL CPluginWindow::UpdateChart (FILE* fp)
{
    MessageBeep (0xFFFFFFFF);

    // Read five lines from the file

    for (int i=0; i<5; i++)
    {
        // First line should contain the VMSTAT signiture

        if (fgets (FileLine, sizeof(FileLine), fp))
        {
            if (i == 0)
                if (strncmp(FileLine, "VMSTAT", sizeof("VMSTAT")-1))
                    return FALSE;
        }
    }
```

After the data of interest is safely stored in FileLine, a Herculean call to sscanf parses the vmstat line:

```
    // Parse out the vmstat data

    sscanf (FileLine, "%d %d %d %d %d %d %d %d %d %d %d %d %d %d %d %d %d %d
%d %d %d %d",
        &vmstat.r, &vmstat.b, &vmstat.w,      // Threads
        &vmstat.avm, &vmstat.fre,     // Memory
        &vmstat.re, &vmstat.at, &vmstat.pi, &vmstat.po,  // Pages
        &vmstat.fr, &vmstat.de,// Pages
   &vmstat.sr, &vmstat.d0, &vmstat.s1, &vmstat.s2, &vmstat.s3, // Pages
        &vmstat.interrupts, &vmstat.syscalls, &vmstat.contextswitch,  // Faults
        &vmstat.user, &vmstat.system, &vmstat.idle);    // CPU
```

Finally, the numbers are multiplied to make future math easier, and the DrawRects method is called to draw the bar chart.

```
    // Make the numbers bigger

    vmstat.user *= 4;
    vmstat.system *= 4;
```

```
    vmstat.idle *= 4;

    CDC* dc = GetDC ();

    DrawRects (dc);

    ReleaseDC (dc);

    return TRUE;
}
```

Drawing the Bar Chart

The method `CPluginWindow::DrawRects` first draws each colored rectangle in proportion to the CPU percentage. Brushes of red, green, and blue are created and selected into the device context. A call to `CDC::Rectangle` draws the colored rectangle:

```
//
// DrawRects - Draw the CPU Monitor bar chart and color keys
//
void CPluginWindow::DrawRects(CDC* dc)
{
    // Draw the bar chart

    CBrush br(RGB(0xFF,0,0));
    dc->SelectObject (br);
    dc->Rectangle (10, 10, vmstat.user+10, 60);

    CBrush br2(RGB(0,0xFF,0));
    dc->SelectObject (br2);
    dc->Rectangle (vmstat.user+10, 10, vmstat.user+vmstat.system+10, 60);

    CBrush br3(RGB(0,0,0xFF));
    dc->SelectObject (br3);
    dc->Rectangle (vmstat.user+vmstat.system+10, 10,
        vmstat.user+vmstat.system+vmstat.idle+10, 60);
```

After the proportional rectangles are drawn, color key rectangles are drawn:

```
    // Draw the color keys

    CRect rect(120,70,200,110);
    dc->SelectObject (br);
    dc->Rectangle (&rect);
    dc->SetBkColor (RGB(0xFF,0,0));
    dc->DrawText ("User", strlen("User"), &rect,
        DT_CENTER | DT_VCENTER | DT_SINGLELINE);

    rect.SetRect(210,70,290,110);
    dc->SelectObject (br2);
    dc->Rectangle (&rect);
    dc->SetBkColor (RGB(0,0xFF,0));
    dc->DrawText ("System", strlen("System"), &rect,
        DT_CENTER | DT_VCENTER | DT_SINGLELINE);

    rect.SetRect(300,70,380,110);
    dc->SelectObject (br3);
    dc->Rectangle (&rect);
```

```
dc->SetBkColor (RGB(0,0,0xFF));
dc->DrawText ("Idle", strlen("Idle"), &rect,
    DT_CENTER ¦ DT_VCENTER ¦ DT_SINGLELINE);
}
```

Handling the Update Button

When the Update button is clicked, a call is made to `OnUpdate`. This method calls into `CCpuMon::RequestUpdate` with the previously saved pointer:

```
//
// OnUpdate - The "Update" button was clicked
//
void CPluginWindow::OnUpdate()
{
    if (pCpuMon)
        if (!pCpuMon->RequestUpdate ())
            AfxMessageBox ("Can't update now !");
}
```

Repainting the Window

The `WM_PAINT` message is handled by `OnPaint` in which the bar chart is redrawn:

```
//
// OnPaint - Redraw bar chart
//
void CPluginWindow::OnPaint()
{
    PAINTSTRUCT ps;

    CDC* dc = BeginPaint (&ps);

    DrawRects (dc);

    EndPaint (&ps);
}
```

Setting Up and Running the CPU Monitor Plug-In

The CPU Monitor plug-in requires quite a bit of setup to run. For one thing, you need have access to a Web Server's CGI file area. Then, upload the included `unixprog.c` and compile with `cc` or whatever is available. Move the executable to a CGI directory and determine what the correct URL path is to execute the program. This plug-in was developed using the following CGI program URL:

```
http://www.swcp.com/zan-bin/vmstat.cgi
```

After you have determined the correct URL to run the CGI program, create a text file with that URL in it. Currently, this plug-in uses the MIME type of `application/x-tex`, so the file extension should be .TEX. To use this MIME type, create the text file with this extension. You should end up with a URL looking something like this:

```
http://www.swcp.com/~zan/cpumon.tex
```

Now open `cpumon.tex` in the Navigator. The plug-in should load and immediately try to run the CGI program. You can embed the plug-in in a Web page. Here is a very simple example of the plug-in embedded in HTML code:

```
<html>
<body>

<h1 align=center>CPU Monitor Plug-in</h1>

<center><p><embed SRC=cpumon.tex WIDTH=420 HEIGHT=120></p></center>

</body>
</html>
```

The Navigator with an embedded version of the CPU Monitor plug-in should look something like the one shown in Figure 19.2. You can see the bar chart with different colors for User, System, and Idle CPU percentage in addition to the Update button.

Figure 19.2.
The CPU Monitor plug-in running in embedded mode.

Conclusion

The sample CPU Monitor plug-in shows a good example of using Navigator's `NPP_GetURL` API. This API communicates with a small CGI program written in C that executes the UNIX `vmstat` program. The output of `vmstat` is given back to the plug-in with a file in Netscape's cache. This output is parsed and displayed with a bar chart on the plug-in window.

What's Next?

The next chapter shows how to use the Microsoft Windows MCIWnd window class to create highly functional, yet simple to code, plug-ins. With very little code, this sample plug-in supports AVI video, WAV audio, and MIDI playback.

CHAPTER 20

A Plug-In with MCIWnd

Introduction

Many media types can be easily supported in your plug-in through the use of MCIWnd. MCIWnd is a window class for controlling multimedia devices. This window class is composed of macros, messages, and functions that provide a simple way for an application to add multimedia capabilities.

When you use MCIWnd, you don't really need to subclass the plug-in window. The MCIWndCreate function takes the plug-in window handle as a parameter and creates another window for media playback. Controls for playback are provided by MCIWnd, avoiding the need for subclassing.

The NPMCIWND plug-in sample supports AVI video, WAV audio, and MIDI playback with the default controls provided by MCIWnd. Because the plug-in window is not subclassed, all playback controls are handled by MCIWnd.

Where to Find the Files

All the necessary files for building NPMCIWND.DLL are located on the CD-ROM. These files are in the \CODE\MCIWND, \CODE\INC, and \CODE\COMMON directories. You will need the files shown in the following lists.

For the directory \CODE\MCIWND, you need these files:

- npshell.cpp: Plug-in entry point methods
- npmciwnd.cpp, npmciwnd.h: The MCIWnd class CMCIWnd
- npmciwnd.def: DLL module definition file
- npmciwnd.rc: Resources
- npmciwnd.mak: The makefile for Microsoft Visual C++

For the directory \CODE\INC, you need these files:

- npapi.h: Plug-in API prototypes and associated structures
- npupp.h: Plug-in API prototypes
- stdafx.h: Standard include files

For the directory \CODE\COMMON, you need these files:

- npwin.cpp: DLL entry point to plug-in API mapping
- stdafx.cpp: Includes standard include files

The Design of the MCIWnd Plug-In

The MCIWnd plug-in's design is quite simple. Aside from common code, only two small source files are required for this plug-in: npmciwnd.cpp and npshell.cpp. The file npwindow.cpp, which is used in many other sample plug-ins in this book, is not required because this plug-in does not subclass Navigator's plug-in window.

This plug-in is file-based. That is, it sets stype to NP_ASFILE during the NPP_NewStream method. NPP_WriteReady and NPP_Write return the standard values for a file-based plug-in, and all processing is done during NPP_StreamAsFile when the file is completely in cache.

As in the CPU Plug-in Sample, the MCIWnd plug-in's class CMCIWnd has a method called GotFileName. This is called during NPP_StreamAsFile to handle processing the file in Navigator's cache. During this method, a new MCIWnd window is created with a call to MCIWndCreate. The sample plug-in currently supports AVI, WAV, and MIDI. A different window and control set are created depending on the type of the file. This sample can support any MCI device by just adding the appropriate MIME type to its resource.

Figure 20.1 shows the MCIWnd plug-in's components. Notice that only one class is used: CMCIWnd. Also note that the MCI drivers communicate directly with the plug-in window.

Figure 20.1.
The components of the MCIWnd *plug-in.*

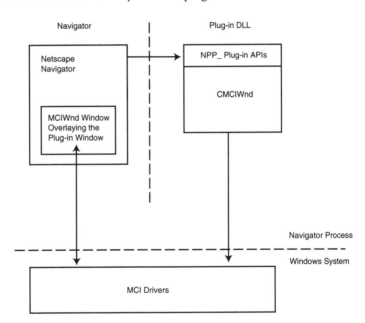

Multiple MIME Types

The MCIWnd sample plug-in supports three MIME types. These types are denoted by "MIMEType" in the plug-in's resource file npmciwnd.rc2. Vertical bars are used to separate each type:

```
VALUE "MIMEType", "video/x-msvideo¦audio/x-wav¦audio/x-midi\0"
```

Each MIME type has an appropriate file extension. In this case, they are AVI, WAV, and MID:

```
VALUE "FileExtents", "avi¦wav¦mid\0"
```

> **TIP**
>
> Remember that if the extension is not registered on the HTTP server to an appropriate MIME type, Navigator does not get the Content-type: designator in the HTTP header. This means your plug-in will load with a local file, but not with an HTTP server file.

Vertical bars also separate the names for the Files of type: section of the file open dialog. With this plug-in are Video, Audio, and MIDI:

```
VALUE "FileOpenName", "Video (*.avi)¦Audio (*.wav)¦MIDI (*.mid)\0"
```

Plug-In Entry Points

As with any plug-in, this sample must handle all of the NPP_ entry points. By handling, you can just return the proper value (if any). The MCIWnd sample uses npshell.cpp to support the standard plug-in API entry points.

Of these, NPP_Initialize, NPP_Shutdown, and NPP_Print simply return without executing any code. NPP_WriteReady and NPP_Write return the proper values to allow for a file-based plug-in.

NPP_New

The NPP_New method creates a CMCIWnd object and attaches a pointer referencing this object to Navigator's instance structure. In addition, the mode is saved. Plug-in instance data is stored in the CMCIWnd object. The parameters argc, argn, and argv, which hold the EMBED tag line attributes, are not parsed in this example.

```
//
// NPP_New - Create a new plug-in instance.
//
NPError NP_LOADDS NPP_New (NPMIMEType pluginType,
    NPP pInstance,
    uint16 mode,
    int16 argc,
    char* argn[],
    char* argv[],
    NPSavedData* saved)
{
    if (pInstance == NULL)
        return NPERR_INVALID_INSTANCE_ERROR;

    // Create a new CMCIWnd object

    CMCIWnd* pMCIWnd = new CMCIWnd (pInstance);

    // Attach it to the instance structure

    pInstance->pdata = pMCIWnd;

    // Save our plug-in's mode
```

```
        pMCIWnd->mode = mode;

        return NPERR_NO_ERROR;
}
```

NPP_Destroy

The plug-in instance is destroyed by a call to NPP_Destroy. During this method, the CMCIWnd object is simply deleted. The destructor of CMCIWnd makes a call to MCIWndDestroy, which closes the MCI device. The instance data pointer pInstance->pdata is set to NULL as a precaution.

```
//
// NPP_Destroy - Destroy our plug-in instance.
//
NPError NP_LOADDS NPP_Destroy (NPP pInstance, NPSavedData** save)
{
        CMCIWnd* pMCIWnd = (CMCIWnd *)pInstance->pdata;

        if (pMCIWnd)
        {
                delete pMCIWnd;
                pInstance->pdata = NULL;
        }
        return NPERR_NO_ERROR;
}
```

NPP_SetWindow

Because there is no subclassing in this plug-in, NPP_SetWindow is quite different from other plug-ins. After the standard checks for the NULL parameter and spurious entries, the Navigator-provided plug-in window handle is saved in the CMCIWnd object. If the handle was already saved, the method CMCIWnd::UpdateWindow is called to redraw the MCIWnd and controls.

```
//
// NPP_SetWindow - Just get the window handle.
//
NPError NP_LOADDS NPP_SetWindow (NPP pInstance, NPWindow* window)
{
        if (!window)
                return NPERR_GENERIC_ERROR;

        if (!pInstance)
                return NPERR_INVALID_INSTANCE_ERROR;

        CMCIWnd* pMCIWnd = (CMCIWnd *)pInstance->pdata;

        if (!pMCIWnd)
                return NPERR_GENERIC_ERROR;

        // Spurious entry - just return

        if (!window->window && !pMCIWnd->hNavigatorWnd)
                return NPERR_NO_ERROR;

        // Get Navigator's window handle
```

```
        if (window->window)
        {
            if (!pMCIWnd->hNavigatorWnd)
                pMCIWnd->hNavigatorWnd = (HWND)window->window;
            else
            {
                pMCIWnd->UpdateWindow (pMCIWnd->hNavigatorWnd);
            }
        }
        return NPERR_NO_ERROR;
}
```

NPP_NewStream

When NPP_NewStream is called, this plug-in sets *stype to NP_ASFILE. This sets up for a file-based plug-in and a future call to NPP_StreamAsFile. The CMCIWnd::Open method is called to notify the object of a new stream.

```
//
// NPP_NewStream - A new stream was created.
//
NPError NP_LOADDS NPP_NewStream(NPP pInstance,
    NPMIMEType type,
    NPStream* pStream,
    NPBool seekable,
    uint16* stype)
{
    if(!pInstance)
        return NPERR_INVALID_INSTANCE_ERROR;

    CMCIWnd* pMCIWnd = (CMCIWnd *)pInstance->pdata;

    *stype = NP_ASFILE;

    if (pMCIWnd)
        pMCIWnd->Open (pStream);

    return NPERR_NO_ERROR;
}
```

NPP_WriteReady and NPP_Write

Like most file-based plug-ins, NPP_WriteReady and NPP_Write are not really used. A large value is returned during NPP_WriteReady to tell Navigator that the plug-in can handle any buffer size. Calls to NPP_Write just return the length.

```
//
// NPP_WriteReady - Returns amount of data we can handle for the next NPP_Write
//
int32 NP_LOADDS    NPP_WriteReady (NPP pInstance, NPStream *stream)
{
    return 0x0FFFFFFF;
}

//
// NPP_Write
//
```

```
int32 NP_LOADDS NPP_Write (NPP pInstance, NPStream *stream,
    int32 offset, int32 len, void *buffer)
{
    return len;
}
```

> **NOTE**
>
> To improve performance, use NPN_Version and check whether the minor version is greater than or equal to 8. If so, Navigator 3.0 is running (Atlas) and you can use NP_ASFILEONLY instead of NP_ASFILE in the preceding NPP_NewStream example. By using this new type, you avoid streaming the file if it is already on a local drive or network. This dramatically improves performance for very large multimedia data files often used with MCIWnd. NPP_WriteReady and NPP_Write are not called with NP_ASFILEONLY. See Chapter 10, "Stream Creation and Destruction," for more information on NP_ASFILEONLY.

NPP_StreamAsFile

When the file is ready for the plug-in, NPP_StreamAsFile is called with the filename. This file might be in either Navigator cache or another directory, depending on the origination. The method CMCIWnd::GotFileName is called to start processing the file.

```
//
// NPP_StreamAsFile
//
void NP_LOADDS NPP_StreamAsFile (NPP pInstance,
    NPStream* stream,
    const char* fname)
{
    CMCIWnd* pMCIWnd = (CMCIWnd *)pInstance->pdata;

    if (pMCIWnd)
        pMCIWnd->GotFileName (fname);
}
```

NPP_DestroyStream

Although this plug-in doesn't need to know when the stream is destroyed, a call is made into a stub method, CMCIWnd::EndOfStream, for any future implementation.

```
//
// NPP_DestroyStream
//
NPError NP_LOADDS NPP_DestroyStream (NPP pInstance,
    NPStream *stream,
    NPError reason)
{
    CMCIWnd* pMCIWnd = (CMCIWnd *)pInstance->pdata;

    if (pMCIWnd)
        pMCIWnd->EndOfStream ();
```

```
        return NPERR_NO_ERROR;
}
```

The CMCIWnd Class

The MCIWnd plug-in has a very simple implementation of its main class, CMCIWnd. This class provides for creating, closing, and updating the MCIWnd window. Here are the methods of this class:

    CMCIWnd::CMCIWnd

    CMCIWnd::~CMCIWnd

    CMCIWnd::Open

    CMCIWnd::GotFileName

    CMCIWnd::UpdateWindow

    CMCIWnd::EndOfStream

Construction and Destruction

The CMCIWnd constructor saves the plug-in instance (which is not used) and zeroes out the members hMCIWnd and hNavigatorWnd. The destructor closes the MCIWnd window with a call to MCIWndDestroy. MCIWndDestroy corresponds to a WM_CLOSE message with wParam and lParam set to zero.

```
/
// Constructor
//
CMCIWnd::CMCIWnd (NPP pInstance)
{
    this->pInstance = pInstance;

    hMCIWnd = hNavigatorWnd = NULL;

}

//
// Destructor
//
CMCIWnd::~CMCIWnd()
{
    if (hMCIWnd)
        MCIWndDestroy (hMCIWnd);
}
```

Open

CMCIWnd::Open saves the stream instance pointer, NPStream*. Other than that, it does nothing. Remember that by saving a pointer to the stream, you can look at things such as the URL at any time. Be careful not to reference the stream after it has been destroyed!

```
//
// Open
//
void CMCIWnd::Open (NPStream* pStream)
{
    this->pStream = pStream;
}
```

GotFileName

When a file is ready, the member GotFileName is called. During this call, a new MCIWnd window is created with MCIWndCreate. After creation, there is a small workaround to force a video window to redraw. If MCIWndGetDevice shows a device type of "AVIVideo", the video is stepped forward one frame.

```
//
// GotFileName
//
void CMCIWnd::GotFileName (const char* fname)
{
    // Open the MCIWnd file

    if (hMCIWnd = MCIWndCreate (hNavigatorWnd, 0, NULL, fname))
    {
        char DeviceName[256];

        if (!MCIWndGetDevice (hMCIWnd, DeviceName, sizeof(DeviceName)))
            if (!strcmp (DeviceName, "AVIVideo"))
                MCIWndStep (hMCIWnd, 1);  // Step because of a bug in MCIWnd
    }
}
```

UpdateWindow

A call to the UpdateWindow method originates from the NPP_SetWindow API. NPP_SetWindow is called when the window needs to be redrawn. During the Updatewindow method, a call to SetWindowPos is made, which forces the Navigator-created plug-in window to the bottom of the z-order. This allows the MCIWnd created window to remain on top.

Additionally, the plug-in window's rectangle is invalidated and updated.

```
//
// UpdateWindow
//
void CMCIWnd::UpdateWindow (HWND hWnd)
{
    RECT rect;

    SetWindowPos (hWnd, HWND_BOTTOM, 0,0,0,0, SWP_NOMOVE | SWP_NOSIZE);

    GetWindowRect (hWnd, &rect);
    InvalidateRect (hWnd, &rect, TRUE);

    ::UpdateWindow (hWnd);
}
```

EndOfStream

`CMciWnd::EndOfStream` does nothing and is provided for any future code.

```
//
// EndOfStream
//
void CMCIWnd::EndOfStream ()
{
}
```

A Bit about `MCIWnd`

`MCIWnd` makes using Windows multimedia devices a simple task. Full motion video can be displayed, complete with controls, by a quick call to `MCIWndCreate`. Other than that, you only need to call `MCIWndDestroy` to close the device.

Although it is simple to use, `MCIWnd` is quite flexible. The following lists cover all of the functions, messages, and macros that can be used with `MCIWnd`.

Window Management

```
MCIWndChangeStyles
MCIWndCreate
MCIWndGetStyles
MCIWndRegisterClass
```

File and Device Management

```
MCIWndClose
MCIWndDestroy
MCIWndEject
MCIWndNew
MCIWndOpen
MCIWndOpenDialog
MCIWndSave
MCIWndSaveDialog
```

Playback Options

```
MCIWndGetRepeat
MCIWndPlay
MCIWndPlayFrom
MCIWndPlayFromTo
MCIWndPlayReverse
MCIWndPlayTo
MCIWndSetRepeat
```

Recording

MCIWndRecord

Positioning

MCIWndEnd

MCIWndGetEnd

MCIWndGetLength

MCIWndGetPosition

MCIWndGetPositionString

MCIWndGetStart

MCIWndHome

MCIWndSeek

MCIWndStep

Pause and Resume Playback

MCIWndGetRepeat

MCIWndPlay

MCIWndPlayFrom

MCIWndPlayFromTo

MCIWndPlayReverse

MCIWndPlayTo

MCIWndSetRepeat

Performance Tuning

MCIWndGetSpeed

MCIWndGetVolume

MCIWndGetZoom

MCIWndSetSpeed

MCIWndSetVolume

MCIWndSetZoom

Image and Palette Adjustments

MCIWndGetDest

MCIWndGetPalette

MCIWndGetSource

MCIWndPutDest

MCIWndPutSource

MCIWndRealize

MCIWndSetPalette

Last Error Retrieval

MCIWndGetError

Event and Error Notification Messages

```
MCIWNDM_NOTIFYERROR
MCIWNDM_NOTIFYMEDIA
MCIWNDM_NOTIFYMODE
MCIWNDM_NOTIFYPOS
MCIWNDM_NOTIFYSIZE
```

Time Formats

```
MCIWndGetTimeFormat
MCIWndSetTimeFormat
MCIWndUseFrames
MCIWndUseTime
MCIWndValidateMedia
```

Status Updates

```
MCIWndGetActiveTimer
MCIWndGetInactiveTimer
MCIWndSetActiveTimer
MCIWndSetInactiveTimer
MCIWndSetTimers
```

Device Capabilities

```
MCIWndCanConfig
MCIWndCanEject
MCIWndCanPlay
MCIWndCanRecord
MCIWndCanSave
MCIWndCanWindow
```

MCI Device Settings

```
MCIWndGetAlias
MCIWndGetDevice
MCIWndGetDeviceID
MCIWndGetFileName
MCIWndGetMode
```

MCI Command-String Interface

```
MCIWndReturnString
MCIWndSendString
```

It looks like Microsoft has everything but the kitchen sink! Feel free to explore MCIWnd and its use in plug-ins. Most MCIWnd calls are very easy to make. For example, this call steps video forward one frame:

```
MCIWndStep (hMCIWnd, 1)
```

You can also create an MCIWnd window without any default controls and make your own controls using the plug-in subclassed window technique discussed in Chapter 17, "A Streaming Audio Sample."

Running the Plug-In

The MCIWnd plug-in is fun to run and enhance. Sliders are provided for seeking, which allows users to randomly scan through media. The video window has controls for scaling, volume, and speed. You can even copy an image to the clipboard or send a string to the MCI device.

A good example of this plug-in's capabilities is shown by embedding all three media types—AVI, WAV, and MIDI—into a single Web page. The following HTML code does this:

```
<html>
<body>

<Body Background="blue_pap.gif">

<h1 align=center>MCIWnd Based Plug-in</h1>

<h2 align=center>Video</h2>

<center><p><embed SRC=sample.avi WIDTH=322 HEIGHT=268></p></center>

<h2 align=center>Wave Audio</h2>

<center><p><embed SRC=outofb.wav WIDTH=300 HEIGHT=28></p></center>

<h2 align=center>MIDI</h2>

<center><p><embed SRC=canyon.mid WIDTH=300 HEIGHT=28></p></center>

</body>
</html>
```

The result of this code should look something like what you see in Figure 20.2.

Figure 20.2.

The MCIWnd *plug-in sample running video, audio, and MIDI.*

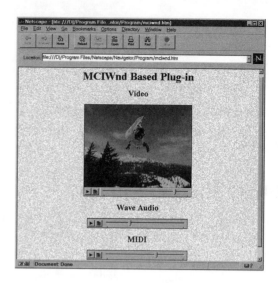

Conclusion

Use MCIWnd to make a full-featured MCI device plug-in capable of supporting multiple data types. The MCIWnd window class is flexible, yet easy to use. You don't have to subclass the Navigator-created plug-in window if you use MCIWnd.

Because the MCIWnd sample plug-in has no use for MFC, it is not linked in. This results in a very small plug-in with huge functionality! Compiled as a retail build (without debugging information), this plug-in is less than 25KB. Not a bad deal for a user, considering it can be downloaded in less than 15 seconds.

What's Next?

Plug-ins can be hidden using the HIDDEN parameter in a plug-in's HTML embed line. The next chapter explores a background MIDI player implemented as a hidden plug-in.

CHAPTER 21

Using MIDI with a Background Plug-In

Introduction

The release of Netscape Navigator 3.*x* gives plug-ins the capability to run in background mode. Background mode is denoted by NP_BACKGROUND during the NPP_New API. This mode has no plug-in window and is for plug-ins that can perform their duties without the need for user interaction through the Navigator.

The Musical Instrument Device Interface (MIDI) allows for recording musical sequences in very small files. MIDI records the actual note value rather than sampling audio with a waveform digitizer. For example, a middle C on a piano can be represented with a single byte of data. MIDI does have its limitations. You can't record voice, and the audio can sound tinny and unrealistic.

For the purposes of a Web page, MIDI can provide a great enhancement with little increase in system and network resources. Popular games such as DOOM use MIDI as background music with great results. MIDI can also be mixed in real-time with waveform data on most audio cards such as the Sound Blaster. DOOM uses this technique for shotgun blasts and monster roars mixed in with eerie background music.

You can easily mix MIDI with waveform also. To prove this, just bring up the MCIWnd sample with a page that has both a .WAV and .MID file embedded in it. You can then play both at the same time! Try making a plug-in that provides for background MIDI with short waveform riffs intermixed. Use this background MIDI player as a base and add waveform support.

Where to Find the Files

All the necessary files for building NPMIDI.DLL are located on the CD-ROM. These files are in the \CODE\MIDI, \CODE\INC and \CODE\COMMON directories. You will need the files shown in the following lists.

For the directory \CODE\MIDI, you need these files:

- npshell.cpp: Plug-in entry point methods
- npmidi.cpp, npmidi.h: The Cmidi class
- npmidi.def: DLL module definition file
- npmidi.rc: Resources
- npmidi.mak: The makefile for Microsoft Visual C++

For the directory \CODE\INC, you need these files:

- npapi.h: Plug-in API prototypes and associated structures
- npupp.h: Plug-in API prototypes

For the directory \CODE\COMMON, you need this file:

■ npwin.cpp: DLL entry point to plug-in API mapping

The Design of the Background MIDI Plug-In

Because the Background MIDI plug-in runs in the background, no plug-in window is needed. This makes the code much simpler—no subclassing, no window class, and no user interaction. The plug-in APIs are routed directly to a CMidi class, which in turn opens the MIDI MCI driver with MCI_OPEN and plays the file with MCI_PLAY.

This plug-in is implemented as file-based, nonstreaming. Most MIDI files are very small and can be quickly downloaded before playing.

Embedding as Hidden

Aside from NP_HIDDEN, this sample can also be run as NP_FULL or NP_EMBED. In the case of full and embedded modes, Navigator creates the appropriate plug-in window, which the MIDI plug-in totally ignores. You probably will only run a hidden plug-in embedded in a page with the appropriate HIDDEN parameter in your HTML code. This parameter prevents Navigator from creating a plug-in window. Embed the sample like this:

```
<embed SRC=canyon.mid HIDDEN>
```

> **NOTE**
>
> The HIDDEN attribute is one of the many attributes you can use with the EMBED tag. Refer to Chapter 7, "Navigator Plug-In Design Considerations," for more information on using HIDDEN and other attributes.

Components

This sample uses only one class to implement the plug-in. The class, CMidi, is called from the standard plug-in APIs. It opens the MIDI MCI driver and plays the MIDI file. As you can see in Figure 21.1, this plug-in has very little interaction with the Navigator.

Figure 21.1.
The components of the Background MIDI Player plug-in.

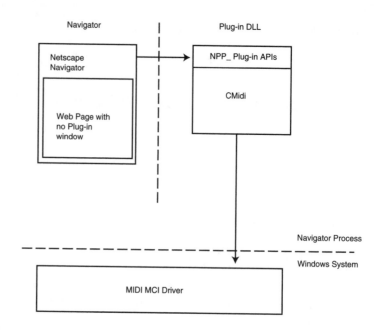

Plug-In Entry Points

Like any plug-in, this one has at least stub code for all plug-in APIs.

Of the methods, only `NPP_New`, `NPP_Destroy`, and `NPP_StreamAsFile` do the work of this sample. The other APIs are provided as either stub code or areas for future enhancement.

NPP_New

The `NPP_New` method creates a `CMidi` object. It passes a pointer to the plug-in's instance, `pInstance`. After that, it saves a pointer to `CMidi` in the Navigator-provided instance structure and saves the mode. The parameters `argc`, `argn`, and `argv`, which would normally contain `EMBED` tag attributes, are not parsed in this example.

```
//
// NPP_New - Create a new plug-in instance.
//
NPError NP_LOADDS NPP_New (NPMIMEType pluginType,
    NPP pInstance,
    uint16 mode,
    int16 argc,
    char* argn[],
    char* argv[],
    NPSavedData* saved)
{
    if (pInstance == NULL)
        return NPERR_INVALID_INSTANCE_ERROR;
```

```
    // Create a new CMidi object

    CMidi* pMidi = new CMidi (pInstance);

    // Attach it to the instance structure

    pInstance->pdata = pMidi;

    // Save our plug-in's mode

    pMidi->mode = mode;

    return NPERR_NO_ERROR;
}
```

NPP_Destroy

This plug-in's instance is destroyed during the NPP_Destroy API. Here, the CMidi object is deleted. Notice the check to make sure that pMidi is not NULL after retrieving it from the Navigator-provided instance structure. Also note that pInstance->pdata is set to NULL after the CMidi object is deleted. Precautions such as these can save your plug-in from trapping in the event of a Navigator calling order error.

```
//
// NPP_Destroy - Destroy our plug-in instance.
//
NPError NP_LOADDS NPP_Destroy (NPP pInstance, NPSavedData** save)
{
    CMidi* pMidi = (CMidi *)pInstance->pdata;

    if (pMidi)
    {
        delete pMidi;
        pInstance->pdata = NULL;
    }
    return NPERR_NO_ERROR;
}
```

NPP_SetWindow

A hidden plug-in is one of the few types in which you can completely ignore the NPP_SetWindow API. As you might remember, the NPP_SetWindow plug-in API allows your plug-in to associate itself with the Navigator-created plug-in window. Because a background plug-in has no window, this method can simply return the following code:

```
//
// NPP_SetWindow - A window was created, resized, or destroyed.
//
NPError NP_LOADDS NPP_SetWindow (NPP pInstance, NPWindow* window)
{
    return NPERR_NO_ERROR;
}
```

NPP_NewStream

When NPP_NewStream is called, this plug-in sets *stype to NP_ASFILE, which sets up for a file-based plug-in and a future call to NPP_StreamAsFile. Navigator 3.0 plug-ins should use NP_ASFILEONLY instead of NP_ASFILE. This flag is documented in Chapter 10, "Stream Creation and Destruction."

After the plug-in type is set, CMidi::Open is called to notify the object of a new stream.

```
//
// NPP_NewStream - A new stream was created.
//
NPError NP_LOADDS NPP_NewStream(NPP pInstance,
    NPMIMEType type,
    NPStream* pStream,
    NPBool seekable,
    uint16* stype)
{
    if(!pInstance)
        return NPERR_INVALID_INSTANCE_ERROR;

    CMidi* pMidi = (CMidi *)pInstance->pdata;

    *stype = NP_ASFILE;

    if (pMidi)
        pMidi->Open (pStream);

    return NPERR_NO_ERROR;
}
```

NPP_WriteReady **and** NPP_Write

Like most file-based plug-ins, NPP_WriteReady and NPP_Write are not really used. A large value is returned during NPP_WriteReady to tell Navigator that the plug-in can handle any buffer size. Calls to NPP_Write just return the length.

```
//
// NPP_WriteReady - Returns amount of data we can handle for the next NPP_Write
//
int32 NP_LOADDS    NPP_WriteReady (NPP pInstance, NPStream *stream)
{
    return 0x0FFFFFFF;
}

//
// NPP_Write
//
int32 NP_LOADDS NPP_Write (NPP pInstance,
    NPStream *stream,
    int32 offset,
    int32 len,
    void *buffer)
{
    return len;
}
```

NPP_StreamAsFile

When the file is ready for the plug-in, NPP_StreamAsFile is called with the filename. This file can be in either Navigator cache or another directory, depending on its origin. The method CMidi::GotFileName is called to start processing the file.

```
//
// NPP_StreamAsFile
//
void NP_LOADDS NPP_StreamAsFile (NPP pInstance,
    NPStream* stream,
    const char* fname)
{
    CMidi* pMidi = (CMidi *)pInstance->pdata;

    if (pMidi)
        pMidi->GotFileName (fname);
}
```

NPP_DestroyStream

Although the NPP_DestroyStream plug-in doesn't need to know when the stream is destroyed, a call is made into a stub method, CMidi::EndOfStream, for any future implementation.

```
//
// NPP_DestroyStream
//
NPError NP_LOADDS NPP_DestroyStream (NPP pInstance,
    NPStream *stream,
    NPError reason)
{
    CMidi* pMidi = (CMidi *)pInstance->pdata;

    if (pMidi)
        pMidi->EndOfStream ();

    return NPERR_NO_ERROR;
}
```

The CMidi Class

The Background MIDI Sample plug-in uses a class called CMidi to implement its main tasks. These tasks include opening, playing, and closing the MIDI file/device. MIDI playback is controlled through the use of the Windows Media Control Interface (MCI). The following are the methods of this class:

```
CMidi::CMidi

CMidi::~CMidi

CMidi::Open

CMidi::GotFileName

CMidi::EndofStream
```

Construction and Destruction

The CMidi constructor saves the plug-in instance (which is not used) and zeroes out the device ID. The destructor closes the MIDI MCI device with a call to mciSendCommand using the MCI_CLOSE flag.

```
//
// Constructor
//
CMidi::CMidi (NPP pInstance)
{
    this->pInstance = pInstance;
    wDeviceID = 0;
}


//
// Destructor
//
CMidi::~CMidi()
{
    MCI_GENERIC_PARMS    Close;

    memset(&Close, 0, sizeof(Close));

    MCIERROR rc = mciSendCommand (wDeviceID,
        MCI_CLOSE,
        MCI_WAIT,
        (ULONG)&Close);
}
```

Open

CMidi::Open saves the stream instance pointer, NPStream*. Additionally, the URL is saved. Although neither of these are used, it's nice to have them around. For example, referring to the URL can tell your plug-in where the file originated (Internet, Intranet, or local drive).

```
//
// Open
void CMidi::Open (NPStream* pStream)
{
//
    this->pStream = pStream;

    strcpy (this->url, pStream->url);
}
```

GotFileName

After the file has been fully downloaded, CMidi::GotFileName is called with the name of that file. This method opens the MIDI MCI device with an element name. The device ID is saved and used to play the MIDI file with MCI_PLAY. Notice that the MCI_PLAY uses an MCI_NOTIFY flag to allow for asynchronous playback.

Normally, you would specify a callback window handle in the MCI_OPEN_PARMS structure's dwCallback member. This window handle allows an MCI driver to post messages to a window indicating device status such as media position, media stopped, and so on. In this example, because the plug-in does not have a window, a notification window is not used. The dwCallback member is set to NULL during a call to memset.

```
//
// GotFileName
//
void CMidi::GotFileName (const char* fname)
{
    // Open the MIDI file

    MCI_OPEN_PARMS Open;

    memset(&Open, 0, sizeof(Open));

    Open.lpstrElementName = fname;

    MCIERROR rc = mciSendCommand (0,
        MCI_OPEN,
        MCI_WAIT | MCI_OPEN_ELEMENT,
        (ULONG)&Open);

    wDeviceID = Open.wDeviceID;

    // Play it async

    MCI_PLAY_PARMS Play;

    memset(&Play, 0, sizeof(Play));

    rc = mciSendCommand (wDeviceID, MCI_PLAY, MCI_NOTIFY, (ULONG)&Play);
}
```

EndOfStream

CMidi::EndOfStream does nothing and is provided for any future code.

```
//
// EndOfStream
//
void CMidi::EndOfStream ()
{
}
```

Running the Plug-In

The MIDI Hidden sample should be run embedded in a page with the HIDDEN attribute specified on the plug-in's command line. This attribute prevents Navigator from creating a plug-in window. The following HTML runs the plug-in in hidden mode:

```
<html>
<body>

<embed SRC=canyon.mid HIDDEN>

<h1 align=center>MIDI Plug-in</h1>

<h2 align=center>This is a hidden plug-in and has no window.</h2>

</body>
</html>
```

Even though this plug-in has no visible aspects, it can really add life to your pages.

Conclusion

MIDI is a great feature to add to Web pages through the use of a MIDI background plug-in. Don't forget that you can mix wave audio with MIDI for some great effects!

Background MIDI is implemented with the `mciSendCommand` Windows API using `MCI_OPEN`, `MCI_PLAY`, and `MCI_CLOSE`. The MIDI music is played asynchronously by using `MCI_NOTIFY` with `MCI_PLAY`. In the `MCI_PLAY_PARMS` structure, `dwCallback` is `0` to prevent the use of a notification window.

What's Next?

This chapter focused on a plug-in without any window, and the next chapter discusses subclassing a plug-in window without using a class library. In the next chapter, the Windows APIs `SetProp` and `GetProp` are used to save and retrieve instance data.

CHAPTER 22

Subclassing without Microsoft's Foundation Class Library

Introduction

Using a class library, such as the Microsoft Foundation Class Library (MFC), for subclassing a Navigator-created plug-in makes the life of a programmer quite simple. A class is derived from CWnd and then subclassed with a call to CWnd::SubclassWindow. This procedure is used in many of the sample plug-ins throughout this book.

In some cases, you might not want to use MFC at all. Whether you want to save on size (statically linking MFC can add well over 50KB to your plug-in) or you just don't have a copy of MFC, it is a straightforward process to subclass without MFC and is worth discussing.

To subclass a window without MFC, you need to use the Windows API SetWindowLong to set and remove a subclassing procedure. This procedure intercepts window messages destined for the plug-in window and can call the old window proc in many cases. Your plug-in's instance data is associated with the window with a call to SetProp, retrieved with GetProp, and removed with RemoveProp. The NPNOMFC plug-in implements this technique to avoid using a class library.

The plug-in covered in this chapter has no real function. It is provided as a template to help you write a plug-in without using a class library to subclass the Navigator-created plug-in window. Simply extend the class CPluginWindow by adding code to the provided stub methods or creating your own new methods.

Where to Find the Files

All the necessary files for building NPNOMFC.DLL are located on the CD-ROM. These files are in the \CODE\NOMFC, \CODE\INC, and \CODE\COMMON directories. You will need the files shown in the following lists.

For the directory \CODE\NOMFC, you need these files:

- npshell.cpp: Plug-in entry point methods
- npwindow.cpp, npwindow.h: The CPluginWindow class
- npnomfc.def: DLL module definition file
- npnomfc.rc: Resources
- npnomfc.mak: The makefile for Microsoft Visual C++

For the directory \CODE\INC, you need these files:

- npapi.h: Plug-in API prototypes and associated structures
- npupp.h: Plug-in API prototypes

For the directory \CODE\COMMON, you need this file:

- npwin.cpp: DLL entry point to plug-in API mapping

The Design of the Non-MFC Plug-In

This plug-in sample is basically a "Hello World" type of plug-in. It prints a short message and URL in the plug-in's window. By doing this, it demonstrates accessing plug-in instance data from a subclassed window procedure. Instance data is maintained in a class called CPluginWindow. This class, unlike other CPluginWindow classes throughout this book's sample code, is not derived from CWnd. It is a base class itself and therefore requires no MFC base.

CPluginWindow is contained in the file npwindow.cpp. This file has a global routine called SubClassFunc, which is used for subclassing the plug-in window. This function handles WM_PAINT where it writes a message with the URL to the plug-in window.

Figure 22.1 shows the components of the Non-MFC subclassing sample.

Figure 22.1.

The components of the Non-MFC subclassing sample.

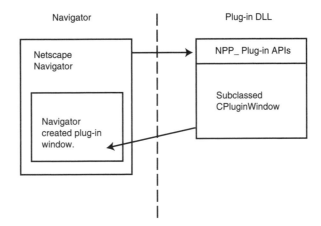

Plug-In Entry Points

Like any plug-in, this one has at least stub code for all the standard plug-in APIs. Because this is a "Hello World" type sample, it does not care about any URL data. Important APIs to this sample are NPP_New, NPP_Destroy, and NPP_SetWindow.

NPP_New

The NPP_New method creates the CPluginWindow object. It passes a pointer to the plug-in's instance, NPP pInstance. After that, it saves a pointer to CPluginWindow in the Navigator-provided instance structure and saves the mode. Because this is a simple example, EMBED tag attributes located in argc, argn, and argv are not parsed.

```
//
// NPP_New - Create a new plug-in instance.
//
```

```
NPError NP_LOADDS NPP_New (NPMIMEType pluginType,
    NPP pInstance,
    uint16 mode,
    int16 argc,
    char* argn[],
    char* argv[],
    NPSavedData* saved)
{
    if (pInstance == NULL)
        return NPERR_INVALID_INSTANCE_ERROR;

    // Create a new CPluginWindow object

    CPluginWindow* pPluginWindow = new CPluginWindow (pInstance);

    // Attach it to the instance structure

    pInstance->pdata = pPluginWindow;

    // Save our plug-in's mode

    pPluginWindow->mode = mode;

    return NPERR_NO_ERROR;
}
```

NPP_Destroy

During the NPP_Destroy API, the window is unsubclassed with a single call to
CPluginWindow::UnsubclassWindow. Remember that this call to UnsubclassWindow is a CPluginWindow
method, not an MFC method as in previous examples. Any window cleanup is performed with a
call to CPluginWindow::CleanupWindow. Finally, the object is deleted and its instance data pointer
is set to NULL.

```
//
// NPP_Destroy - Destroy our plug-in instance.
//
NPError NP_LOADDS NPP_Destroy (NPP pInstance, NPSavedData** save)
{
    CPluginWindow* pPluginWindow = (CPluginWindow *)pInstance->pdata;

    if (pPluginWindow)
    {
        if (pPluginWindow->hWindow)
        {
            // Unsubclass the window, clean it up and delete it.

            pPluginWindow->UnsubclassWindow ();
            pPluginWindow->CleanupWindow();
        }

        delete pPluginWindow;
        pInstance->pdata = NULL;
    }
    return NPERR_NO_ERROR;
}
```

NPP_SetWindow

The NPP_SetWindow implementation is somewhat standard. Instance data is retrieved and spurious entries are checked for. The difference is that no object is created. Because it is the only object used in this plug-in, CPluginWindow was created during NPP_New.

Instead of new object creation, the plug-in window handle is saved, and the window is subclassed and initialized.

```
//
// NPP_SetWindow - A window was created, resized, or destroyed.
//
NPError NP_LOADDS NPP_SetWindow (NPP pInstance, NPWindow* window)
{
    if (!window)
        return NPERR_GENERIC_ERROR;

    if (!pInstance)
        return NPERR_INVALID_INSTANCE_ERROR;

    // Get instance data

    CPluginWindow* pPluginWindow = (CPluginWindow *)pInstance->pdata;

    if (!pPluginWindow)
        return NPERR_GENERIC_ERROR;

    // Spurious entry - just return

    if (!window->window && !pPluginWindow->hWindow)
        return NPERR_NO_ERROR;

    // Window should have been destroyed, but because of a bug in
    // Navigator, we consider this a spurious entry.

    if (!window->window && pPluginWindow->hWindow)
        return NPERR_NO_ERROR;

    if (!pPluginWindow->hWindow && window->window)
    {
        pPluginWindow->hWindow = (HWND)window->window;
        pPluginWindow->SubclassWindow ();

        pPluginWindow->InitWindow ();
    }

    // Redraw the window.

    InvalidateRect (pPluginWindow->hWindow, NULL, TRUE);
    UpdateWindow (pPluginWindow->hWindow);

    return NPERR_NO_ERROR;
}
```

NPP_NewStream

When NPP_NewStream is called, this plug-in sets stype to NP_ASFILE. This sets up for a file-based plug-in and a future call to NPP_StreamAsFile. The CPluginWindow::Open method is called to notify the object of a new stream. This method is typical of most file-based plug-in samples in this book.

```
//
// NPP_NewStream - A new stream was created.
//
NPError NP_LOADDS NPP_NewStream(NPP pInstance,
    NPMIMEType type,
    NPStream* pStream,
    NPBool seekable,
    uint16* stype)
{
    if(!pInstance)
        return NPERR_INVALID_INSTANCE_ERROR;

    CPluginWindow* pPluginWindow = (CPluginWindow *)pInstance->pdata;

    *stype = NP_ASFILE;

    if (pPluginWindow)
        pPluginWindow->Open (pStream);

    return NPERR_NO_ERROR;
}
```

> **NOTE**
>
> If your plug-in requires Navigator 3.0 and above, you might want to use NP_ASFILEONLY instead of NP_ASFILE in the preceding example. See Chapter 10, "Stream Creation and Destruction," for more information on this new Navigator 3.0 parameter.

NPP_WriteReady **and** NPP_Write

Like most file-based plug-ins, NPP_WriteReady and NPP_Write are not really used. A large value is returned during NPP_WriteReady to tell Navigator that the plug-in can handle any buffer size. Calls to NPP_Write just return the length. If you decide to use NP_ASFILEONLY as mentioned in the previous note, these methods will not be called and no file data will be streamed.

```
//
// NPP_WriteReady - Returns amount of data we can handle for the next NPP_Write
//
int32 NP_LOADDS    NPP_WriteReady (NPP pInstance, NPStream *stream)
{
    return 0x0FFFFFFF;
}
```

```
//
// NPP_Write
//
int32 NP_LOADDS NPP_Write (NPP pInstance,
    NPStream *stream,
    int32 offset,
    int32 len,
    void *buffer)
{
    return len;
}
```

NPP_StreamAsFile

When the file is ready for the plug-in, NPP_StreamAsFile is called with the filename. This file can be in either Navigator cache or another directory, depending on its origination. The method CPluginWindow::GotFileName is called to start processing the file. This particular plug-in does nothing with the filename in CPluginWindow::GotFileName.

```
//
// NPP_StreamAsFile
//
void NP_LOADDS NPP_StreamAsFile (NPP pInstance,
    NPStream* stream,
    const char* fname)
{
    CPluginWindow* pPluginWindow = (CPluginWindow *)pInstance->pdata;

     if (pPluginWindow)
        pPluginWindow->GotFileName (fname);
}
```

NPP_DestroyStream

Although this plug-in doesn't need to know when the stream is destroyed, a call is made to a stub method, CPluginWindow::EndOfStream, for any future implementation.

```
//
// NPP_DestroyStream
//
NPError NP_LOADDS NPP_DestroyStream (NPP pInstance,
    NPStream *stream,
    NPError reason)
{
    CPluginWindow* pPluginWindow = (CPluginWindow *)pInstance->pdata;

     if (pPluginWindow)
        pPluginWindow->EndOfStream ();

    return NPERR_NO_ERROR;
}
```

The CPluginWindow Class

The CPluginWindow class contains the instance data for the plug-in. It also handles window subclassing and unsubclassing in addition to stub methods provided for future code if you use this example as a template. CPluginWindow contains the following methods:

```
CPluginWindow::CPluginWindow

CPluginWindow::~CPluginWindow

CPluginWindow::Open

CPluginWindow::GotFileName

CPluginWindow::InitWindow

CPluginWindow::EndOfStream

CPluginWindow::CleanupWindow

CPluginWindow::SubclassWindow

CPluginWindow::UnsubclassWindow
```

Construction and Destruction

The CPluginWindow constructor saves the plug-in instance (which is not used) and zeroes out the window handle. The destructor does nothing.

```
//
// Constructor
//
CPluginWindow::CPluginWindow (NPP pInstance)
{
    this->pInstance = pInstance;
    hWindow = NULL;
}

//
// Destructor
//
CPluginWindow::~CPluginWindow()
{
}
```

Open

The Open method is called from NPP_NewStream. The plug-in saves the stream instance pointer and copies the URL. The URL is later displayed in the plug-in window for this "Hello World" example.

```
//
// Open
//
void CPluginWindow::Open (NPStream* pStream)
{
```

```
    this->pStream = pStream;

    strcpy (this->url, pStream->url);
}
```

Stub Methods

InitWindow, GotFileName, EndOfStream, and CleanupWindow are stub methods of CPluginWindow for future code. InitWindow is called from NPP_SetWindow, GotFileName is called from NPP_StreamAsFile, EndOfStream is called from NPP_DestroyStream, and CleanupWindow is called from NPP_Destroy. Look at another sample such as the one in Chapter 19, "The CPU Monitor Plug-In," to see an implemention example of these methods.

```
//
// InitWindow
//
void CPluginWindow::InitWindow()
{
}
//
// GotFileName
//
void CPluginWindow::GotFileName (const char* fname)
{
}
//
// EndOfStream
//
void CPluginWindow::EndOfStream ()
{
}
//
// CleanupWindow
//
void CPluginWindow::CleanupWindow ()
{
}
```

SubclassWindow

CPluginWindow::SubclassWindow is called from NPP_SetWindow to subclass the plug-in window. This method calls SetWindowLong with a window handle, GWL_WNDPROC index, and address of the plug-in's global routine SubClassFunc. GWL_WNDPROC allows SetWindowLong to index into the window's data area where the window procedure address is stored and replace the address. The returned old window procedure address is saved in CPluginWindow::lpfnOldWndProc.

After subclassing, the CPluginWindow object is attached to the window by calling SetProp with the window handle, the property name, and a reference to the CPluginWindow object.

```
//
// SubclassWindow
```

```
//
void CPluginWindow::SubclassWindow ()
{
    lpfnOldWndProc = (FARPROC)SetWindowLong (hWindow,
        GWL_WNDPROC,
        (DWORD)SubClassFunc);

    SetProp (hWindow, PROPERTY_NAME, (HANDLE)this);
}
```

UnsubclassWindow

CPluginWindow::UnsubclassWindow is called from NPP_Destroy. The method removes the property attachment with RemoveProp and removes the subclass with SetWindowLong. SetWindowLong takes the window handle, GWL_WNDPROC, and the previously saved old window procedure. Notice that this call to SetWindowLong replaces the old window procedure that was previously saved with lpfnOldWndProc during the CPluginWindow::SubclassWindow method.

```
//
// UnsubclassWindow
//
void CPluginWindow::UnsubclassWindow ()
{
    RemoveProp (hWindow, PROPERTY_NAME);

    SetWindowLong (hWindow, GWL_WNDPROC, (DWORD)lpfnOldWndProc);
}
```

A Global Subclassing Procedure

The global procedure used for subclassing the plug-in's window is located in the same file as the CPluginWindow class. The procedure, SubClassFunc, gets a pointer to the CPluginWindow object with a call to GetProp.

The window message WM_PAINT is handled with text, including the URL, being drawn on the window.

The end of the routine calls CallWindowProc with the address of the old window procedure. This allows the old procedure to handle any messages that SubClassFunc does not.

```
//
// SubClassFunc
//
LONG WINAPI SubClassFunc (HWND hWnd, WORD Message, WORD wParam, LONG lParam)
{
    CPluginWindow* pPluginWindow = (CPluginWindow*)GetProp (hWnd, PROPERTY_NAME);

    switch(Message)
    {
    case WM_PAINT:
    {
        char buff[1024];
```

```
        sprintf (buff, "\n\n   The plug-in has successfully subclassed the
➥Navigator window!\n\n   URL = %s",
            pPluginWindow->url);

        PAINTSTRUCT    ps;

        HDC    hDC = BeginPaint (hWnd, &ps);
        int rc = DrawText (hDC, buff, strlen(buff), &ps.rcPaint, 0);
        EndPaint (hWnd, &ps);

          break;
    }
    default:
        break;
    }

    return CallWindowProc (pPluginWindow->lpfnOldWndProc,
        hWnd,
        Message,
        wParam,
        lParam);
}
```

Running the Plug-In

This plug-in currently uses the fictitious MIME type of x-tiny/x-plugin and a file extension of
.TIN. Just create a file with the extension .TIN on your local disk drive, and open it with the
Navigator. You should see something like the screen shown in Figure 22.2.

Figure 22.2.

*The Non-MFC subclassing
plug-in in action.*

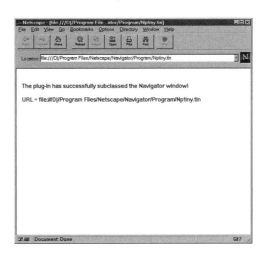

Conclusion

If you want to make a really small plug-in or don't want to use a class library, use a global window procedure to subclass the Navigator-created plug-in window with the Windows API SetWindowLong.

Attach your instance data to the plug-in's window using SetProp. Retrieve that data with GetProp. Remove the window property with RemoveProp.

What's Next?

LiveConnect, introduced with the release of Netscape's 3.0 Navigator SDK, allows communication between Java, JavaScript, and plug-ins. The next chapter examines Netscape's LiveConnect sample. This sample requires the use of a Java compiler and Netscape's javah tool.

CHAPTER 23

Netscape's LiveConnect Sample

Introduction

With the release of Netscape's 3.0 Navigator SDK comes a LiveConnect sample for playing AVI movies. This sample shows how to integrate JavaScript, Java, and Navigator plug-ins with LiveConnect.

LiveConnect provides communication among JavaScript, Java, and Navigator plug-ins by letting each language call the methods of the other language. Therefore, a plug-in can call a Java method, Java can call a plug-in method, JavaScript can call a Java method, and Java can call a JavaScript method. Because there is no connection between plug-ins and JavaScript, you must use Java to connect these two. To see this visually, look at Figure 23.1.

Figure 23.1.

The LiveConnect interface between plug-ins, Java, and JavaScript.

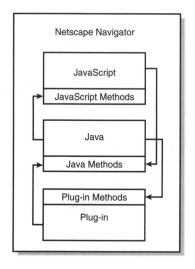

At first glance, Netscape's LiveConnect example might seem overwhelming, but using this chapter to break it up into small components should help you understand how it works. One thing you might notice right away is that the sample does not use an Integrated Development Environment (IDE) to build the components. Most of today's Java tools are command-line based, so Netscape uses a makefile to build the sample. Other new things are the addition of a Java compiler (javac) and Java header/stub generator (javah). These new tools are used with a C++ compiler (cl), linker (link), and resource compiler (rc) from Microsoft.

Where to Find the Files

Netscape's FTP servers are the best place to find the files needed to build this sample. That way, you'll be sure to get the most up-to-date tools and headers. The new SDK can be found on any one of Netscape's FTP servers in the PUB/NAVIGATOR/SDK directory.

For example, to get the Windows SDK, use this address:

`ftp://ftp3.netscape.com/pub/navigator/sdk/windows/nspi30.zip`

If you are developing for Windows, unzip this file using an unzip program that can handle long filenames. After you unzip the file, the following directories are created:

- ■ BIN: This directory contains Netscape's `javah` tool for generating headers and stub code for Java to plug-in glue.
- ■ CLASSES: This directory contains the .zip with current Java classes.
- ■ COMMON: This directory contains common C++ code for plug-ins in cpwin.cpp.
- ■ DOC: This directory contains the latest plug-in SDK documentation in HTML format.
- ■ INCLUDE: This directory contains headers for the Java Runtime Interface (JRI) and standard plug-in headers.
- ■ LIB: This directory contains the current JRI library, jrt3221.lib.
- ■ SAMPLE: This directory contains sample code for the AVI sample and a plug-in shell.

Get a Java Compiler

You also need to get a command-line based Java compiler. This example works with the `javac` compiler from Sun Microsystems. You can get this from `http://java.sun.com`.

The Design of the LiveConnect AVI Sample

Netscape's LiveConnect sample is based on the same plug-in design found in the sample plug-ins in this book. The Navigator created plug-in window is subclassed with an object called `CPluginWindow`. Video is controlled through MCI with a `CAvi` object, and plug-in APIs are handled through a file called `npshell.cpp`.

Here are some of the differences between Netscape's LiveConnect sample and this book's code samples found in Chapters 17 through 22:

- ■ No C++ class library such as Microsoft's Foundation Class Library (MFC) is used. Netscape's 2.x Plug-in SDK made use of MFC, but the 3.x SDK does not. Also, the Microsoft Visual C++ IDE is no longer used. A standard `makefile` is incorporated instead of the IDE. You can change this sample to use an IDE and compile the Java stuff externally.
- ■ Java communication is added. Native plug-in methods are contained in avijava.cpp. Stub code and headers are added with AviObserver.c and AviPlayer.c. This stub code communicates with the Java class and interfaces `AviPlayer` and `AviObserver`, respectively.
- ■ A Java applet or JavaScript program is used to control the media instead of the plug-in 2.x SDK technique of subclassing plug-in windows controls. (Chapter 17, "A Streaming Audio Sample," shows a plug-in using C++ to handle buttons.)

Components

Looking at the block diagram in Figure 23.2, you can see how Java attaches to a plug-in with LiveConnect. Notice that this diagram is divided into four sections: Netscape Navigator, Java and JavaScript Interpreters, Plug-in DLL, and Windows System. Arrows show the calling paths to each code module. Figure 23.2 is a more detailed view of the same concept shown in Figure 23.1. You might want to refer to Figure 23.2 while reading through this chapter, because much of this chapter is organized to match this figure.

Figure 23.2.

The components of the LiveConnect AVI sample.

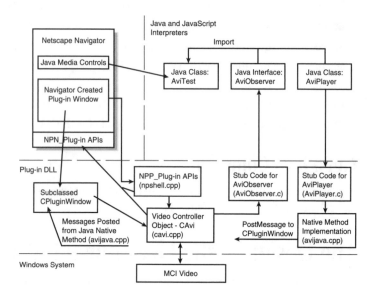

The Java Applet

The Java applet uses two classes and an interface to implement Java control over the plug-in. The classes are `AviTest` and `AviPlayer`. The Java interface is `AviObserver`. Of these, `AviTest` creates and maintains a user interface, `AviObserver` is called from the plug-in, and `AviPlayer` calls into the plug-in.

AviTest

The Java code shown in Listing 23.1 implements the test applet (AviTest.class) for this sample. Notice that `AviObserver` and `AviPlayer` classes are imported. Also, Play and Stop buttons are created and handled. For more specific information on this code, *Core Java* from The SunSoft Press Java Series is suggested reading.

Listing 23.1. The Java code to implement a user interface for Netscape's LiveConnect sample.

```java
import AviObserver;
import AviPlayer;
import java.awt.Panel;
import java.awt.TextField;
import java.awt.Button;
import java.awt.Event;
import java.awt.BorderLayout;
import java.awt.Frame;
import java.applet.Applet;
import netscape.javascript.JSObject;

public class AviTest extends Applet implements AviObserver{
    MediaControl control;

    public void init() {
        setLayout(new BorderLayout());
        add("Center", control = new MediaControl(getDocument()));
        control.enable();
    }

    public static void main(String args[]) {
        Frame f = new Frame("AviTest");
        AviTest aviTest = new AviTest();

        aviTest.init();

        f.add("Center", aviTest);
        f.resize(300, 30);
        f.show();
    }

    public void onStop() {
        control.resetButton();
    }

    public void onPositionChange(int newPosition) {
        control.updateFrame(newPosition);
    }

    public JSObject getDocument() {
        return (JSObject)JSObject.getWindow(this).getMember("document");
    }

}

class MediaControl extends Panel {
    TextField s;
    Button play;
    Button stop;

    JSObject document;

    public MediaControl(JSObject doc) {
        document = doc;

        add(play = new Button("Play"));
```

continues

Listing 23.1. continued

```java
            add(stop = new Button("Stop"));
            add(s = new TextField("0", 4));
            stop.disable();
    }

    public void updateFrame(int frame) {
        s.setText(String.valueOf(frame));
    }

    public void resetButton() {
        play.enable();
        stop.disable();
    }

    public boolean action(Event ev, Object arg) {
        if (ev.target instanceof Button) {
            AviPlayer avi = (AviPlayer)document.getMember("avi");

            String label = (String)arg;
            if (label == "Play") {
                // look AviPlayer.java for exaplanation
                avi.play(true);
                play.disable();
                stop.enable();
                return true;
            }
            else {
                // look AviPlayer.java for exaplanation
                avi.stop(true);
                stop.disable();
                play.enable();
                return true;
            }
        }
        return false;
    }
}
```

AviObserver

If you refer back to Figure 23.2, you'll see a Java class interface called AviObserver for the plug-in DLL. This Java class is used for events coming from the AVI plug-in, such as media event notifications (media stopped, position advisories, and so on). The following code shows how the AviObserver interface handles calls from the plug-in via stub code in AviObserver.c:

```c
// java interface for events coming from the avi plugin
// any object implementing this interface may register itself into the
// AviPlayer to get notifications (see advise function in AviPlayer)

interface AviObserver {

    public void onStop();
```

```
    public void onPositionChange(int newPosition);
}
```

AviPlayer

Look again at Figure 23.2, and notice the Java class `AviPlayer`. This Java class calls into native C/C++ methods located in AviPlayer.c and avijava.cpp. The code for the `AviPlayer` Java class is given in Listing 23.2. This code held a large comment from Netscape developers that detailed a problem with another thread calling MCI video. This code comment is now printed in the following warning box.

The `AviPlayer` Java class is run by the Navigator Java Interpreter, which is on a different thread than the plug-in APIs called from Navigator. Apparently, Windows MCI does not allow a different thread to make MCI calls for controlling video. This is why Netscape had to post window messages to `CPluginWindow` instead of calling that object directly (see Figure 23.2).

A WARNING FROM THE NETSCAPE DEVELOPERS

For AVI methods with MCI drivers, an instance of an AVI driver belongs to the thread that created it. When an applet tries to call one of the `play`, `stop`, `seek`, `rewind`, `forward`, `frameForward`, and `frameBack` functions (see Listing 23.2), MCI fails to execute the command because the applet is in a different thread than the one in which the AVI instance was created (which is the main thread when it loads the plug-in). The `isAsync` argument is used to see whether the function can be called directly (`isAsync = false`) or whether a message needs to be posted in order to execute the function.

This problem could happen every time. In some applets, you try to access (directly or indirectly) thread-safe data from within another thread. This usually doesn't happen because your data is in the java class, so it is available from other applets. However, when you have native functions hiding data (the plug-in is a very good example of this), this problem might occur.

It would be nice if the MCI drivers were not so strict, and why do they need to be?

Listing 23.2. Java code to implement the `AviPlayer` Java class.

```
import netscape.plugin.Plugin;
import AviObserver;

public class AviPlayer extends Plugin {

    // used to fire avi asynchronous events like OnStop or OnPositionChange.
    // AviObserver is an interface (see AviObserver.java)

    private AviObserver observer;
```

continues

Listing 23.2. continued

```
    public AviObserver getObserver() {
        return observer;
    }

    // the object interested in listening the avi must register here.
    // timeout defines the time that occurs beetwen two OnPositionChange events

    public boolean advise(AviObserver o, int timeout) {
        System.err.println("called advise "+o+" "+timeout);
        if (observer == null)
            observer = o;
        else
            return false;

        setTimeOut(timeout);
        return true;
    }

    //\\//\\//\\//\\//\\//\\//\\//\\//\\//\\//\\//\\//\\//\\//\\//.
    // those are all native.
    // check AviPlayer.c/.h for stubs and prototypes information
    // check avijava.cpp for native implementation

    // set the timeout for the position checking timer

    public native void setTimeOut (int timeout);

    public native boolean play (boolean isAsync);
    public native boolean stop (boolean isAsync);
    public native boolean seek (boolean isAsync, int position);
    public native boolean rewind (boolean isAsync);
    public native boolean forward (boolean isAsync);
    public native boolean frameForward (boolean isAsync);
    public native boolean frameBack (boolean isAsync);
}
```

Stub Code and Headers with `javah`

When you build this sample, stub code and headers are generated to connect the Java interface, AviObserver, and Java class, AviPlayer, to the appropriate C++ code implemented with avijava.cpp and cavi.cpp. You can see how the stub code fits in the mix by looking back at Figure 23.2.

Native Plug-In Methods for Java

A *native* Java method is one that is implemented in another more machine-dependent language such as C++. Native code is implemented in the file avijava.cpp. These methods are called from a Java interpreter thread and therefore must access the plug-in's instance through a call to getPeer. This instance handle is set by the system.

After the instance structure is retrieved, a pointer to the CPluginWindow object is dereferenced. If the call is asynchronous (which it must be for MCI video because of the previously mentioned thread problem), a message is posted to the plug-in window with a call to PostMessage. CPluginWindow handles these posted messages because it has previously subclassed the plug-in window.

AviPlayer_setTimeOut

The native Java method AviPlayer_setTimeOut sets the frequency for the video update position. This method is not implemented by the previous Java code.

```
extern "C" JRI_PUBLIC_API(void)
native_AviPlayer_setTimeOut (JRIEnv* env,
    struct AviPlayer* self,
    JRIMethodThunk* method,
                jint timeout)
{
    NPP instance = (NPP)self->getPeer(env);
    CPluginWindow* pPluginData = (CPluginWindow*)instance->pdata;
    pPluginData->GetAviStream().SetFrequency(timeout);
}
```

AviPlayer_play

AviPlayer_play plays the video. A call to this C++ method originates from clicking on the Java-created play button.

```
native_AviPlayer_play (JRIEnv* env,
    struct AviPlayer* self,
    JRIMethodThunk* method,
    jbool isAsync)
{
    NPP instance = (NPP)self->getPeer(env);
    CPluginWindow* pPluginData = (CPluginWindow*)instance->pdata;
    if (isAsync) {
        ::PostMessage(*pPluginData, WM_COMMAND, MAKEWPARAM(ID_VIDEO_PLAY, 0), 0);
        return TRUE;
    }
    else
        return pPluginData->GetAviStream().Play();
}
```

AviPlayer_stop

A call to AviPlayer_stop stops the video. This call results from clicking on the Java-created stop button.

```
extern "C" JRI_PUBLIC_API(jbool)
native_AviPlayer_stop (JRIEnv* env,
    struct AviPlayer* self,
    JRIMethodThunk* method,
    jbool isAsync)
```

```
{
    NPP instance = (NPP)self->getPeer(env);
    CPluginWindow* pPluginData = (CPluginWindow*)instance->pdata;
    if (isAsync) {
        ::PostMessage(*pPluginData, WM_COMMAND, MAKEPARAM(ID_VIDEO_STOP, 0), 0);
        return TRUE;
    }
    else
        return pPluginData->GetAviStream().Stop();
}
```

AviPlayer_seek

AviPlayer_seek allows seeking within the video file. As in all of these methods, notice the call to
PostMessage to prevent the MCI driver multithreading bug discussed previously.

```
extern "C" JRI_PUBLIC_API(jbool)
native_AviPlayer_seek (JRIEnv* env,
    struct AviPlayer* self,
    JRIMethodThunk* method,
    jbool isAsync,
    jint position)
{
    NPP instance = (NPP)self->getPeer(env);
    CPluginWindow* pPluginData = (CPluginWindow*)instance->pdata;
    if (isAsync) {
        ::PostMessage(*pPluginData, WM_COMMAND, MAKEPARAM(ID_VIDEO_SEEK, 0), 0);
        return TRUE;
    }
    else
        // CAvi::Seek(..)
        return pPluginData->GetAviStream().Seek(position);
}
```

AviPlayer_rewind

The AviPlayer_rewind method rewinds the AVI video to the first frame. Notice that each of these
methods in this section have a parameter for isAsync. This parameter determines whether the
method can call the MCI video driver on the current thread, or whether it must post a window
message to effectively switch threads.

```
extern "C" JRI_PUBLIC_API(jbool)
native_AviPlayer_rewind (JRIEnv* env,
    struct AviPlayer* self,
    JRIMethodThunk* method,
    jbool isAsync)
{
    NPP instance = (NPP)self->getPeer(env);
    CPluginWindow* pPluginData = (CPluginWindow*)instance->pdata;
    if (isAsync) {
        ::PostMessage(*pPluginData, WM_COMMAND, MAKEPARAM(ID_VIDEO_REWIND, 0), 0);
        return TRUE;
    }
    else
        return pPluginData->GetAviStream().Rewind();
}
```

AviPlayer_forward

AviPlayer_forward moves the video to the last video frame. This is like rewind, but it goes to the first frame rather than the last.

```
extern "C" JRI_PUBLIC_API(jbool)
native_AviPlayer_forward (JRIEnv* env,
    struct AviPlayer* self,
    JRIMethodThunk* method,
    jbool isAsync)
{
    NPP instance = (NPP)self->getPeer(env);
    CPluginWindow* pPluginData = (CPluginWindow*)instance->pdata;
    if (isAsync) {
        ::PostMessage(*pPluginData, WM_COMMAND, MAKEWPARAM(ID_VIDEO_FORWARD, 0), 0);
        return TRUE;
    }
    else
        return pPluginData->GetAviStream().Forward();
}
```

AviPlayer_frameForward

AviPlayer_frameForward enables you to step the video forward a single frame.

```
extern "C" JRI_PUBLIC_API(jbool)
native_AviPlayer_frameForward(JRIEnv* env,
    struct AviPlayer* self,
    JRIMethodThunk* method,
    jbool isAsync)
{
    NPP instance = (NPP)self->getPeer(env);
    CPluginWindow* pPluginData = (CPluginWindow*)instance->pdata;
    if (isAsync) {
        ::PostMessage(*pPluginData, WM_COMMAND,
➥MAKEWPARAM(ID_VIDEO_FRAME_BACK, 0), 0);
        return TRUE;
    }
    else
        return pPluginData->GetAviStream().FrameForward();
}
```

AviPlayer_frameBack

Just like you can step a frame forward with AviPlayer_frameForward, you can step backward with AviPlayer_frameBack.

```
extern "C" JRI_PUBLIC_API(jbool)
native_AviPlayer_frameBack (JRIEnv* env,
    struct AviPlayer* self,
    JRIMethodThunk* method,
                jbool isAsync)
{
    NPP instance = (NPP)self->getPeer(env);
    CPluginWindow* pPluginData = (CPluginWindow*)instance->pdata;
    if (isAsync) {
        ::PostMessage(*pPluginData, WM_COMMAND,
```

```
↪MAKEWPARAM(ID_VIDEO_FRAME_FORWARD, 0), 0);
        return TRUE;
    }
    else
        return pPluginData->GetAviStream().FrameBack();
}
```

CPluginWindow

CPluginWindow contains a window procedure that handles messages from the native Java methods in avijava.cpp and handles standard window messages from the plug-in window. This C++ class also creates a CAvi object, subclasses itself to the plug-in window, and implements a menu.

The Window Procedure

The window procedure handles mouse messages, palette changes, and commands from the Java native method. While you are looking at Listing 23.3, notice that both window messages originating from Java (WM_COMMAND) and direct mouse commands (WM_LBUTTONDOWN and WM_RBUTTONDOWN) are handled. This is a good example of how a plug-in can have both a Java and a C++ implemented user interface at the same time!

Listing 23.3. The window procedure CPluginWindow::PluginWndProc.

```
LRESULT CALLBACK
CPluginWindow::PluginWndProc(HWND hWnd, UINT Msg, WPARAM WParam, LPARAM lParam)
{
    // pull out the instance object receiving the message
    CPluginWindow* pluginObj = (CPluginWindow*)GetProp(hWnd,
↪CPluginWindow::_ThisLookUp);

    // message switch
    switch (Msg) {

        case WM_LBUTTONDOWN:
        {
            POINT p;
            p.x = LOWORD(lParam);
            p.y = HIWORD(lParam);
            pluginObj->OnLButtonDown(WParam, &p);
        break;
        }

        case WM_RBUTTONDOWN:
        {
            POINT p;
            p.x = LOWORD(lParam);
            p.y = HIWORD(lParam);
            pluginObj->OnRButtonDown(WParam, &p);
        break;
        }

        case WM_PAINT:
```

```
{
    PAINTSTRUCT  PaintStruct;
    ::BeginPaint(hWnd, &PaintStruct);
    pluginObj->OnPaint();
    ::EndPaint(hWnd, &PaintStruct);
break;
}

case WM_PALETTECHANGED:
    pluginObj->OnPaletteChanged((HWND)WParam);
break;

//\\//\\//\\//\\//\\//\\//\\//\\//\\//\\//\\//\\//\\//\\//.
// the following two messages are used from the CAvi class
//
// MM_MCINOTIFY informs about a stop event
case MM_MCINOTIFY:
    pluginObj->GetAviStream().OnStop();
break;

// WM_TIMER is used to update the position status
case WM_TIMER:
    pluginObj->GetAviStream().OnPositionChange();
break;
//\\//\\//\\//\\//\\//\\//\\//\\//\\//\\//\\//\\//\\//\\//.

// menu handling
// pass to CPluginWindow instance? (too much work...)
//
// WARNING
// those ids are also used from the native functions (avijava.cpp)
// when the flag isAsync is setted to TRUE
// (see avijava.cpp and AviPlayer.java)
case WM_COMMAND:
    if (!HIWORD(WParam)) {
        switch LOWORD(WParam) {
            case ID_VIDEO_PLAY:
                //pluginObj->GetAviStream().Play();
                pluginObj->OnLButtonDown(0, 0);
            return 0;
            case ID_VIDEO_STOP:
                pluginObj->GetAviStream().Stop();
            return 0;
            case ID_VIDEO_REWIND:
                pluginObj->GetAviStream().Rewind();
            return 0;
            case ID_VIDEO_FORWARD:
                pluginObj->GetAviStream().Forward();
            return 0;
            case ID_VIDEO_FRAME_BACK:
                pluginObj->GetAviStream().FrameBack();
            return 0;
            case ID_VIDEO_FRAME_FORWARD:
                pluginObj->GetAviStream().FrameForward();
            return 0;
            // this is hidden to the menu but it's used from
            // the java class in asynchronous mode (see AviPlayer.java
```

continues

Listing 23.3. continued

```
                        // and avijava.cpp)
                        case ID_VIDEO_SEEK:
                            pluginObj->GetAviStream().Seek(lParam);
                        return 0;
                }
        }
        default:
        return CallWindowProc(pluginObj->GetWndProc(),
            hWnd, Msg, WParam, lParam);
    };
    return 0;
}
```

Constructor

The constructor initializes values, saves the mode, and creates a new CAvi object for MCI video control.

```
CPluginWindow::CPluginWindow (BOOL bAutoStart,
    BOOL bLoop,
    uint16 mode,
    NPP instance)
{
    // initialized in SetWindow
    _hPluginWnd = 0;
    _pfnDefault = 0;

    _mode = mode;
    // make an avi object
    // passing the NPP instance down is necessary because of the
    // java callback in CAvi (see CAvi::OnStop() and CAvi::OnPositionChange()
    _pAvi = new CAvi(bAutoStart, bLoop, instance);
}
```

Destructor

The destructor deletes the CAvi object and removes the window subclass and property.

```
CPluginWindow::~CPluginWindow()
{
    // delete the avi object
    delete _pAvi;
    // restore the old window proc and delete the property
    if (_pfnDefault) {
        ::SetWindowLong(_hPluginWnd, GWL_WNDPROC, (LONG)_pfnDefault);
        ::RemoveProp(_hPluginWnd, CPluginWindow::_ThisLookUp);
    }
}
```

CPluginWindow::SetWindow

SetWindow is called from NPP_SetWindow in npshell.cpp. This method stores the window handle and subclasses the window procedure. It also saves a pointer to CPluginWindow in the window property with SetProp.

```
void
CPluginWindow::SetWindow(HWND hWnd)
{
    hPluginWnd = hWnd;

    // subclass

    pfnDefault = (WNDPROC)::SetWindowLong (hWnd,
        GWL_WNDPROC,
        (LONG)CPluginWindow::PluginWndProc);
    // register "this" with the window structure
    ::SetProp(hWnd, CPluginWindow::_ThisLookUp, (HANDLE)this);
}
```

CPluginWindow::OnLButtonDown

A call to CPluginWindow::OnLButtonDown originates from handling a WM_LBUTTONDOWN in the window procedure. This method can either stop the video or play it depending on the video state and position.

```
void
CPluginWindow::OnLButtonDown(UINT uFlags, LPPOINT pPoint)
{
    if (_pAvi->isPlaying()) {
        // if plying, stop
        _pAvi->Stop();
    }
    else {
        // if stopped, play
        DWORD dwPos, dwLen;
        dwPos = _pAvi->GetPosition();
        dwLen = _pAvi->GetLength();

        if (dwPos >= dwLen)
            _pAvi->Rewind();
        _pAvi->Play();
    }
}
```

CPluginWindow::OnRButtonDown

If the user clicks the right mouse button over the video window, the CPluginWindow::OnRButtonDown method brings up a popup menu for video control. When this menu is up, the user can control the video through the menu in the same way as with Java-created buttons.

```
void
CPluginWindow::OnRButtonDown(UINT uFlags, LPPOINT pPoint)
```

```
{
    UINT uState;

    //  Create the popup.
    HMENU hPopup = ::CreatePopupMenu();
    if(hPopup == 0)  {
        return;
    }

    if(_pAvi->isPlaying())
        uState = MF_GRAYED;
    else
        uState = MF_ENABLED;

    ::AppendMenu(hPopup, uState, ID_VIDEO_PLAY, "Play...");
    ::AppendMenu(hPopup, !uState, ID_VIDEO_STOP, "Pause...");

    //  Separator
    ::AppendMenu(hPopup, MF_SEPARATOR, 0, 0);

    uState = MF_ENABLED;
    ::AppendMenu(hPopup, uState, ID_VIDEO_REWIND,  "Rewind (Start of movie)...");
    ::AppendMenu(hPopup, uState, ID_VIDEO_FORWARD, "Forward (End of movie)...");

    //  Separator
    ::AppendMenu(hPopup, MF_SEPARATOR, 0, 0);

    ::AppendMenu(hPopup, uState, ID_VIDEO_FRAME_BACK,  "Frame Back...");
    ::AppendMenu(hPopup, uState, ID_VIDEO_FRAME_FORWARD, "Frame Forward...");

    ::ClientToScreen(_hPluginWnd, pPoint);
    ::TrackPopupMenu(hPopup,
                        TPM_LEFTALIGN | TPM_RIGHTBUTTON,
                        pPoint->x,
                        pPoint->y,
                        0,
                        _hPluginWnd,
                        NULL);
}
```

CPluginWindow::OnPaint

If the video needs repainting, a WM_PAINT message handled in the window procedure results in a call to CPluginWindow::OnPaint. This method simply calls the video object's update method.

```
void
CPluginWindow::OnPaint()
{
    _pAvi->Update();
}
```

CPluginWindow::OnPaletteChange

Palette changes are indicated by a `WM_PALETTECHANGED` window message that results in a call to the `CPluginWindow::OnPaletteChanged` method. The video control object is called to realize the current palette.

```
void
CPluginWindow::OnPaletteChanged(HWND hFocusWnd)
{
    //  Don't do this if we caused it to happen.
    if(hFocusWnd != _hPluginWnd)   {
        _pAvi->Realize();
    }
}
```

CAvi

The `CAvi` class is called by `CPluginWindow` to control AVI video files through MCI. This class calls back Java to notify of video stop and position change. MCI commands are sent to the MCI AVI driver with the Windows `mciSendCommand` API. Remember that MCI needs to be called on the same thread for video.

Constructor

The constructor saves the plug-in instance and initializes members. Notice the flags for autostart (bAutoStart) and looping (bLoop).

```
CAvi::CAvi (BOOL autoStart, BOOL bLoop, NPP instance)
{
    _pluginInstance = instance;
    _mDeviceID = 0;
    _hMovieWnd = 0;

    _bLoop = bLoop;
    _bAutoStart = autoStart;
    _bPlaying = FALSE;

    _uTimeOut = 0;
    _uTimerID = ++s_InstanceCount;
}
```

Destructor

The destructor closes the video device by calling `CAvi::Close`, and the MCI video driver is closed with an `MCI_CLOSE` message.

```
CAvi::~CAvi ()
{
    Close();
}
```

CAvi::Open

CAvi::Open opens the MCI video device and saves the device ID. A window handle (hWnd) is passed to the method so that the video driver can use it for displaying video. Also, the filename (Filename) that contains the name of the AVI file is passed in as the second parameter. The MCI driver is opened with MCI_OPEN and the window handle is associated with MCI_WINDOW.

```
BOOL CAvi::Open (HWND hWnd, LPCSTR Filename)
{
    DWORD RetCode;
    MCI_ANIM_OPEN_PARMS OpenParms;
    MCI_ANIM_WINDOW_PARMS WindowParms;

    // Close any device that is already open.
    if (_mDeviceID){
        Close ();
    }

    // Open a device for playback.

    OpenParms.dwCallback = NULL;
    OpenParms.wDeviceID = 0;
    OpenParms.lpstrDeviceType = NULL;
    OpenParms.lpstrElementName = Filename;
    OpenParms.lpstrAlias = 0;
    OpenParms.dwStyle = WS_CHILD ¦ WS_VISIBLE;
    OpenParms.hWndParent = hWnd;

    if (RetCode = mciSendCommand (0, MCI_OPEN,
        (DWORD) MCI_OPEN_ELEMENT ¦
         MCI_ANIM_OPEN_PARENT ¦
         MCI_ANIM_OPEN_WS,
        (DWORD)(LPVOID)&OpenParms)) {
            char szBuf[256];
            mciGetErrorString(RetCode, szBuf, 256);
            MessageBox(NULL, szBuf, "AVI Plugin: Error Opening Device!", MB_OK);
            return FALSE;
        }
    // The device was opened, cache the device ID.

    _mDeviceID = OpenParms.wDeviceID;

    // set and cache the AVI window handle

    WindowParms.dwCallback = NULL;
    WindowParms.hWnd = hWnd;
    WindowParms.nCmdShow = SW_SHOW;
    WindowParms.lpstrText = (LPSTR) NULL;

    if (RetCode = mciSendCommand (_mDeviceID,
                                  MCI_WINDOW,
                                  MCI_ANIM_WINDOW_HWND,
                                  (DWORD)(LPVOID)&WindowParms)) {
        return FALSE;
    }
    _hMovieWnd = WindowParms.hWnd;
```

```
    // start playing if auto start defined

    if (_bAutoStart)
        Play();

    return TRUE;
}
```

CAvi::Close

CAvi::Close closes the MCI video device. The close is performed by sending an MCI_CLOSE message via the mciSendCommand MCI API. After the close, playing status is set to false and the video device ID is set to 0.

```
void CAvi::Close (void)
{
    // Closing a device ID will stop the video playback.

    if (_mDeviceID)
        mciSendCommand (_mDeviceID, MCI_CLOSE, 0L, NULL);

    _bPlaying = FALSE;
    _mDeviceID = 0;
}
```

CAvi::Play

CAvi::Play starts the video playback asynchronously. It also sets a timer for position tracking. Video playback is started with the MCI_PLAY command. The video window (hMovieWnd) is notified when the play is complete.

```
BOOL CAvi::Play ()
{
    DWORD RetCode, dwFlags = MCI_NOTIFY;     // notify a window proc when
                                             // the play status change (like stop)
    MCI_ANIM_PLAY_PARMS PlayParms;

    // if no device open return
    if (!_mDeviceID)
        return FALSE;

    // Start playback using the MCI_PLAY command.
    PlayParms.dwCallback = (DWORD)_hMovieWnd;
    PlayParms.dwFrom = PlayParms.dwTo = 0;

#ifdef WIN32
    if (_bLoop)
        dwFlags = MCI_DGV_PLAY_REPEAT;
#endif
    if (RetCode = mciSendCommand (_mDeviceID,
                                  MCI_PLAY,
                                  dwFlags,
                                  (DWORD)(LPVOID)&PlayParms)) {
        char szBuf[256];
```

```
        mciGetErrorString(RetCode,szBuf,256);
        MessageBox(NULL, szBuf, "MCI Play Error", MB_OK);

        return FALSE;
    }

    // start the timer so we can track down the position
    if (_uTimeOut)
        SetTimer(_hMovieWnd, _uTimerID, _uTimeOut, NULL);

    _bPlaying = TRUE;

    return TRUE;
}
```

CAvi::Stop

CAvi::Stop sends an MCI_STOP to stop video playback.

```
BOOL CAvi::Stop (void)
{
    // Stop playback

    if (_mDeviceID && mciSendCommand (_mDeviceID, MCI_STOP, 0L, NULL)) {
        return FALSE;
    }

    return TRUE;
}
```

CAvi::Seek

CAvi::Seek sends an MCI_SEEK to seek within the AVI file. The seek position is indicated by the dwSeekPosition parameter, which is passed into this method.

```
BOOL CAvi::Seek (ULONG dwSeekPosition)
{
    MCI_SEEK_PARMS seekParams;
    seekParams.dwTo = dwSeekPosition;

    if (_mDeviceID && mciSendCommand(_mDeviceID,
                                     MCI_SEEK,
                                     MCI_TO,
                                     (DWORD)(LPVOID)&seekParams)) {
        return FALSE;
    }

    return TRUE;
}
```

CAvi::Rewind

`CAvi::Rewind` rewinds the video to the beginning and displays the first frame. Notice that a rewind is accomplished with an `MCI_SEEK` message using the `MCI_SEEK_TO_START` flag.

```
BOOL CAvi::Rewind (void)
{
    // Use the MCI_SEEK command to return to the beginning of the file.
    if (_mDeviceID && mciSendCommand (_mDeviceID,
                        MCI_SEEK,
                        MCI_SEEK_TO_START,
                        NULL)) {
        return FALSE;
    }

    return TRUE;
}
```

CAvi::Forward

`CAvi::Forward` forwards the video to the last frame and displays it. When the video is at the end of the `MCI_SEEK` message with an `MCI_SEEK_TO_END` flag, private methods `FrameBack` and `FrameForward` are called to avoid a display bug in the video driver. Whatever it takes!

```
BOOL CAvi::Forward (void)
{
    // Use the MCI_SEEK command to go to the end of the file.
    if (_mDeviceID && mciSendCommand (_mDeviceID,
                        MCI_SEEK,
                        MCI_SEEK_TO_END,
                        NULL)) {
        return FALSE;
    }

    FrameBack();
    FrameForward();

    return TRUE;
}
```

CAvi::FrameForward

`CAvi::FrameForward` moves the video forward one frame. This is done with the `MCI_STEP` message using the `MCI_ANIM_STEP_FRAMES` flag. `StepParms.dwFrames` is set to 1 to allow for single-frame stepping.

```
BOOL CAvi::FrameForward (void)
{
    MCI_ANIM_STEP_PARMS StepParms;

    StepParms.dwFrames = 1L;
    if (_mDeviceID && mciSendCommand (_mDeviceID,
                    MCI_STEP,
```

```
                              MCI_ANIM_STEP_FRAMES,
                              (DWORD)(LPVOID)&StepParms)) {
        return FALSE;
    }

    return TRUE;
}
```

CAvi::FrameBack

CAvi::FrameBack moves the video back one frame. This method is very similar to CAvi::FrameForward, but it uses the MCI_ANIM_STEP_REVERSE flag to step backward one frame.

```
BOOL CAvi::FrameBack (void)
{
    MCI_ANIM_STEP_PARMS StepParms;

    // Use MCI_STEP to move back one frame.

    StepParms.dwFrames = 1L;

    if (_mDeviceID && mciSendCommand (_mDeviceID,
                        MCI_STEP,
                        MCI_ANIM_STEP_REVERSE,
                        (DWORD)(LPVOID)&StepParms)) {
        return FALSE;
        }

    return TRUE;
}
```

Sizing, Positioning, and Updating

Sizing, positioning, and updating the video are handled by CAvi with the following methods:

CAvi::GetLength

CAvi::GetPosition

CAvi::GetWidth

CAvi::GetHeight

CAvi::Center

CAvi::Update

CAvi::Realize

These methods are beyond the scope of this chapter. You should check CAVI.CPP to see how they work.

CAvi::SetFrequency

The CAvi::SetFrequency method changes the timer value for position updates. The method first stops the old timer with a call to KillTimer and then sets a new timer with SetTimer using the timer frequency passed into the method as uTimer. The actual WM_TIMER timer messages are sent to the main window procedure by the Windows subsystem.

```
void
CAvi::SetFrequency(UINT uTimer)
{
    if (_bPlaying && _uTimeOut)
        KillTimer(_hMovieWnd, _uTimerID);

    _uTimeOut = uTimer;

    if (_uTimeOut && _bPlaying)
        SetTimer(_hMovieWnd, _uTimerID, _uTimeOut, 0);
}
```

CAvi::OnStop

CAvi::OnStop is called when the video is stopped. The Java stub code located in AviObserver.c is called, which bubbles up to the Java Interface AviObserver method onStop. Notice the calls to new Navigator 3.0 plug-in APIs: NPN_GetJavaPeer and NPN_GetJavaEnv. These calls are documented in Chapter 14, "LiveConnect."

```
void
CAvi::OnStop()
{
    AviPlayer* javaAviInst;
    JRIEnv* env;

    // load the java instance representing the plugin instance

    javaAviInst = (AviPlayer*)NPN_GetJavaPeer(_pluginInstance);
    env = NPN_GetJavaEnv();

    // find the listener if any (observer on AviPlayer java class;
    // AviPlayer.java)

    AviObserver* observer = javaAviInst->getObserver(env);

    // if time out is non zero we set a timer on play.

    if (_uTimeOut) {
        KillTimer(_hMovieWnd, _uTimerID);
        if (observer)
            observer->onPositionChange(env, GetPosition());
    }

    if (observer)
        observer->onStop(env);

    _bPlaying = FALSE;
}
```

CAvi::OnPositionChange

`CAvi::OnPosition` sends position change events to the Java stub code located in AviObserver.c. These events bubble up to the Java interface `AviObserver` method `OnPositionChange`.

```
void
CAvi::OnPositionChange()
{
    AviPlayer* javaAviInst;
    JRIEnv* env;

    javaAviInst = (AviPlayer*)NPN_GetJavaPeer(_pluginInstance);
    env = NPN_GetJavaEnv();

    AviObserver* observer = javaAviInst->getObserver(env);

    if (observer)
        observer->onPositionChange(env, GetPosition());
}
```

Plug-In Entry Points

Netscape's LiveConnect sample supports all the standard 2.*x* plug-in APIs. You can look at any other sample code in this book to see how these APIs work. For the purposes of this chapter, a new 3.*x* plug-in API called `NPP_GetJavaClass` is used.

NPP_GetJavaClass

`NPP_GetJavaClass` is used to associate a Java class with a plug-in (discussed in Chapter 14). Within this plug-in implemented API, the Java environment is retrieved with a call to `NPN_GetJavaEnv`. The information returned from this call is needed for all Java Runtime Interface (JRI) calls. After getting the Java environment, a call is made to initialize the native C implemented Java class with `init_AviPlayer`. This initialization method was created by Netscape's `javah` tool. If your plug-in is not using Java, a `NULL` is returned from the `NPP_GetJavaClass` API.

```
jref
NPP_GetJavaClass(void)
{

    JRIEnv* env = NPN_GetJavaEnv();

    return init_AviPlayer(env);

}
```

Running the Sample with JavaScript

To get the whole thing started, Netscape uses an HTML file with some embedded JavaScript. This script brings in both the Java applet and the plug-in with an EMBED tag:

```
<html>
<head>
<script language="JavaScript">

<!--

function setup() {
    document.avi.advise(document.controller, 500);
}

//-->

</script>
</head>

<body onLoad="setup()">

<center>
<h1>Avi Plugin test using a Java Applet</h1>

<hr>

<applet name=controller code=AviTest.class width=400 height=30 mayscript>
</applet>

<hr>

<embed    name=avi SRC="sample.avi" WIDTH=100 HEIGHT=100>

<hr>

<a href="AviTest.java">The source.</a>
</center>
```

Figure 23.3 shows what the sample looks like when it is running. Notice the Java-created buttons and the plug-in video window with C++ created menu controls.

Figure 23.3.

Netscape's LiveConnect sample in action.

Conclusion

You should be familiar with Java in order to use LiveConnect with your plug-in. This chapter has intentionally left out JavaScript because it has no direct interface with plug-ins and only confuses the matter. JavaScript does have plug-in specific methods that you might want to look into if you are using JavaScript.

You should find it very helpful to study Figure 23.2 while reading through this chapter. Each block in the figure corresponds to a section in the chapter.

You might have noticed that there were no code listings for plug-in 2.*x* APIs from npshell.cpp. This chapter is really about LiveConnect. Look at any other sample in this book for explanation of 2.*x* APIs.

At the time of this writing, LiveConnect is still in beta. You might notice some discrepancies between this book and the plug-in SDK with which you are working. Concentrate on the LiveConnect concept rather than each line of code. You might even find some bugs if you look carefully. Be sure to get the latest plug-in SDK!

What's Next?

Do you ever wonder what the heck Netscape is doing on the WinSock layer? If so, check out the next chapter detailing Socket Spy, a technique for "spying" on a WinSock application's network data flow.

CHAPTER 24

Debugging with the Socket Spy

Introduction

Netscape Navigator communicates with the Internet through a generic socket interface. In Windows 95, this interface is implemented as a DLL called WSOCK32.DLL. This DLL provides an API for all socket-based applications ranging from Web browsers to telnet applications. Any application that uses this socket DLL simply loads it and calls the socket routines. Multiple applications can use WSOCK32.DLL at the same time.

A Netscape Navigator plug-in module normally does not use the Windows socket interface directly. A plug-in uses the plug-in API to communicate its needs to the Navigator, which in turn uses sockets to fulfill any network-related requests.

In many cases, it is nice to know what data the Navigator is reading from and writing to the socket interface. This data can be very helpful in debugging plug-in problems. The Socket Spy enables you to easily monitor this data flow using a standard source-level debugger. It also writes out this data to the files send.dat and recv.dat for each Navigator session. The Socket Spy is implemented as a DLL called WSOCK00.DLL. This DLL is inserted between the Navigator and the socket interface by making Navigator load WSOCK00.DLL instead of WSOCK32.DLL. To do this, you must edit NETSCAPE.EXE with a binary editor and change wsock32 to wsock00. This technique works for any application that uses WSOCK32.DLL and is explained in more detail later in this chapter.

The Socket Interface

Every day more and more socket-based applications are appearing on the scene. These applications can be Web browsers, FTP programs, telnet applications, and any other software that wants to talk on the Internet. In Windows 95, these applications all use the dynamic link library, WSOCK32.DLL, for socket communication. This DLL is shipped with Windows 95, along with a TCP/IP stack. Figure 24.1 shows WinSock interface with the WSOCK32.DLL WinSock DLL.

Figure 24.1.
WinSock applications and the socket interface.

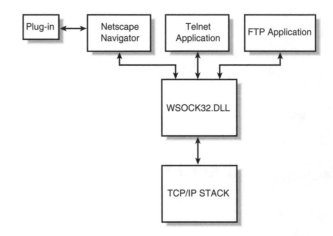

Tricking Socket Applications

The Socket Spy is implemented by changing the name of the socket DLL within the socket application. This is done using a binary editor on the program executable. With the editor, all occurrences of the string wsock32 are changed to wsock00. After you have modified the socket program, it loads WSOCK00.DLL, thinking that it is really WSOCK32.DLL. Because the Socket Spy DLL has all the proper entry points, the socket application links to the new DLL with no problems. Figure 24.2 shows how the Socket Spy DLL, WSOCK00.DLL, intercepts socket calls to and from Netscape's Navigator. Notice that the new DLL does not replace WSOCK32.DLL but acts as an intermediary between the socket application and the WSOCK32.DLL. Also notice that other WinSock applications still have direct access to the original WinSock DLL.

> **WARNING**
>
> This practice of modifying executables is strictly for in-house debugging because the executable checksums will be incorrect. Virus detection software really hates this!

Figure 24.2.
Winsock applications with the Socket Spy.

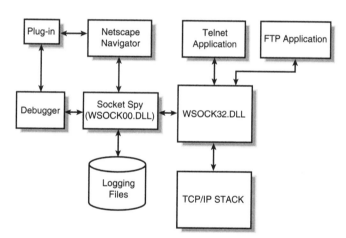

Using the Socket Spy with Netscape

You can use the Socket Spy with any WinSock application. To use Socket Spy with Netscape's Navigator in a debugging session, you must edit the Navigator's binary executable with binary editor and compile the Socket Spy DLL in debug.

Editing NETSCAPE.EXE

To set up the Socket Spy for use with Netscape, first find the file NETSCAPE.EXE. This file should be located in the directory above the plugins directory. Make sure to make a backup copy of NETSCAPE.EXE. Now get your favorite binary editor that can handle large files, and open the file. Use the editor's search facility and search for all occurrences of the string wsock32. Navigator 2.*x* and 3.*x* have only one such string. Change wsock32 to wsock00 and save the file. A good shareware binary editor is Hedit 1.2 by Yuri Software, which is shown in Figure 24.3.

Figure 24.3.

Changing wsock32 *to* wsock00 *with Hedit 1.2 by Yuri Software.*

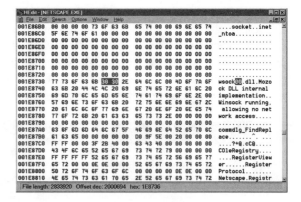

If you don't have a binary editor but you know the offset of the string within the file, you can use Microsoft Visual C to make the change. For example, Navigator 3.0 Beta 2 has the string at offset 0x1E8730. Select the menu item File|Open and pick Open As Binary (see Figure 24.4) in the lower portion of the Open dialog. Don't use the automatic open mode because it opens the file as Resources, which is not what you want.

Figure 24.4.

Opening a file as binary with Microsoft Visual C++ 4.0.

After the file is open and you can see the standard hexadecimal display, go to the offset with the Edit|Go To menu. Figure 24.5 shows the offset 0x1E8730 entered after Offset is selected in the list box.

Now change wsock32 to wsock00 and save the file.

Figure 24.5.
The Go To dialog in Microsoft Visual C++ 4.0.

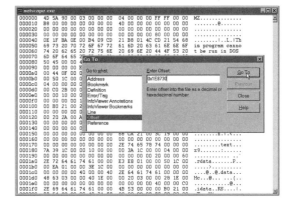

Getting the Files and Building

The next step is copying the files from the CD to a directory on your hard drive. The following files are located in the \CODE\SOCKSPY directory and should be copied:

SOCKSPY.CPP

SOCKCPY.H

SOCKSPY.DEF

SOCKSPY.MAK

Now build the DLL. With Visual C++, set your Output file name to [drive]: \windows\system\wsock00.dll. This allows the Navigator to find the DLL. Figure 24.6 shows how to set the Output filename with Microsoft's Developer Studio.

Figure 24.6.
Setting the output filename in Microsoft Visual C++ 4.0.

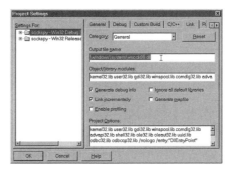

Also set the Executable for debug session and Working directory in the Debug area of your build settings. Figure 24.7 shows how to set the executable and working directory for D:\Program Files\Netscape\Navigator\Program\netscape.exe.

Figure 24.7.

Setting the executable and working directory.

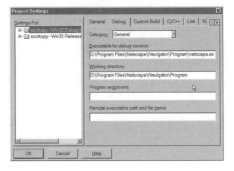

Now verify that things are working properly by setting a breakpoint in SOCKSPY.CPP on the WSAStartup routine and running the Navigator from within the debugger. Figure 24.8 shows this breakpoint with the Microsoft Debugger.

Figure 24.8.

Setting a breakpoint on WSAStartup.

When you have that working, you can set breakpoints in any of the socket routines while debugging your plug-in!

Under the Hood

The Socket Spy DLL is kind of an odd creature. Because the routines within the Spy DLL have the same names as the WSOCK32 routines, it can't use the standard wsock32.lib to build the Spy DLL. Instead, each API address must be saved to a function pointer using GetProcAddress. This is done during the DLL initialization routine, DllEntryPoint. You might want to consult Chapter 4, "Helper Applications and Network Communications," for a quick refresher on WinSock APIs.

The following code listing shows WinSock APIs being mapped to Socket Spy routines:

```
//
// This routine is called when your DLL is loaded.
//
BOOL WINAPI DllEntryPoint (HINSTANCE  hinstDLL,     // handle of DLL module
    DWORD  fdwReason,    // reason for calling function
    LPVOID  lpvReserved)
{

if (fdwReason == DLL_PROCESS_ATTACH)
{
if (!ulAttachCount++)
{
    HINSTANCE h;

    // Load the real winsock library

    if (!(h = LoadLibrary ("wsock32.dll")))
        return FALSE;

    // Get all the APIs

    pfnWinSock.accept = (DEFaccept)GetProcAddress (h, "accept");
    pfnWinSock.bind = (DEFbind)GetProcAddress (h, "bind");
    pfnWinSock.closesocket = (DEFclosesocket)GetProcAddress (h, "closesocket");
    pfnWinSock.connect = (DEFconnect)GetProcAddress (h, "connect");
    pfnWinSock.getsockname = (DEFgetsockname)GetProcAddress (h, "getsockname");
    pfnWinSock.getpeername = (DEFgetpeername)GetProcAddress (h, "getpeername");
    pfnWinSock.getsockopt = (DEFgetsockopt)GetProcAddress (h,
                "getsockopt");
    pfnWinSock.htonl = (DEFhtonl)GetProcAddress (h, "htonl");
    pfnWinSock.htons = (DEFhtons)GetProcAddress (h, "htons");
    pfnWinSock.inet_addr = (DEFinet_addr)GetProcAddress (h, "inet_addr");
    pfnWinSock.inet_ntoa = (DEFinet_ntoa)GetProcAddress (h, "inet_ntoa");
    pfnWinSock.ioctlsocket = (DEFioctlsocket)GetProcAddress (h, "ioctlsocket");
    pfnWinSock.listen = (DEFlisten)GetProcAddress (h, "listen");
    pfnWinSock.ntohl = (DEFntohl)GetProcAddress (h, "ntohl");
    pfnWinSock.ntohs = (DEFntohs)GetProcAddress (h, "ntohs");
    pfnWinSock.recv = (DEFrecv)GetProcAddress (h, "recv");
    pfnWinSock.recvfrom = (DEFrecvfrom)GetProcAddress (h, "recvfrom");
    pfnWinSock.select = (DEFselect)GetProcAddress (h, "select");
    pfnWinSock.send = (DEFsend)GetProcAddress (h, "send");
    pfnWinSock.sendto = (DEFsendto)GetProcAddress (h, "sendto");
    pfnWinSock.setsockopt = (DEFsetsockopt)GetProcAddress (h, "setsockopt");
    pfnWinSock.shutdown = (DEFshutdown)GetProcAddress (h, "shutdown");
    pfnWinSock.socket = (DEFsocket)GetProcAddress (h, "socket");
    pfnWinSock.gethostbyaddr = (DEFgethostbyaddr)GetProcAddress (h,
        "gethostbyaddr");
    pfnWinSock.gethostbyname = (DEFgethostbyname)GetProcAddress (h,
        "gethostbyname");
    pfnWinSock.getprotobyname = (DEFgetprotobyname)GetProcAddress (h,
        "getprotobyname");
    pfnWinSock.getprotobynumber = (DEFgetprotobynumber)GetProcAddress (h,
        "getprotobynumber");
    pfnWinSock.getservbyname = (DEFgetservbyname)GetProcAddress (h,
        "getservbyname");
    pfnWinSock.getservbyport = (DEFgetservbyport)GetProcAddress (h,
        "getservbyport");
```

```
    pfnWinSock.gethostname = (DEFgethostname)GetProcAddress (h,
        "gethostname");
    pfnWinSock.WSAAsyncSelect = (DEFWSAAsyncSelect)GetProcAddress (h,
        "WSAAsyncSelect");
    pfnWinSock.WSAAsyncGetHostByAddr = (DEFWSAAsyncGetHostByAddr)
        GetProcAddress (h, "WSAAsyncGetHostByAddr");
    pfnWinSock.WSAAsyncGetHostByName = (DEFWSAAsyncGetHostByName)
        GetProcAddress (h, "WSAAsyncGetHostByName");
    pfnWinSock.WSAAsyncGetProtoByNumber = (DEFWSAAsyncGetProtoByNumber)
        GetProcAddress (h, "WSAAsyncGetProtoByNumber");
    pfnWinSock.WSAAsyncGetProtoByName = (DEFWSAAsyncGetProtoByName)
        GetProcAddress (h, "WSAAsyncGetProtoByName");
    pfnWinSock.WSAAsyncGetServByPort = (DEFWSAAsyncGetServByPort)
        GetProcAddress (h, "WSAAsyncGetServByPort");
    pfnWinSock.WSAAsyncGetServByName = (DEFWSAAsyncGetServByName)
        GetProcAddress (h, "WSAAsyncGetServByName");
    pfnWinSock.WSACancelAsyncRequest = (DEFWSACancelAsyncRequest)
        GetProcAddress (h, "WSACancelAsyncRequest");
    pfnWinSock.WSASetBlockingHook = (DEFWSASetBlockingHook)
        GetProcAddress (h, "WSASetBlockingHook");
    pfnWinSock.WSAUnhookBlockingHook = (DEFWSAUnhookBlockingHook)
        GetProcAddress (h, "WSAUnhookBlockingHook");
    pfnWinSock.WSAGetLastError = (DEFWSAGetLastError)
        GetProcAddress (h, "WSAGetLastError");
    pfnWinSock.WSASetLastError = (DEFWSASetLastError)
        GetProcAddress (h, "WSASetLastError");
    pfnWinSock.WSACancelBlockingCall = (DEFWSACancelBlockingCall)
        GetProcAddress (h, "WSACancelBlockingCall");
    pfnWinSock.WSAIsBlocking = (DEFWSAIsBlocking)
        GetProcAddress (h, "WSAIsBlocking");
    pfnWinSock.WSAStartup = (DEFWSAStartup)GetProcAddress (h, "WSAStartup");
    pfnWinSock.WSACleanup = (DEFWSACleanup)GetProcAddress (h, "WSACleanup");
    pfnWinSock.WSARecvEx = (DEFWSARecvEx)GetProcAddress (h, "WSARecvEx");
    pfnWinSock.__WSAFDIsSet = (DEF__WSAFDIsSet)
        GetProcAddress (h, "__WSAFDIsSet");
    }
    }
    return TRUE;
}
```

All of the wsock32 API pointers are saved to a structure called WinSock. When an application such as Netscape's Navigator calls the Socket Spy, the appropriate wsock32 API is called. For example, if the Navigator calls the socket API connect, it is routed to the real API saved with pfnWinSock.connect:

```
int PASCAL FAR connect (SOCKET s,
    const struct sockaddr FAR *name,
    int namelen)
{
    return pfnWinSock.connect (s, name, namelen);
}
```

In this case, the typedef for the function prototype is declared as follows:

```
typedef int (WINAPI *DEFconnect) (SOCKET s, const struct sockaddr *name, int
➥namelen);
```

The WinSock structure member is as follows:

```
DEFconnect connect;
```

This design enables you to put a breakpoint in any of the socket APIs or even add code.

The Data Files

The Socket Spy creates and writes to data files during its normal operation. These files are created during WSAStartup, which is always called by a socket application:

```
int PASCAL FAR WSAStartup (WORD wVersionRequired, LPWSADATA lpWSAData)
{
    if (!hSend)
        hSend = CreateFile ("send.dat", GENERIC_WRITE, FILE_SHARE_READ, 0,
            CREATE_ALWAYS, FILE_ATTRIBUTE_NORMAL | FILE_FLAG_WRITE_THROUGH, 0);

    if (!hRecv)
        hRecv = CreateFile ("recv.dat", GENERIC_WRITE, FILE_SHARE_READ, 0,
            CREATE_ALWAYS, FILE_ATTRIBUTE_NORMAL | FILE_FLAG_WRITE_THROUGH, 0);

     int rc = pfnWinSock.WSAStartup (wVersionRequired, lpWSAData);

    return rc;
}
```

Notice that the files are created as FILE_SHARE_READ. This allows another application to read the data as the Socket Spy is writing it. For example, if you have a UNIX-like tail program, you can watch the data as it comes across. Try this:

```
tail -f send.dat
```

After creation, the send.dat file is written to during the send API. The send.dat file captures to disk all data transferred via the send API called by the WinSock application. You can put a breakpoint in this routine to view send buffers while debugging. The following code shows socket data as it is written to disk by the Windows WriteFile API. After the data is written to file, the WinSock API is called via the pfnWinSock.send function pointer:

```
//
// Netscape uses this routine to send data. Put a breakpoint here and
// take a look at the buffer.
//
int PASCAL FAR send (SOCKET s, const char FAR * buf, int len, int flags)
{
    // Write the buffer to our debug file

    DWORD bytesWritten;

    if (hSend)
        BOOL rc = WriteFile (hSend, buf, len, &bytesWritten, 0);

    // Send the data

    int rc = pfnWinSock.send (s, buf, len, flags);

    return rc;
}
```

Just like the send.dat data file, the recv.dat data file also captures data to disk but does it in the reverse direction (from the network to the WinSock application). Notice that the WinSock recv API is called by the pfnWinSock.recv function pointer before data is written to file with the Windows WriteFile API. Again, you might want to put a breakpoint here to view socket data on the fly:

```
//
// Netscape uses this routine to receive data. Put a breakpoint here and
// take a look at the buffer.
//
int PASCAL FAR recv (SOCKET s, char FAR * buf, int len, int flags)
{
    // Receive the data

    int bytesRecv = pfnWinSock.recv (s, buf, len, flags);

    if (bytesRecv != SOCKET_ERROR)
    {
        // Write the data to our debug file

        DWORD bytesWritten;

        if (hRecv)
            BOOL rc = WriteFile (hRecv, buf, bytesRecv, &bytesWritten, 0);
    }

    return bytesRecv;
}
```

The WSACleanup WinSock API is called when a Windows WinSock application is finished using Windows sockets. During this time, the Socket Spy closes its data files, send.dat and recv.dat, with the Windows API CloseHandle:

```
int PASCAL FAR WSACleanup(void)
{
    if (hSend)
        CloseHandle (hSend);

    if (hRecv)
        CloseHandle (hRecv);

    return pfnWinSock.WSACleanup ();
}
```

Running the Socket Spy

Don't be afraid to leave the Socket Spy in place with the modified version of the Navigator. It's nice to take a peek at the data files occasionally to see what Navigator is up to. For example, when running the CPU Monitor Plug-in Sample, the send.dat file shows the GET request sent to the HTTP server that runs a CGI program:

```
GET /zan-bin/vmstat.cgi HTTP/1.0
Connection: Keep-Alive
User-Agent: Mozilla/3.0B2 (Win95; I)
```

```
Pragma: no-cache
Host: www.swcp.com
Accept: image/gif, image/x-xbitmap, image/jpeg, image/pjpeg, */*
```

The CGI program called `vmstat.cgi` performs a `vmstat` on the UNIX end and sends back the output. This output can be seen in the `recv.dat` file:

```
HTTP/1.0 200 Document follows
Date: Sun, 14 Apr 1996 20:05:57 GMT
Server: NCSA/1.4.2
Content-type: text/plain

VMSTAT 1 second intervals.
 procs     memory            page                    disk          faults      cpu
 r b w   avm   fre  re at  pi  po  fr  de  sr d0 s1 s2 s3  in  sy  cs us sy id
 0 0 0     0  1280   0  5   3   3   1   0  16  4  8 10  0 223 607 134 20 25 55
 0 0 0     0  1280   0  0  32   0   0   0   0  0  1  0  0 112 319  79  3 10 87
```

These data files were helpful in developing the CPU Monitor Sample.

Conclusion

Modify a socket application executable with a binary editor to make it load WSOCK00.DLL instead of WSOCK32.DLL. This allows the Socket Spy to filter all socket APIs. Put breakpoints in the Socket Spy source file `sockspy.cpp` and look at data buffers. Add code to Socket Spy for special debugging needs.

Allow the modified version of Netscape's Navigator to run at all times. The performance impact is negligible.

Feel free to try Socket Spy with any Windows 95 socket applications.

What's Next?

Part IV of this book, "Plug-In Programming Resources for Windows," gives step by step instructions for building a Navigator plug-in with the Borland, Microsoft, and Watcom C++ compilers. This section starts with an introduction to the Windows C++ compilers and moves on to separate chapters for each compiler.

PART IV

Plug-In Programming Resources for Windows

25   About Windows C++ Compilers

26   Writing a Plug-In with Borland C++ 5.*x*

27   Writing a Plug-In with Microsoft Visual C++ 4.*x*

28   Writing a Plug-In with Watcom C++ 10.*x*

CHAPTER 25

About Windows C++ Compilers

Introduction

Chapters 26, 27, and 28 cover building Netscape Navigator plug-ins with the Borland, Microsoft, and Watcom C++ compilers. As with the rest of this book's samples, all plug-ins are targeted for Windows 95/NT.

For these examples, source code is used from the previous plug-in samples, which means that there is no source code on the CD-ROM for the Borland or Watcom environments. If you are a Borland or Watcom developer, don't worry. The next chapters give very detailed instructions on building a plug-in with these environments using Microsoft source code as a base.

A few anomalies are involved when writing plug-ins using different development environments. Resources, routine exporting, function declarations, and calling conventions can give a plug-in developer premature gray hair.

Resources

As you probably already know, Navigator looks for the `MIMEType`, `FileExtents`, and `FileOpenName` resources in your plug-in. These resource values are defined with a version block in the .rc file.

Borland and Microsoft enable you to create a version resource with their respective resource editors. In Chapters 26, 27, and 28, you'll see how to do this. With Microsoft, the version block header must be changed to Windows Multilingual. Borland defaults to this.

Watcom's resource editor cannot create a version resource. However, its resource compiler can compile one. Just copy one of the .rc files from the CD-ROM for use with Watcom.

Calling Conventions

Calling conventions tend to change for different compilers. Stack argument order and register versus stack calling must be properly defined for each compiler. Because the plug-in API bypasses standard Windows DLL calling conventions in the interest of cross-platform support, special attention must be paid to calling conventions for each compiler. Additionally, changes need to be made to the Windows DLL calling conventions in order for the Borland and Watcom compilers to work properly.

Plug-In Methods

If you remember from Chapter 8, API mapping was discussed. API mapping hides the Windows plug-in DLL interface from Netscape's Navigator, making both the Navigator and plug-in code portable across the Macintosh, UNIX, and Windows platforms. Navigator gets pointers to NPP type plug-in methods and gives the plug-ins pointers to NPN type methods. After this is done, the Navigator and plug-in call each other directly through the use of these function pointers.

All of this works great until you try to use a compiler with the wrong default calling convention, which results in a serious trap! Navigator calls your plug-in methods using the _cdecl calling convention. This convention is used by the Microsoft compiler in which Netscape's Navigator was written. The _cdecl calling convention passes arguments on the stack from right to left, with the last argument pushed first. Some compilers use a register-based calling convention as the default. Passing function parameters through registers is faster than using the stack.

If you have a compiler that uses a register-based calling convention (most notably, the Watcom compiler), you can either define all the plug-in methods as _cdecl or simply change the compiler switches to use a stack-based convention as default.

Windows 95 DLL Entry Points

Another difference that you should be aware of is the calling convention for your plug-in's DLL entry points. For example, in Windows 95 the DLL entry points are defined as WINAPI. This boils down to _stdcall. In _stdcall, arguments are pushed from right to left, with the last argument first, such as _cdecl. This is very different from Windows 3.1 DLLs, which use the _pascal convention. In _pascal, arguments are pushed on the stack in reverse order, with the first argument pushed first.

extern "C"

With the Microsoft compiler, it is enough to declare the DLL entry points as external C in the header. The Watcom and Borland compilers need an additional extern "C" before the actual routine.

Exporting

Both Borland and Microsoft use a module definition, or .DEF, file to export the DLL routines. Watcom has something called a librarian command file that is similar to a .DEF file. Creating this file is covered in detail in Chapter 28, "Writing a Plug-In with Watcom C++ 10.*x*."

Class Libraries

Both Microsoft and Watcom come with the Microsoft Foundation Class Library (MFC). Borland ships with the Object Windows Library (OWL). Although the Microsoft example uses a class library, the Watcom and Borland examples do not. Adding class library support to Borland and Watcom is left to the reader as an exercise, because it is beyond the scope of this book.

Conclusion

With a few tweaks, the Borland and Watcom C++ compilers are acceptable alternatives for Netscape Navigator plug-in development. If your Borland or Watcom plug-in produces either compile or runtime errors, be sure to check your resources and calling conventions.

What's Next?

Read on to learn how to build a plug-in from scratch with the Borland, Microsoft, and Watcom compilers. The next three chapters include plenty of screen shots taken with Borland C++ 5.0, Microsoft Visual C++ 4.0, and Watcom C/C++ 10.6.

CHAPTER 26

Writing a Plug-In with Borland C++ 5.x

Introduction

Borland C++ 5 provides a good alternative to Microsoft for Windows plug-in developers. Borland's Integrated Development Environment (IDE) allows a plug-in developer to edit, compile, run, and debug a plug-in without leaving the environment. Resources required for plug-in DLLs are easily edited within the IDE. Borland ships a number of libraries in the product, including Standard C++, Standard C, Services, Container Class, WinSys, ObjectComponents Framework (OCF), and ObjectWindows Library (OWL). OWL also has Windows Sockets classes for direct socket communications using TCP/IP.

This chapter is a step by step guide to building a Netscape Navigator plug-in using Borland C++ 5. The example does not use a class library such as OWL. It is based on the Non-MFC sample found earlier in Chapter 22. Using OWL and its `TWindow` class to develop a plug-in is discussed after the example.

Where to Find the Files

If you want to build this sample plug-in, you need to create a directory and put in it some files borrowed from the Non-MFC sample on the CD-ROM. These files are in the \CODE\NOMFC, \CODE\INC, and \CODE\COMMON directories. You need the files shown in the following lists.

For the \CODE\NOMFC directory, you need these files:

- npshell.cpp: Plug-in entry point methods.
- npwindow.cpp, npwindow.h: The `CPluginWindow` class.

For the \CODE\INC directory, you need these files:

- npapi.h: Plug-in API prototypes and associated structures.
- npupp.h: Plug-in API prototypes.

For the \CODE\COMMON directory, you need this file:

- npwin.cpp: DLL entry point to plug-in API mapping.

Put all five files in the same directory to match this example.

Preparing the Files for the Borland Compiler

After you copy the files to a new directory, a few modifications must be made so that the Borland compiler works properly. First, you must change the included header file paths and then reprototype the DLL entry points.

1. All the CPP files include Netscape headers in relative paths for the Microsoft example. Change these to local, like this:

```
#include "..\inc\npapi.h"
```

should be

```
#include "npapi.h"
```

You can also delete the `include` of stdafx.h in npwin.cpp. This file is for Microsoft's class library and is not needed for Borland.

2. The file npwin.cpp contains three exported functions:

```
NPError WINAPI NP_EXPORT NP_GetEntryPoints(NPPluginFuncs* pFuncs)
NPError WINAPI NP_EXPORT NP_Initialize(NPNetscapeFuncs* pFuncs)
NPError WINAPI NP_EXPORT NP_Shutdown()
```

Borland needs these to be public externals. Put an `extern "C"` in front of each routine:

```
extern "C" NPError WINAPI NP_EXPORT NP_GetEntryPoints(NPPluginFuncs* pFuncs)
extern "C" NPError WINAPI NP_EXPORT NP_Initialize(NPNetscapeFuncs* pFuncs)
extern "C" NPError WINAPI NP_EXPORT NP_Shutdown()
```

The Example

The next three sections give step by step instructions for creating a plug-in from scratch with Borland's IDE. The first section shows you how to set up a new project that creates a Windows plug-in DLL. The next section shows how to build the plug-in. Lastly, the third section covers testing and debugging your Borland built plug-in.

Setting Up the Project

Your first task is to create the project with all the appropriate files. Steps 1 through 7 and their associated figures show how to create the project with the Target Expert, create and modify a new resource, add new files, and modify the library definition file for new Windows DLL entry points.

Step 1: Create a New Project

After you have started the Borland IDE, use the File|New|Project menu item to create a new project. Now the Target Expert should be up. Specify your project path and name in the top entry field. In Figure 26.1, you can see a project path and name of `d:\src\plugin\npplugin`. This should be the same path in which you put the files previously. To make your life easier, begin the project name with `np`. Navigator requires plug-in DLLs to begin with `np` or the plug-in will not be loaded. It's a good idea to follow this convention throughout your project.

Select a Target Type of Dynamic Library (.DLL). Platform should be Win32, and Target Model should be GUI. Deselect all class libraries and pick Static for linkage. The New Target dialog should look like the dialog shown in Figure 26.1.

Figure 26.1.
Using the Target Expert.

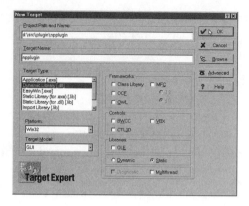

Step 2: Delete npplugin.cpp

For the purposes of this example, npplugin.cpp is not needed and should be deleted. Right-click on this file in the view and select Delete Node. Figure 26.2 shows the menu that results from a right mouse click and the option to delete a node (file, in this case) is highlighted.

Figure 26.2.
Deleting a node.

Step 3: Add a New Resource

Double-click the resource file npplugin.rc in the project view. This brings up the resource editor. Select Resource|New from the main menu. This menu item is highlighted in Figure 26.3.

Figure 26.3.
Creating a new resource.

Step 4: Make a VERSIONINFO Resource

The Netscape Navigator looks for a VERSIONINFO resource in the DLL to determine the plug-in's MIME type, file extension, and file open name. Create a VERSIONINFO resource by selecting the VERSIONINFO item in the New Resource dialog and clicking OK as shown in Figure 26.4.

Figure 26.4.
Creating a VERSIONINFO *resource.*

Step 5: Add the Plug-In's Resource Information

Add your plug-in's resource information. In this example, the MIME type is x-any/x-mimetype. The file extension is .ext, and the file open name is Test Plug-in (*.ext). Remember that this is a fictitious MIME type and it won't work on an HTTP server without the proper configuration. For the purposes of this example, files are opened on the local drive, which loads your plug-in based on extension rather than MIME type. Figure 26.5 shows the new resource information as a highlighted block of text. Save and close the resource file after adding the new information.

Figure 26.5.
Adding the plug-in's resources.

```
VERSIONINFO_1 VERSIONINFO
FILEVERSION 1, 0, 0, 0
PRODUCTVERSION 1, 0, 0, 0
FILEOS VOS_NT_WINDOWS32
FILETYPE VFT_APP
{
  BLOCK "StringFileInfo"
  {
    BLOCK "040904E4"
    {
      VALUE "CompanyName", "My Company\000\000"
      VALUE "FileDescription", "Description from .def file here\000"
      VALUE "FileVersion", "1.00\000\000"
      VALUE "InternalName", "Application name\000"
      VALUE "LegalCopyright", "Copyright © My Company 1996\000\000"
      VALUE "OriginalFilename", ".exe file name here\000"
      VALUE "MIMEType", "x-any/x-mimetype\000"
      VALUE "FileExtents", ".ext\000"
      VALUE "FileOpenName", "Test Plug-in (*.ext)\000"
    }
  }

  BLOCK "VarFileInfo"
  {
    VALUE "Translation", 0x409, 1252
  }
}
```

Step 6: Edit the .DEF File

In the library definition file (npplugin.def, created by the Target Expert), define the library name and its three exported routines: NP_GetEntryPoints, NP_Initialize, and NP_Shutdown. Figure 26.6 shows how the library definition file should look for Borland.

Figure 26.6.
Editing the .DEF file.

Step 7: Add the Files

Right-click on your project view and select Add node. This menu is the same one that is used to delete a node in Figure 26.2. When the Add to Project List dialog comes up (see Figure 26.7), select the files npshell.cpp, npwin.cpp, and npwindow.cpp. Click on the Open button to add them to your project.

Figure 26.7.
Selecting files.

Compiling the Project

Steps 1 through 5 show how to compile the project. First, the project is compiled with a full build and warnings are examined. Then, the DLL output directory is changed and the project is relinked to create a DLL in the Navigator's `plugin` directory.

Step 1: Build the Project

In the main menu, select Project|Build all to build the whole project. Figure 26.8 shows the location of the Build all menu item. This will be the first build. Later, the DLL output directory will be changed to the Navigator's home directory and the project will be relinked.

Figure 26.8.
Start building the project.

Step 2: Build Complete

When the build is complete, your status should be Success. There will be some warnings for unused parameters. You should see something similar to Figure 26.9 with 297,348 lines compiled and 21 warnings.

Figure 26.9.

The Building npplugin - Complete dialog.

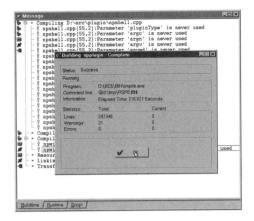

Step 3: Examine the Warnings

Take a look at the warnings. Most are from npshell.cpp. This file contains the plug-in entry points. You can get rid of these warnings by changing the warning level in the compiler options. Most warnings (as shown in Figure 26.10) should be parameter never used.

Figure 26.10.

Looking at the warnings.

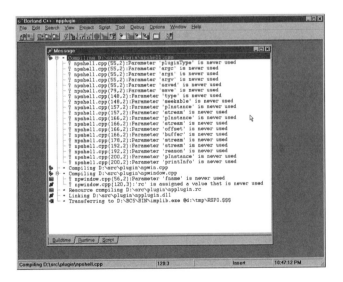

Step 4: Change the Final Output Directory

Select Options|Project in the main menu to bring up the project options. Figure 26.11 shows where this menu item is located.

Make the Final Output Directory the Navigator's `plugins` directory. This allows you to debug the plug-in. Figure 26.12 shows that directory path on this machine:

```
d:\Program Files\Netscape\Navigator\Program\plugins
```

Figure 26.11.

Bringing up project options.

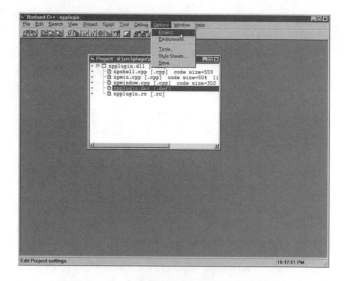

Figure 26.12.

Changing the final output directory.

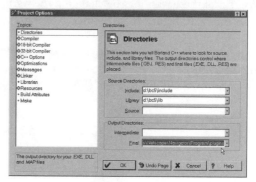

Step 5: Make the Project

Now that the DLL output directory is changed, make the project, which causes it to relink the DLL and write the DLL to the new output directory. You can use the toolbar button for this, as shown in Figure 26.13.

Figure 26.13.

Making the project.

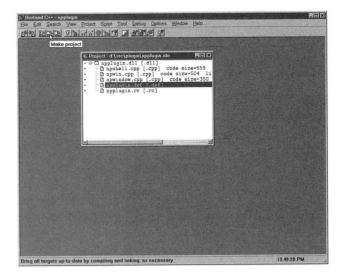

Testing Your Project

To test and debug the Borland created plug-in, you need to create a test file, set a breakpoint in Borland's debugger, load the Navigator executable, and verify the plug-in's resource data. If all goes well, you should be able to hit the breakpoint and display the data filename. The following steps 1 through 8 show how to do this.

Step 1: Create a Test File

Use a text editor to create a test file. Although this plug-in won't read it, the file must have some data in it or Navigator produces an error and the plug-in is not loaded. Make sure you save the file with the proper file extension indicated in the resource. In this case, it is .ext.

Step 2: Set a Breakpoint

Open the npshell.cpp file and set a breakpoint by clicking in the left margin. In Figure 26.14, a breakpoint is set in the NPP_StreamAsFile API, which will be called with the name of the test file.

Figure 26.14.
Setting a breakpoint.

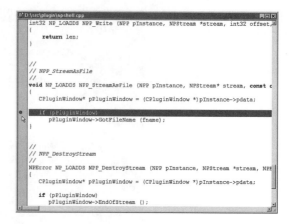

Step 3: Load the Program

Using the Debug|Load menu, bring up the Load Program dialog. Figure 26.15 shows the location of this menu item.

Figure 26.15.
Bringing up the Load Program dialog.

When the Load Program dialog is up, use the Browse button, find the Navigator executable, and click OK to load it. Figure 26.16 shows Navigator loading from the following path:

```
d:\Program Files\Netscape\Navigator\Program\netscape.exe
```

No arguments are required.

Figure 26.16.
Loading the Navigator.

Step 4: Run the Program

Start the Navigator using the Debug|Run menu. Figure 26.17 shows the location of this menu item.

Figure 26.17.
Running the program.

Watch Navigator come up. Figure 26.18 shows Atlas Preview Release 2 initializing.

Figure 26.18.
Atlas comes up.

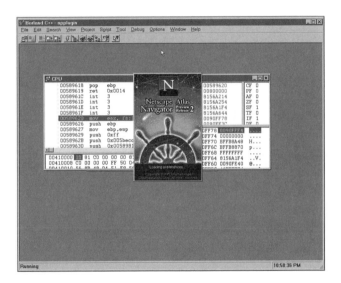

Step 5: Verify the Plug-In's Resources

First, verify that the plug-in's resource data is correct by bringing up Help|About Plug-ins in the Navigator. Figure 26.19 shows the location of this menu item. The fact that your plug-in is listed in Help|About Plug-ins does not mean that it will execute; it only means that your resources are correct. Navigator does not load a plug-in DLL to get this information.

Figure 26.19.
Using About Plug-ins.

In Figure 26.20, you can see that Navigator has found this plug-in. Verify the MIME type and suffixes. In this case, the MIME type is x-any/x-mimetype and suffixes are ext.

Figure 26.20.
Finding the plug-in.

Step 6: Open the Test File

With File|Open File on the Navigator, prepare to open the test file created earlier. Figure 26.21 shows the location of this menu item.

Figure 26.21.
Opening a local file.

Make sure that the proper file type is in the Files of type drop down. Figure 26.22 shows how to select a file type of Test Plug-in (*.ext).

Figure 26.22.
Files of type.

Step 7: Hit the Breakpoint

After the test file is opened, you should hit your breakpoint. Verify the filename. Figure 26.23 shows how to hit the breakpoint and see that the data filename is d:\src\plugin\data.ext.

Figure 26.23.

Hitting the breakpoint.

Step 8: Hello World

This sample displays a message indicating that it has subclassed the plug-in window and the URL. In Figure 26.24, you can see that the plug-in is displaying "The plug-in has successfully subclassed the Navigator window!" with URL = file:///D¦/src/plugin/data.ext. That funky URL is Netscape's way of locating a file on your local disk drive.

Figure 26.24.

Displaying a message and URL.

All Done

Well, that was really stimulating, wasn't it? This plug-in example doesn't rock the world with its functionality, but hopefully it will help you get started with Borland C++ 5. Most large Borland plug-in endeavors need to use the OWL class library.

Using OWL

The preceding example was based on the Microsoft Non-MFC sample. This sample does not use a class library such as Microsoft's MFC or Borland's OWL. Although a sample using OWL is beyond the scope of this book, here is some minimal information.

Navigator creates a window for the plug-in to use. A handle to this window is provided during the NPP_SetWindow API. You can effectively subclass this window using OWL by creating a TWindow with a valid window handle in NPP_SetWindow. For example, using the wave audio sample, a window derived from OWL's TWindow can be created like this:

```
pWave->pWindow = new TPluginWindow (pWave, (HWND)window->window, ::Module);
```

In this case, the TPluginWindow constructor passes on the window handle and module to TWindow like this:

```
//
// Constructor
//
CPluginWindow::CPluginWindow (CWave *pWave, HWND hWnd, TModule* module)
    : TWindow (hWnd, module)
{
    this->pWave = pWave;
}
```

Within CPluginWindow, controls can be created in the normal OWL fashion and a response table can be set up.

Conclusion

Use the preceding step by step guide to build a very simple Borland-based plug-in module. Don't forget to modify the source files as outlined in the beginning of this chapter. As you get better with Borland (or if you are already an expert), add the OWL class library.

What's Next?

The next chapter takes you through a similar step by step example of building a plug-in with Microsoft's Visual C++ 4.*x*.

CHAPTER 27

Writing a Plug-In with Microsoft Visual C++ 4.x

Introduction

This book's examples were written and compiled with Microsoft's Visual C++ 4.0. Additionally, the Netscape Plug-in SDK was also written in Visual C++. This development environment includes many tools such as Visual Workbench, App Studio, AppWizard, ClassWizard, and several others. All the functionality needed to build and test a plug-in is included in Visual C++: text editor, compiler, linker, resource editor, and debugger. The Microsoft Foundation Class Library (MFC), included with the product, is somewhat of an industry standard. MFC, as shown in many of this book's examples, makes plug-in development much simpler.

Although the book contains many examples using Visual C++, none of the examples explains how to create a plug-in from scratch. This chapter contains a step by step example of how to write a plug-in starting with files from the Server CPU Monitor example. Complete screen shots show all settings and procedures needed to build a plug-in. If you are relatively new to Visual C++, this is the chapter for you. Many hours of frustration can be avoided by following these simple steps.

It's interesting to note that this example does not use the MFC AppWizard (dll). For Netscape Navigator plug-in development, there is no need to overcomplicate your project by using the AppWizard. This example adds MFC later with the project settings. There is one important thing to remember if you use the sans AppWizard method to create an MFC plug-in: Be sure to define a global instance of CWinApp. In this example, it is done in the file npshell.cpp:

```
CWinApp theApp;
```

Defining CWinApp initializes MFC. If you forget to do this, you'll see some very odd assertions while running your plug-in!

Where to Find the Files

If you want to follow along with the example, you need to get the files shown in the following lists from the Server CPU Monitor sample.

For the \CODE\CPUMON directory, you need these files:

- npcpumon.cpp, npcpumon.h: The main object, CCpuMon.
- npshell.cpp: Plug-in entry point methods.
- npwindow.cpp, npwindow.h: The CPluginWindow class.
- npcpumon.def: The DLL module definition file.

For the \CODE\INC directory, you need these files:

- npapi.h: Plug-in API prototypes and associated structures.
- npupp.h: Plug-in API prototypes.

For the \CODE\COMMON directory, you need these files:

- npwin.cpp: DLL entry point to plug-in API mapping.
- stdafx.cpp: Includes standard headers.

Put all files in the same directory to match this example.

Modifying the Files

After you copy the files to a new directory, change the header `include` paths. All the CPP files except stdafx.cpp include a relative path for stdafx.h. Change these to local:

```
#include "..\inc\stdafx.h"
```

should be

```
#include "stdafx.h"
```

The Example

The next three sections give step by step instructions for creating a plug-in from scratch with MicroSoft's IDE. The first section shows you how to set up a new project that creates a Windows plug-in DLL. Then, the next section shows how to build the plug-in. Lastly, the third section covers testing and debugging your Microsoft built plug-in.

Setting up the Project

To set up a project for Visual C++, first you must create a new project with the proper project types. Then, create and change the resource file. Finally, you add the source files and change the build settings. Steps 1 through 7 demonstrate this.

Step 1: Create a New Project

First, start the Developer Studio by double-clicking on the Microsoft Developer Studio icon. After that moment of great excitement, create a new Project Workspace with File|New in the main menu. Figure 27.1 shows Project Workspace selected in the New dialog.

Figure 27.1.
Creating a New Project Workspace.

Step 2: Select the Project Type

Select Dynamic-Link Library with the name of npcpumon, Win32, and the location of the directory in which your files are stored. Figure 27.2 shows the project of name npcpumon in location d:\src\cpumon for platform Win32 and a type of Dynamic-Link Library.

Figure 27.2.
Creating a new DLL.

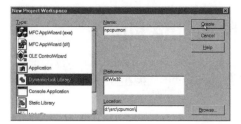

Step 3: Create the Resource

Now that you have a project, create a resource by using the Insert|Resource menu item. The location of this menu item is shown in Figure 27.3.

Figure 27.3.
Inserting a resource.

Select a resource type of Version and click OK. Figure 27.4 shows the resource type of Version selected.

Figure 27.4.
Selecting Version resource type.

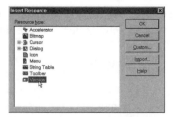

Step 4: Change the Resource Block-Header Properties

You need to change the Block Header properties to Windows, Multilingual. If you don't do this, your plug-in will not be recognized by the Navigator! Double-click on the block header to bring up the properties dialog. In Figure 27.5, you can see that the language ID is English (United States) and the code page is Windows, Multilingual. After these modifications are complete, save the resource as npcpumon.rc.

Figure 27.5.
Changing the Block-Header properties.

Step 5: Add the Plug-In's Resource Information

Next, open the resource as Text. You do this so that you can add your plug-in specific information to the version block. The resource editor is not capable of adding new information in the version block, so you must use the text editor. Figure 27.6 shows how to change the Open As drop-down to Text.

Figure 27.6.
Opening the resource as text.

Add the MIME type, file extension, and file open name to the resource. This example uses `application/x-tex`, `tex`, and `CPU Monitor (*.tex)`, respectively. In Figure 27.7, you can see this new information as a highlighted block of text.

Figure 27.7.
Adding the plug-in resource information.

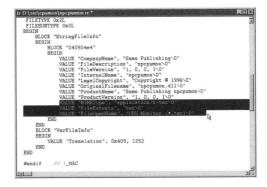

Step 6: Adding the Files

Add the files for the Server CPU Monitor to the project with the Insert|Files into Project menu item. Figure 27.8 shows the location of this menu item. These files are npcpumon.cpp, npcpumon.def, npcpumon.rc, npshell.cpp, npwin.cpp, npwindow.cpp, and stdafx.h.

Figure 27.8.

Bringing up the Insert Files dialog.

You can select all the files at the same time by holding down the Ctrl key. Figure 27.9 shows all the files highlighted.

Figure 27.9.

The Insert Files into Project dialog.

Step 7: Changing Build Settings

Bring up the Project Settings dialog by selecting the Build|Settings main menu item. Figure 27.10 shows this menu item.

Figure 27.10.

Bringing up the Project Settings dialog.

In the General tab area (see Figure 27.11), select "Use MFC in a Static Library" to add the MFC library to the project. You probably should statically link to MFC, rather than dynamically link, to avoid conflicts with Netscape's linkage of MFC.

Figure 27.11.

Statically linking to MFC.

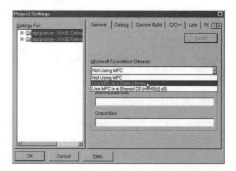

Put in the Netscape Navigator path, executable, and working directory in the Debug tab area. This enables you to run Navigator for debugging the plug-in. Figure 27.12 shows the following Navigator path:

```
d:\Program Files\Netscape\Navigator\Program\netscape.exe
```

Figure 27.12.
Pathing in Navigator.

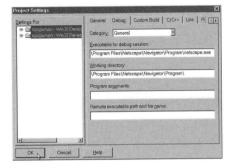

Now switch to the C/C++ tab area (see Figure 27.13). Under Category Preprocessor, add the pre-processor definition _USRDLL. This is required by MFC.

Figure 27.13.
Adding _USRDLL.

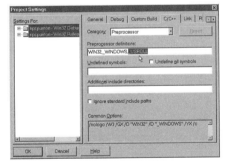

Switch to the Link tab area (see Figure 27.14). Set the Output filename to reflect the path of the Navigator's plugins directory and the name of the plug-in.

Figure 27.14.
Setting the plug-in's Output directory.

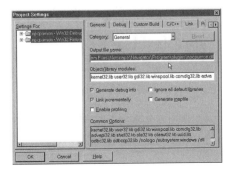

Compiling the Project

To build the plug-in, the next two steps show how to start a full build and check the output for errors.

Step 1: Build the Plug-In

Using Build|Build npcpumon.dll or Build|Rebuild All in the main menu, build the plug-in DLL. Figure 27.15 shows the location of these menu items.

Figure 27.15.
Starting a build.

Step 2: Check the Build Output

Upon completion, the output should look something like what you see in Figure 27.16, with 0 errors and 0 warnings.

Figure 27.16.
Build output.

Testing Your Project

The next seven steps show how to debug this newly created plug-in. To do this, you must create a test file, set a breakpoint, run the Navigator, and open the test file.

Step 1: Create a Test File

The Server CPU Monitor sample plug-in needs a file with the extension .tex opened in Navigator to load the plug-in. Normally, this file would contain the URL of a CGI program that returns server statistics. (See Chapter 19, "The CPU Monitor Plug-In," for further information.) For the purposes of this example, just create a dummy file with garbage in it with a .tex extension.

> **NOTE**
>
> The extension .tex and MIME type `application/x-tex` were picked almost randomly to use with the Server CPU Monitor. That way, the server configuration did not have to change in order to try the sample. Use this MIME type and extension for testing only!

Step 2: Set a Breakpoint

Set a breakpoint in the code. A good place for the breakpoint is in the `NPP_StreamAsFile` API in the file npshell.cpp. This API will be called with the name of your test file. In Figure 27.17, a breakpoint is set by clicking on the hand in the toolbar.

Figure 27.17.
Setting a breakpoint.

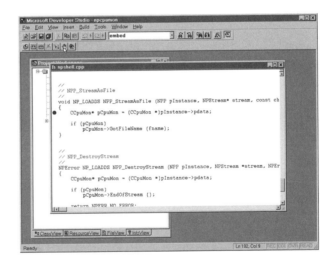

Step 3: Run Navigator

Run Navigator by clicking on the Run button. A warning error is produced because netscape.exe does not contain debugging information. Just click OK. This warning error is shown in Figure 27.18.

Figure 27.18.
Running Netscape Navigator.

Step 4: Verify the Plug-In Resource Information

Verify that your plug-in's resources have been properly read by Navigator with the Help|About Plug-ins menu item. Figure 27.19 shows the location of this menu item.

WARNING

Just because you can see your resources in About Plug-ins does not mean that the plug-in DLL is loadable. Navigator pulls these resources from the plug-in DLL without loading it. This can create confusion if, say, you forget to add a .def file to your project. Without the .def file exporting the entry points, Navigator can't load the plug-in, but you can see it in Help|About Plug-ins!

Figure 27.19.
About Plug-ins.

Step 5: Open the Test File

Use the File|Open File menu item in Navigator to open the test file. In Figure 27.20, you can see the location of this menu item.

Figure 27.20.
Bringing up the File Open dialog.

Make sure that CPU Monitor (*.tex) is in the Files of type section. Select this type, as shown in Figure 27.21, to display the test file. Then, select the test file and open it.

Figure 27.21.
Verify files of type.

Step 6: Hit the Breakpoint

If all has gone well, you should hit the breakpoint set previously. Verify the test filename by bringing up a QuickWatch on fname. You can do this by right-clicking on the fname variable. In Figure 27.22, fname is shown as d:\src\cpumon\cpumon.tex.

Figure 27.22.
Hitting the breakpoint.

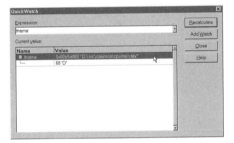

Step 7: Assertion Time

Because there was garbage and not a URL in the test file, you get an assertion (shown in Figure 27.23). To avoid this, you need to run the CPU Monitor sample in the configuration outlined in Chapter 19 or just add code to avoid this error.

Figure 27.23.
The assertion is displayed.

Conclusion

If you are using this chapter as a basis for a new plug-in, you should replace the files npcpumon.cpp and npcpumon.h with files of your own. Of course, rename the project and files to reflect your plug-in. Don't forget that the plug-in DLL must begin with np or it will not be loaded by the Navigator!

What's Next?

The next chapter takes you through a similar step by step example of building a plug-in with Watcom C++ 10.*x*.

CHAPTER 28

Writing a Plug-In with Watcom C++ 10.x

Introduction

Watcom's C++ 10.6 comes with the standard components expected of a modern GUI compiler. Visual Programmer, debugger, browser, profiler, source editor, resource editor, Spy, DDESpy, Heap Walker, and Zoom are part of the list. The Watcom product also includes a licensed version of MFC 3.2 with source code. Although the following example does not use MFC, it should be a straightforward task to compile one of the sample plug-ins in this book that uses MFC.

Compared to other Integrated Development Environments, Watcom's IDE is somewhat less integrated than Microsoft or Borland. Both the debugger and the resource editor are located outside of the IDE. Watcom's real power probably lies under the hood with tight, fast code generation. Powersoft (makers of Watcom C++) has announced something called Optima++ Developer. This is a rapid application development (RAD) environment that simplifies the use of C++ and Java languages to build client/server and Web-enabled applications. Time will tell whether Optima++ is appropriate for developing plug-ins.

In any case, with a few tweaks the current Watcom IDE is quite capable of generating a plug-in for Netscape's Navigator.

Where to Find the Files

This example builds on the MCIWnd sample found previously in the book and on the CD-ROM. Refer to Chapter 20, "A Plug-In with MCIWnd," for more details on its implementation. If you want to build this example, get the files shown in the following lists from the CD-ROM and put them all in a single directory.

For the \CODE\MCIWND directory, you need these files:

- npmciwnd.cpp, npmciwnd.h: The main object, CMCIWnd.
- npshell.cpp: Plug-in entry point methods.
- npmciwnd.rc: Plug-in resources.

For the \CODE\INC directory, you need these files:

- npapi.h: Plug-in API prototypes and associated structures.
- npupp.h: Plug-in API prototypes.

For the \CODE\COMMON directory, you need this file:

- npwin.cpp: DLL entry point to plug-in API mapping.

Put all files in the same directory to match this example.

Modifying the Files

For the Watcom compiler, you need to make a few changes to the source files. First, change the `include` paths to local. Then, change the syntax for the `sizeof` operator in NPWIN.CPP. Finally, change the entry point definitions. The next three sections detail these changes.

The Includes

After you copy the files to a new directory, change the header `include` paths. All the CPP files except stdafx.cpp include a relative path for stdafx.h. Change these to local:

```
#include "..\inc\stdafx.h"
```

should be

```
#include "stdafx.h"
```

The `sizeof` Operator

In the file npwin.cpp, put parentheses around `NPPluginFuncs` where it is used with the `sizeof` operator.

Change the line

```
if (pFuncs->size < sizeof NPPluginFuncs)
```

to this:

```
if (pFuncs->size < sizeof (NPPluginFuncs))
```

Change the Entry Point Definitions

Again in npwin.cpp, change all three entry point definitions.

Change the lines

```
NPError WINAPI NP_EXPORT NP_GetEntryPoints(NPPluginFuncs* pFuncs)
NPError WINAPI NP_EXPORT NP_Initialize(NPNetscapeFuncs* pFuncs)
NPError WINAPI NP_EXPORT NP_Shutdown()
```

to these:

```
extern "C" NPError WINAPI NP_GetEntryPoints(NPPluginFuncs* pFuncs)
extern "C" NPError WINAPI NP_Initialize(NPNetscapeFuncs* pFuncs)
extern "C" NPError WINAPI NP_Shutdown()
```

The Example

The next three sections give step by step instructions for creating a plug-in from scratch with Watcom's IDE. The first section shows you how to set up a new project that creates a Windows plug-in DLL. The next section shows how to build the plug-in. Lastly, the third section covers testing and debugging your Watcom-built plug-in.

Setting Up the Project

To set up your project for a Watcom-based plug-in, you need to create the project, set the target, add the proper source files, create a librarian command file, and change some compiler and linker switches. Steps 1 through 7 detail these tasks.

Step 1: Create a New Project

After starting Watcom's IDE by double-clicking on the IDE icon, create a new project with the File|New Project main menu item. Name the new project npmciwnd.wpj, and create it in the directory in which your modified files are stored. In Figure 28.1, you can see the Enter Project Filename dialog for this information.

Figure 28.1.
Project name and location.

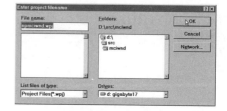

Step 2: Create a New Target

Name the new target npmciwnd and select environment Win32. Make the Image Type Dynamic Link Library (.dll). If you plan to use MFC later on, you should select at that time MFC-32bit (3.2) in the dialog shown in Figure 28.2.

Figure 28.2.
Target Name, Environment, and Image Type.

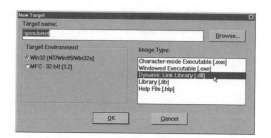

Step 3: Add the Source Files

Now that you have a new project, add source files with the Sources|New Source main menu item, as shown in Figure 28.3.

Figure 28.3.
The New Source menu item.

When the Add Files dialog appears, add the files npmciwnd.cpp, npshell.cpp, npwin.cpp, and npmciwnd.rc, which are the source files needed for the MCIWnd example. Just click the Add All button as shown in Figure 28.4.

Figure 28.4.
The Add Files dialog.

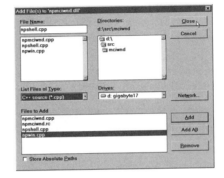

Step 4: Verify Resources

The Watcom Resource Editor is not capable of generating a version resource. No problem. Just use the .rc file from the Microsoft example and change it in the text editor. Watcom's resource compiler generates the proper resource from the Microsoft-produced file. You need not change the .rc file for this example. In Figure 28.5, the plug-in specific resources are shown in highlighted text.

Figure 28.5.
Verifying the .rc file.

```
#endif
 FILEOS 0x40004L
 FILETYPE 0x2L
 FILESUBTYPE 0x0L
BEGIN
    BLOCK "StringFileInfo"
    BEGIN
        BLOCK "040904e4"
        BEGIN
            VALUE "CompanyName", "Your Company, Inc.\0"
            VALUE "FileDescription", "MCIWnd Plug-in\0"
            VALUE "FileVersion", "0.0.0.1\0"
            VALUE "InternalName", "Whatever\0"
            VALUE "LegalCopyright", "Copyright Your Company. 1995, 1996\0"
            VALUE "LegalTrademarks", "ZanTop\0"
            VALUE "OriginalFilename", "npmciwnd.dll\0"
            VALUE "ProductName", "MCIWnd Plug-in\0"
            VALUE "ProductVersion", "0.0.0.1\0"
            VALUE "MIMEType", "video/x-msvideo|audio/x-wav|audio/x-midi\0"
            VALUE "FileExtents", "avi|wav|mid\0"
            VALUE "FileOpenName", "Video (*.avi)|Audio (*.wav)|MIDI (*.mid)\0"
        END
    END
    BLOCK "VarFileInfo"
    BEGIN
        VALUE "Translation", 0x409, 1200
```

Step 5: Create a Librarian Command File

Create a librarian command file for the Watcom linker. Each line in this file corresponds to an exported DLL routine. The format for these lines is as follows:

```
++sym.dll_name[.export_name][.ordinal]
```

In this format, `sym` is the name of the symbol in the DLL, `dll_name` is the name of the DLL, `export_name` is the external name of the export, and `ordinal` is the ordinal number that can be used instead of the name.

To be consistent with this example, name this file export.lbc. Watcom uses a library command file instead of a .DEF file to define DLL entry points. The contents of this file, as you can see in Figure 28.6, should be the following three lines:

```
++_NP_GetEntryPoints@4.npmciwnd.NP_GetEntryPoints.1
++_NP_Initialize@4.npmciwnd.NP_Initialize.2
++_NP_Shutdown@0.npmciwnd.NP_Shutdown.1
```

NOTE

Those funky ampersands followed by numbers are notation for the `__stdcall` alias. With `__stdcall`, all C symbols are suffixed by @nnn, where nnn is the sum of the argument sizes. The library command file names these symbols to the proper external name. You can see the symbol names in your .map file.

Figure 28.6.

The contents of the Librarian command file.

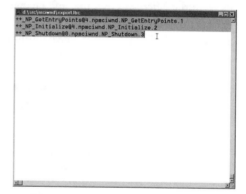

Step 6: Change the C++ Compiler Switches

Bring up the C++ Compiler Switches dialog with the Options|C++ Compiler switches main menu item. Figure 28.7 shows the location of this menu.

Figure 28.7.

Bring up the C++ compiler switches.

Your plug-in needs to use stack-based calling instead of register-based calling as a default because the Navigator directly calls your plug-in APIs. Navigator expects stack-based calling conventions. In Figure 28.8, you can see the compiler switches "10. Memory Model and Processor Switches" with 80386 stack-based calling selected, along with the default 32-bit flat memory model.

Figure 28.8.

Setting to 80386 stack-based calling.

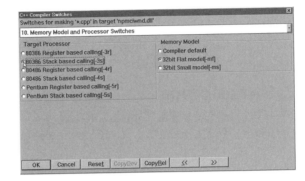

Step 7: Change the Link Switches

Bring up the linker switches dialog with the Options|Link Switches main menu item. Under the Export names section, fill in the name of your previously created export.lbc file with a leading equal sign. In Figure 28.9, the Export name is set to =export.lbc.

Figure 28.9.

Adding the export definition file.

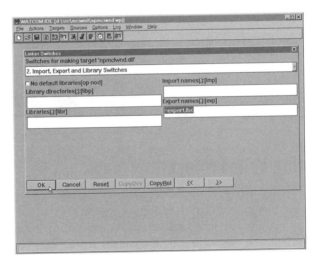

Compiling the Project

To build the plug-in, the next two steps show how to start a full build and check the output for errors.

Step 1: Build the Plug-In

With the Target|Make main menu item, start building the plug-in. Figure 28.10 shows the location of this menu item.

Figure 28.10.
Building the plug-in.

Step 2: Check for Errors

A number of warnings are printed from nonreferenced symbols. Don't worry about these. Look for any fatal errors. In Figure 28.11, you can see these warnings.

Figure 28.11.
Checking for errors.

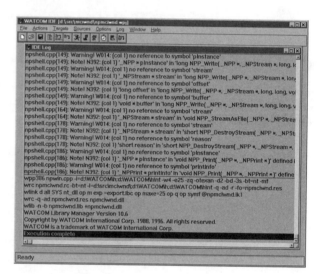

Testing Your Project

The Watcom debugger, unlike the Microsoft and Borland debuggers, is a separate debugger. To test your plug-in, you need to change the debugger's startup directory, load and run Netscape, set any breakpoints, and then restart the Navigator. Watcom's debugger requires this first Navigator load so that you can set breakpoints for the second run. Steps 1 through 8 detail these instructions.

Step 1: Change the Debugger's Startup Directory

When you have successfully built the plug-in DLL, copy it to the `plugins` directory under the Navigator program. After that, open the Properties of Watcom's Windowed Debugger.

To make it easy for the debugger to find your source files, make the start directory your plug-in's source file directory.

Step 2: Start the Debugger and Load Netscape

Start the debug session by browsing for netscape.exe. Click OK when it is found. Figure 28.12 shows the New Program dialog used to start Netscape.

Figure 28.12.
Loading netscape.exe.

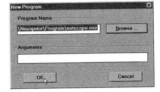

Step 3: Run Netscape

You need to load the plug-in twice in order to set a breakpoint. For the first time, select Run|Go on the main menu (see Figure 28.13).

Figure 28.13.
The Run|Go menu item that is used to run Netscape.

Step 4: Verify the Resource Data

While the Navigator is up, make sure that the plug-in's resource data is correct by bringing up the About Plug-ins dialog with Help|About Plug-ins (see Figure 28.14).

Figure 28.14.
Bringing up About Plug-ins.

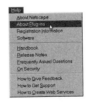

For this plug-in, About Resources should show MIME types of audio/x-midi, audio/x-wav, and video/x-msvideo. You can see these MIME types in Figure 28.15.

Figure 28.15.

Supported MIME types.

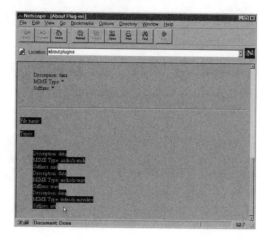

Step 5: Play an AVI File

After you have verified the plug-in's resource information, open an AVI file from within the Navigator. You can also use wave or midi. The first file open loads your plug-in. Figure 28.16 shows how to play a video that comes with Windows 95. Now that you've loaded the plug-in one time, exit the Navigator with File|Exit.

Figure 28.16.

Playing the video.

Step 6: Find the Modules

After exit, the debugger should be aware of your plug-in module. As in Figure 28.17, you should see the plug-in's source files listed in the Modules window. Double-click on one of them to see the source.

Figure 28.17.
Finding the modules.

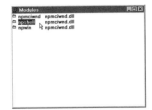

Step 7: Set a Breakpoint

Now you can set a breakpoint. In Figure 28.18, a breakpoint is set in the NPP_StreamAsFile API.

Figure 28.18.
Setting a breakpoint.

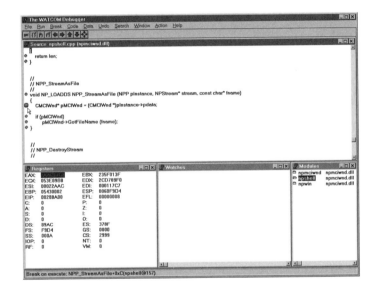

Step 8: Restart, Go, and Hit the Breakpoint

After breakpoints are set, restart the Navigator and Go again with the debugger's main menu items: Run|Restart and Run|Go.

If all went well, you should hit the breakpoint on this run. In Figure 28.19, the AVI filename is checked after hitting the breakpoint.

Figure 28.19.
Hitting the breakpoint.

Conclusion

Here are the most important things to remember when porting to the Watcom compiler:

- Change to a stack-based calling convention.
- Create a librarian response file instead of a .DEF file.
- Add the response file to your linker switches.
- Add extern "C" to the exported routines.
- Make the debugger run in your plug-in directory by changing its properties.
- Load the plug-in twice for debugging. The first time is to get to your source for setting breakpoints, and the second time is for hitting those breakpoints.

Remember that Watcom ships with MFC. Try to port one of the MFC examples in this book to Watcom.

What's Next?

The appendices are next, which include a listing of Netscape's product line, a listing of many of the currently available plug-ins, and a glossary of terms. Many of the plug-ins listed in Appendix B are included on the CD-ROM.

PART V

Appendixes

A   Netscape's Product Line
B   Today's Wide World of Plug-Ins
C   Glossary of Terms

Netscape's Product Line

Introduction

Netscape Communications Corporation is an extremely aggressive and fast-moving company. A fast product development cycle combined with new product acquisitions and Internet distribution has made a sizable software product line for a very new company. For a newcomer to Netscape development, the task of learning the Netscape products, which now number more than 30, can take a significant amount of precious time. This appendix takes a snapshot of Netscape's product line as it exists in May of 1996.

Netscape's current product line can be divided into the following four sections:

    Navigator

    Collabra Share

    Commercial applications

    Servers

For additional details on these products, check out the following address:

```
http://home.netscape.com/comprod/netscape_products.html
```

Navigator

Plug-in developers are mostly concerned with Netscape's Navigator line, whose products (as of 2.0 and excluding UNIX) all support plug-in code modules. Navigator and its add-ons are considered client applications in the client/server software model. At the time of this writing, Navigator products include the following:

    Navigator 2.*x*

    Navigator Gold 2.*x*

    Navigator 3.0 Beta

    Navigator Personal Edition

    Navigator Dial-Up-Kit

    Netscape Power Pack for Windows

    Netscape SmartMarks

    Netscape Chat

If you are developing a Navigator plug-in, make sure to take note throughout this book of the API differences between Navigator 2.*x* and Navigator 3.*x*.

Navigator 2.*x*

With the introduction of Navigator 2.0, Netscape set a new standard for Web browsers. This product combines Web browsing with e-mail, newsgroups, chat, and FTP.

Here are the new end-user features:

- Improved multimedia performance with features such as client-side image mapping, progressive JPEG support, GIF animation, and multiple data streaming
- Integrated e-mail so that mail can be read and sent from within the browser
- Integrated newsgroups so that you can read your news from within the browser
- FTP file upload so that you can use FTP upload and download from within the browser
- Bookmarks that are improved with aliases and hierarchical menus

Here are the new developer features:

- Frames enables you to divide a Web page into separate regions.
- Plug-ins are code modules that can be used to extend the browser's capabilities.
- Navigator 2.0 was the first Web browser to support Java applets based on Sun Microsystem's Java language.
- JavaScript is an easy to use scripting language, based on Java.

Navigator Gold 2.x

Navigator Gold builds on the Navigator's code base by adding a what-you-see-is-what-you-get (WYSIWYG) Web page editor. This editor avoids the complexities of HTML. Gold's current features are as follows:

- Web Page Editor: An easy word processor-like Web page editor.
- Drag-and-drop: Things such as graphics and links can be dragged from other Web pages to yours.
- Publish: Upload your whole Web page project, including all needed files, with one button.
- JavaScript: A JavaScript program editor.
- Netscape Page Starter Site: Tools, templates, and instructions to help you with your first Web page.
- Netscape Gold Rush Tool Chest: A collection of home page templates.
- Netscape Page Wizard: Helps you create a Web page with fill in the blank questions.

Navigator 3.0 Beta

Navigator 3.0 Beta will be a released product by the time you read this book. Navigator 3.0 extends 2.x by adding a series of applets and plug-ins, in addition to enhancing features such as JavaScript, security, and cache capabilities. Here are the new features:

- LiveAudio is a plug-in that supports a variety of audio file formats.
- LiveVideo is a plug-in that supports .AVI format video files.

■ Live3D is a plug-in that supports VRML viewing.

■ QuickTime is a plug-in for Macintosh QuickTime movie viewing.

■ CoolTalk is an Internet telephone with chat and shared whiteboard capabilities.

■ Java and JavaScript enhancements provide dynamic images and loaded plug-in detection.

■ LiveConnect is a means of communication and interaction between Java, JavaScript, and Navigator plug-ins.

■ Netscape Administration Kit enables you to set and lock user configurations.

■ Enhanced security supports the Secure Socket Layer (SSL) 3.0 and includes a personal identity certificate.

■ New HTML tags provide table background colors and plug-in embedding.

■ Also updated and improved are frame navigation, mail, news, caching, Macintosh support, and UNIX support.

Navigator Personal Edition

Netscape's Navigator Personal Edition is Navigator 2.0 packaged for retail sales. It includes all the software needed to get on the Internet, in addition to several promotional offers.

Navigator Dial-Up-Kit

The Navigator Dial-Up-Kit is for Internet Service Providers or companies that want to make it easy for their customers/employees to connect to the Internet. This product includes Navigator 2.0. The kit includes the following items:

Windows 3.1

Netscape Navigator 2.*x* (16 bit)

Shiva PPP, NTS TCP/IP, and dialer

Account Setup Wizard

Windows 95

Netscape Navigator 2.*x* (32 bit)

Account Setup Wizard (configures Windows 95 dial-up networking)

Online hypermedia manual for Netscape Navigator

Both Platforms

128-bit encryption for United States and Canada

40-bit encryption for International

Printed configuration guide

Electronic *Getting Started* manual

Netscape Navigator Log Kit

You can modify this product for your customers by preconfiguring things such as dial-up parameters, dialer name, wizards, Navigator Preferences, read me files, and documentation.

Netscape Power Pack for Windows

Netscape's Power Pack 2.0 is a set of utilities that add to Navigator's functionality. This product will have a retail version in CD-ROM format in addition to an electronic version. Current utilities include the following:

- Netscape SmartMarks 2.0: A software agent that downloads Web pages for later viewing, saving connection costs.
- INSO CyberSpell for Netscape Mail: Spell-checker for Navigator e-mail.
- Norton Antivirus Internet Scanner: Checks all downloaded Internet files for viruses.
- Netscape Chat 2.0: A chat utility for Navigator.

Plug-Ins

The Power Pack CD-ROM version also includes a collection of plug-ins for Navigator 2.*x* and above. The following plug-ins are currently included:

- ASAP WebShow by Software Publishing Corporation: View business presentations within Web pages.
- Astound Web Player by Gold Disk: Play back multimedia presentations created with Astound and Studio M.
- CarbonCopy/Net by Microcom: Access and control other PCs over the Internet.
- EarthTime/Lite by Starfish Software: Tell time around the world at a glance.
- Envoy by Tumbleweed Software: View formatted Envoy documents.
- FIGleaf Inline Lite by Carberry Technology: View and zoom a wide variety of raster and vector graphics formats.
- FormulaOne/NET by Visual Components: Embed and manipulate live spreadsheets and charts.
- Lightning Strike by InfinitOp: View compressed Web image files.
- Netscape Live3D by Netscape Communications: View 3-D VRML documents.
- RealAudio by Progressive Networks: Listen to live and rebroadcast audio on the Internet.
- Shockwave for Director by Macromedia: Play Macromedia Director animations and presentations.
- VDOLive by VDOnet: View real-time video over the Internet.
- VRScout VR Browser by Chaco Communications: Display 3-D VRML documents from the Web.
- WIRL 3D Browser by VREAM: Browse VRML sites.
- Word Viewer by Inso Corporation: View Microsoft Word documents.

Netscape SmartMarks

Netscape SmartMarks is an advanced bookmarking and Web monitoring utility for Navigator users. This product enables you to track Web pages and notifies you when they are updated. Here are the key features of this product:

- Web Monitoring gives automatic notification of Web page updates.
- Web Site Bulletins allow Web site authors to send bulletins to SmartMark users.
- Internet Directory Search provides a point-and-click interface for the most popular Internet directory services.
- Bookmark Management helps you manage bookmarks with folders, and it supports sort, rename, show, and hide.

Netscape Chat

Netscape Chat supports real-time communications for Navigator users. It enables you to interact with existing IRC chat servers or a Netscape Community System Chat Server. Here are the key features:

Share URLs with other users.

Multiple chat modes for one to one, one to many, and many to many.

Share and exchange multimedia files.

Multiple chat rooms.

Integrated with Netscape's Navigator.

Collabra Share

Collabra Share is a company-wide solution for electronic organization. It includes discussion forums for such things as product development, management, IS help desks, and customer service. The product also includes a variety of software agents for mail, news, Lotus Notes, and replication. Collabra Share currently consists of the following elements:

Collabra Share for Windows and Macintosh

Collabra Share Mail Agent

Collabra Share Internet News Group Agent

Collabra Share Agent for Lotus Notes

Collabra Share Replication Agent

Check out Netscape's product information at `http://www.netscape.com` for more information on Collabra share.

Commercial Applications

Netscape's Commercial Applications, as the name implies, are for making money. Electronic malls, storefronts, publishing services, chat services, bulletin board services, and mail are made easy to implement for the purpose of generating revenue for your company. These are the current Commercial Applications:

> Merchant System
>
> Publishing System
>
> Community System
>
> IStore

Merchant System

Netscape's Merchant System uses Netscape Commerce Server in conjunction with Netscape Navigator to provide an Internet retailer with a merchandising system that is easy to implement, manage, and scale. Here are the key features:

- Product Loading and Updates: Products can be loaded using a `Name:Value` pair structured file format.
- Staging Server: Merchants can review product displays before approving them for consumer viewing.
- Shopping Baskets: A virtual shopping basket allows customers to keep a basket containing product stock-keeping units (SKUs), quantity, and attributes of each product selected for purchase.
- Search Capabilities: Customers can search for a given product.
- Credit Card and Order Processing: This feature uses secure encryption over the Internet or X.25 PAD and leased lines for secure credit card authorization with First Data Corporation's (FDC) Envoy Corporation authorization center.
- Electronic Mail-Order Services: This feature provides Integrated Privacy Enhanced Mail (PEM) for secure deliveries of order fulfillment data to merchants.
- Monitoring Shopping and Sales Activity: This feature lets merchants see which products are being viewed and how many customers are visiting the store.

Publishing System

Netscape's Publishing System helps you publish information on the Internet and bill for that information. Here are the key features:

- Registration: A set of login and registration templates that can be used for access control, promotions, and advertising.

- Access Control: Lets the content providers control access to their information, whether it be a free or a charge area.
- Document Management: Tools are provided to tag, convert, and load documents into Netscape's Publishing System.
- Product Definition: Tracks billable areas.
- Billing Services: Supports billing options for fee-based services such as basic subscriptions, premium services, or pay-per-access.
- Search Capability: Provides text search.
- Credit Card Processing: Includes a Credit Card Gateway for secure credit card processing.

Community System

Netscape's Community System enables you to provide commercial services such as bulletin boards, Usenet news, online chat, and electronic mail. Here are the key product features:

- Chat Services include an Internet Relay Chat (IRC) server and Netscape Chat client.
- Bulletin Board Services include secure public and private discussion groups.
- Electronic Mail Services include an integrated Netscape Mail Server.
- Registration and Membership provides login and registration templates.
- Access Control provides access permissions for news groups and chat rooms.

IStore

IStore is an entry-level solution for an Internet store front. Here are the key features:

- Product Display: Store departments, product inventory, product images, and prices are easily implemented.
- Store Manager: This feature lets merchants set up a store quickly by providing easy entry for tax rates, shipping charges, merchant ID, and terminal ID.
- Online Credit Card Processing: This feature includes Netscape's secure online credit card processing system.
- Order Processing: Order information can be viewed quickly by the customer and merchant.

Servers

Netscape offers a good variety of servers across a number of platforms. Servers such as Web, mail, news, and proxy are complemented with administrative tools and languages. The current servers are as follows:

> SuiteSpot
>
> FastTrack
>
> Enterprise Server
>
> Proxy Server
>
> News Server
>
> Mail Server
>
> Catalog Server
>
> Commerce Server
>
> Communications Server

SuiteSpot

Netscape's SuiteSpot is a collection of servers geared toward an internal corporate Intranet. SuiteSpot includes the following servers:

- Enterprise Server is a World Wide Web server.
- Netscape LiveWire Pro is used for building live online applications.
- Mail Server is an electronic mail server.
- News Server is an external or internal news groups.
- Proxy Server filters access to Web documents.
- Catalog Server is used for creating and managing catalogs of Internet resources.

FastTrack

The FastTrack server is a quick means of setting up your Web site. It includes the following features:

- Installation and Setup Wizards: These include an automated installation and configuration agent.
- Intuitive Server Management: This feature provides remote management, online help, and detailed reports.
- Easy Authoring and Publishing: This feature comes with Navigator Gold for creating Web pages.
- Security: This includes flexible access control and Secure Sockets Layer 3.0.
- Development: This feature includes support for Java and JavaScript; high-performance server extensions with Netscape Server APIs (NSAPI); and CGI and WinCGI support.

Enterprise Server

Enterprise server is another more robust server collection from Netscape. It includes the following features:

Navigator Gold

Integrated full-text search

Version control with MKS

Transparent multiple domains

Server-parsed HTML

HTML footers

Remote administration

Simple Network Management Protocol (SMTP) support

Summary reports

Advanced logging

Configuration rollback

Common Server Manager

Java and JavaScript support

CGI support

Third generation HTTP engine

High-performance caching

Enhanced HTTP standards, including byte range extensions (key for plug-in developers) and HTTP keep alives

Proxy Server

Netscape's Proxy Server controls access to restricted network resources and caches frequently used documents. Here are its features:

- Replication-On-Demand: Replicates Web documents in cache. Allows batch retrieval and automatic cache refresh.
- Content Filtering: Grants access to external resources based on username/password.
- Enterprise Management: Provides secure, cross-platform administration with SNMP support and configuration rollback.
- Performance: Supports new standards such as byte range extensions and HTTP keep alives. Uses cache sizes up to 128GB and can handle over 70 million URLs.
- Security: Uses SSL 3.0, reverse proxying, transaction logging, and automatic response for unavailable networks.
- Fail-over: Routes HTTP requests to a secondary proxy if the primary is unavailable.

News Server

Netscape's News Server enables users to create secure public and private discussion groups and gives you the following benefits:

Network News Transport (NNTP) over TCP/IP

News feeds from Usenet newsgroups

Secure communications with SSL

MIME type and image formats

Extra product components, including programs to feed articles to the news server, receive articles, transmit articles, and purge articles.

Mail Server

Netscape's mail server is a messaging system that supports remote clients, enhanced performance, enhanced security, open standards, and intuitive server management. Current Netscape Mail Server Technical Specifications are as follows:

■ Supports open Internet-protocols including HTTP, HTML, POP3, IMAP4, and SMTP.

■ Handles multimedia and other electronic attachments via MIME.

■ Supports a wide variety of POP3 and IMAP4 mail clients.

■ Conforms to RFCs 821, 822, 974, 1123, 1521, 1651, 1725, 1730, and 1760.

■ Supports Secure Sockets Layer 3.0.

■ Allows remote messaging through IMAP4.

■ Administration via HTML or e-mail forms.

■ Program delivery features allow incoming mail to activate a preconfigured script or program to process the content of the message.

■ Expands to accommodate proprietary mail protocols such as Microsoft Mail.

■ Allows creation of multiple reply options for vacation notices and absence reminders through an auto-reply feature.

■ Does not require a separate host to deliver mail.

■ Supports both domain-based and host-based mail addressing.

Catalog Server

Catalog Server allows your organization to put together a catalog of Internet resource such as documents, e-mail addresses, and file archives. Here are the current features:

■ Automatically collects and indexes Internet resources

■ Provides customized views

■ Standard "Harvest" index format

- Relational and full text searching
- Turnkey "What's New" and "What's Popular"
- Open standards support any Web server

Commerce Server

Netscape's Commerce Server provides for secure electronic commerce and communications on the Internet and other TCP/IP networks.

> **NOTE**
>
> Because Commerce Server is an older server, you will probably buy one of the next generation servers listed previously. These newer servers have a superset of the following listed features.

Current technical specifications are as follows:

- Supports industry-standard HTTP/1.0 protocol
- Serves HTML documents and supports MIME typing through filename extensions
- CGI/1.1-compliant
- Integrated security using SSL, which incorporates public key cryptographic technology from RSA Data Security
- Enhanced user authorization, including HTTP/1.0 access authorization, IP and DNS-based access control, local access control, user-controlled passwords, and named groups
- Netscape Server Application Programming Interface (NSAPI) for programmable access to a suite of server application functions and a dynamic loading interface
- Documentation and tutorials make it easy to use the NSAPI and integrate with other applications
- Dynamic process management yields faster response times and increased throughput, efficiency, and reliability
- Intuitive graphical user interface using Netscape Navigator for installation, configuration, and management
- Extensive online documentation provides context-sensitive help
- Support for multiple IP addresses allows a server to support multiple domain names
- Windows NT version runs as an NT service
- Log analysis tools allow summaries of log information so that it can be used to better manage server functions
- Configuration by file, directory, shell wildcard pattern, or template

- Configurable logging options, including the use of syslog facilities, and client accesses are logged in the common logfile format
- Custom error messages
- Multiple-user public information directories with variable paths
- Customizable server-parsed HTML

Communications Server

Communications Server is an HTTP server for HTML documents on the Internet and internal TCP/IP networks.

> **NOTE**
>
> Because Communications Server is an older server, you will probably buy one of the next generation servers listed previously. These newer servers have a superset of the following listed features.

Current technical specifications are as follows:

- Supports industry-standard HTTP/1.0 protocol and serves all HTTP-compatible clients
- Serves HTML documents and supports MIME typing through filename extensions —
- CGI/1.1 compliant
- Enhanced user authorization, including HTTP/1.0 access authorization, IP and DNS-based access control, local access control, user-controlled passwords, and named groups
- Netscape Server Application Programming Interface (NSAPI) for programmatic access to a suite of server application functions and a dynamic loading interface, and the documentation and tutorials make easy the use of the NSAPI and integration with other applications
- Dynamic process management yields faster response times and increased throughput, efficiency, and reliability
- Intuitive graphical user interface using Netscape Navigator for installation, configuration, and management, and the extensive online documentation provides context-sensitive help
- Support for multiple IP addresses, allowing a server to support multiple domain names
- Windows NT version runs as an NT service
- Log analysis tools allow summaries of log information and application to server management functions
- Configuration by file, directory, shell wildcard pattern, or template, and the templates allow a set of configuration parameters to be created and applied to multiple directories (such as all user directories)

- Configurable logging options, including the use of syslog facilities, and client accesses are logged in common logfile format
- Custom error messages
- Multiple-user public information directories with variable paths
- Customized error messages
- Customizable server-parsed HTML

Conclusion

By the time you read this, many of Netscape's products and their features might have changed. Be sure to check the following address for current information:

`http://home.netscape.com/comprod/netscape_products.html`

What's Next?

Appendix B takes a look at some of the more popular Navigator plug-ins as of May 1996.

Today's Wide World of Plug-Ins

Introduction

For a development kit that has only been out for about five months at the time of this writing, there sure are a lot of Navigator plug-ins out there!

The following pages list plug-ins that are available as of May 1996. This list is divided into the following categories:

- Image Viewers
- Document Viewers
- Presentation
- Animation
- 3-D and VRML
- Audio
- Video
- Utilities

With no further ado, here they are!

Image Viewers

Plug-in: ABC QUICKSILVER

Company: Micrografx

Platforms: Windows 95/NT

URL: `http://www.micrografx.com`

The ABC QUICKSILVER plug-in from Micrografx lets you interact with Web page graphics. You can also create these new object graphics using tools from Micrografx.

Plug-in: CMX Viewer

Company: Corel

Platforms: Windows 95/NT

URL: `http://www.corel.com`

Corel offers the CMX Viewer plug-in that allows viewing of Corel vector format CMX files. Vector format graphics are smaller in size than raster graphics such as JPEG.

Plug-in: DWG/DXF

Company: SoftSource

Platforms: Windows 95/NT

URL: `http://www.softsource.com`

SoftSource has created a plug-in called DWB/DXF that enables you to view AutoCAD (DWG) and DXF drawings on a Web page. The graphics are in vector format and are scaleable.

Plug-in: FIGleaf Inline

Company: Carberry Technology/EBT

Platforms: Windows 95/NT

URL: `http://www.ct.ebt.com`

Carberry Technologies plug-in offering called FIGLeaf Inline allows the Navigator to view several graphical file formats, including CGM, GIF, JPEG, PNG, TIFF, CCITT GP4, BMP, WMF, EPSF, Sun Raster, and RGB. Graphics viewing is enhanced with scrollbars, image rotation, and multipage file support.

Plug-in: Fractal Viewer

Company: Iterated Systems

Platforms: Windows 95/NT, Windows 3.1, Macintosh

URL: `http://www.iterated.com`

The Iterated Systems Fractal Viewer plug-in allows you to view graphics compressed with Iterated's Fractal Image Format. Image controls such as zoom, stretch, flip, and rotate are also provided. Check out Chapter 2, "Netscape Navigator Plug-Ins," for more on this plug-in.

Plug-in: InterCAP InLine

Company: InterCAP Graphics Systems

Platforms: Windows 95/NT

URL: `http://www.intercap.com`

A plug-in called InterCAP InLine is offered from InterCAP Graphics Systems. This plug-in expands on the company's MetaLink RunTime CGM viewer to bring this format to the Web. CGM is a vector file format smaller than a conventional bitmap. This plug-in also provides zooming, panning, and animation.

Plug-in: KEYview for Windows

Company: FTP Software

Platforms: Windows 95/NT, Windows 3.1

URL: `http://www.ftp.com`

FTP Software claims support for almost 200 types of file formats. Formats such as MS Word, WordPerfect, Excel, EPS, and PCX are supported. Copy, paste, and convert options are also supported for each of KEYview's supported formats.

Plug-in: Lightning Strike

Company: Infinet Op

Platforms: Windows 95/NT, Windows 3.1, Macintosh

URL: `http://www.infinop.com`

Lightning Strike is a plug-in from Infinet Op that offers an image compression technology based on wavelet compression. Infinet Op claims higher compression and better image quality for its compression format.

Plug-in: Shockwave for FreeHand

Company: Macromedia

Platforms: Windows 95/NT, Windows 3.1, Macintosh

URL: `http://www.macromedia.com`

Macromedia's Shockwave for FreeHand plug-in is an interactive viewer for FreeHand art. You can pan and zoom this vector graphic format. Support is also included for 24-bit color images.

Plug-in: SVF

Company: SoftSource

Platforms: Windows 95/NT

URL: `http://www.softsource.com`

The SVF plug-in from SoftSource lets you view graphics in Simple Vector Format (SVF). Pan, zoom, and image layers are supported. You can also include HTML hyperlinks in an SVF file.

Plug-in: ViewDirector

Company: TMS

Platforms: Windows 95/NT

URL: `http://www.tmsinc.com`

TIFF and other image support is provided from a company called TMS with its ViewDirector plug-in. Features such as zoom, pan, and rotate are supported.

Plug-in: Wavelet Image Viewer

Company: Summus

Platforms: Windows 95/NT, Windows 3.1

URL: `http://www.summus.com`

Summus supports wavelet-based image compression with its plug-in called Wavelet Image Viewer. High compression ratios with good image quality are possible with this image viewer.

Plug-in: WHIP!

Company: Autodesk

Platforms: Windows 95/NT

URL: `http://www.autodesk.com`

You can view 2-D vector data with WHIP! from Autodesk. This plug-in uses the same viewing engine as AutoCAD Release 13 to display vector file formats. Zoom, pan, and embedded URLs are supported.

Document Viewers

Plug-in: Acrobat Amber Reader

Company: Adobe

Platforms: Windows 95/NT, Windows 3.1, Macintosh

URL: `http://www.adobe.com`

To view Portable Document Format (PDF) files in the Navigator, you can use the Acrobat Amber Reader plug-in from Adobe. The PDF file format is compact and platform-independent.

Plug-in: Chemscape Chime

Company: MDL Information Systems

Platforms: Windows 95/NT, Windows 3.1, Macintosh, PowerMac

URL: `http://www.mdli.com`

Using the Chemscape Chime plug-in lets scientists display 2-D and 3-D chemical structures with the Navigator.

Plug-in: Envoy

Company: Tumbleweed Software

Platforms: Windows 95/NT, Windows 3.1, Macintosh, PowerMac

URL: `http://www.twcorp.com`

The Envoy document viewer plug-in from Tumbleweed Software lets you view documents created with the Tumbleweed Publishing Essentials. This document format supports fonts, graphics, and layouts. Additionally, a developer's kit is provided for viewer customization.

Plug-in: Formula One/NET

Company: Visual Components

Platforms: Windows 95/NT, Windows 3.1

URL: http://www.visualcomp.com

The Formula One/NET plug-in from Visual Components lets you view a Microsoft Excel spread-sheet. This plug-in supports live charts, embedded URLs, text and number formatting, calculations, buttons, and controls.

Plug-in: Word Viewer

Company: Inso Corporation

Platforms: Windows 95/NT, Windows 3.1

URL: http://www.inso.com

Inso Corporation offers the Word Viewer plug-in to view Microsoft 6.0 and 7.0 documents. Copy and print are also supported. See Chapter 2 for more on this plug-in.

Presentation

Plug-in: ASAP WebShow

Company: Software Publishing Corporation

Platforms: Windows 95/NT, Windows 3.1

URL: http://www.spco.com

Another plug-in featured in Chapter 2 of this book, SPC's ASAP WebShow, lets you view presentation documents created with ASAP WordPower. This plug-in supports printing, downloading, and viewing reports and presentations.

Plug-in: Astound Web Player

Company: Gold Disk

Platforms: Windows 95/NT, Windows 3.1

URL: http://www.golddisk.com

Gold Disk provides Navigator support for multimedia documents created with its Astound or Studio M software with the Astound Web Player plug-in. This document format supports animation, graphics, audio, video, and interactivity. Slide viewing on the fly is supported using full streaming capabilities of the plug-in API.

Plug-in: PowerMedia

Company: RadMedia

Platforms: Windows 95/NT, Windows 3.1

URL: http://www.radmedia.com

The PowerMedia plug-in from RadMedia enables you to author and view multimedia documents geared toward business communications. Some business uses of this plug-in are presentations, training, kiosks, and demos.

Animation

Plug-in: mBED

Company: mBED Software

Platforms: Windows 95/NT, Windows 3.1, Macintosh, PowerMac

URL: http://www.mbed.com

The mBED file format for animated Web page graphics is supported with the mBED plug-in from mBED Software. These graphics are both animated and interactive.

Plug-in: Shockwave for Authorware

Company: Macromedia

Platforms: Windows 95/NT, Windows 3.1, Macintosh

URL: http://www.macromedia.com

Another plug-in from Macromedia, Shockwave for Authorware, provides Navigator support for Authorware courses and pieces. Animation, buttons, URLs and streaming images, movies, and sound are supported.

Plug-in: Shockwave for Director

Company: Macromedia

Platforms: Windows 95/NT, Windows 3.1, Macintosh

URL: http://www.macromedia.com

One of the most popular multimedia presentation applications is Director from Macromedia. You can use the company's Shockwave for Directory plug-in to view Director files through the Navigator. Support for buttons, animation, URLs, movies, and sound is provided with this plug-in.

Plug-in: Sizzler

Company: Totally Hip

Platforms: Windows 95/NT, Windows 3.1, Macintosh, PowerMac

URL: `http://www.totallyhip.com`

Streaming animation is provided by the Sizzler plug-in from Totally Hip. The company also has a tutorial for converting QuickTime movies and PIC files to Sizzler files. See Chapter 2 for more on this plug-in.

3-D and VRML

Plug-in: Live3D

Company: Netscape

Platforms: Windows 95/NT, Windows 3.1

URL: `http://www.netscape.com`

Starting with Navigator 3.0, the Live3D plug-in is included with Netscape's Navigator for viewing virtual worlds written in the VRML language. This plug-in supports 3-D text, background images, texture animation, morphing, viewpoints, collision detection, gravity, and RealAudio streaming sound. This plug-in is featured in Chapter 2.

Plug-in: Topper

Company: Kinetix

Platforms: Windows 95/NT

URL: `http://www.ktx.com`

Kinetix has extended VRML with its new Virtual Reality Behavior Language (VRBL). This new specification enables users to add animation to VRML. The 3-D Studio and 3-D Studio MAX tools from the company let you create 3-D scenes for viewing with the Topper plug-in.

Plug-in: Viscape

Company: Superscape

Platforms: Windows 95/NT

URL: `http://www.superscape.com`

The Viscape plug-in from Superscape is an interactive 3-D viewer plug-in. Object grabbing, walkthroughs, and sound are supported.

Plug-in: VR Scout VRML

Company: Chaco Communications

Platforms: Windows 95/NT

URL: `http://www.chaco.com`

Another VRML viewer called VR Scout VRML from Chaco Communications supports the full 1.0 VRML standard for flying through virtual worlds.

Plug-in: VRealm

Company: Integrated Data Systems

Platforms: Windows 95/NT

URL: `http://www.ids-net.com`

Integrated Data Systems offers the VRealm Navigator plug-in that supports VRML virtual worlds. Additional features such as object behaviors, gravity, collision detection, autopilot, and multimedia are added with this plug-in.

Plug-in: Whurlplug

Company: Apple

Platforms: Macintosh

URL: `http://product.info.apple.com/qd3d/3Dsample.HTML`

The Macintosh-based plug-in, Whurlplug from Apple, lets you interact with 3-D models. This plug-in uses Apple's QuickDraw 3-D API for 3-D rendering, picking, and navigation.

Plug-in: WIRL Virtual Reality Browser

Company: VREAM

Platforms: Windows 95/NT

URL: `http://www.vream.com`

VREAM's WIRL Virtual Reality Browser plug-in supports the VRML standard. It also adds support for object behaviors, multimedia capabilities, and world authoring.

Audio

Plug-in: Crescendo

Company: Live Update

Platforms: Windows 95/NT, Windows 3.1, Macintosh

URL: `http://www.liveupdate.com`

The MIDI file format is supported by Live Update's Crescendo plug-in. This plug-in gives a Web page background MIDI with CD player controls.

Plug-in: Echospeech

Company: Echo Speech Corporation

Platforms: Windows 95/NT, Windows 3.1

URL: `http://www.echospeech.com`

The Echospeech plug-in from Echo Speech Corporation provides for high-quality compressed speech.

Plug-in: MacZilla

Company: Knowledge Engineering

Platforms: Macintosh

URL: `http://maczilla.com`

Knowledge Engineering is offering the MacZilla plug-in for supporting a multitude of file formats such as Quicktime, MIDI, WAV, AU, AIFF, MPEG, and AVI.

Plug-in: RapidTransit

Company: FastMan

Platforms: Windows 95/NT, Windows 3.1, Macintosh

URL: `http://monsterbit.com/rapidtransit`

FastMan claims compression of up to 40 to 1 with its RapidTransit plug-in. Additionally, full CD-quality sound can be compressed to 10 to 1 or better.

Plug-in: RealAudio

Company: Progressive Networks

Platforms: Windows 95/NT, Windows 3.1, Macintosh

URL: `http://www.realaudio.com`

The RealAudio plug-in from Progressive Networks is one of the more popular audio decompression plug-ins. See Chapter 5 for more information on this plug-in.

Plug-in: Talker

Company: MVP Solutions

Platforms: Macintosh

URL: `http://www.mvpsolutions.com`

Talker, a Macintosh-only plug-in from MVP Solutions, uses text to speech technology to actually read you a Web page.

Plug-in: ToolVox

Company: Voxware

Platforms: Windows 95/NT, Windows 3.1, Macintosh

URL: `http://www.voxware.com`

The ToolVox plug-in from Voxware decompresses streaming audio at up to 53 to 1 compression ratios. This is one of the best compression ratios available and works well for speech.

Video

Plug-in: ACTION

Company: Open2u

Platforms: Windows 95/NT

URL: `http://www.open2u.com`

MPEG movies are supported with the ACTION plug-in from Open2U.

Plug-in: CoolFusion

Company: Iterated Systems

Platforms: Windows 95/NT

URL: `http://www.iterated.com`

Iterated Systems' CoolFusion plug-in supports streaming video. This plug-in uses the AVI file format.

Plug-in: MovieStar

Company: Intelligence At Large

Platforms: Windows 95/NT, Macintosh

URL: `http://www.beingthere.com`

Quicktime movies both in Windows and Macintosh are supported with the MovieStar plug-in from Intelligence At Large. The plug-in supports autoplay and looping among other HTML configurations.

Plug-in: PreVU

Company: InterVU

Platforms: Windows 95/NT

URL: `http://www.intervu.com`

MPEG movies are supported with the PreVU plug-in from InterVU. This plug-in supports both streaming and full-speed cached video viewing.

Plug-in: VDOLive

Company: VDOnet

Platforms: Windows 95/NT, Windows 3.1

URL: `http://www.vdolive.com`

VDOnet's VDOlive plug-in is currently one of the most popular video plug-ins for the Web. VDOnet claims real-time frame rates of 10 to 15 frames per second with a 28.8kbps modem for the VDOLive plug-in.

Plug-in: ViewMovie QuickTime

Company: Ivan Cávero Belaúnde

Platforms: Macintosh

URL: `http://www.well.com/user/ivanski`

Macintosh QuickTime movies are supported with the ViewMovie QuickTime plug-in from Ivan Cávero Belaúnde.

Utilities

Plug-in: ActiveX

Company: NCompass

Platforms: Windows 95/NT, Windows 3.1, Macintosh

URL: `http://www.ncompasslabs.com`

You can use ActiveX controls (formerly OLE) in your Web page with the ActiveX plug-in from NCompass. Most standard programming languages can generate ActiveX controls as applets. Support for Active Document viewing is also provided by this plug-in.

Plug-in: Carbon Copy/Net

Company: Microcom

Platforms: Windows 95/NT, Windows 3.1, Macintosh

URL: `http://www.microcom.com`

Remotely access your PC or Macintosh with the Carbon Copy/Net plug-in from Microcom. This plug-in supports remote file access, document viewing/editing, and running applications.

Plug-in: EarthTime

Company: Starfish Software

Platforms: Windows 95/NT

URL: `http://www.starfishsoftware.com`

A plug-in called EarthTime from Starfish Software displays an animated map so that you can see the local time in eight geographic locations. This plug-in is featured in Chapter 2.

Plug-in: ISYS HindSite

Company: ISYS/Odyssey Development

Platforms: Windows 95/NT, Windows 3.1

URL: `http://www.isysdev.com`

To track every Web page you have ever visited, use the ISYS HindSite plug-in from ISYS/Odyssey Development. You can perform text searches for saved Web pages. Time-frame for saving URLs can be set.

Plug-in: Look@Me

Company: Farallon

Platforms: Windows 95/NT

URL: `http://www.farallon.com`

Farallon offers the Look@Me plug-in, which enables you to view another Look@Me user's screen. This plug-in is based on Timbukto Pro and supports complete interaction with another user's computer. A stand-alone version of Look@Me is also available.

Plug-in: OpenScape

Company: Business@Web

Platforms: Windows 95/NT

URL: `http://www.busweb.com`

The OpenScape plug-in from Business@Web supports OLE/OCX. You can use Visual Basic scripting in conjunction with this plug-in for your Web pages.

Plug-in: PointCast Network

Company: PointCast

Platforms: Windows 95/NT, Windows 3.1

URL: http://www.pointcast.com

The PointCast Network plug-in from PointCast lets you view the current news, weather, stock quotes, sports, and more within the Navigator. PointCast also has a popular stand-alone version of this software.

Plug-in: QuickServer

Company: Wayfarer Communications

Platforms: Windows 95/NT

URL: http://www.wayfarer.com

Wayfarer Communications offers the QuickServer plug-in that provides for high-performance client-server applications developed with Visual Basic, PowerBuilder, C++, and Java.

Glossary of Terms

ACM: Audio Compression Manager. Used in Microsoft Windows for runtime audio compression and decompression.

API: Application Programming Interface. A very structured and well-documented interface for extending operating systems and applications.

ASCII: American National Standard Code for Information Interchange. A standard code consisting of 7-bit characters used to represent alphanumeric values.

Atlas: Netscape's code name for Navigator 3.0.

AVI: Audio Video Interleave. A file format used to store full motion video with its associated audio track.

AWT: Alternative Window Toolkit. A Java class library for basic GUI programming.

base class: In C++, a class that is not derived from another class.

browser: An application used to find and display World Wide Web pages or "surf the net."

BSD: Berkeley Software Distribution. Inventors of network sockets, along with many UNIX flavors.

bytecode: In the Java language, this is platform-independent binary data generated by Java compilers, which is interpreted later to run a Java applet or application.

cache: Buffer or file storage that contains frequently accessed data in a faster, but usually smaller, device.

CERN: The European Laboratory for Particle Physics. Invented the World Wide Web.

CGI: Common Gateway Interface. An interface to a Web server that allows browser clients to communicate with specialized server programs.

class: In C++, a collection of data types including both data members and methods.

class library: In C++, a collection of classes that typically inherit from each other to form a hierarchical library.

CODEC: Short for compressor/decompressor. Used to describe runtime compression and decompression code modules typically used for audio and video.

critical section: A term used in multithreaded programming referring to a code section that can only be accessed by a single thread at any given time.

DDE: Dynamic Data Exchange. In Windows, a technique for interprocess communication using window messages.

deadlock: In multithreaded programming, a situation in which a thread attempts to access a resource but access will never be granted. The thread remains frozen for the life of the process.

DLL: Dynamic Link Library. In Windows, a code module that is loaded at runtime by a given process.

EMBED: An HTML tag used to embed a Navigator plug-in within a Web page.

FIFO: First-In-First-Out.

FILO: First-In-Last-Out.

FTP: File Transfer Protocol. A protocol used for transferring files with TCP/IP, typically on the Internet.

GUI: Graphical User Interface.

heap: A large block of process memory typically managed by a runtime library. Application memory requests are satisfied from the heap and its runtime routines.

helper application: Refers to an application used to "help" Web browsers display an unknown media type.

HIDDEN: An HTML tag used to define a hidden type Navigator plug-in.

HTML: HyperText Markup Language. A text-based interpreted language used to define a Web page.

HTTP: HyperText Transmission Protocol. The protocol used for communications between a Web client and server.

IANA: Internet Assigned Numbers Authority. Approves and tracks media types for use in the MIME specification.

IDE: Integrated Development Environment. A development environment that provides access to all tools needed for software development in a single application.

instance: An entity that belongs to a particular class of entities. For example, several copies of the same program are considered instances of that program.

instance data: Private data that is associated with an instance.

Internet: A world-wide network of computers, networks, and gateways that uses the TCP/IP protocol suite to function as a single virtual network.

Intranet: An internal corporate network or LAN, usually using TCP/IP to function as a mini Internet.

IP Address: A 32-bit address assigned to hosts in a TCP/IP network.

IRC: Internet Relay Chat. Provides real-time chatting over the Internet by typing on the keyboard.

ISI: Information Sciences Institute. Part of the University of Southern California that operates IANA among other things.

Java: A new language developed by Sun Microsystems that is geared toward platform independence and especially well suited to the Internet.

Java Applet: Java bytecode that is downloaded and interpreted in a Web browser.

JavaScript: An interpreted text-based scripting language developed by Netscape in conjunction with Sun. This language has a heavy Java influence.

MCI: Media Control Interface. In Windows, a generic interface to many media types and devices.

MCIWnd: In Windows, a window class that implements a large number of macros and routines to simplify MCI development.

method: In C++, a term used to refer to a function within a particular class. Also used to refer to a Netscape Navigator Plug-in API.

MFC: Microsoft Foundation Class Library.

MIDI: Musical Instrument Device Interface. Musical information is encoded in a series of bytes that determine such things as note, duration, and attack velocity.

MIME: Multipurpose Internet Mail Extensions. An extendible standard defining a large number of media types that exist today.

Mosaic: The name of the first popular Web browser, which was developed by NCSA.

Mozilla: The mascot of Netscape's Navigator. Mozilla is a small, fire-breathing, Godzilla-like creature.

Navigator: The name of Netscape's highly successful Web browser.

NCSA: National Center for Supercomputing Applications. Funded by the University of Illinois, this organization wrote NCSA Mosaic.

NSAPI: Netscape API. A collection of programming interfaces for Netscape's server line of software products.

OLE: Object Linking and Embedding. Developed by Microsoft, this mechanism allows applications to communicate and share code resources.

overrun: In data streaming, this indicates that the data producer has produced more data than the consumer can manage.

OWL: Object Windows Library. A Windows GUI class library written by Borland.

Page: In this book, refers to either a Web page or a 4096-byte memory page.

PCM: Pulse Code Modulation. Refers to a common technique for digitizing audio data.

POP3: A standard for remotely reading e-mail across a network.

PPP: Point-to-Point-Protocol. A serial packet protocol commonly used to connect computers to the Internet through modems.

process: A single application or program that usually has a separate CPU context.

protocol: A set of rules that defines a method of communication across a network.

Resource: In Windows, data that is attached to a code module or program.

RFC: Request For Comment. A document proposing a new Internet standard.

SDK: Software Development Kit.

socket: A simplified, generic connection to a TCP/IP network originated by Berkeley Software Distribution.

software agent: A software program that intelligently performs its duties without human interaction.

SSL: Secure Sockets Layer. Offered by Netscape to provide better network security.

stream: A continuous data flow from one device to another.

TCP/IP: Transmission Control Protocol/Internet Protocol. The networking standard used on the Internet.

Telnet: A communications protocol for connecting locally to other computers across the Internet.

thread: A separate CPU context that is part of a process.

TWIP: One twentieth of a printer's point. A unit of measurement in Windows.

undderrun: In data streaming, this indicates that the data consumer has consumed all the data that the producer has produced.

URL: Universal Resource Locator. A standardized format to describe the location of a Web resource.

V*x*D: In Windows, a virtual device driver.

WinCGI: For Windows, a method of writing CGI programs using languages such as Visual Basic.

WinSock: Windows implementation of network sockets.

worker thread: A thread that is created for a task that usually has no user interaction.

World Wide Web: A network of HTTP servers that provide information in a variety of media through the use of the HTML language.

Index

A

ABC QUICKSILVER Web site, 370

About Plug-ins command (Help menu), 54

accept (WinSock routine), 29

ACM (Audio Compression Manager), 185, 384
   streaming data, 180

Acrobat Amber Reader Web site, 373

ACTION Web site, 379

ActiveX Web site, 380

addresses
   global routines, 267
   IP, 385
   processes, Windows 95, 137
   virtual memory, resolving, 139

adjustCursorEvent, 170

agents, 387

AllocateBuffers method, 204
   CBufferCircular class, 207
   CBufferFIFO class, 213

Alternative Window Toolkit (AWT), 384

American National Standard Code for Information Interchange (ASCII), 384

Andreessen, Marc, 149

animation plug-ins, 11, 375-376

AnyEmptyBuffers method, 204
   CBufferCircular class, 208
   CBufferFIFO class, 214

AnyFullBuffers method, 205
   CBufferCircular class, 209-210
   CBufferFIFO class, 215

APIs (Application Programming Interfaces), 52, 70, 384
   CloseHandle, 306
   DeleteCriticalSection, 188
   EnterCriticalSection, 188
   GetJavaClass, 158
      LiveConnect sample plug-in, 294
   GetProp (instance data), 167
   Heap Memory, 139
   InitializeCriticalSection, 188
   LeaveCriticalSection, 188

mapping, 79, 312
calls, 72-73
memory management, 136
Windows 95, 137
Memory Mapped File, 138
methods, managing data
streams, 56
NP ASFILE, creating files,
125
NPN DestroyStream,
109-110
NPN GetURL, 98-112
Server CPU Monitor, 219
NPN GetURLNotify,
114-116
NPN MemAlloc, 140-141
NPN MemFlush, 142-143
NPN MemFree, 141-142
NPN NewStream, 108-109
NPN PostURL, 98-114
NPN PostURLNotify,
116-117
NPN RequestRead, 131-132
NPN Status, 146
NPN UserAgent, 146
NPN Write, 132-133
streams, 127
NPP Destroy, Server CPU
Monitor, 222
NPP DestroyStream, 96,
107-108
parameters, 97
Server CPU Monitor, 225
NPP GetJavaClass, 158
NPP GetJavaEnv, 159
NPP GetJavaPeer, 160
NPP HandleEvent, 175-176
Macintosh window events,
170
NPP New, 250
Server CPU Monitor, 221
NPP NewStream, 105-106
Server CPU Monitor, 223
NPP Print, 169-172, 175
NPP SetWindow, 165,
170-172
instance data, 167
Server CPU Monitor, 222

NPP StreamAsFile, 124,
130-131
Server CPU Monitor,
219, 224
NPP URLNotify, 117-119
NPP Write
processing data, 122-123
Server CPU Monitor, 224
NPP WriteReady, 127-130
allocating buffers, 122
Server CPU Monitor, 224
platform independance,
development
considerations, 62
plug-ins, 70, 74
entry points, 252-255,
261
prefixes, 52
RemoveProp, instance data,
167
RequestRead, searching
remote files, 126
SetProp, instance data, 167
SetWindowLong, 165, 260
streams, writing, 122
version numbers, 72
NPN Version function, 84
Virtual Memory, 138
waveOutOpen, 194
windows, targeting, 104
WinSock, 29-31
WSACleanup (WinSock),
306
see also functions
applets
AviObserver, 274
compared to plug-ins, 55
Java, 386
application (MIME type), 19
Application Programming
Interface *see* APIs
applications
CGI, POST HTTP method,
99, 102
helper, 28-29, 385
NCAPI, 32
processes, 386
Socket Spy, 31
software agents, 387

argc argument (NPP New
function), 81
argn argument (NPP New
function), 81
arguments
NPP New function
(HTML), 81-82
stacks, order, 312
argv argument (NPP New
function), 81
ASAP WebShow plug-in, 359
Web site, 11, 374
ASCII (American National
Standard Code for
Information Interchange),
384
assisted installation, 57
PLUGINSPAGE attribute
(<EMBED> HTML tag),
64
AssociateInstance routine,
instance data, 167
Astound Web Player plug-in,
359
Web site, 374
Atlas, 384
attributes
adding, 64
case-sensitivity, 40
<EMBED> HTML tag,
63-65
HEIGHT, 55
HIDDEN, 251
WIDTH, 55
HTML tags, 40
RealAudio, 40-50
audio
autostart parameters, 186
buffers
returning, 192
threads, 184
compression, 185
devices, creating worker
threads, 197
drivers
callback routines, 194
opening, 194
files, WAV plug-ins, 79

MIDI, 250
playback, 196-197
  pausing, 197
plug-ins, 13, 377-379
  autostart, 200
  configuring buffers, 199
  designing, 184-185
  entry points, 185
  NPWAVE, 184
  running, 199-200
streaming, bandwidth
  considerations, 61-62
Audio Compression Manager,
  see **ACM**
audio (MIME type), 19
audio plug-ins, underrun
  errors, 190
Audio Streamer sample plug-
  in, 180
Audio Video Interleave, *see*
  AVI
autostart, audio plug-ins, 200
AUTOSTART attribute
  (<EMBED> HTML tag),
  RealAudio plug-in, 48
autostart parameters, audio
  plug-ins, 186
autostart plug-ins, FillBuffer
  method, 189-190
AVI (Audio Video Interleave),
  384
methods, MCI driver
  problems, 277
playing (LiveConnect), 272
plug-ins, 13
AviObserver interface, 274
LiveConnect sample plug-in,
  276
AviPlayer class, LiveConnect
  sample plug-in, 277
AviTest class, LiveConnect
  sample plug-in, 274-276
AWT (Alternative Window
  Toolkit), 384

B

Background MIDI plug-in,
  251
background mode, plug-ins,
  250
bandwidth
audio, streaming, 61-62
NPWAVE plug-in, 185
requirements, 60-61
bar charts
drawing, 231-232
Server CPU Monitor,
  updating, 228
bDataUnderrun flag (buffers),
  190
Berkeley sockets, 29
Berkeley Software
  Distribution (BSD), 384
bind (WinSock routine), 29
blank target window option,
  104
Borland C++ 5, 316
plug-ins
  adding project files, 320
  adding resources, 318-319
  adding VERSIONINFO
    resources, 318
  building, 320
  changing output
    directories, 321
  compiling, 320
  creating, 317
  creating DLLs, 322
  editing library definition
    files, 319
  project creation, 317-318
  project setup, 317
  testing, 323-327
  warnings, 320-321
breakpoints
Borland plug-ins, creating,
  323
creating Visual C++ plug-
  ins, 337
Socket Spy sample plug-in,
  setting, 302
Browser keyword (MIME
  types), configuring, 23

browsers, 384
plug-ins
  instances, 78
  support, 50
  Web sites, 8
printing, 164
status messages, 146
usage statistics, Web sites,
  148
windows, creating, 164
BrowserWatch Web site, 8,
  148
BSD (Berkeley Software
  Distribution), 384
buffers
allocating
  circular, 205
  methods, 204
audio
  returning, 192
  threads, 184
audio plug-ins, configuring,
  199
bDataUnderrun flags, 190
checking availability, 189
circular, 205-206
classes
  methods, 204-205
  streaming data, 180
data streams, 56
FIFO, 212
  methods, 212-216
freeing, methods, 204
headers, 189, 205
linked lists, 212
methods, 254
streaming, 204
streams
  allocating, 122
  secondary management
    schemes, 123
see also memory
building
projects, Borland plug-ins,
  320
Visual C++ plug-ins,
  changing settings, 334-335
warnings, Borland plug-ins,
  320-321

buttons, *see* **command buttons**
byte range requests, 126
  linked lists, building, 126
  seekable streams, 96
bytecodes, 384
BytesReady method, 34

C

C++ programming language
  plug-ins
    development, 60
    file locations, 316
caches, 384
  size, changing, 125
caching
  FIFO, 125
  files, 125
  systems, 57
callback routines, audio
  drivers, 194
calling
  conventions
    compiling, 312
    registers, 313
  Java methods, 155
  routines, 73-74
CallWindowProc method,
  166
CarbonCopy/Net plug-in, 359
  Web site, 380
case-sensitivity, HTML tag
  attributes, 40
Catalog Server, 365
CAvi class
  construction, 287
  destruction, 287
  LiveConnect sample plug-in,
    287
  objects
    construction, 284
    destruction, 284
CBitmapButton class, 198
CBuffer objects, 189
CBufferCircular class,
  205-206
  methods, 206-212

CBufferFIFO class, 212
  methods, 212-216
CButton objects, creating,
  198
CCpuMon class, Server CPU
  Monitor, 219
CCpuMon objects
  construction, 225
  deleting, 222
  destruction, 225
  methods, 225-228
  saving, 221
CCriticalSection objects, 188
CERN (European Laboratory
  for Particle Physics), 384
CGI (Common Gateway
  Interface), 384
  applications, POST HTTP
    method, 99
  client/servers, designing, 66
  Server CPU Monitor sample
    plug-in, 181
  server statistics, obtaining,
    219
  Socket Spy sample plug-in,
    running, 306
  support, planning, 60
  vmstat command, running,
    220-221
  WinCGI, 387
Chemscape Chime Web site,
  373
child windows, event
  handling, 55
circular buffers, 205-206
class libraries, 313
  subclassing, 260
classes, 384
  AviPlayer (LiveConnect
    sample plug-in), 277
  AviTest (LiveConnect
    sample plug-in), 274-276
  buffers, 204
    methods, 204-205
    streaming data, 180
  CAvi (LiveConnect sample
    plug-in), 287
  CBitmapButton, 198

CBufferCircular, 205-206
  methods, 206-212
  CBufferFIFO, 212
  methods, 212-216
  CCpuMon (Server CPU
    Monitor), 219
  CMCIWnd
    construction, 242
    destruction, 242
    GotFileName method,
      243
    MCIWnd plug-in, 242
    Open method, 242
  CMidi, 251, 255
    construction, 256
    destruction, 256
  CNetscapeMemObject, 83
  constructors, buffers, 204
  CPluginWindow, 261
    construction, 266
    destruction, 266
    LiveConnect sample plug-
      in, 282-287
    message maps, 196
    methods, 266
    Server CPU Monitor, 219
  CWave
    attaching to instance
      structures, 186
    methods, 187
    new operator, 188
  destructors, buffers, 204
  instances, 385
  Java
    accessing fields, 155
    accessing methods, 155
  MCIWnd, 236, 386
  netscape.plugin.Plugin, 156
  subclassing, 260
  windows, creating with
    MFC, 167
CleanupWindow method, 262
  CPluginWindow objects,
    229
client/servers
  CGI (Server CPU Monitor
    sample plug-in), 181
  plug-ins, designing, 66

Close method, 34-35
  CAvi class, 289
  NPWAVE plug-in, 191-192
  Server CPU Moitor, 228
CloseHandle API, 306
closesocket (WinSock routine), 29
closing, MCI video devices, 289
CMCIWnd class
  construction, 242
  destruction, 242
  GotFileName method, 243
  MCIWnd plug-in, 242
  Open method, 242
CMCIWnd objects, creating, 238-239
CMidi objects
  creating, 252-253
  deleting, 253
CMidi class, 251-255
  construction, 256
  destruction, 256
CMidi method, 256
CMX Viewer Web site, 370
CNetscapeMemObject class, 83
code
  samples, 180
    Audio Streamer, 180
    Server CPU Monitor, 181
  stub, AviObserver class, 278
CODECs, 384
Collabra Share, 360
command buttons
  creating (NPWAVE plug-in), 198
  Play, creating, 274-276
  Stop, creating, 274-276
  Update, handling, 232
command-line interface options, MCIWnd plug-in, 246
commands
  fflush (vmstat), 220
  Help menu, About Plug-ins, 54

  vmstat, 218-220
    fflush command, 220
    parsing data, 228-231
    printf header, 221
Commerce Server, 366
Commercial Applications, 361-362
Common Gateway Interface, *see* **CGI**
communications (Internet) WinSock, 29-31
Communications Server, 367
Community System, 362
compatibility
  Java, plug-ins, 272
  LiveConnect, 62
  methods, LiveConnect, 154
  multiplatform, development considerations, 62
  NPN DestroyStream API, 109
  NPN GetURL API, 110
  NPN GetURLNotify API, 114
  NPN NewStream API, 108
  NPN PostURL API, 112
  NPN PostURLNotify API, 116
  NPN RequestRead API, 131-132
  NPN Write API, 132-133
  NPP DestroyStream API, 107
  NPP GetJavaClass API, 158
  NPP GetJavaEnv API, 159
  NPP GetJavaPeer API, 160
  NPP HandleEvent API, 175-176
  NPP NewStream API, 105
  NPP Print API, 172, 175
  NPP SetWindow API, 170-172
  NPP StreamAsFile API, 130-131
  NPP URLNotify API, 117
  NPP Write API, 128, 130
  NPP WriteReady API, 127-128

compiling, 74
  Borland plug-ins, preparing files, 316-317
  calling conventions, 312
  Java Web site, 273
  projects
    Borland plug-ins, 320
    Visual C++ plug-ins, 336
    Watcom C++ plug-in, 347-348
    changing switches, 346
components, plug-ins, 52
compression
  audio files, 185
  CODEC, 384
  lossy, 62
  modems, audio streaming, 61
configuring
  buffers, audio plug-ins, 199
  MIME types, 22-23
    adding new, 23
    automated, 23
    plug-ins, 23
connect (WinSock routine), 29
CONSOLE attribute (<EMBED> HTML tag), RealAudio plug-in, 48-49
construction
  CAvi class, 287
  CCpuMon object, 225
  CMCIWnd class, 242
  CMidi class, 256
  CPluginWindow, Cavi objects, 284
  CPluginWindow class, 266
  CPluginWindow object, 229
Constructor methods
  CBufferCircular class, 206
  CBufferFIFO class, 212
constructors
  classes, buffers, 204
  CWave class, 188
  Plugin, netscape.plugin.Plugin class, 157

Content-Type MIME header field, 20
CONTROLS attribute (<EMBED> HTML tag), RealAudio plug-in, 40
CONTROLS=ALL attribute (<EMBED> HTML tag), RealAudio plug-in, 41
CONTROLS=ControlPanel attribute (<EMBED> HTML tag), RealAudio plug-in, 42
CONTROLS=InfoPanel attribute (<EMBED> HTML tag), RealAudio plug-in, 42
CONTROLS=InfoVolumePanel attribute (<EMBED> HTML tag), RealAudio plug-in, 42
CONTROLS=PlayButton attribute (<EMBED> HTML tag), RealAudio plug-in, 44
CONTROLS=PositionField attribute (<EMBED> HTML tag), RealAudio plug-in, 46
CONTROLS=PositionSlider attribute (<EMBED> HTML tag), RealAudio plug-in, 45
CONTROLS=StatusBar attribute (<EMBED> HTML tag), RealAudio plug-in, 43
CONTROLS=StatusField attribute (<EMBED> HTML tag), RealAudio plug-in, 47
CONTROLS=StopButton attribute (<EMBED> HTML tag), RealAudio plug-in, 45
CONTROLS=VolumeSlider attribute (<EMBED> HTML tag), RealAudio plug-in, 45
CoolFusion Web site, 379

CPluginWindow class, 261
Cavi objects
construction, 284
destruction, 284
construction, 266
destruction, 266
LiveConnect sample plug-in, 282-287
message maps, 196
methods, 266
Server CPU Monitor, 219
CPluginWindow object
construction, 229
creating, 186, 261
destruction, 229
subclassing, 195
windows, attaching, 267
CPluginWindow objects
repainting, 232
Server CPU Monitor, 228
subclassing, 222
windows, subclassing, 168
Crescendo Web site, 377
critical sections (multithreading), 384
creating, 188
CBuffer, protecting, 189
current target window option, 104
CWave class
creating, new operator, 188
instance structures, attaching, 186
methods, 187
multithreading, 188
CWinApp objects, MFC initialization, 198
CWnd (children), creating, 186

D

data buffers, memory, 83
data files (MIME types), testing, 24
databases (routines), WinSock, 30

DDE (Dynamic Data Exchange), 32-33, 384
implementation Web site, 33
topics, 32-33
deadlocks (multithreading), 384
debugging
plug-ins, 24
socket interfaces, Socket Spy sample plug-in, 182, 298
delete operator, memory management, 138
DeleteCriticalSection API, 188
deleting
CCpuMon objects, 222
CMCIWnd objects, 239
CMidi objects, 253
npplugin.cpp, 318
objects, 262
designing plug-ins, MCIWnd, 236-237
destroy method, netscape.plugin.Plugin class, 157
destruction
CAvi class, 287
CCpuMon object, 225
CMCIWnd class, 242
CMidi class, 256
CPluginWindow, Cavi objects, 284
CPluginWindow class, 266
CPluginWindow object, 229
Destructor method
CBufferCircular class, 206
CBufferFIFO class, 213
destructors (classes), buffers, 204
development (plug-ins)
bandwidth, support, 61
MFC AppWizard, 330
MIME types
conflicts, 65
support for multiple, 65

planning, 60
  client/server design, 66
  HTML considerations,
    63-65
  Navigator version support,
    61
  platform compatibility, 62
  selecting programming
    languages, 60-61
  streaming compared to file-
    based plug-ins, 66
devices
  audio, creating worker
    threads, 197
  classes, MCIWnd, 236
  management, MCIWnd
    plug-in, 244
  multimedia
    designing, 236-237
    MIME types, 237-238
    plug-in entry points, 238
  settings, MCIWnd plug-in,
    246
  sharing multiple instances,
    199
  status, posting messages, 257
disk-based caching, 57
displaying error messages, 147
DLLs (Dynamic Link
  Libraries), 384
  creating Borland plug-ins,
    322
  entry points
    external, 313
    NPWIN.CPP, 71
    Windows 95, 313
  exporting, 313
  headers, 71
  plug-ins, 164
    loading, 70
    Windows 95, 140
  programming languages, 60
  Socket Spy sample plug-in,
    creating, 301
document viewers, 9, 373-374
drawing bar charts, 231-232
DrawRects method,
  CPluginWindow objects,
  231-232

drivers (audio), opening, 194
dwCallback function, 257
DWG/DXF Web site, 370
Dynamic Data Exchange, *see*
  DDE
Dynamic Link Libraries, *see*
  DLLs

E

e-mail, POP3, 386
EarthTime Lite plug-in, 359
EarthTime Web site, 13, 381
Echospeech Web site, 378
editing
  library definition files, 319
  NETSCAPE.EXE, 299-300
  resource files, 333
  WinSock executable file,
    299
<EMBED> HTML tag, 40,
  52, 385
  attributes, 55, 63-65
    adding, 64
embedding plug-ins
  hiding, 251
  printing, 169
EndOfStream method, 257
  CCpuMon object, 226
  MCIWnd plug-in, 241, 244
  NPWAVE plug-in, 190
EnterCriticalSection API, 188
Enterprise server, 364
entry points
  DLLs
    external, 313
    Windows 95, 313
  LiveConnect sample plug-in,
    294
  Server CPU Monitor,
    221-225
  Watcom C++ plug-ins,
    changing definitions, 343
Envoy plug-in, 359
  Web site, 373
error messages, displaying,
  147

errors (underrun), audio plug-
  ins, 190
European Laboratory for
  Particle Physics (CERN),
  384
EventRecord structure,
  Macintosh window events,
  170
events
  adjustCursorEvent, 170
  getFocusEvent, 170
  handling
    LiveConnect sample plug-
      in, 276
    windows, 55
  loseFocusEvent, 170
  synchronization,
    multithreading, 192
exporting DLLs, 313
extensions, WinSock, 31

F

FastTrack server, 363
fflush command (vmstat), 220
fields
  headers
    Content-Type, 20
    MIME, 18
  Java class, accessing, 155
  User Agent, 146
    HTTP servers, 148-149
FIFO (First In First Out),
  125, 385
  buffers, 212
  methods, 212-216
FIGleaf Inline Lite plug-in,
  359
  Web site, 371
File Transfer Protocol (FTP),
  385
file-based plug-ins, 9, 66
file-based streams, processing,
  124
files
  audio, compression, 185
  AVI, playing, 272

Borland plug-ins, modifying, 316-317

C++ plug-ins, locations, 316

caching, 125

creating, NP ASFILE API, 125

data
debugging plug-ins, 24
Socket Spy sample plug-in, 305

extensions, MIME, 18

formats, plug-ins, 8

librarian command (Watcom C++ plug-in), 346

LiveConnect sample plug-in, locations, 272-273

local, fully qualified paths, 124

management, MCIWnd plug-in, 244

memory mapped, 139

names, parsing URLs, 124

NETSCAPE.EXE, editing, 299-300

NPMCIWND.DLL, locations, 236

NPMIDI.DLL, locations, 250-251

NPNOMFC.DLL, locations, 260

npplugin.cpp, deleting, 318

npshell.cpp, 185

NPWAVE.DLL, locations, 184

NPWIN.CPP, 71

npwin.cpp, 185

projects, adding to Borland plug-ins, 320

rc, 312

recv.dat (Socket Spy sample plug-in), 306

remote, searching, 126

resources
adding to Borland plug-ins, 318-319
adding VERSIONINFO to Borland plug-ins, 318
creating, 312

send.dat (Socket Spy sample plug-in), 305

Server CPU Monitor sample plug-in, 218
locations, 330-331

socket data, reading, 99

Socket Spy sample plug-in, locations, 301

streaming, progress indicators, 147-148

test
creating, 323
creating for Visual C++ plug-ins, 336

Visual C++ plug-ins
adding, 333
modifying paths, 331

Watcom C++ plug-in
adding, 344
locations, 342
modifying, 343

WAV, 79

WSOCK00.DLL, 298

WSOCK32.DLL, 298

FillBuffer method, autostart plug-ins, 189-190

FILO (First-In-Last-Out), 385

filters, creating, 97-98

First In First Out, *see* **FIFO**

First-In-Last-Out (FILO), 385

flags
bDataUnderrun, buffers, 190
buffer headers, 205
kill, worker threads, 192

formats (files), plug-ins, 8

forms
creating, NPN PostURL API, 102
HTML code, 100-102

FormulaOne/NET plug-in, 359
Web site, 374

Forward method
AviPlayer class, 281
CAvi class, 291

Fractal Viewer Web site, 9, 371

FrameBack method
AviPlayer class, 281
CAvi class, 292

FrameForward method
AviPlayer class, 281
CAvi class, 291

FreeBuffers method, 204
CBufferCircular class, 208
CBufferFIFO class, 213

FTP (File Transfer Protocol), 385

functions
dwCallback, 257
malloc, 139
MCIWndCreate, 236
memory management, 138
NPN MemAlloc, 83
NPN Version, 84, 90-91
NPN_MemAlloc, 81
NPP Destroy, 82, 88-90
NPP Initialize, 79, 84-85
NPP New, 80, 86-88
NPP Shutdown, 79, 85-86
parameters, passing with registers, 313
pfnWinSock.send, 305
pointers, structures, 72
SubClassFunc, 261
see also APIs; methods

G

garbage collection, 158

General Protection Faults (GPFs), 82

GET method, 99

GetContentEncoding method, 34

GetContentLength method, 34

GetContentType method, 34

GetErrorMessage method, 34

GetExpires method, 34

GetFlagFancyFTP method, 34

GetFlagFancyNews method, 34

GetFlagShowAllNews method, 34

getFocusEvent, 170
gethostbyaddr (WinSock database routine), 30
gethostbyname (WinSock database routine), 30
gethostname (WinSock database routine), 30
GetInstance routine, instance data, 167
GetLastFullBuffer method, 205
  CBufferCircular class, 210-211
GetLastFullBuffers method, CBufferFIFO class, 215
GetLastModified method, 34
GetNextEmptyBuffer method, 205
  CBufferCircular class, 209
  CBufferFIFO class, 214
GetNextFullBuffer method, 193, 205
  CBufferCircular class, 210
GetNextFullBuffers method, CBufferFIFO class, 215
GetPassword method, 34
GetPeer method, netscape.plugin.Plugin class, 157
getpeername (WinSock routine), 29
GetProp API, instance data, 167
getprotobyname (WinSock database routine), 30
getprotobynumber (WinSock database routine), 30
getservbyname (WinSock database routine), 30
getservbyport (WinSock database routine), 30
GetServerStatus method, 34
getsocketname (WinSock routine), 29
getsocketopt (WinSock routine), 29
GetStatus method, 34
GetUsername method, 34

GetWindow method, netscape.plugin.Plugin class, 157
global memory, 158
global routines, addressing, 267
GlobalAlloc method, 139
GotFileName method, 237, 256
  CCpuMon object, 226-228
  CMCIWnd class, 243
GPFs (General Protection Faults), 82
GUIs (Graphical User Interfaces), 385

H

headers
  AviObserver class, LiveConnect sample plug-in, 278
  Block Headers, changing properties, 332
  buffers, 189, 205
  Content-Type, 20
  DLLs, 71
  fields, MIME, 18
  include paths, modifying, 331, 343
  printf (vmstat command), 221
  version blocks, 312
Heap Memory API, 139
heaps, 385
HEIGHT attribute (<EMBED> HTML tag), 55, 63
Help menu, About Plug-ins command, 54
helper applications, 28-29, 385
  NSAPI, 32
Helpers configuration screen, 22
HIDDEN attribute (<EMBED> HTML tag), 63, 251

<HIDDEN> HTML tag, 385
HTML (HyperText Markup Language), 385
  arguments, NPP New function, 81-82
  development considerations, 63-65
  forms, 100-102
  LiveConnect sample plug-in, running, 294-295
  tags
    attributes, 40
    <EMBED>, 40, 52, 63, 64, 65, 385
    <HIDDEN>, 385
    <NOEMBED>, 50
    plug-in compatibility, 40
    RealAudio attributes, 40-42, 45-50
htonl (WinSock routine), 29
htons (WinSock routine), 29
HTTP (HyperText Transmission Protocol), 385
  methods
    GET, 99
    POST HTTP, 99, 102
  servers
    methods, 98-99
    User Agent fields, 148-149
HyperText Markup Language, *see* HTML
HyperText Transmission Protocol, *see* HTTP

I

IANA (Internet Assigned Numbers Authority), 18, 385
  media types, 20-22
  MIME types, submitting new, 18
  Web site, 20
IDE (Integrated Development Environment), 385
image (MIME type), 19
images, viewers, 9, 370-373

inet addr (WinSock routine),
30
inet ntoa (WinSock routine),
30
**Information Sciences Institute
(ISI)**
init method,
netscape.plugin.Plugin class,
157
initialization (MFC),
CWinApp objects, 198
Initialize method, 35
InitializeCriticalSection API,
188
initializing
CPluginWindow objects,
222
plug-ins, 79
variables, CWave class, 188
windows, 263
InitWindow method
command buttons, creating,
198
CPluginWindow objects,
229
Inso Corporation Web site,
10
installing plug-ins, assisted,
57
instance data, 54
plug-ins, 78-79
pointers, NPP New
function, 80-81
retrieving, 263
saving, NPP Destroy
function, 82-83
**instance parameter, stream
destruction, 97**
**instance pointers (streams),
saving, 242, 266**
instances, 54-55, 385
communication between, 55
creating, NPWAVE plug-in,
186
data, 385
linked lists, 167
MFC pointers, 168

LiveConnect sample plug-in,
saving, 287
multiple, 199-200
sharing devices, 199
plug-ins
creating, 52
destroying, 82
streams, structures, 95
subclassing, destroying, 166
windows, obtaining data,
166-167
**Integrated Development
Environment (IDE), 385**
InterCAP InLine Web site,
371
interfaces, 52
AviObserver, LiveConnect
sample plug-in, 276
LiveConnect, 154, 272
WinSock, 298
Internet, 385
protocols, 29
**Internet Assigned Numbers
Authority,** *see* **IANA**
Internet Protocol, *see* **IP**
Internet Relay Chat (IRC),
385
Intranet, 385
**ioctlsocket (WinSock
routine), 30**
IP (Internet Protocol), 29
addresses, 385
IRC (Internet Relay Chat),
385
isActive method,
netscape.plugin.Plugin class,
157
IsFinished method, 34
**ISI (Information Sciences
Institute), 20, 385**
**ISPs (Internet Service
Providers), bandwidth
considerations, 61**
IStore, 362
ISYS HindSite Web site, 381

J

Java, 385
applets, 386
AviObserver, 274
classes
accessing fields, 155
accessing methods, 155
compilers, Web sites, 273
garbage collection, 158
interfaces, support, 60
LiveConnect, 182
compatibility, 62
methods
calling from plug-ins, 155
native, 278-279
type names, 156
plug-ins, compatibility, 272
primitive types, 156
**Java code to implement a user
interface for Netscape's
LiveConnect sample
(listing), 275-276**
**Java code to implement the
AviPlayer Java class (listing),
277-278**
Java Runtime Interface (JRI),
52
JavaScript, 386
LiveConnect sample plug-in,
running, 294-295
JRI (Java Runtime Interface),
52

K-L

**KEYview for Windows Web
site, 371**
**keywords, Browser
(configuring MIME types),**
23
kill flags, worker threads, 192
LeaveCriticalSection API, 188
**librarian command files
(Watcom C++ plug-in),
creating, 346**

libraries
    classes, 313, 384
        subclassing, 260
    definition files, editing, 319
Lightning Strike plug-in, 359
    Web site, 372
link switches (Watcom C++ plug-in), changing, 347
linked lists, instance data, 167
listen (WinSock routine), 30
listings
    Java code to implement a user interface for Netscape's LiveConnect sample, 275-276
    Java code to implement the AviPlayer Java class, 277-278
    window procedure CPluginWindow: :PluginWndProc, 282-284
Live3D plug-ins, 12
    Web site, 376
LiveAudio, MIME types, 65
LiveCache, 57
LiveConnect, 52-53, 154, 182
    AVI files, playing, 272
    Java compatibility, 62
    methods, 53
    platform independance, development considerations, 62
LiveConnect sample plug-in
    AviObserver class, 276
        headers, 278
        stub code, 278
    AviPlayer class, 277
    AviTest class, 274-276
    CAvi class, 287
    CPluginWindow class, 282-287
    design, 273
        components, 274
    entry points, 294
    files, locations, 272-273
    Java interface, AviObserver, 274

    PluginWndProc procedure, 282-284
    running, 294-295
loading
    plug-ins, 52
        checking, 140
        development, 25
        dynamically, 70
        MIME types, 78
        parsing resource information, 54
    TYPE attribute (<EMBED> HTML tag), 64
LocalAlloc method, 139
Look@Me Web site, 381
loops (infinite), threads, 192
loseFocusEvent, 170
lossy compression, 62

M

Macintosh
    memory, flushing, 136
    windows
        event handling, 55
        events, 170
        subclassing, 170
MacZilla Web site, 378
mail server, 365
malloc function, 139
mapping
    APIs, 79, 312
        calls, 72-73
    memory, 139
    WinSock APIs, Socket Spy routines, 302-306
mBED Web site, 375
MCI (Media Control Interface), 255, 386
    drivers, AVI methods problems, 277
    MIDI devices, opening, 256
    video devices
        closing, 289
        opening, 288
        playing, 289-290
        rewinding, 291
        stopping, 290

MCI OPEN PARMS structure, 257
MCIWnd class, 236, 386
MCIWnd plug-in
    designing, 236-237
    entry points, 238-242
    functionality, 244, 247
    MIME types, 237-238
    multimedia controller, 181
    performance considerations, 241
    resource file, MIMEtype syntax, 237-238
    running, 247
    Watcom C++, file locations, 342
    windows, creating, 243
MCIWndCreate method, 236-243
MCIWndDestroy method, 239, 242
MCIWndGetDevice method, 243
Media Control Interface, *see* **MCI**
Media Type Registration Procedure Web site, 25
media types, IANA approved, 20-22
memory
    allocating, 81
        circular buffers, 206-212
        NPN MemAlloc method, 136
        saving instance data, 83
    buffers
        freeing, 208
        methods, 254
    data buffers, 83
    freeing, NPN MemFree method, 136
    garbage collection, 158
    global, 158
    heap, 385
    Macintoshes, flushing, 136
    management
        APIs, 136
        audio driver callback routines, 195

functions, 138
layers, 138
Windows 95, 137
protection faults, avoiding,
208
see also buffers
**Memory Mapped File API,
138**
memory mapped files, 139
memory-based caching, 57
Merchant System, 361
message maps
CPluginWindow class, 196
OnPlay method, 168
OnStop method, 168
subclassing windows,
167-168
message MIME type, 19
messages, displaying, 147
methods, 386
AllocateBuffers, 204
CBufferCircular class, 207
CBufferFIFO class, 213
AnyEmptyBuffers, 204
CBufferCircular class, 208
CBufferFIFO class, 214
AnyFullBuffers, 205
*CBufferCircular class,
209-210*
CBufferFIFO class, 215
APIs
managing data streams, 56
prefixes, 52
buffers, 204-205
BytesReady, 34
calling,
netscape.plugin.Plugin
class, 157
CallWindowProc, 166
CbufferCircular class,
206-212
CBufferFIFO class, 212-216
CCpuMon object, 225-228
CleanupWindow, 262
*CPluginWindow objects,
229*

Close, 34-35
CAvi class, 289
CWave class, 187
*NPWAVE plug-in,
191-192*
Server CPU Moitor, 228
CMidi, 256
compatibility, LiveConnect,
154
constructors
CBufferCircular class, 206
CBufferFIFO class, 212
CPluginWindow class, 266
CWave class, 187
destroy,
netscape.plugin.Plugin
class, 157
destructors
CBufferCircular class, 206
CBufferFIFO class, 213
DrawRects,
CPluginWindow objects,
231-232
EndOfStream, 257
CCpuMon object, 226
*MCIWnd plug-in, 241,
244*
NPWAVE plug-in, 190
FillBuffer
*autostart plug-ins,
189-190*
NPWAVE plug-in, 187
Forward
CAvi class, 291
AviPlayer class, 281
FrameBack
AviPlayer class, 281
CAvi class, 292
FrameForward
AviPlayer class, 281
CAvi class, 291
FreeBuffers, 204
CBufferCircular class, 208
CBufferFIFO class, 213
GetContentEncoding, 34
GetContentLength, 34
GetContentType, 34
GetErrorMessage, 34

GetExpires, 34
GetFlagFancyFTP, 34
GetFlagFancyNews, 34
GetFlagShowAllNews, 34
GetLastFullBuffer, 205
*CBufferCircular class,
210-211*
CBufferFIFO class, 215
GetLastModified, 34
GetNextEmptyBuffer, 205
CBufferCircular class, 209
CBufferFIFO class, 214
GetNextFullBuffer, 193,
205
CBufferCircular class, 210
CBufferFIFO class, 215
GetPassword, 34
GetPeer,
netscape.plugin.Plugin
class, 157
GetServiceStatus, 34
GetStatus, 34
GetUsername, 34
GetWindow,
netscape.plugin.Plugin
class, 157
GlobalAlloc, 139
GotFileName, 237, 256
*CCpuMon object,
226-228*
CMCIWnd class, 243
init, netscape.plugin.Plugin
class, 157
Initialize, 35
InitWindow
*CPluginWindow objects,
229*
*creating command buttons,
198*
isActive,
netscape.plugin.Plugin
class, 157
IsBufferAvailable,
NPWAVE plug-in, 187
IsFinished, 34
Java
accessing, 155
calling from plug-ins, 155

native, *278-279*
type names, *156*
LiveConnect, 53
LocalAlloc, 139
MCIWndCreate, 237, 243
MCIWndDestroy, 239, 242
MCIWndGetDevice, 243
NPN DestroyStream, 66
NPN GetURL, 66
NPN GetURLNotify, 66
NPN MemAlloc, 136
NPN MemFlush, 136
NPN MemFree, 136
NPN NewStream, 66
NPN PostURL, 66
NPN PostURLNotify, 66
NPN RequestRead, 56
NPN Version, MCIWnd
    plug-in, 241
NPP Destroy, 253, 262
    *deleting CMCIWnd
    objects, 239*
    NPWAVE plug-in, 187
    subclassing windows, 262
NPP DestroyStream, 56,
    255, 265
    MCIWnd plug-in, 241
    *NPWAVE plug-in, 187,
    191*
NPP EndOfStream, 265
NPP GetJavaClass, 53
NPP GotFileName, 265
NPP HandleEvent, 55
NPP Initialize, 72
    NPWAVE plug-in, 186
NPP New, 252-253,
    261-262
    *creating CMCIWnd
    objects, 238-239*
    creating instances, 54
    NPWAVE plug-in, 186
NPP NewStream, 56, 237,
    240, 254, 264
    NPWAVE plug-in, 186
NPP SetWindow, 253, 263
    creating windows, 55
    NPWAVE plug-in, 186
    *saving window handles,
    239-240*

NPP ShutDown, NPWAVE
    plug-in, 187
NPP StreamAsFile, 237,
    255, 265
    MCIWnd plug-in, 241
NPP URLNotify, 66
NPP Write, 56, 237, 254
    MCIWnd plug-in, 240
    NPWAVE plug-in, 187
NPP WriteReady, 237, 254,
    264-265
    MCIWnd plug-in, 240
    NPWAVE plug-in, 187
OLE, 33-35
OnButtonDown
    *CPluginWindow class,
    285-286*
OnPaint
    *CPluginWindow class,
    286*
    *CPluginWindow objects,
    232*
OnPaletteChange,
    CPluginWindow class, 287
OnPause, NPWAVE plug-
    in, 197
OnPlay
    message maps, 168
    *NPWAVE plug-in,
    196-197*
OnPositionChange, CAvi
    class, 294
OnStop
    CAvi class, 293
    message maps, 168
OnUpdate, Server CPU
    Monitor, 228
Open, 34-35, 240
    CAvi class, 288-289
    CCpuMon object, 226
    CMCIWnd class, 242
    CMidi class, 256
    CWave class, 186
    saving pointers, 266
overloaded, symbol names,
    156
Pause, 197

Play
    AviPlayer class, 279
    CAvi class, 289-290
    *NPWAVE plug-in,
    196-197*
PlayTheAudio, 190
plug-ins, 312
    calling form Java, 156
prefaces, 185
Read, 34
Ready, 35
RegisterProtocol, 35
RegisterViewer, 35
Registry, 35
RemoveProp, 268
RequestUpdate, Server CPU
    Monitor, 228
Resolve, 34
ReturnUsedBuffer, 205
    CBufferFIFO class, 216
returnUsedBuffer,
    CBufferCircular class,
    211-212
Rewind
    AviPlayer class, 280
    CAvi class, 291
Seek
    AviPlayer class, 280
    CAvi class, 290
SendDataToDriver, 193
servers, HTTP, 98-99
SetFlagFancyFTP, 34
SetFlagFancyNews, 34
SetFlagShowAllNews, 34
SetFrequency, CAvi class,
    292
SetPassword, 34
setTimeOut, AviPlayer class,
    279
SetUsername, 34
SetWindow,
    CPluginWindow class, 285
SetWindowLong, 267
ShowProgress, 147-148
Stop
    AviPlayer class, 279
    CAvi class, 290

StoreData, instance data, 168

stream types, changing, 56

stubs, subclassing windows, 267

subclassing windows, 164

SubclassWindow, 168, 267

UnSubclassWindow, 168, 262, 268

UpdateChart, CPluginWindow objects, 230-231

UpdateWindow, 239
   MCIWnd plug-in, 243

URLs, 98-99

video
   players, 278-282
   updating, 292

VirtualAlloc, 139

Write, 35

see also functions

MFCs (Microsoft Foundation Class Libraries), 313, 386

CCriticalSection object, 188

initialization, CWinApp objects, 198

subclassing, 167-168, 260

windows, creating classes, 167

MFC AppWizard, 330

Microsoft Developer Network, memory management, 139

Microsoft Foundation Class Libraries, *see* **MFCs**

MIDI (Musical Instrument Device Interface), 181, 250, 386

background sample, 181

MCI devices, opening, 256

plug-ins, Background, 251

waveform audio, mixing, 250

MIME (Multipurpose Internet Mail Extensions), 18, 386

application type, 19

audio type, 19

configuring, 22-23
   adding new, 23
   automated, 23
   plug-ins, 23

conflicts, 65

data files
   debugging plug-ins, 24
   SCR attribute (<EMBED> HTML tag), 64

file extensions, 18

headers, fields, 18

history, 18-19

identifying, NPP New function, 80

image type, 19

LiveAudio, 65

MCIWnd plug-in, 237-238

message type, 19

multimedia controller plug-ins, 181

multipart type, 19

multiple, support, 65

new, submitting, 18

plug-ins, 18, 24-52
   development, 24
   loading, 78
   registering, 25

resource information, adding to Borland plug-ins, 319

Server CPU Monitor, 227

standards, 18-19

streams, creating, 94-95

support, 60

text type, 19

top-level types, 19

video type, 19

modems, data compression, 61-62

modes

background, plug-ins, 250

NP HIDDEN, 251

NPP New function, 81

plug-ins, 55

modules, *see* **plug-ins**

Mosaic, 386

MovieStar Web site, 379

Mozilla, 149, 386

multi-instance plug-ins, 49

multimedia

audio
   autostart, 200
   designing plug-ins, 184-185
   entry points, 185
   MIDI, 250
   plug-ins, 13, 184
   running plug-ins, 199-200
   streaming, 61-62

audio drivers, opening, 194

AVI files, playing, 272

compression, lossy, 62

controller plug-ins
   MCIWnd class, 181

devices
   designing plug-ins, 236-237
   MCIWnd class, 236
   plug-in entry points, 238
   plug-in MIME types, 237-238

error retreival, MCIWnd plug-in, 245

palette adjustments, MCIWnd plug-in, 245

performance tuning, MCIWnd plug-in, 245

playback options, MCIWnd plug-in, 244-245

plug-ins
   functionality, 244, 247
   performance considerations, 241
   running, 247

recording, MCIWnd plug-in, 245

video, plug-ins, 13

multipart MIME type, 19

Multipurpose Internet Mail Extensions, *see* **MIME**

multithreading, critical sections, 384

creating, 188

CWave class, 188

deadlocks, 384

plug-ins, shutting down, 191-192

synchronization events, 192

Windows 95, 188

worker threads, CWave plug-in, 192-193

Musical Instrument Device Interface, *see* MIDI

N

National Center for Supercomputing Applications, *see* NCSA

native methods, Java, 278-279

Navigator, 356, 386

Power Pack 2.0, 359

Socket Spy sample plug-in, 299

status line, 146

streaming, 66

versions, plug-in development, 61

Navigator 2, 356-357

Navigator 3 Beta, 357-358

Navigator Dial-Up-Kit, 358-359

Navigator Gold 2, 357

Navigator Personal Edition, 358

NCAPI (Netscape Client API), 32

NCSA (National Center for Supercomputing Applications), 386

Fill-Out Form Support Page Web site, 100

Net, *see* Internet

Netscape, 356

Commercial Applications, 361-362

servers, 362-368

Web site, 12

Netscape API (NSAPI), 386

Netscape Chat, 360

Netscape Client API (NCAPI), 32

Netscape Live3D plug-in, 359

Netscape Plug-in:Navigator Defined API (NPN), 70

Netscape Plug-in:Plug-in Defined API (NPP), 70

Netscape SmartMarks, 360

NETSCAPE.EXE, editing, 299-300

netscape.plugin.Plugin class, 156

subclassing, 158

networks

bandwidth support, 61

WinSock, 387

new operator

CWave class, creating, 188

memory management, 138

overloading, 83

new target window option, 104

News Server, 365

<NOEMBED> HTML tag, 50

NOLABEL attribute (<EMBED> HTML tag), RealAudio plug-in, 50

NP ASFILE, 237, 264

NP ASFILE API, creating files, 125

NP ASFILE value (stype parameter), 96

NP ASFILEONLY, 124, 264

NP ASFILEONLY value (stype parameter), 96

NP BACKGROUND mode, 81

NP EMBED mode, 81

NP EMBED type plug-ins, printing, 169

NP FULL mode, 81

NP FULL type plug-ins, printing, 169-170

NP GetEntryPoints routine, 73-74

NP HIDDEN mode, 251

NP Initialize routine, 71-72

NP NORMAL value (stype parameter), 96

NP SEEK value (stype parameter), 96

NPByteRange structure, 126

NPCPUMON.DLL, file locations, 218

NPEmbedPrint structure, 169

NPMCIWND.DLL, file locations, 236

NPMIDI.DLL, file locations, 250-251

NPN, (API prefix), 52

NPN DestroyStream API, 66, 75, 109-110

NPN GetJavaEnv API, 75

NPN GetJavaPeer API, 53, 75

NPN GetURL API, 66, 75, 98-99, 110-112

Server CPU Monitor, 219

windows, targeting, 104

NPN GetURLNotify API, 66, 75, 114-116

NPN MemAlloc API, 75, 81-83, 136, 140-141

NPN MemFlush API, 75, 136, 142-143

NPN MemFree API, 75, 136, 141-142

NPN NewStream API, 66, 75, 108-109

NPN PostURL API, 75, 98-99, 112-114

bugs, Navigator version 2, 103-104

forms, creating, 102

windows, targeting, 104

NPN PostURL method, 66

NPN PostURLNotify API, 66, 75, 116-117

NPN preface, plug-in methods, 185

NPN RequestRead API, 56, 75, 131-132

files, searching remote, 126

NPN RequestRead method, 56

NPN Status API, 75, 146

NPN UserAgent API, 75, 146

NPN Version API, 75, 84, 90-91
MCIWnd plug-in, 241
NPN Write API, 75, 132-133
streams, 127
NPNetscapeFuncs structure, 71-72
NPNOMFC.DLL, file locations, 260
NPP, (API prefix), 52
plug-in methods, 185
NPP Close method, CWave class, 187
NPP Destroy API, 74, 82, 88-90, 253, 262
CMCIWnd objects, deleting, 239
NPWAVE plug-in, 187
Server CPU Monitor, 222
subclassing windows, 262
NPP DestroyStream API, 56, 74, 96, 107-108, 255, 265
MCIWnd plug-in, 241
NPWAVE plug-in, 187, 191
parameters, 97
Server CPU Monitor, 225
NPP EndOfStream method, 265
NPP FillBuffer method, NPWAVE plug-in, 187
NPP GetJavaClass API, 53, 75, 158
LiveConnect sample plug-in, 294
NPP GetJavaEnv API, 53, 159
NPP GetJavaPeer API, 160
NPP GotFileName method, 265
NPP HandleEvent API, 55, 75, 175-176
window events, Macintosh, 170
NPP Initialize API, 72, 75, 79, 84-85
npplugin.cpp, deleting, 318
NPWAVE plug-in, 186
NPP IsBufferAvailable method, NPWAVE plug-in, 187

NPP New API, 75, , 80, 86-88, 250-253, 261-262
instances, creating, 54
NPWAVE plug-in, 186
CMCIWnd objects, creating, 238-239
Server CPU Monitor, 221
NPP NewStream API, 56, 75, 105-106, 237, 240, 254, 264
NPWAVE plug-in, 186
Server CPU Monitor, 223
NPP Print API, 75, 169-175
NPP SetWindow API, 75, 165, 170-172, 253, 263
instance data, 167
NPWAVE plug-in, 186
Server CPU Monitor, 222
window handles, saving, 239-240
windows, creating, 55
NPP Shutdown API, 74-75, 79, 85-86
NPWAVE plug-in, 187
NPP StreamAsFile API, 75, 124, 130-131, 237, 255, 265
MCIWnd plug-in, 241
Server CPU Monitor, 219, 224
NPP URLNotify API, 66, 75, 117-119
NPP Write API, 56, 75, 128-130, 237, 254
MCIWnd plug-in, 240
NPWAVE plug-in, 187
Server CPU Monitor, 224
NPP WriteReady API, 75, 127-128, 237, 254, 264-265
buffers, allocating, 122
MCIWnd plug-in, 240
NPWAVE plug-in, 187
processing data, 122-123
Server CPU Monitor, 224
NPPluginFuncs structure, 73-74
NPPrint structure
embedded plug-ins, 169
problems, 169
NPRES DONE (stream destruction), 97

NPRES NETWORK ERR (stream destruction), 97
NPRES USER BREAK (stream destruction), 97
NPSavedData, 82
npshell.cpp, 185
NPStream structure, 95, 256
NPWAVE plug-in, 184
audio drivers, callback routines, 194
closing, 191-192
designing, 184-185
entry points, 185
multithreading, 188
running, 199-200
user interface, 195-196
NPWAVE.DLL, file locations, 184
NPWIN.CPP, 71, 185
NSAPI (Netscape API), 386
ntohl (WinSock routine), 30
ntohs (WinSock routine), 30

O

Object Linking and Embedding, *see* OLE
Object Windows Library, *see* OWL
objects
CBuffer, 189
CButton, creating, 198
CCpuMon
deleting, 222
saving, 221
CCriticalSection, 188
CMCIWnd, creating, 238-239
CMidi
creating, 252-253
deleting, 253
CPluginWindow
attaching to windows, 267
creating, 186, 261
subclassing, 168, 195
CWinApp, MFC initialization, 198
deleting, 262
streams, notifying, 254

offset parameter, NPP Write API, 123
OLE (Object Linking and Embedding), 386
  automation, 35
  methods, 33
OnButtonDown method, CPluginWindow class, 285-286
OnPaint method
  CPluginWindow class, 286
  CPluginWindow objects, 232
OnPaletteChange method, CPluginWindow class, 287
OnPause method, NPWAVE plug-in, 197
OnPlay method
  message maps, 168
  NPWAVE plug-in, 196-197
OnPositionChange method, CAvi class, 294
OnStop method
  CAvi class, 293
  message maps, 168
OnUpdate method, Server CPU Monitor, 228
Open method, 34, 35, 240
  CAvi class, 288-289
  CCpuMon object, 226
  CMCIWnd class, 242
  CMidi class, 256
  CWave class, 186
  pointers, saving, 266
opening
  devices, MIDI, 256
  MCI video devices, 288
  pointers, stream instances, 256
OpenScape Web site, 381
operators
  memory management, 138
  new
    creating CWave class, 188
    overloading, 83
  sizeof, Watcom C++ plug-in, 343
output directories, changing (Borland plug-ins), 321

overloaded methods, symbol names, 156
overloading, new operator, 83
overrun (streaming), 386
OWL (Object Windows Library), 313, 386
  Borland plug-ins, 328

P

pages, virtual memory, 138-139
painting
  CPluginWindow objects, repainting, 232
  video, 286
palettes, video, 287
PALETTE attribute (<EMBED> HTML tag), 63
parameters
  instance, stream destruction, 97
  reason, stream destruction, 97
  seekable, 96
  stream, stream destruction, 97
  stype, 96
parent target window option, 104
parsing
  URLs, filenames, 124
  vmstat command, 228-231
paths
  include, modifying, 331
  include headers, modifying, 343
Pause method, 197
PCM (Pulse Code Modulation), 386
pfnWinSock.send function, 305
platform independence, development considerations, 62
platforms (compatibility), development considerations, 62

Play command buttons, creating, 274-276
Play method
  CAvi class, 289-290
  NPWAVE plug-in, 196-197
play method, AviPlayer class, 279
playing, MCI video devices, 289-290
PlayTheAudio method, 190
Plug-in Native Methods, 156
Plug-in SDK Web site, 57
plug-ins, 8, 35, 52
  address spaces, size, 137
  animation, 11
  APIs, 70, 74
    entry points, 252-255
  ASAP WebShow, 11
  audio, 13
    autostart parameters, 186
    NPWAVE, 184
  autostart, FillBuffer method, 189-190
  Background MIDI, 251
  background mode, 250
  Borland C++ 5
    adding resources, 318-320
    adding VERSIONINFO resources, 318
    building, 320
    changing output directories, 321
    compiling, 320
    creating, 317
    creating DLLs, 322
    editing library definition files, 319
    project creation, 317-318
    project setup, 317
    testing, 323-327
    warnings, 320-321
  browsers, support, 50
  categories, 8
  code modules, 52
  compared to applets, 55
  components, 52
  debugging, 24
  designing, non-MFC, 261

development
  loading, 25
  planning, 60
  version support, 60-61
embedded, window size, 52
embedding
  hidden, 251
  troubleshooting, 79
entry points, 261
file-based, 9, 264
Fractal Viewer, 9
global destruction, 79
hidden, running, 257-258
HTML tags, compatibility, 40
image viewers, 9
initializing, 79
instance data, 78-79
instances
  destroying, 82
  multiple, 79, 199-200
Live 3D, 12
LiveConnect, 52
loading, 52
  checking, 140
  parsing resource information, 54
MCIWnd
  designing, 236-237
  entry points, 238-242
  functionality, 244, 247
  performance considerations, 241
  resource files, 237-238
  running, 247
methods, calling from Java, 156
MIME types, 18, 24
  configuring, 23
  development, 24
  loading, 78
  registering, 25
modes, 55
  NPP New function, 81
multi-instance, 49
multimedia devices
  designing, 236-237
  entry points, 238
  MIME types, 237-238

Navigator Power Pack 2.0, 359
NPWAVE
  designing, 184-185
  entry points, 185
  running, 199-200
presentation, 11
RealAudio, HTML tag attributes, 40-50
streaming, 9, 52
system resources, allocating per instance, 78, 80
utility, 13
version numbers, NPN Version function, 84
video, 13
viewers, documents, 9
Visual C++
  adding files, 333
  changing Block Header properties, 332
  changing build settings, 334-335
  compiling, 336
  creating, 331
  creating resources, 332
  editing resource files, 333
  project creation, 331
  project setup, 331
  project types, 332
  testing, 336-339
VRML, 12
WAV files, 79
Web site, 8
window subclassing, running, 269
Windows 95, DLLs, 140
Word Viewer, 10
Plugin constructor, netscape.plugin.Plugin class, 157
PLUGINS folder, 52
PLUGINSPAGE attribute (<EMBED> HTML tag), 64
PluginWndProc procedure
  LiveConnect sample plug-in, 282-284
Point-to-Point-Protocol (PPP), 386

PointCast Network Web site, 382
pointers
  buffer headers, 205
  functions, structures, 72
  instance data, 54
    MFC, 168
    NPP New function, 80-81
  memory
    data buffers, 83
    mapping, 139
  streams
    opening, 256
    saving, 242
    types, 94-95
POP3 , (e-mail), 386
POST HTTP method, 99, 102
Power Pack 2.0, 359
PowerMedia Web site, 375
PPP (Point-to-Point-Protocol), 386
prefixes, APIs, 52
presentation plug-ins, 11, 374-375
PreVU Web site, 380
primitive types, Java, 156
printf header, vmstat command, 221
printing, 164, 169-170
  NP EMBED type plug-ins, 169
  NP FULL type plug-ins, 169-170
  windows, coordinate conversions, 170
procedures (SubclassFunc), subclassing windows, 165
processes, 386
  address space, Windows 95, 137
programming
  processes, 386
  streams, 387
  threads, 387
  WinCGI, 387
programming languages
  Borland C++ 5, 316
  selecting, 60-61

Visual C++ 4, 330
Watcom C++, 342
progress indicators,
  streaming, 147-148
projects
  Borland C++ plug-ins
    adding project files, 320
    adding resources, 318-319
    adding VERSIONINFO
      resources, 318
    building, 320
    changing output
      directories, 321
    compiling, 320
    creating, 317-318
    creating DLLs, 322
    editing library definition
      files, 319
    setup, 317
    testing, 323-327
    warnings, 320-321
  Visual C++ plug-ins
    adding files, 333
    changing Block Header
      properties, 332
    changing build settings,
      334-335
    compiling, 336
    creating, 331
    creating resources, 332
    editing resource files, 333
    setup, 331
    testing, 336-339
    types, 332
  Watcom C++ plug-ins
    creating, 344
    setup, 344
properties
  Block Headers, changing,
    332
  lists, obtaining instance data,
    167
protocols, 387
  FTP, 385
  IP, 29
  TCP, 29
  Telnet, 387
Proxy Server, 364

Publishing System, 361
Pulse Code Modulation
  (PCM), 386

Q-R

QuickServer Web site, 382

RapidTransit Web site, 378
rc file, 312
Read method, 34
Ready method, 35
RealAudio, 359
  HTML tag attributes, 40-50
  Web site, 40, 378
reason parameter, stream
  destruction, 97
recording music (MIDI), 250
recv (WinSock routine), 30
recv.dat file (Socket Spy
  sample plug-in), 306
recvfrom (WinSock routine),
  30
registering plug-ins, MIME
  types, 25
RegisterProtocol method, 35
registers (function
  parameters), passing, 313
RegisterViewer method, 35
Registry, methods, 35
RemoveProp API, instance
  data, 167, 268
reports (vmstat command),
  Server CPU monitor, 220
Request for Comments
  (RFCs), 22, 387
RequestUpdate method,
  Server CPU Moitor, 228
Resolve method, 34
resources, 387
  Borland plug-ins
    adding, 318-319
    verifying, 325
    VERSIONINFO, 318
  creating, 312
  editing, 333
  MCIWnd plug-in,
    MIMEType syntax,
    237-238

Visual C++ plug-ins,
  verifying, 337
Watcom C++ plug-in,
  verifying, 345
ReturnUsedBuffer method,
  205
  CBufferCircular class,
    211-212
ReturnUsedBuffers method,
  CBufferFIFO class, 216
Rewind method
  AviPlayer class, 280
  CAvi class, 291
rewinding MCI video devices,
  291
RFCs (Request for
  Comments), 22, 387
  Web site, 22
routines
  AssociateInstance, instance
    data, 167
  callback, audio drivers, 194
  calling, 73-74
  GetInstance, instance data,
    167
  global, addressing, 267
  NP GetEntryPoints, 73-74
  NP Initialize, 71
  NPP Shutdown, 74
  see also functions
running
  Borland plug-ins, 324
  LiveConnect sample plug-in,
    294-295
  Socket Spy sample plug-in,
    306-307

S

Safe Subclassing in Win32
  (document), 167
saving
  CCpuMon objects, 221
  data, NPP Destroy function,
    82-83
  instance pointers, streams,
    266
  instances, LiveConnect
    sample plug-in, 287

SCR attribute (<EMBED> HTML tag), 64
SDKs (Software Development Kits), 387
  Windows, ftp sites, 273
searching remote files, 126
Secure Sockets Layer (SSL), 387
Seek method
  AviPlayer class, 280
  CAvi class, 290
seekable
  parameter, 96
  streams, 56-57
    byte range requests, 96
    checking, 126
    offset values, 126
    performance
      considerations, 56
seeking (streaming), byte range requests, 126
select (WinSock routine), 30
self target window option, 104
send (WinSock routine), 30
send.dat file (Socket Spy sample plug-in), 305
SendDataToDriver method, 193
sendto (WinSock routine), 30
sequential streams, 56-57
Server CPU Monitor
  APIs
    NPP Destroy, 222
    NPP DestroyStream, 225
    NPP New, 221
    NPP NewStream, 223
    NPP SetWindow, 222
    NPP StreamAsFile, 224
    NPP Write, 224
    NPP WriteReady, 224
  bar charts, updating, 228
  entry points, 221-225
  running, 233
  setup, 232
  vmstat command, 220

Server CPU Monitor sample plug-in, 181, 218, 227
  files
    design, 219
    locations, 218, 330-331
    servers, 362-368
  CGI applications, POST HTTP method, 99, 102
  HTTP, User Agent fields, 148-149
  methods
    HTTP, 98-99
    POST HTTP, 99, 102
  seekable streams, support, 96
  statistics
    plug-in design, 219
    retrieving, 218
SetFlagFancyFTP method, 34
SetFlagFancyNews method, 34
SetFlagShowAllNews method, 34
SetFrequency method, CAvi class, 292
SetPassword method, 34
SetProp API, instance data, 167
setsocketopt (WinSock routine), 30
setTimeOut method, AviPlayer class, 279
setup, Server CPU Monitor, 232-233
SetUsername method, 34
SetWindow method, CPluginWindow class, 285
SetWindowLong API, 165, 260
SetWindowLong method, 267
Shockwave, 11
Shockwave for Authorware Web site, 375
Shockwave for Director plug-in, 359
  Web site, 375
Shockwave for FreeHand Web site, 372
ShowProgress method, 147-148

shutdown (WinSock routine), 30
sizeof operator, Watcom C++ plug-in, 343
Sizzler Web site, 11, 376
slide show viewers, 11
socket (WinSock routine), 30
Socket Spy, 31
  Navigator, 299
Socket Spy sample plug-in, 182, 298
  breakpoints, setting, 302
  data files, creating, 305
  DLL file, creating, 301
  files, locations, 301
  NETSCAPE.EXE.editing, 299-300
  running, 306-307
  WinSock, editing executable, 299
  WinSock API, mapping routines, 302-306
sockets, 387
  Berkeley, 29
  NCAPI, 32
  Socket Spy, 31
  Windows 95, reading data files, 99
  WinSock, 29-31
software
  agents, 387
Software Development Kits, *see* SDKs
SSL (Secure Sockets Layer), 387
stacks (arguments), order, 312
statistics, servers
  plug-in design, 219
  retrieving, 218
status line, 146
Stop command buttons, creating, 274-276
Stop method
  AviPlayer class, 279
  CAvi class, 290
stopping MCI video devices, 290
StoreData method, instance data, 168

stream parameter (stream destruction), 97
streams, 387
audio
Audio Streamer sample plug-in, 180
bandwidth considerations, 61, 62
Server CPU Monitor sample plug-in, 181
buffers, 204
classes, 180
allocating, 122
secondary management schemes, 123
caching, FIFO, 125
creating, 94, 97-98
types, 94-95
data, 55-56
processing, 122-123
destroying, 96-97, 123, 255
ending, 95
file-based
creating local files, 125
processing, 124
instance structures, 95
instances (pointers)
opening, 256
saving, 242, 266
multiple
management, 56
tracking, 95
Navigator, 66
objects, notifying, 254
overrun, 386
performance considerations, Navigator version 2, 125
plug-ins, 9, 52, 66
programming, planning, 60
progress indicators, 147-148
seekable, 56, 57
byte range requests, 96
checking, 126
offset values, 126
seeking, byte range requests, 126
sequential, 56, 57
stype parameter, values, 96

types
changing, 56
invalid fields, 95
underrun, 387
windows, targeting, 104
writing APIs, 122
structures
buffer headers, 205
EventRecord, Macintosh window events, 170
function pointers, 72
MCI OPEN PARMS, 257
NPByteRange, 126
NPEmbedPrint, 169
NPNetscapeFuncs, 71-72
NPPluginFuncs, 73-74
NPPrint, embedded plug-ins, 169
NPStream, 95
streams, instances, 95
WNDCLASS, 164
stub
code (AviObserver class), LiveConnect sample plug-in, 278
methods (windows), subclassing, 267
stype parameter, 96
SubClassFunc function, 261
windows, subclassing, 165
subclassing, 260
CPluginWindow objects, 195, 222
instances, destroying, 166
MFC, 167-168
netscape.plugin.Plugin class, 158
windows, 164-166, 181, 263
global, 268-269
LiveConnect sample plug-in, 285
Macintosh, 170
message maps, 167-168
methods, 164
NPWAVE plug-in, 186
running plug-ins, 269
stub methods, 267
troubleshooting, 168

SubclassWindow method, 168, 267
SuiteSpot server, 363
SVF Web site, 372
synchronization events, multithreading, 192
syntax
Content-Type MIME header field, 20
<EMBED> HTML tag, 40, 63
Java methods, calling from plug-ins, 155
NPN DestroyStream API, 109
NPN GetURL API, 110
NPN GetURLNotify API, 115
NPN NewStream API, 108
NPN PostURL API, 112
NPN PostURLNotify API, 116
NPN RequestRead API, 131
NPN Status API, 150-151
NPN Write API, 133
NPP DestroyStream, 107
NPP GetJavaClass API, 158
NPP GetJavaEnv API, 159
NPP GetJavaPeer API, 160
NPP HandleEvent API, 175
NPP NewStream, 105
NPP Print API, 173
NPP SetWindow API, 171
NPP StreamAsFile API, 130
NPP URLNotify API, 118
NPP Write API, 128
NPP WriteReady API, 127
system resources
allocating, per instance, 80
freeing, global destruction, 79
plug-ins, allocating, 78

T

tags, HTML
attributes, 40
<EMBED>, 40, 52, 63-65, 385

<HIDDEN>, 385
<NOEMBED>, 50
RealAudio attributes, 40-50
Talker Web site, 378
**Target Expert (Borland C++
5), projects**
creation, 317
setup, 317
targets
Watcom C++ plug-in,
creating, 344
windows, APIs, 104
**TCP (Transmission Control
Protocol), 29**
**TCP/IP (Transmission
Control Protocol/Internet
Protocol), 387**
Telnet, 387
test files
Borland plug-ins, creating,
323-326
Visual C++ plug-ins
creating, 336
opening, 338
testing
projects, Borland plug-ins,
323-327
Visual C++ plug-ins,
336-339
Watcom C++ plug-in,
348-351
text (MIME type), 19
threads, 387
buffers, audio, 184
loops, infinite, 192
multithreading, Windows
95, 188
worker, 387
creating, 197
CWave plug-in, 192-193
ToolVox Web site, 379
topics, DDE, 32-33
Topper Web site, 376
Totally Hip Web site, 11
**Transmission Control
Protocol (TCP), 29**
**Transmission Control
Protocol/Internet Protocol
(TCP/IP), 387**

troubleshooting
plug-ins
embedding, 79
*Socket Spy sample plug-in,
182*
subclassing, unsubclassing
windows, 168
virtual memory, APIs, 136
TWIPs, 387
**TYPE attribute (<EMBED>
HTML tag), 64**

U

undderrun (streaming), 387
errors, audio plug-ins, 190
**UNITS attribute (<EMBED>
HTML tag), 64**
**Universal Resource Locators,
see URLs**
**UnSubclassWindow method,
168, 262, 268**
**Update command button
(CPluginWindow objects),
handling, 232**
**UpdateChart method,
CPluginWindow objects,
230-231**
UpdateWindow method, 239
MCIWnd plug-in, 243
updating
bar charts, Server CPU
Monitor, 228
video, methods, 292
**URLs (Universal Resource
Locators), 387**
filenames, parsing, 124
methods, 98-99
requesting, GET method, 99
Server CPU Monitor, setup,
232
streams, creating, 95
User Agent fields, 146
utilities, plug-ins, 13, 380-382

V

values
offset, seekable streams, 126
stype parameter, streaming,
96
**variables, initializing (CWave
class), 188**
VDOLive plug-in, 359
VDOLive Web site, 380
version block headers, 312
version numbers, APIs, 72
**VERSIONINFO resource
files, creating (Borland plug-
ins), 318**
video
AVI files, plug-ins, 13
MCI devices
closing, 289
opening, 288
playing, 289-290
rewinding, 291
stopping, 290
painting, 286
palettes, 287
players, methods, 278-282
plug-ins, 13, 379-380
updating, methods, 292
video (MIME type), 19
videos, playing, 285-286
ViewDirector Web site, 372
viewers
document, 373-374
documents, 9
images, 370-373
plug-ins, 9
slide show, 11
**ViewMovie QuickTime Web
site, 380**
virtual memory
addresses, resolving, 139
allocating, 139
management, APIs, 136
pages, 138-139
Virtual Memory API, 138
**Virtual Reality Modeling
Language, *see* VRML**
VirtualAlloc method, 139
Viscape Web site, 376

Visual C++
include paths, modifying, 331
plug-ins
adding files, 333
changing Block Header properties, 332
changing build settings, 334-335
compiling, 336
creating, 331
creating resources, 332
editing resourcce files, 333
project creation, 331
project setup, 331
project types, 332
testing, 336-337, 339
Visual C++ 4, 330
plug-ins, file locations, 330-331
vmstat command, 218-220
data, parsing, 228-231
fflush command, 220
printf header, 221
running, CGI, 220-221
VR Scout VRML Web site, 377
VRealm Web site, 377
VRML (Virtual Reality Modeling Language), 12
plug-ins, 376-377
VRScout plug-in, 359
VxDs (virtual device drivers), 387

W

Watcom C++, 342
plug-ins
adding source files, 344
changing entry point definitions, 343
compiling, 347-348
creating, 343-351
file locations, 342
modifying files, 343
modifying header include paths, 343

project creation, 344
project setup, 344
sizeof operator, 343
target creation, 344
testing, 348-351
WAV files, plug-ins, 79
waveform audio (MIDI), mixing, 250
Wavelet Image Viewer Web site, 372
waveOutOpen API, 194
Web browsers, Mosaic, 386
Web sites
ABC QUICKSILVER, 370
Acrobat Amber Reader, 373
ACTION, 379
ActiveX, 380
ASAP WebShow, 11, 374
Astound Web Player, 374
BrowserWatch, 8, 148
Carbon Copy/Net, 380
Chemscape Chime, 373
CMX Viewer, 370
CoolFusion, 379
Crescendo, 377
DDE implementation, 33
DWG/DXF, 370
EarthTime, 381
Earthtime, 13
Echospeech, 378
Envoy, 373
FIGleaf Inline, 371
Formula One/NET, 374
Fractal Viewer, 9, 371
IANA, 20
Inso Corporation, 10
InterCAP InLine, 371
ISYS HindSite, 381
Java compilers, 273
KEYview for Windows, 371
Lightning Strike, 372
Live3D, 376
Look@Me, 381
MacZilla, 378
mBED, 375
Media Type Registration Procedure, 25
MovieStar, 379

NCSA Fill-Out Form Support Page, 100
Netscape, 12
OpenScape, 381
Plug-in SDK, 57
plug-ins, 8
PointCast Network, 382
PowerMedia, 375
PreVU, 380
QuickServer, 382
RapidTransit, 378
RealAudio, 40, 378
RFCs, 22
Shockwave for Authorware, 375
Shockwave for Director, 375
Shockwave for FreeHand, 372
Sizzler, 11, 376
SVF, 372
Talker, 378
ToolVox, 379
Topper, 376
Totally Hip, 11
VDOLive, 380
ViewDirector, 372
ViewMovie QuickTime, 380
Viscape, 376
VR Scout VRML, 377
VRealm, 377
Wavelet Image Viewer, 372
WHIP!, 373
Whurlplug, 377
WIRL Virtual Reality Browser, 377
Word Viewer, 374
while loops infinite (threads), 192
WHIP! Web site, 373
Whurlplug Web site, 377
WIDTH attribute (<EMBED> HTML tag), 55, 64
WinCGI, 387
window procedure CPluginWindow::PluginWndProc (listing), 282-284

Windows
programming languages, DLLs, 60
resource, 387
WinCGI, 387
windows
child, event handling, 55
classes, MCIWnd, 236
creating, 55
handles, saving, 239-240
initializing, 263
instances, obtaining data, 166-167
MCIWnd plug-in
creating, 243
management, 244
MFCs, creating classes, 167
printing embedded plug-ins, 170
redrawing, 243
size
embedded plug-ins, 52
HEIGHT attribute (<EMBED> HTML tag), 63
UNITS attribute (<EMBED> HTML tag), 64
WIDTH attribute (<EMBED> HTML tag), 64
sizing, 164
streams, targeting, 104
subclassing, 164-166, 181, 263
CPluginWindow objects, 168
global, 268-269
LiveConnect sample plug-in, 285
Macintosh, 170
message maps, 167-168
methods, 164
NPWAVE plug-in, 186

running plug-ins, 269
stub methods, 267
unsubclassing, troubleshooting, 168
visibility, HIDDEN attribute (<EMBED> HTML tag), 63
Windows 95
DLLs, entry points, 313
memory management, 137
layers, 138
multithreading, 188
plug-ins, DLLs, 140
processes, address spaces, 137
virtual memory, pages, 138-139
Windows SDK ftp site, 273
WinSock, 29-31, 387
database routines, 30
editing, executable, 299
extensions, 31
routines, 29-30
WinSock APIs (Socket Spy sample plug-in), mapping routines, 302-306
WIRL 3D Browser plug-in, 359
WIRL Virtual Reality Browser Web site, 377
WNDCLASS structures, 164
WOM CLOSE audio driver message, 194
WOM DONE audio driver message, 195
WOM OPEN audio driver message, 195
Word Viewer plug-in, 10, 359
Word Viewer Web site, 374
worker thread, 387
worker threads, creating
NPWAVE plug-in, 197
CWave plug-in, 192-193
World Wide Web, *see* WWW

Write method, 35
WSAAsyncGetHostByAddr (WinSock extension), 31
WSAAsyncGetHostByName (WinSock extension), 31
WSAAsyncGetProtoByName (WinSock extension), 31
WSAAsyncGetProtoByNumber (WinSock extension), 31
WSAAsyncGetServByName (WinSock extension), 31
WSAAsyncGetServByPort (WinSock extension), 31
WSAAsyncSelect (WinSock extension), 31
WSACancelAsyncRequest (WinSock extension), 31
WSACancelBlockingCall (WinSock extension), 31
WSACleanup (WinSock extension), 31
WSACleanup API, (WinSock), 306
WSAGetLastError (WinSock extension), 31
WSAIsBlocking (WinSock extension), 31
WSASetBlockingHook (WinSock extension), 31
WSASetLastError (WinSock extension), 31
WSAStartup (WinSock extension), 31
WSAUnhookBlockingHook (WinSock extension), 31
WSOCK00.DLL, 298
WSOCK32.DLL, 298
WWW (World Wide Web), 387
browsers
creating windows, 164
status messages, 146
usage statistics Web sites, 148

Teach Yourself Netscape 2 Web Publishing in a Week

— Wes Tatters

Teach Yourself Netscape 2 Web Publishing in a Week is the easiest way to learn how to produce attention-getting, well-designed Web pages for the Netscape environment. It is intended for non-technical people, and will be equally of value to users on the Macintosh, Windows, and UNIX platforms. For new HTML developers, the book will provide a solid grounding in HTML and Web publishing principles, while providing special focus on the possibilities presented by the Netscape environment.

Teaches how to create attention-grabbing pages with Netscape extensions.

Explores ways to use Netscape Navigator Gold 2.0 editor to create all kinds of Web pages.

Explains frames, plug-ins, Java applets, and JavaScript.

Covers Netscape

Price: $39.99 USA/$56.95 CDN   *User Level: Casual - Accomplished*
ISBN: 1-57521-068-1   672 pp.

Internet/Web Publishing

HTML, JAVA, CGI, VRML, SGML Web Publishing Unleashed

— William Stanek

Includes sections on how to organize and plan your information, design pages, and become familiar with hypertext and hypermedia. Choose from a range of applications and technologies, including Java, SGML, VRML, and the newest HTML and Netscape extensions.

The CD contains software, templates, and examples to help you become a successful Web publisher.

Teaches how to convey information on the Web using the latest technology—including Java.

Readers learn how to integrate multimedia and interactivity into their Web publications.

Covers the World Wide Web

Price: $49.99 USA/$70.95 CDN   *User Level: Casual - Expert*
ISBN: 1-57521-051-7   960 pp.

Organize and plan your information, design pages, and become familiar with hypertext and hypermedia!

Internet/Web Publishing

Java Unleashed

— Michael Morrison, et al.

Java Unleashed is the ultimate guide to the year's hottest new Internet technologies, the Java language and the HotJava browser from Sun Microsystems. Java Unleashed is a complete programmer's reference and a guide to the hundreds of exciting ways Java is being used to add interactivity to the World Wide Web.

Includes helpful and informative CD-ROM

Describes how to use Java to add interactivity to Web presentations

Shows readers how Java and HotJava are being used across the Internet

Covers Java 1.1

Price: $49.99 USA/$70.95 CDN   User Level: Casual - Accomplished - Expert
ISBN: 1-57521-049-5   1,008 pp.

Learn how to program Java to add interactivity to the World Wide Web

Internet Programming

Laura Lemay's Web Workshop: Netscape Navigator Gold 3

— Laura Lemay & Ned Snell

Netscape Gold and JavaScript are two powerful tools used to create and design effective Web pages. This book details not only design elements, but also how to use the Netscape Gold WYSIWYG editor. The included CD-ROM contains editors and code from the book, making the reader's learning experience a quick and effective one.

CD-ROM includes editors and all the source code from the book

Teaches how to program within Navigator Gold's rich Netscape development environment

Explores elementary design principles for effective Web page creation

Covers Web publishing

Price: $39.99 USA/$56.95 CDN   User Level: Casual - Accomplished
ISBN: 1-57521-128-9   400 pp.

Internet/General

Netscape 3 Unleashed, Second Edition

— Dick Oliver

Readers learn how to fully exploit the new features of this latest version of Netscape—the most popular Web browser in use today.

CD-ROM includes source code from the book and powerful utilities

Teaches how to install, configure, and use Netscape Navigator 3.0

Covers how to add interactivity to Web pages with Netscape

Covers Netscape 3

Price: $49.99 USA/$70.95 CDN   User Level: Accomplished - Expert
ISBN: 1-57521-164-5   950 pp.

Internet/Online/Communications

Netscape 2 Unleashed

— Dick Oliver, et al.

This book provides a complete, detailed, and fully fleshed-out user manual for Netscape, covering all facets of its implementation and how businesses and institutions are using it effectively.

Gives a full description of the evolution of Netscape from its inception to today, and its cutting edge developments with Macromedia, Adobe Acrobat, and HTML 3.0

Offers detailed discussions of the Communication Server, Commerce Server, News Server, and Proxy Server with case studies

Covers Netscape Client and Server

Price: $49.99 USA/$70.95 CDN   User Level: Casual - Accomplished - Expert
ISBN: 1-57521-007-X   922 pp.

Internet/General

Teach Yourself Borland C++ 5 in 21 Days, Third Edition

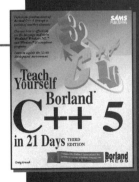

— Craig Arnush

Updated and revised, this book shows readers how to use the language and how to write beginner-level programs.

Author is a member of Team Borland and has access to the most frequently asked questions from the Borland help line

Uses the successful *Teach Yourself* elements, including Workshop and Q&A sections, quizzes, and shaded syntax boxes

Covers Version 5

Price: $39.99 USA/$56.95 CDN   User Level: New - Casual
ISBN: 0-672-30756-1   864 pp.

Replaces previous edition ISBN: 0-672-30598-4, $29.99 USA/$42.95 CDN

Programming

Teach Yourself Visual C++ 4 in 21 Days

— Nathan & Ori Gurewich

This book merges the power of the best-selling *Teach Yourself* series with the knowledge of Namir Shammas, a renowned expert in code, creating the most efficient way to learn Visual C++. In just 21 days it will transform a novice into a knowledgeable programmer.

CD-ROM included

Provides all the training needed to write code in just days

The hands-on approach makes the reader learn by doing, and not just reading

Question and Answer section sheds light on common programming problems

Covers the latest version for Windows

Price: $35.00 USA/$49.95 CDN   User Level: New - Casual
ISBN: 0-672-30795-2   840 pp.

Become a Visual C++4 programmer in just a matter of days!

Programming

Tom Swan's Mastering Borland C++ 5, Premier Edition

— Tom Swan

The new release of Borland C++ 5.0 includes valuable tools developers are craving. Tools such as new object-oriented scripting, a new C++ language environment that lets you control the IDE completely, and debugger control. With all those and many other new features, developers will turn to *Mastering Borland C++ 5.0, Premier Edition* to receive the latest , most accurate information on how to exploit these new features in their programs.

CD-ROM includes source code from the book and powerful utilities

Provides a complete introduction and thorough coverage of intermediate and advanced topics

Includes hundreds of working examples

Covers Borland C++ 5.0

Price: $59.99 USA/$84.95 CDN   User Level: Casual - Accomplished - Expert
ISBN: 0-672-30802-9   1,088 pp.

Replaces previous edition ISBN 0-672-30546-1 $49.99 USA/$67.99 CDN

The latest, most accurate information on how to exploit these new features in their programs!

Programming

Delphi 2 Unleashed, Second Edition

— *Charlie Calvert*

This book helps every programmer get the most from the latest version of Delphi. And it reveals all the latest information including how to develop client/server applications, multimedia programs, and advanced Windows programming in an easy-to-understand style.

Included CD-ROM contains source code from the book and sample applications

Teaches the components of object-oriented programming

Covers Windows 95 and multimedia programming

Covers latest version of Delphi

Price: $59.99 USA/$84.95 CDN   User Level: Accomplished - Expert
ISBN: 0-672-30858-4   1,440 pp.

Replaces previous edition ISBN: 0-672-30499-6

Learn how to develop client/server applications, multimedia programs, and advanced Windows programs!

Programming

Teach Yourself Delphi 2 in 21 Days

— *Dan Osier*

This unique book presents Delphi programming in logical, easy-to-follow sequences that have made the *Teach Yourself* series a bestseller. The reader begins learning the basics of Delphi and then moves on to more advanced topics.

Guides the reader through a system for learning a programming language in a set period of time

Question & Answer sections answer the most commonly asked questions

Includes a detailed study of looping, records, arrays, branching, data manipulation, and more

Covers Delphi 2

Price: $35.00 USA/$49.95 CDN   User Level: New - Casual
ISBN: 0-672-30863-0   736 pp.

Begin programming in chapter one! Shaded boxes with handy references make finding key information easy and efficient.

Programming

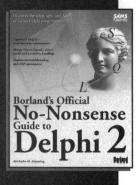

Borland's No-Nonsense Guide to Delphi 2

— Michelle Manning

This book contrasts itself against others by providing an in-depth, no-nonsense study of Delphi—just the facts. Written for casual programmers, *Borland's No-Nonsense Guide to Delphi 2* gives the readers the essential information they need on topics as varied as developing client/server applications, multimedia programs, and advanced Windows programming.

Skips the fluff and delivers straightforward, insightful direction

Essential examples provide an excellent foundational study of Delphi's features

Special review sections highlight only the most important information

Covers latest version of Delphi

Price: $25.00 USA/$35.95 CDN   User Level: Casual
ISBN: 0-672-30871-1   416 pp.

Written for casual programmers, *Borland's No-Nonsense Guide to Delphi 2* gives you the essential information you need.

Programming

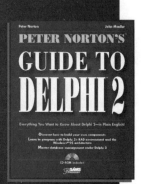

Peter Norton's Guide to Delphi 2

— Peter Norton & John Mueller

Peter Norton's name is synonymous with PC expertise and this book dispenses his knowledge in a fast, hands-on style that will teach you everything about Delphi 2. By the time you finish this book you will be programming with Delphi in the new 32-bit environment.

CD-ROM included

Covers the new 32-bit environment

Unique, fast paced hands-on approach makes learning easy

Covers Delphi

Price: $49.99 USA/$70.95 CDN   User Level: New - Casual
ISBN: 0-672-30898-3   816 pp.

By the time you finish this book you will be programming with Delphi in the new 32-bit environment.

Programming

Delphi 2 Developer's Guide, Second Edition

— Steve Teixiera & Xavier Pacheco

This book empowers the reader with the ability to capitalize on the growing movement toward GUI (Graphical User Interface)-based applications. The reader will become adept at exploiting Delphi 2's tools and commands and will learn how to create object-oriented programs.

CD-ROM contains product demos and all of the source code from the book

Demonstrates practical applications through the use of step-by step written procedures

Details Delphi 2's tools for efficient OOP

Covers latest version of Delphi 2

Price: $59.99 USA/$84.95 CDN   User Level: Casual - Accomplished - Expert
ISBN: 0-672-30914-9   1,368 pp.

Replace previous edition: ISBN: 0-672-30704-9, $49.99 USA/$70.95 CDN

Become adept at exploiting Delphi 2's tools and commands and learn how to create object-oriented programs.

Programming

Developing PowerBuilder 5 Applications, Fourth Edition

— Bill Hatfield

Capitalizing on the success of the previous edition, *Developing PowerBuilder 5 Applications, Fourth Edition* is a hands-on guide for developers who want to create their own real-world applications. It details all the new changes to PowerBuilder, giving programmers the essential information they need to exploit PowerBuilder 5's powerful features.

CD-ROM includes all the source code from the book and various PowerBuilder applications

Teaches how to exploit PowerBuilder 5's new features

Programmers will master user interface design, PowerScript programming, debugging, and database design

Covers PowerBuilder 5

Price: $59.99 USA/$84.95 CDN   User Level: Beginner - Intermediate
ISBN: 0-672-30916-5   864 pp.

Exploit PowerBuilder 5's new features and maximize your programming power!

Client/Server

Visual C++ 4 Unleashed

— Viktor Toth

This is the perfect book for advanced Visual C++ programmers. Its 900 pages explore the most advanced topics while its enclosed CD-ROM allows the user to quickly learn by working through the programs in the book. It not only covers the new release of Visual C++ and its capabilities but also teaches LAN programming, OLE, DLLs, OLE Automation, and how to update old programs to the new version of Visual C++.

Enclosed CD-ROM contains source code and illustrative programs from the book

Explores the capabilities of the new Visual C++ release

Provides extensive information on such advanced topics as I/O timers, LAN programming, and Windows 95 applications

Covers Visual C++ 4

Price: $49.99 USA/$70.95 CDN   User Level: Accomplished - Expert
ISBN: 0-672-30874-6   912 pp.

Explore the capabilities of the new Visual C++ release!

Programming

Add to Your Sams.net Library Today
with the Best Books for Internet Technologies

ISBN	Quantity	Description of Item	Unit Cost	Total Cost
1-57521-164-5		Netscape 3 Unleashed, Second Ed. (Book/CD-ROM)	$49.99	
0-672-30914-9		Delphi 2 Developer's Guide, Second Edition (Book/CD-ROM)	$59.99	
1-57521-128-9		Laura Lemay's Web Workshop: Netscape Navigator Gold 3 (Book/CD-ROM)	$39.99	
0-672-30916-5		Developing PowerBuilder 5 Applications, Fourth Edition (Book/CD-ROM)	$59.99	
0-672-30898-3		Peter Norton's Guide to Delphi 2 (Book/CD-ROM)	$49.99	
0-672-30802-9		Tom Swan's Mastering Borland C++ 5, Premier Edition (Book/CD-ROM)	$59.99	
1-57521-049-5		Java Unleashed (Book/CD-ROM)	$49.99	
1-57521-051-7		Web Publishing Unleashed (Book/CD-ROM)	$49.99	
0-672-30858-4		Delphi 2 Unleashed, Second Ed. (Book/CD-ROM)	$59.99	
1-57521-068-1		Teach Yourself Netscape 2.0 Web Publishing in a Week (Book/CD-ROM)	$39.99	
		Shipping and Handling: See information below.		
		TOTAL		

Shipping and Handling: $4.00 for the first book, and $1.75 for each additional book. If you need to have it NOW, we can ship product to you in 24 hours for an additional charge of approximately $18.00, and you will receive your item overnight or in two days. Overseas shipping and handling adds $2.00. Prices subject to change. Call between 9:00 a.m. and 5:00 p.m. EST for availability and pricing information on latest editions.

201 W. 103rd Street, Indianapolis, Indiana 46290

1-800-428-5331 — Orders   1-800-835-3202 — FAX   1-800-858-7674 — Customer Service

Book ISBN 1-57521-098-3

CD-ROM Install

Technical Support from Macmillan

We can't help you with Windows or Macintosh problems or software from third parties, but we can assist you if a problem arises with the CD-ROM itself.

E-mail Support: Send e-mail to `support@mcp.com`.

CompuServe: `GO SAMS` to reach the Macmillan Computer Publishing forum. Leave us a message, addressed to SYSOP. If you want the message to be private, address it to *SYSOP.

Telephone: (317) 581-3833

Fax: (317) 581-4773

Mail:

> Macmillan Computer Publishing
> Attention: Support Department
> 201 West 103rd Street
> Indianapolis, IN 46290-1093

Here's how to reach us on the Internet:

World Wide Web (The Macmillan Information SuperLibrary):

`http://www.mcp.com/samsnet`

What's on the Disc

The companion CD-ROM contains all the source code and project files developed by the author, plus an assortment of third-party tools and utilities.

Windows 3.1/NT Installation Instructions

1. Insert the CD-ROM disc into your CD-ROM drive.
2. From File Manager or Program Manager, choose Run from the File menu.
3. Type `<drive>CDSETUP` and press Enter, where `<drive>` corresponds to the drive letter of your CD-ROM. For example, if your CD-ROM is drive D:, type `D:CDSETUP` and press enter.
4. Follow the on-screen instructions in the installation program. Files will be installed to a directory named \PNE, unless you choose a different directory during installation.

CDSETUP creates a Windows program manager group called *Programming Netscape Plug-ins.* This group contains icons for exploring the CD-ROM.

Windows 95 Installation Instructions

If Windows 95 is installed on your computer and you have the AutoPlay feature enabled, the Guide to the CD-ROM program starts automatically whenever you insert the disc into your CD-ROM drive.

Macintosh Installation Instructions

1. Insert the CD-ROM disc into your CD-ROM drive.
2. When an icon for the CD appears on your desktop, open the disc by double-clicking on its icon.
3. Double-click on the icon named Guide to the CD-ROM, and follow the directions that appear.